Piecemeal acquisitions

+ Disposals – share of Net assets at Disposal + minorits.

Managerial Paper P8

FINANCIAL ANALYSIS

For exams in 2009

CIMA

Practice & Revision Kit

In this January 2009 new edition

- We discuss the **best strategies** for revising and taking your CIMA exams

- We show you how to be well prepared for the **2009 exams**

- We give you **lots of great guidance** on tackling questions

- We include **genuine student answers** with BPP commentary

- We show you how you can **build your own exams**

- We provide you with **three** mock exams including the **November 2008 exam**

BPP's **i-Pass** product also supports this paper.

BPP
LEARNING MEDIA

First edition 2005
Fifth edition January 2009

ISBN 9780 7517 6552 6
(previous ISBN 9780 7517 5192 5)

British Library Cataloguing-in-Publication Data
A catalogue record for this book
is available from the British Library

Published by

BPP Learning Media Ltd
BPP House, Aldine Place
London W12 8AA

www.bpp.com/learningmedia

Printed in the United Kingdom

We are grateful to the Chartered Institute of
Management Accountants for permission to reproduce
past examination questions. The answers to past
examination questions have been prepared by BPP
Learning Media Ltd.

Your learning materials, published by BPP Learning
Media Ltd, are printed on paper sourced from
sustainable, managed forests.

Contents

Question index

The headings in this checklist/index indicate the main topics of questions, but questions often cover several different topics.

Preparation questions, listed in italics, provide you with a firm foundation for attempts at exam-standard questions.

Questions set under the old syllabus *Financial Reporting (FR)*, are included because their style and/or content are similar to those that appear in the Paper P8 exam.

Planning your question practice

Our guidance from page xxv shows you how to organise your question practice, either by attempting questions from each syllabus area or by **building your own exams** – tackling questions as a series of practice exams.

Extra guidance

You can find additional guidance on a number of questions in this kit on BPP's website:

www.bpp.com/cima/extra-question-guidance

Topic index

Listed below are the key Paper P8 syllabus topics and the numbers of the questions in this Kit covering those topics.

If you need to concentrate your practice and revision on certain topics or if you want to attempt all available questions that refer to a particular subject, you will find this index useful.

Note that Section A questions are not included in this index.

Syllabus topic	Question numbers
Actuarial deficits and surpluses	42, 43, 44, 45
Asset valuation (alternative approaches to)	37
Consolidation	
• Acquisitions	3-9, 15-23, 59, Mock 1 Q3, Mock 2 Q2
• Associates	11, 12, 59
• Income statement	13, 21, Mock 1 Q6
• Balance sheet	16, 18
• Disposals	15
• Equity method	11
• Foreign currency translation	24, 25, 26, 27
• Group cash flow statement	28, 29, 30, 31
• Joint ventures	10, 11
• Proportionate consolidation method	11
• Subsidiaries	3-9, 15-23
• Multi-entity structures	15-23
Creative accounting	Mock 2 Q6
Earnings per share	59, 63-66
Environmental issues	35, 36, 70, 71, 77
Financial instruments	37, 38, 39, 40, 41
Global Reporting Initiative	70
Human resource accounting	75
Hyperinflation	33, 34, Mock 1 Q2
Intellectual capital	75
IAS 7	28, 29, 30, 31
IAS 19	42-45
IAS 21	24-27
IAS 27	3-9, 15-23
IAS 28	59
IAS 29	Mock 1 Q2
IAS 31	14
IAS 32	23
IAS 33	63-66

Syllabus topic	Question numbers
IAS 37	35
IAS 39	37-41
IFRS 2	53
IFRS 3	Mock 1 Q3
IFRS 8	67, 68, 69, Mock 1 Q7
Interpretation of financial statements	48, 49, Mock 1 Q5
Pension schemes	42-45
Ratio analysis	48-60
Regulatory framework	1, 2
Retirement benefits	42-45
Revenue recognition	46
Segment analysis	Mock 1 Q7
Substance over form	Mock 2 Q6
US GAAP/IFRS	Mock 1 Q4

Using your BPP Learning Media Practice and Revision Kit

Tackling revision and the exam

You can significantly improve your chances of passing by tackling revision and the exam in the right ways. Our advice is based on recent feedback from CIMA examiners. You may be surprised to know that much examiner advice is the same whatever the exam, and the reasons why many students fail don't vary much between subjects and exam levels.

- We look at the dos and don'ts of revising for, and taking, CIMA exams. Making the most of your revision time can make a big, big difference to how well-prepared you are for the exam

- We focus on Paper P8; we discuss revising the syllabus, what to do (and what not to do) in the exam, how to approach different types of question and ways of obtaining easy marks

Selecting questions

We provide signposts to help you plan your revision.

- A full **question index**

- A **topic index** listing all the questions that cover key topics, so that you can locate the questions that provide practice on these topics, and see the different ways in which they might be examined

- A **BPP question plan** highlighting the most important questions and explaining why you should attempt them

- **Build your own exams**, showing you how you can practise questions in a series of exams

Making the most of question practice

At BPP we realise that you need more than just questions and model answers to get the most from your question practice.

- Our **Top tips** provide essential advice on tackling questions, presenting answers and the key points that answers need to include

- We show you how you can pick up **Easy marks** on questions, as we know that picking up all readily available marks often can make the difference between passing and failing

- We summarise **Examiner's comments** to show you how students who sat the exam coped with the questions

- We refer to the **BPP 2008 Study Text** for detailed coverage of the topics covered in each question

- We provide extra help and annotated student answers for certain questions on BPP Learning Media's website, www.bpp.com/learningmedia

Attempting mock exams

There are three mock exams that provide practice at coping with the pressures of the exam day. We strongly recommend that you attempt them under exam conditions. **Mock exam 1** reflects the question styles and syllabus coverage of the exam; **Mock exam 2** is the actual May 2007 exam and **Mock exam 3** is the actual November 2008 exam. To help you get the most out of doing these exams, we not only provide help with each answer, but also guidance on how you should have approached the whole exam.

How to revise

☑ Plan your revision

At the start of your revision period, you should draw up a **timetable** to plan how long you will spend on each subject and how you will revise each area. You need to consider the total time you have available and also the time that will be required to revise for other exams you're taking.

☑ Practise Practise Practise

The **more exam-standard questions** you do, the **more likely you are to pass** the exam. Practising full questions will mean that you'll get used to the time pressure of the exam. When the time is up, you should note where you've got to and then try to complete the question, giving yourself practice everything that the question tests.

☑ Revise enough

Make sure that your revision covers the breadth of the syllabus, as in most papers most topics could be examined in a compulsory question. However it is true that some topics are **key** – they often appear in compulsory questions or are a particular interest of the examiner – and you need to spend sufficient time revising these. Make sure you know the **basics** – the fundamental calculations, proformas and report layouts.

☑ Deal with your difficulties

Difficult areas are topics you find dull and pointless, or subjects that you found problematic when you were studying them. You mustn't become negative about these topics; instead you should build up your knowledge by reading the **Passcards** and using the **Quick quiz** questions in the Study Text to test yourself. When practising questions in the Kit, go back to the Text if you're struggling.

☑ Learn from your mistakes

Having completed a question you must try to look at your answer critically. Always read the **Top tips** guidance in the answers; it's there to help you. Look at **Easy marks** to see how you could have quickly gained credit on the questions that you've done. As you go through the Kit, it's worth noting any traps you've fallen into, and key points in the **Top tips** or **Examiner's comments** sections, and referring to these notes in the days before the exam. Aim to learn at least one new point from each question you attempt, a technical point perhaps or a point on style or approach.

☑ Read the examiners' guidance

We refer throughout this Kit to **Examiner's comments**; these are available on CIMA's website. As well as highlighting weaknesses, examiners' reports often provide clues to future questions, as many examiners will quickly test again areas where problems have arisen. CIMA's website also contains articles that are relevant to this paper, which you should read.

☑ Complete all three mock exams

You should attempt the **Mock exams** at the end of the Kit under **strict exam conditions** to gain experience of selecting questions, managing your time and producing answers.

How NOT to revise

☒ Revise selectively

Examiners are well aware that some students try to forecast the contents of exams, and only revise those areas that they think will be examined. Examiners try to prevent this by doing the unexpected, for example setting the same topic in successive sittings or setting topics in compulsory questions that have previously only been examined in optional questions. Remember you have little choice of questions in most CIMA exams.

☒ Spend all the revision period reading

You cannot pass the exam just by learning the contents of Passcards, Course Notes or Study Texts. You have to develop your **application skills** by practising questions.

☒ Audit the answers

This means reading the answers and guidance without having attempted the questions. Auditing the answers gives you **false reassurance** that you would have tackled the questions in the best way and made the points that our answers do. The feedback we give in our answers will mean more to you if you've attempted the questions and thought through the issues.

☒ Practise some types of question, but not others

Although you may find the numerical parts of certain papers challenging, you shouldn't just practise calculations. These papers will also contain written elements, and you therefore need to spend time practising written question parts as well.

☒ Get bogged down

Don't spend a lot of time worrying about all the minute detail of certain topic areas, and leave yourself insufficient time to cover the rest of the syllabus. Remember that a key skill in the exam is the ability to **concentrate on what's important** and this applies to your revision as well.

☒ Overdo studying

Studying for too long without interruption will mean your studying becomes less effective. A five minute break each hour will help. You should also make sure that you are leading a **healthy lifestyle** (proper meals, good sleep and some times when you're not studying).

How to PASS your exams

☑ Prepare for the day

Make sure you set at least one alarm (or get an alarm call), and allow plenty of time to get to the exam hall. You should have your route planned in advance and should listen on the radio for potential travel problems. You should check the night before to see that you have pens, pencils, erasers, watch, calculator with spare batteries, also exam documentation and evidence of identity.

☑ Select the right questions

You should select the optional questions you feel you can answer **best**, basing your selection on the topics covered, the requirements of the question, how easy it will be to apply the requirements and the availability of easy marks.

☑ Plan your three hours

You need to make sure that you will be answering the correct number of questions, and that you spend the right length of time on each question – this will be determined by the number of marks available. Each mark carries with it a **time allocation** of **1.8 minutes**. A 25 mark question therefore should be selected, completed and checked in 45 minutes. With some papers, it's better to do certain types of question first or last.

☑ Read the questions carefully

To score well, you must follow the requirements of the question, understanding what aspects of the subject area are being covered, and the tasks you will have to carry out. Make sure you are aware of what the **question verbs require**; CIMA provides a table of verbs used together with their meaning as part of the question paper (see p xxiii in this Kit). The requirements will also determine what information and examples you should provide. Reading the question scenarios carefully will help you decide what **issues** to discuss, what **techniques** to use, **information** and **examples** to include and how to **organise** your answer.

☑ Plan your answers

Five minutes of planning plus twenty-five minutes of writing is certain to earn you more marks than thirty minutes of writing. Consider when you're planning how your answer should be **structured**, what the **format** should be and **how long** each part should take.

Confirm before you start writing that your plan makes **sense**, covers **all relevant points** and does not include **irrelevant material.**

☑ Show evidence of judgement

Remember that examiners aren't just looking for a display of knowledge; they want to see how well you can **apply** the knowledge you have. Evidence of application and judgement will include writing answers that only contain **relevant** material, using the material in scenarios to **support** what you say, **criticising** the **limitations** and **assumptions** of the techniques you've used and making **reasonable recommendations** that follow from your discussion.

☑ Stay until the end of the exam

Use any spare time to **check and recheck** your script. This includes checking you have filled out the candidate details correctly, you have labelled question parts and workings clearly, you have used headers and underlining effectively and spelling, grammar and arithmetic are correct.

How to FAIL your exams

☒ Don't do enough questions

If you don't attempt sufficient questions on the paper, you are making it harder for yourself to pass the questions that you do attempt. If for example you don't do a 20 mark question, then you will have to score 50 marks out of 80 marks on the rest of the paper, and therefore have to obtain 63% of the marks on the questions you do attempt. Failing to attempt all of the paper is symptomatic of poor time management, poor question selection or failure to revise the whole syllabus.

☒ Include irrelevant material

Markers are given detailed mark guides and will not give credit for irrelevant content. Therefore you should **NOT** braindump into your answer all you know about a broad subject area; the markers will only give credit for what is **relevant**, and you will also be showing that you lack the ability to **judge what's important.** Similarly forcing irrelevant theory into every answer won't gain you marks, nor will providing uncalled for features such as situation analyses, executive summaries and background information.

☒ Fail to use the details in the scenario

General answers or reproductions of old answers that don't refer to what is in the scenario in **this** question won't score enough marks to pass.

☒ Copy out the scenario details

Examiners see **selective** use of the right information as a key skill. If you copy out chunks of the scenario that aren't relevant to the question, or don't use the information to support your own judgements, you won't achieve good marks.

☒ Don't do what the question asks

Failing to provide all the examiner asks for will limit the marks you score. The question part may include two requirements and you should answer **both**, not just the first one. If the requirements specify you should present your work in a certain format (memo, report) there will be marks for doing so, and you will not obtain these marks if you do not use the format specified. You will also decrease your chances by not providing an answer with enough **depth** – producing a single line bullet point list when the examiner asks for a discussion.

☒ Present your work poorly

Markers will only be able to give you credit if they can read your writing. There are also plenty of other things as well that will make it more difficult for markers to reward you. Examples include:

* Not using black or blue ink
* Not showing clearly which question you're attempting
* Scattering question parts from the same question throughout your answer booklet
* Not showing clearly workings or the results of your calculations

Paragraphs that are too long or which lack headers also won't help markers and hence won't help you.

Revising P8

Knowledge

Section A, and to a certain extent, Section B requires you to demonstrate knowledge as much as application. Some of the objective test questions can be very straightforward as they are testing your knowledge of the syllabus. However, the examiner has commented that whereas some excellent answers are normally produced at the top end, a substantial minority of candidates appear to have virtually no useable knowledge of the syllabus.

Explanation

As well as stating your knowledge, you will also sometimes be asked to demonstrate the more advanced skill of explaining the requirements of accounting standards. Explaining means providing simple definitions and covering the reasons why regulations have been made and what the problems are that the standards are designed to counter. You'll gain higher marks if your explanations are clearly focussed on the question and you can supplement your explanations with examples.

Calculations

The examiner does not usually set purely numerical questions. It is more likely that you will have to use calculations to support your explanations or arguments. It goes without saying that all workings should be shown and referenced. Not only is it professional, but it enables the examiner to give you credit by following through your answer if you make a mistake early on.

Interpretation and recommendation

As discussed above, you may have to interpret and draw conclusions from any figures or ratios you have calculated. Your arguments should be logical and structured.

Question practice

You should use the Passcards and any brief notes you have to revise these topics, but you mustn't spend all your revision time passively reading. Question practice is vital; doing as many questions as you can in full will help develop your ability to analyse scenarios and produce relevant discussion and recommendations. The revision plan on page (xxv) tells you what questions cover so that you can choose appropriate questions covering the whole range of technical areas.

Passing the P8 exam

Cover the whole syllabus?

Ideally, yes. The examiner has stated that any syllabus topic could be examined. In view of the weighting, however, it makes sense to focus most of your efforts on groups and financial analysis. Leaving topics out is not advisable, but if you are forced to do this through lack of time, then make sure you do not leave out any aspects of these very important topics. At least get an overview of any topic not covered, by skim reading or reading Passcards.

Practise

Our text gives you ample opportunity to practise by providing questions within chapters, quick quiz questions and questions in the exam question bank at the end. In addition the BPP Practice and Revision Kit provides lots more question practice. It's particularly important to practise:

- Banks of objective test questions so that you get used to doing a number together
- Ten mark questions, mostly knowledge based with some calculations
- Longer scenario questions, of the type to be found in Section C

Develop time management skills

The examiner has identified time management as being a problem, with some candidates not leaving themselves enough time to do the shorter calculations. Particularly therefore towards the end of your course, you need to practise all types of question, only allowing yourself the time you will be given in the exam.

Develop business awareness

Candidates with good business awareness can score well in a number of areas.

- Reading articles in CIMA's *Financial Management* magazine and the business press will help you understand the practical rationale for accounting standards and make it easier for you to apply accounting requirements correctly

- Looking through the accounts of major companies will familiarise you with the contents of accounts and help you comment on key figures and changes from year-to-year

The verdict

The examiner has said that a very broad spectrum of marks is produced. Some excellent papers and some which are less than excellent! In the latter case, lack of knowledge often lets candidates down. Please make sure that doesn't happen to you!

Exam information

Format of the paper

		Number of marks
Section A:	Up to 10 multiple choice and other objective test questions, 2-4 marks each	20
Section B:	3 compulsory questions, 10 marks each	30
Section C:	2 out of 3 questions, 25 marks each	50
		100

Time allowed: 3 hours

A number of Section A questions may be based on a common scenario. Section A may contain questions of the conventional 'multiple choice' format, but may also include other forms of objective test question. Generally, the multiple choice format is likely to account for not more than 60% of Section A questions. Other possibilities include:

(a) Filling in a blank in a sentence.

(b) Listing items in a rank order.

(c) Stating a definition (in not more than .... words).

(d) Identifying a key issue (eg advantage/disadvantage) (in not more than .... words).

(e) Calculating one specific figure eg profit for the period/absorption cost per product.

(f) Completing a blank or partially completed prescribed format using terms and/or number eg published account format.

(g) Identifying a specific term describing action/valuation seen in a scenario.

(h) Matching items together or with a description eg 'are the following cash or non-cash items' – identifying depreciation as non-cash or inventory as a current asset.

(i) Interpreting/analysing numerical or graphical data.

November 2008

Section A

1   Seven objective test questions ranging across the syllabus

Section B

2   Intellectual capital: advantages of recognising intellectual assets on the balance sheet and reasons for non-recognition
3   Basic and diluted earnings per share with a bonus issue
4   Calculation of retained earnings and minority interest for group with two subsidiaries

Section C

5   Consolidated income statement, balance sheet and statement of changes in equity for a group with a foreign subsidiary
6   Financial analysis – report with ratios in support of application for a loan
7   Adjustments for incorrect accounting treatment of sale and repurchase, factoring and preference shares; recalculation of ratios

This paper is Mock Exam 3 in this Kit.

May 2008

Examiner's comments

In Section A, which contains questions of varying degrees of difficulty, many candidates scored highly in the early questions 1.1, 1.2 and 1.3 and not so well in later questions. There was some confusion over the unwinding of the discount in 1.7 and very few wholly correct answers to the last question, 1.8.

In Section B, candidates made basic errors in the calculation of consolidation adjustments in question two. The numerical part of question three on derivatives was well answered, as was question four on the convergence project.

In Section C, questions five and seven were financial analysis questions and question six required the preparation of a relatively straightforward consolidated cash flow statement. The well prepared scored highly in this question. In question five, many candidates failed to appreciate the critical cash shortage of the rapidly expanding company. In question seven, some candidates provided little more than a description of how the ratios were calculated.

November 2007

May 2007

Section A

1   9 multiple choice and OT questions covering the whole syllabus

Section B

2   Calculation of goodwill consolidated earnings and minority interest
3   Calculation of group earnings per share in respect of alternative acquisition scenarios
4   Preparation of paper discussing the progress of the convergence project

Section C

5   Analysis of financial statements with emphasis on difference between cash and profit
6   Financial analysis including adjustment for transactions with issues relating to substance over form
7   Consolidated income statement including adjustments for bond and related finance costs.

This paper is Mock Exam 2 in this Kit.

November 2006

Examiner's comments

The examiner noted that the examination produced some good papers with candidates scoring well on Question one, two, and in some cases, three.

In Section A candidates struggled with sub-question 1.5 which required the calculation of finance costs.

In Section B candidates showed a lack of relevant technical knowledge on IAS 19 *Employee benefits* examined in Question four.

In Section C, each of the questions tested two different syllabus areas. The examiner noted that candidates should expect more of this type of question in future. The least popular question in this section was Question six as it appeared that candidates were unsure about the accounting for joint ventures.

The examiner noted, that despite clearly set out rules, candidates continue to start and finish more than one question on a single page.

May 2006

Examiner's comments

The examiner was pleased to see some excellent papers, but said that a significant number of candidates seemed to find the paper difficult. The main problem was time pressure, but in some cases this was the candidate's own fault for demonstrating poor exam technique.

Section A was generally well done. However, there were problems with the hybrid financial instrument question in Section 1.6. Some answers were too long. Section B had two fully written questions and one which required only calculations. The calculation question was answered better than the written one. Section C had two analysis questions and a fairly complex consolidation with a part-disposal. The disposal caused confusion, and candidates who chose both analysis questions tended to fair better.

Many candidates fell down on exam technique. For example, they wasted time on introductions or did not show workings.

November 2005

Section A	Question in this Kit
1 7 multiple choice and OT questions covering the whole syllabus	82

Section B	
2 Current cost accounting	Mock exam 1 Q2
3 Calculation of goodwill with fair values	Mock exam 1 Q3
4 Role of IFRS	Mock exam 1 Q4

Section C	
5 Ratio analysis and limitations	50
6 Consolidated cash flow statement	30
7 Analysis of segment report; limitations of segment reporting	69

Examiner's comments

As in May 2005, the examiner was pleased to report that there were some excellent papers. Unfortunately a substantial minority of candidates showed very poor preparation and lack of knowledge. Time pressure was not as much of an issue this time round.

Marks for Section A varied, with some candidates scoring full marks. The minority interest in Question 1.1 caused problems, as did the acquisition journal in Question 1.7. Section B contained two fully written questions and one requiring calculations. Question 2 on accounting for changing price levels was not well answered, and Question 4 on international harmonisation even less so, with some answers vague and general. Question 3 produced good answers. In Section C, the first analysis question (5) elicited some very good answers, although some contained what the examiner called an 'all-purpose ratio set'. Question 6 was well answered, but Question 7 was often rushed.

Poor housekeeping may have jeopardised some candidates' chances, for example identifying questions by the wrong number.

May 2005

Examiner's comments

The examiner noted a wide range of marks with some really excellent papers and a fair number where candidates 'appeared to have virtually no useable knowledge of the syllabus'.

Section A marks ranged from 0 to 20. Answers to Question 1.8 were often wordy, rather than being in the form of journal entries as requested. Section B contained a question requiring candidates to classify some financial assets in accordance with IAS 39. A few candidates did well, but most did not, and were vague and general. This section also contained a consolidation question with a part disposal, which was quite well done. The other question, on EPS and P/E, was well answered on the calculation part, but not on the written. In Section C, all questions were well answered.

The examiner emphasised that candidates should cover all areas of the syllabus.

Pilot paper

What the examiner means

The table below has been prepared by CIMA to help you interpret exam questions.

Learning objective	Verbs used	Definition	Examples in the Kit
1 Knowledge What you are expected to know	• List • State • Define	• Make a list of • Express, fully or clearly, the details of/facts of • Give the exact meaning of	19
2 Comprehension What you are expected to understand	• Describe • Distinguish • Explain • Identify • Illustrate	• Communicate the key features • Highlight the differences between • Make clear or intelligible/state the meaning of • Recognise, establish or select after consideration • Use an example to describe or explain something	34 22 40
3 Application How you are expected to apply your knowledge	• Apply • Calculate/compute • Demonstrate • Prepare • Reconcile • Solve • Tabulate	• To put to practical use • To ascertain or reckon mathematically • To prove with certainty or to exhibit by practical means • To make or get ready for use • To make or prove consistent/ compatible • Find an answer to • Arrange in a table	8 9
4 Analysis How you are expected to analyse the detail of what you have learned	• Analyse • Categorise • Compare and contrast • Construct • Discuss • Interpret • Produce	• Examine in detail the structure of • Place into a defined class or division • Show the similarities and/or differences between • To build up or complete • To examine in detail by argument • To translate into intelligible or familiar terms • To create or bring into existence	14 11 2 50
5 Evaluation How you are expected to use your learning to evaluate, make decisions or recommendations	• Advise • Evaluate • Recommend	• To counsel, inform or notify • To appraise or assess the value of • To advise on a course of action	39 33

Useful websites

The websites below provide additional sources of information of relevance to your studies for *Management Accounting – Decision Management.*

- BPP   www.bpp.com/learningmedia

  For details of other BPP material for your CIMA studies

- CIMA   www.cimaglobal.com

  The official CIMA website

- *Financial Times*   www.ft.com

- *The Economist*   www.economist.com

- *Wall Street Journal*   www.wsj.com

Using your BPP products

This Kit gives you the question practice and guidance you need in the exam. Our other products can also help you pass:

- **Learning to Learn Accountancy** gives further valuable advice on revision

- **Passcards** provide you with clear topic summaries and exam tips

- **Success CDs** help you revise on the move

- **i-Pass CDs** offer tests of knowledge against the clock

- **Learn Online** is an e-learning resource delivered via the Internet, offering comprehensive tutor support and featuring areas such as study, practice, email service, revision and useful resources

You can purchase these products by visiting www.bpp.com/mybpp.

Visit our website www.bpp.com/cima/learnonline to sample aspects of Learn Online free of charge.

Planning your question practice

We have already stressed that question practice should be right at the centre of your revision. Whilst you will spend some time looking at your notes and the Paper P8 Passcards, you should spend the majority of your revision time practising questions.

We recommend two ways in which you can practise questions.

- Use **BPP's question plan** to work systematically through the syllabus and attempt key and other questions on a section-by-section basis

- **Build your own exams** – attempt the questions as a series of practice exams

These ways are suggestions and simply following them is no guarantee of success. You or your college may prefer an alternative but equally valid approach.

BPP's question plan

The plan below requires you to devote a **minimum of 35 hours** to revision of Paper P8. Any time you can spend over and above this should only increase your chances of success.

Step 1   **Review your notes** and the chapter summaries in the Paper P8 **Passcards** for each section of the syllabus.

Step 2   **Answer the key questions** for that section. These questions have boxes round the question number in the table below and you should answer them in full. Even if you are short of time you must attempt these questions if you want to pass the exam. You should complete your answers without referring to our solutions.

Step 3   **Attempt the other questions** in that section. For some questions we have suggested that you prepare **answer plans or do the calculations** rather than full solutions. Planning an answer means that you should spend about 40% of the time allowance for the questions brainstorming the question and drawing up a list of points to be included in the answer.

Step 4   **Attempt Mock exams 1, 2 and 3** under strict exam conditions.

Syllabus section	2008 Passcards chapters	Questions in this Kit	Comments	Done ☑
Regulation	1	1	Do an answer plan only. This question requires you to discuss the degree of comparability that accounting standards help to achieve and would give valuable background in answering financial analysis questions later on.	
		2	Do an answer plan only. This is a useful question on the Operating and Financial Review.	
Consolidated financial statements	2, 3, 4, 5	7	Answer in full. This will set the scene for more complicated questions.	☐
		8	Do an answer plan only.	☐
		13	Answer in full. An excellent question on consolidation.	☐
Associates and joint ventures	6	19	Answer in full. Useful question that provides revision of the treatment of different types of investments.	☐
		12	Answer in full. Excellent question on associates.	☐
Multi-entity structures; changes in composition	7, 8	20	Answer in full. A big question with lots of notes. Useful for practising exam technique. Keep to the time allowed.	☐
		21	Answer if you have time.	☐
Foreign currency translation	9	24	Answer in full. A good preparation question.	☐
		25	Answer in full. Gives good practice in translating a company's balance sheet and preparing consolidated accounts.	
Consolidated cash flow statements	10	28	Answer in full. A good preparation question.	☐
		30	Answer in full. Lots of information to plough through. Looks complicated but is straightforward if you work through it logically.	☐
Off-balance sheet finance	16	35 36	Answer in full. Both questions provide excellent practice in deciding the true nature of transactions and applying IAS 37.	☐

Syllabus section	2008 Passcards chapters	Questions in this Kit	Comments	Done ☑
Financial instruments	13	37	Answer in full. A good preparation question on balance sheet valuations.	☐
		40	Answer in full. A good part examination question that provides a short discussion of IASs 32 and 39 followed by the use of IAS 39 in practice.	
Employee benefits	12	42	Answer in full. A good preparation question for this difficult topic.	☐
		44	A good recent examination question.	
International issues	19	72	Answer in full. A good discussion question on US GAAP versus IAS.	☐
		74	Do an answer plan only.	☐
Ratio and trend analysis	17	48 49	Answer in full. Do these two preparation questions before moving to examination style questions.	☐
		55	Answer in full. Remember to write a report (use the correct format). Only quote those ratios that are relevant to the report. Remember to include all ratios used as an appendix to the report.	
		51	Do an answer plan only.	☐
Earnings per share	15	65	Answer in full. A thorough and very practical test of IAS 33.	☐
Segment reporting	15	67	Answer in full. A useful exercise in report writing, as well as testing your knowledge of IAS 14.	☐
		68	Do an answer plan only. A good practical example of an exam question. Do not neglect part (a).	☐
Miscellaneous standards	11, 14	46	Do an answer plan only for this question on revenue recognition.	☐
		68	Do an answer plan only for this question on segment reporting.	☐
		53	Answer this question in full as it includes the topical and highly examinable area of share based payment.	
Environmental issues	18	70	Do an answer plan only. A comprehensive question, covering everything you are likely to meet. Do an answer plan but learn our answer carefully.	☐
		71	Answer in full. Useful past exam question.	☐

Build your own exams

Having revised your notes and the BPP Passcards, you can attempt the questions in the Kit as a series of practice exams. You can organise the questions in the following ways:

- Either you can attempt complete old papers; recent papers are listed below.

	P8								
	Pilot paper	May '05	Nov '05	May '06	Nov '06	May '07	Nov '07	May '08	Nov '08
Section A									
1	80	81	82	83	84	ME2 Q1	85	86	ME3 Q1
Section B									
2	64	65	ME1 Q2	2	27	ME2 Q2	66	9	ME3 Q2
3	8	21	ME1 Q3	13	75	ME2 Q3	45	41	ME3 Q3
4	39	40	ME1 Q4	47	44	ME2 Q4	77	76	ME3 Q4
Section C									
5	25	55	50	20	22	ME2 Q5	59	61	ME3 Q5
6	53	12	30	56	14	ME2 Q6	23	31	ME3 Q6
7	54	71	69	57	58	ME2 Q7	60	62	ME3 Q7

- Or you can make up practice exams, either yourself or using the mock exams that we have listed below.

	Practice exams							
	1	2	3	4	5	6	7	8
Section A								
1	79	80	81	82	83	84	85	86
Section B								
2	35	39	40	2	47	64	41	45
3	13	21	27	22	6	65	76	9
4	64	65	75	73	39	40	77	66
Section C								
5	53	58	55	56	57	44	31	23
6	14	12	20	26	30	21	59	60
7	70	71	36	34	47	57	61	62

- Whichever practice exams you use, you must attempt **Mock exams 1, 2 and 3** at the end of your revision.

Questions

REGULATORY FRAMEWORK

Questions 1 and 2 cover the regulatory framework, the subject of Part A of the BPP Study Text for Paper 8.

1 Preparation question: Prescriptive standards

Consider the following statement.

'Accounting standards permit such a wide variety of different accounting policies and practices that it would be wrong to assume any significant degree of comparability between companies' statutory accounts.'

Required

Discuss this statement, commenting on the extent to which comparability is achieved in practice and reaching a conclusion as to whether more prescriptive standards should be introduced.

2 MNO (5/06)   18 mins

You are the assistant to the Finance Director of MNO, a medium-sized listed entity that complies with International Financial Reporting Standards. One of MNO's directors has proposed the publication of an Operating and Financial Review (OFR) as part of the annual financial statements. Most of the directors know very little about the OFR, and the Finance Director has asked you to produce a short briefing paper on the topic for their benefit.

Required

Write the briefing paper, which should discuss the following issues.

(a)   Any relevant regulatory requirements for an OFR
(b)   The purpose and, in outline, the typical content of an OFR
(c)   The advantages and drawbacks of publishing an OFR from the entity's point of view   **(10 marks)**

GROUP ACCOUNTS

Questions 3 to 31 cover group accounts, the subject of Part B of the Study Text for Paper 8.

3 Section A questions: Group accounts (1)   36 mins

1   The following diagram shows the structure of a group:

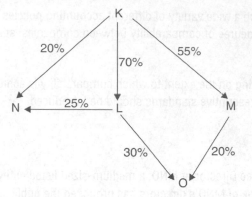

On the basis of this information, what are the two subsidiaries of K?

(2 marks)

2   Tiger has the following shares in issue:

10,000 25c ordinary shares
5,000 $1 preferred shares
5,000 $1 'A' ordinary shares (non-voting)

Leopard owns the following shares in Tiger:

6,500 25c ordinary shares
5,000 $1 preferred shares
2,500 $1 'A' ordinary shares (non-voting)

What is Leopard's effective interest in Tiger?

(2 marks)

3   Consul owns the following equity shareholdings in other entities.

Admiral	25%
Sultan	20%
Warrior	30%

Consul has a seat on the board of each entity.

Consul is the largest shareholding in Admiral (no other shareholdings are larger than 10%).

Another entity owns 25% of the equity shares in Sultan and also has a seat on its board. No other individual or entity owns more than 5% of the equity share capital of Sultan.

Another entity holds 70% of Warrior's equity and has a seat on its board.

Which entities are associates of Consul?

A   Admiral only
B   Admiral and Sultan
C   Admiral and Warrior
D   Admiral, Sultan and Warrior

(2 marks)

4 A group structure is shown below:

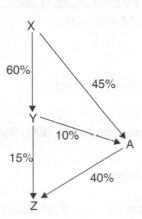

X

60%   45%

Y   10%   A

15%

40%

Z

What proportion of Z is controlled by X?

A   19%
B   29%
C   37%
D   55%   (1 mark)

5   ST has owned 100% of the equity share capital of UV and WX for many years.

(1)   UV operates in a country in Central Africa. During the current reporting period, civil war has broken out in this country. Essential services have been severely disrupted and it has been impossible to communicate with local personnel for several months. This situation is unlikely to be resolved in the near future.

(2)   WX is an insurance company. The rest of the group extracts and processes mineral ores. The directors of ST have decided that WX should be sold and are actively seeking a buyer.

Which of these subsidiaries must be excluded from consolidation?   (2 marks)

6   The summarised balance sheets of Falcon and Kestrel at 31 December 20X8 were as follows:

	Falcon	Kestrel
	$m	$m
Net assets (at fair values)	68	25
Share capital	10	10
Reserves	58	15
	68	25

On 1 January 20X8 Falcon purchased 80% of the equity share capital of Kestrel for $24 million. The fair value of the net assets of Kestrel was $20 million at that date. The goodwill arising on consolidation was impaired by 100%.

Calculate the amount of reserves to be included in the consolidated balance sheet at 31 December 20X8.
                                                                                          (3 marks)

7   Harrow acquired 270,000 $1 ordinary shares in Slough on 1 January 20X9 at a cost of $400,000. At that date, Slough had 300,000 $1 ordinary shares in issue and its reserves were $50,000.
The amount of goodwill arising on consolidation is:

A $50,000
B $80,000
C $85,000
D $130,000   (2 marks)

8   Ploughshare acquired 80% of the equity share capital of Sword on 30 September 20X1. On 31 December 20X1, the share capital and reserves of Sword were:

	$'000
Ordinary shares of 50c each	300
Retained earnings at 1 January 20X1	80
Retained profit for the year ended 31 December 20X1	40
	420

The profits of Sword have accrued evenly throughout 20X1. Goodwill arising on the acquisition was $20,000.

What was the cost of the investment in Sword?   (3 marks)

9   AB acquired a 60% holding in CD many years ago. At 31 December 20X3 AB held inventory with a book value of $30,000 purchased from CD at cost plus 20%.

The effect on the consolidated income statement for the year is:

	Group profit	Minority interest
A	Reduced by $3,000	Reduced by $2,000
B	Reduced by $3,600	Reduced by $2,400
C	Reduced by $5,000	No effect
D	Reduced by $6,000	No effect

(1 mark)

10   XY owns 75% of the issued equity share capital of PQ. At the year end, XY held inventory valued at $160,000 and PQ held inventories valued at $90,000. The inventories held by XY included $20,000 of goods purchased from PQ at a profit margin of 30%. There was also inventories in transit between the two entities; this amounted to a further $10,000 at selling price.

At what value should inventories appear in the consolidated balance sheet?   (2 marks)

(Total = 20 marks)

4 Section A questions: Group accounts (2)   36 mins

1   X owns 80% of Y and 75% of Z. At 31 December 20X5, the three entities had declared the following dividends for the year ended on that date:

	$
X	60,000
Y	30,000
Z	20,000

X had also paid an interim dividend of $15,000.

What is the total liability for dividends payable in the consolidated balance sheet at 31 December 20X5?

(2 marks)

The following information is relevant for questions 2 and 3

Hardy has a 90% subsidiary, Lawrence. During the year ended 31 December 20X2 Lawrence sold goods to Hardy for $25,000, which was cost plus 25%. At 31 December 20X2 $10,000 of these goods remained unsold.

2   In the consolidated income statement for the year ended 31 December 20X2, revenue will be reduced by:

A $18,750
B $20,000
C $22,500
D $25,000

(1 mark)

3   In the consolidated income statement for the year ended 31 December 20X2, gross profit will be reduced by:

A $1,800
B $2,000
C $2,250
D $2,500   (1 mark)

4   Pumpkin has held 90% of the equity share capital of Squash for many years. Cost of sales for each entity for the year ended 31 December 20X3 was as follows:

                                                                                         $
Pumpkin   100,000
Squash   80,000

During the year, Squash sold goods costing $5,000 to Pumpkin for $8,000. At the year end, all these goods remained in inventory.

What figure should be shown as cost of sales in the consolidated income statement of the Pumpkin group for the year ended 31 December 20X3?   (3 marks)

5   Parent owned 80% of the issued equity share capital of Subsidiary. For the year ended 31 December 20X6 Subsidiary reported a net profit of $55 million. During 20X6 Subsidiary sold goods to Parent for $15 million at cost plus 20%. At the year end half these goods are still held by Parent.

In the consolidated income statement for the year ended 31 December 20X6 the minority interest is:

A $8 million
B $10.7 million
C $10.75 million
D $11 million   (2 marks)

6   River owns 80% of the ordinary share capital and 30% of the preferred share capital of Stream. The capital structure of Stream is as follows:

                                                                                         $
$1 ordinary shares   2,000,000
10% $1 preferred shares   1,000,000

River and Stream made profits after tax of $900,000 and $400,000 respectively for the year ended 31 December 20X8 after adjusting for all intra-group items.

What is the total retained profit for the group for the year?   (2 marks)

7   Strachey owns 75% of the equity shares in Bell. At 31 July 20X2, the inventory of Strachey was valued at $420,000 and included goods costing $60,000 that it had purchased from Bell at cost plus 20%.

At 31 July 20X2, inventories were was valued at $445,000 in the consolidated balance sheet of the Strachey group.

At 31 July 20X2, what is the inventory figure in the balance sheet of Bell?   (3 marks)

8   Woolf acquired 80% of the share capital of Stephen on its incorporation many years ago. No goodwill arose on the acquisition. At 31 December 20X9, the retained earnings of Woolf were $202,000 and the consolidated retained earnings of the Woolf group were $230,000.

During the year ended 31 December 20X9, Stephen had sold goods to Woolf for $25,000. The goods originally cost $20,000.

What were the retained earnings of Stephen at 31 December 20X9?   (3 marks)

Outlook has one subsidiary. On 1 January 20X7 Outlook purchased 30% of the share capital of View for $12 million. The summarised balance sheet of View at 31 December 20X7 was as follows:

	$m
Net assets (at book value)	30
Share capital: $1 ordinary shares	10
Retained earnings at 1 January 20X7	15
Profit for the year ended 31 December 20X7	5
	30

At 1 January 20X7 the fair value of the net assets of View was $5 million greater than their book value. The difference relates to land which is still owned by View at 31 December 20X7.

Using the equity method, at what value is the investment in View shown in the consolidated balance sheet of the Outlook group at 31 December 20X7? **(3 marks)**

(Total = 20 marks)

5 Develop

18 mins

You are the accountant responsible for training at Develop, an entity with a number of investments throughout the world. A key financial reporting task is to prepare consolidated financial statements and this forms an important aspect of the training of new accountants.

A recently-employed trainee has sent you this memorandum.

I have just attended my first training course and have learned the mechanics of how to treat subsidiaries, associates, and trade investments in the consolidated accounts. I'm reasonably comfortable with the numbers, but the concepts baffle me. Why does the exercise of adding together the balance sheets of our entity with those of our subsidiaries give our shareholders useful financial information? Why do we treat associates differently – I find the concept of adding together all the net assets and showing our share as one amount particularly confusing? I'm happier with the treatment of trade investments, at least I can see that the figure is what we paid to buy the shares. Why not do this for all our investments? I don't need a detailed explanation of the mechanics, which I'm already reasonably happy with.

Required

Draft a reply to your trainee that explains the principles underpinning the preparation of consolidated financial statements. You should clearly explain why subsidiaries, associates and trade investments are treated differently and why the information is of benefit to the shareholders of the investor. **(10 marks)**

6 Fair values

18 mins

You are a recently qualified CIMA accountant. A trainee who reports to you has raised the following issue.

I've just attended my second training course and a couple of things confused me. First of all, we were told that the net assets of newly-acquired subsidiaries need to be revalued to fair value at the date of acquisition. I don't see how this can produce sensible results unless the net assets of other group members are revalued at the same time.

Required

Draft a reply to this second trainee that explains the rationale behind fair value adjustments. You do NOT need to explain the detailed mechanics of fair value adjustments. **(10 marks)**

7 Preparation question: Simple consolidation

(handwritten: FVA = 1200)

P acquired 80% of S on 1 January 20X4 for $20,000,000 when its equity was $13,800,000 (share capital $1,500,000, retained earnings $12,300,000). The fair value of S at that date was $1,200,000 more than its book value, the difference being attributable to the value of the property, plant and equipment, being depreciated over a remaining useful life of 10 years from 1 January 20X4. P acquired 30% of A on 1 January 20X6 for $1,900,000 when the balance on its equity was $4,000,000 (share capital $1,000,000, retained earnings $3,000,000).

(handwritten margin: 30% P, A 80%, S)

During the year ended 31 December 20X7, S sold goods to P which cost $1,000,000 for $1,500,000. One quarter of these goods remain unsold at the end of the year. A sold goods to P which cost $500,000 for $700,000. All of the goods remain unsold at the end of the year. *(handwritten: PuP ADJ)*

An impairment test conducted at the year end revealed impairment losses of $800,000 relating to the recognised goodwill of S. No impairment losses had previously been recognised. The Group recognises impairment losses in other expenses. No impairment losses to date have been necessary for the investment in A.

(handwritten: current year impairment)

(handwritten: If P sold to A, any PuP will be added to cos.)

INCOME STATEMENTS FOR THE YEAR ENDED 31 DECEMBER 20X7

	P	S	A
	$'000	$'000	$'000
Revenue	200,000	150,000	44,000
Cost of sales	(120,000)	(90,000)	(31,000)
Gross profit	80,000	60,000	13,000
Other expenses	(30,000)	(30,000)	(4,000)
Profit before tax	50,000	30,000	9,000
Income tax expense	(20,000)	(10,500)	(3,000)
Profit for the period	30,000	19,500	6,000

STATEMENT OF CHANGES IN EQUITY FOR THE YEAR ENDED 31 DECEMBER 20X7

	Total equity		
	P	S	A
	$'000	$'000	$'000
Balance at 31.12.20X6	51,100	20,500	11,000
Profit for the period	30,000	19,500	6,000
Balance at 31.12.20X7	81,100	40,000	17,000

Equity at 31 December 20X7 comprises:

	P	S	A
Share capital	2,900	1,500	1,000
Retained earnings	78,200	38,500	16,000
	81,100	40,000	17,000

(handwritten: RE)

Required

Prepare the consolidated income statement and statement of changes in equity (total) for the year ended 31 December 20X7.

Helping hands

1   Lay out a proforma income statement as shown below, leaving plenty of space. Alternatively, use and fill in the one below.

2   Lay out the workings you think you'll need.

3   Fill in the easy numbers given in the question.

4   Work out the more complicated numbers using the workings.

5   Keep all your work very neat and tidy to make it easy to follow. Cross reference all your workings to the balance sheet.

P GROUP
CONSOLIDATED INCOME STATEMENT FOR THE YEAR ENDED 31 DECEMBER 20X7

$'000

Revenue
Cost of sales
Gross profit
Other expenses
Share of profit of associate
Profit before tax
Income tax expense
Profit for the period

Attributable to:
  Equity holders of the parent
  Minority interest

CONSOLIDATED STATEMENT OF CHANGES IN EQUITY FOR THE YEAR ENDED 31 DECEMBER 20X7

	Equity attributable to equity holders of the parent	Minority interest	Total equity
	$'000	$'000	$'000
Balance at 31 December 20X6			
Profit for the period			
Balance at 31 December 20X7			

8 XYZ (Pilot paper)   18 mins

XYZ is a listed entity engaged in the provision of recruitment services, preparing financial statements to 30 June each year. Part of the directors' long term strategy is to identify opportunities for the takeover of other related businesses. In 20X1, the directors decided to expand their operations into the second major city of the country in which XYZ operates by taking over an existing recruitment agency. On 1 July 20X1, XYZ paid $14,700,000 for 80% of the shares in the successful AB Agency. At that date, AB had 1,000,000 shares in issue at a nominal value of $1 each, and retained earnings were $2,850,000. At the date of acquisition, AB's brand name was valued by specialists at $2,900,000 and following the acquisition it has been recognised in the consolidated financial statements of XYZ. Apart from retained earnings, AB has no other reserves.

AB has continued to be very successful and, therefore XYZ's directors have been seeking further acquisitions. On 1 April 20X7, XYZ gained control of a small on-line recruitment business, paying $39.60 per share to acquire 60,000 out of 100,000 issued shares in the CD Agency. The nominal value of each share in CD is $1. CD's retained earnings at 1 July 20X6 were $700,000; at 30 June 20X7, they were $780,000. CD paid no dividends during the year ended 30 June 20X7. CD's profits can be assumed to accrue evenly over time. Since acquisition CD has continued to produce growth in both profit and market share.

The directors follow the treatment accounting required for goodwill arising on consolidation by IFRS 3 *Business combinations*. XYZ has no investments other than those in AB and CD.

Required

(a)   Calculate the balance of goodwill on acquisition to be included in the consolidated financial statements of
       XYZ for the year ended 30 June 20X8.   **(6 marks)**

(b)   What is the accounting treatment required by IFRS 3 *Business Combinations?* Will this have any impact on
       retained earnings?   **(4 marks)**

(Total marks = 10)

9 AAY (5/08)

Summarised statements of changes in equity for the year ended 31 March 2008 for AAY and its only subsidiary, BBZ, are shown below:

	AAY	BBZ
	$'000	$'000
Balance at 1 April 2007	662,300	143,700
Profit for the period	81,700	22,000
Dividends	(18,000)	(6,000)
Balance at 31 March 2008	726,000	159,700

Notes

1   AAY acquired 80% of the issued share capital of BBZ on 1 April 2005, when BBZ's total equity was $107·7 million. The first dividend BBZ has paid since acquisition is the amount of $6 million shown in the summarised statement above. The profit for the period of $81,700 in AAY's summarised statement of changes in equity above does not include its share of the dividend paid by BBZ.

2   The only consolidation adjustment required is in respect of intra-group trading. BBZ regularly supplies goods to AAY. The amount included in the inventory of AAY in respect of goods purchased from BBZ at the beginning and end of the accounting period was as follows:

1 April 2007	$2 million
31 March 2008	$3 million

BBZ earns a profit on intra-group sales of 25% on cost.

Required

Prepare a summarised consolidated statement of changes in equity for the AAY Group for the year ended 31 March 2008.

(10 marks)

10 Preparation question: Joint venture

	Top Co	Notch Co
	$'000	$'000
Non-current assets		
Property, plant and equipment	70,000	45,000
Investment in Notch	12,000	
	82,000	45,000
Current assets	93,000	52,000
	175,000	97,000
Equity		
Share capital	50,000	5,000
Retained earnings	74,000	65,000
	124,000	70,000
Current liabilities	51,000	27,000
	175,000	97,000

Top Co acquired a 25% interest in Notch Co six years ago when the balance on Notch Co's retained earnings was $35,000,000. Top Co has joint control of Notch together with three other parties.

Required

Prepare the consolidated balance sheet of Top Co incorporating Notch under the proportionate consolidation method. No impairment losses have been necessary to date.

TOP GROUP: CONSOLIDATED BALANCE SHEET

$'000

Non-current assets
Property, plant and equipment
Goodwill

Current assets

Equity
Share capital
Retained earnings

Current liabilities

11 Textures

45 mins

Textures Co was incorporated in 20W5 to manufacture artificial limbs. Its financial year end is 30 November 20X6. It exports more than 60% of its output. It has a number of overseas subsidiaries.

It has developed a number of arrangements to support its export sales. These include agreements with Pills Co, Eduaid Co and Bracos Co, and Computer Control Co. Information on the agreements is as follows.

1   *Agreement with Pills Co*

An agreement was made in 20X2 with Pills Co, a pharmaceutical company, to jointly fund on a 50:50 basis an entity, Textures & Pills Joint Venture, to operate a marketing office in Asia which would advise on each of the company's products but not trade in the products. Both Textures and Pills have guaranteed to meet liabilities if the other party fails to meet its share of costs and risks.

Accounts prepared for Textures & Pills Joint Venture for the year ended 30 November 20X6 showed the following.

	$'000
Property, plant and equipment	
Premises	300
Current assets	
Bank and cash	30
	330
Capital	
As at 1 December 20X5	
Textures Ltd	211
Pills Co	211
	422
Less expenses	92
As at 30 November 20X6	330

2   *Agreement with Eduaid and Bracos*

Textures entered into an agreement on 1 December 20X1 with Eduaid, an entity that manufactured educational equipment, and Bracos, a South American lawyer, to set up under their joint control an unincorporated import undertaking in South America to trade as Eurohelp. Textures had an effective 30% interest in Eurohelp. The balance sheet of Textures as at 30 November 20X6 showed an investment at cost in Eurohelp of $750,000.

BPP
LEARNING MEDIA

The balance sheet of Eurohelp for the year ended 30 November 20X6 showed the following.

	$'000
Non-current assets	7,500
Net current assets	1,100
	8,600
Capital account	
As at 30 November 20X5	6,750
Retained profit for the year	1,850
	8,600

Textures has used proportionate consolidation to account for its interest in Eurohelp since entering into the agreement.

3 *Agreement with Computer Control*

Textures entered into an agreement on 1 December 20X3 with Computer Control to jointly control Afrohelp, an entity in which each investor held a 50% interest. Afrohelp assembled mechanical products from Textures and automated them with control equipment from Computer Control.

The joint venture has been proportionately consolidated by each investor entity. One of the newly appointed non-executive directors has questioned whether the investment in Afrohelp should be treated as a quasi-subsidiary and consolidated.

On 1 November 20X6 Textures sold inventory costing $110,000 to Afrohelp for $162,000. This inventory was unsold at 30 November 20X6.

Required

(a) (i) Explain the advantages and disadvantages of using equity accounting to account for associates in consolidated accounts. **(4 marks)**

(ii) Discuss the advantages and disadvantages of using proportionate consolidation to account for joint ventures. **(5 marks)**

(b) (i) Explain how the joint activity of Textures & Pills Joint Venture would be dealt with in the accounts of Textures as at 30 November 20X6. **(3 marks)**

(ii) Calculate the retained profit of Eurohelp as at 1 December 20X5 that would be included in the consolidated retained earnings brought forward in the accounts of Textures at 30 November 20X6. **(2 marks)**

(c) Assuming that you are the Finance Director of Textures:

(i) Advise the non-executive director of the conditions that would need to be satisfied to avoid Afrohelp being treated as a quasi-subsidiary as at 30 November 20X6. **(6 marks)**

(ii) Contrast the treatment of the unrealised gain on the sale of inventory to Afrohelp on consolidating Afrohelp as an associate compared to a quasi-subsidiary. **(5 marks)**

(Total marks = 25)

12 AJ (5/05)   45 mins

AJ is a law stationery business. In 20X2, the majority of its board of directors was replaced. The new board decided to adopt a policy of expansion through acquisition. The balance sheets at 31 March 20X5 of AJ and of two entities in which it holds substantial investments are shown below.

	AJ		BK		CL	
	$'000	$'000	$'000	$'000	$'000	$'000
Non-current assets						
Property, plant and equipment	12,500		4,700		4,500	
Investments	18,000		–		1,300	
		30,500		4,700		5,800
Current assets						
Inventories	7,200		8,000		–	
Trade receivables	6,300		4,300		3,100	
Financial assets	–		–		2,000	
Cash	800		–		900	
		14,300		12,300		6,000
		44,800		17,000		11,800
Equity						
Called up share capital ($1 shares)		10,000		5,000		2,500
Reserves		14,000		1,000		4,300
		24,000		6,000		6,800
Non-current liabilities						
Loan notes		10,000		3,000		–
Current liabilities						
Trade payables	8,900		6,700		4,000	
Income tax	1,300		100		600	
Short-term borrowings	600		1,200		400	
		10,800		8,000		5,000
		44,800		17,000		11,800

NOTES TO THE BALANCE SHEETS

Note 1 – Investment by AJ in BK

On 1 April 20X2, AJ purchased $2 million loan notes in BK at par.

On 1 April 20X3, AJ purchased 4 million of the ordinary shares in BK for $7.5 million cash, when BK's reserves were $1.5 million.

At the date of acquisition of the shares, BK's property, plant and equipment included land recorded at a cost of $920,000. At the date of acquisition the fair value of the land was $1,115,000. No other adjustments in respect of fair value were required to BK's assets and liabilities upon acquisition. BK has not recorded the fair value in its own accounting records.

Note 2 – Investment by AJ in CL

On 1 October 20X4, AJ acquired 1 million shares in CL, a book distributor, when the reserves of CL were $3.9 million. The purchase consideration was $4.4 million. Since the acquisition, AJ has had the right to appoint one of the five directors of CL. The remaining shares in CL are owned principally by three other investors.

No fair value adjustments were required in respect of CL's assets or liabilities upon acquisition.

Note 3 – Goodwill on consolidation

Since acquiring its investment in BK, AJ has adopted the requirements of IFRS 3 *Business combinations* in respect of goodwill on consolidation. During March 20X5, it conducted an impairment review of goodwill. As a result, the goodwill element of the investment in CL is unaltered, but the value of goodwill on consolidation in respect of BK is now $1.7 million.

Note 4 – Intra-group trading

BK supplies legal books to AJ. On 31 March 20X5, AJ's inventories included books purchased at a total cost of $1 million from BK. BK's mark-up on books is 25%.

Required

(a) Explain, with reasons, how the investments in BK and CL will be treated in the consolidated financial statements of the AJ group.

(5 marks)

(b) Prepare the consolidated balance sheet for the AJ group at 31 March 20X5. Full workings should be shown.

(20 marks)

(Total = 25 marks)

13 ST (5/06)

18 mins

The income statements of ST and two entities in which it holds investments are shown below for the year ended 31 January 20X6.

	ST	UV	WX
	$'000	$'000	$'000
Revenue	1,800	1,400	600
Cost of sales	(1,200)	(850)	(450)
Gross profit	600	550	150
Operating expenses	(450)	(375)	(74)
Profit from operations	150	175	76
Finance cost	(16)	(12)	–
Interest income	6	–	–
Profit before tax	140	163	76
Income tax expense	(45)	(53)	(26)
Profit for the period	95	110	50

Note 1: investments by ST

Several years ago ST acquired 70% of the issued ordinary share capital of UV. On 1 February 20X5, ST acquired 50% of the issued share capital of WX, an entity set up under a contractual arrangement as a joint venture between ST and one of its suppliers. The directors of ST have decided to adopt a policy of proportionate consolidation wherever appropriate and permitted by International Financial Reporting Standards.

Note 2: UV's borrowings

During the financial year ended 31 January 20X6, UV paid the full amount of interest due on its 6% debenture loan of $200,000. ST invested $100,000 in the debenture when it was issued three years ago.

Note 3: Intra-group trading

During the year, WX sold goods to ST for $20,000. Half of the goods remained in ST's inventories at 31 January 2006. WX's gross profit margin on the sale was 20%.

Required

Prepare the consolidated income statement of the ST group for the year ended 31 January 20X6. **(10 marks)**

14 SDB (11/06)

45 mins

A friend of yours has recently been left a portfolio of investments by a relative. The portfolio includes 150 shares in SDB, a listed entity that designs, manufactures and supplies houses in kit form for export to developing countries. Having recently received the financial statements of the entity for the financial year ended 31 July 20X6, your friend, who has some basic knowledge of accounting, has asked you to clarify certain points for him, and to provide him with a brief report on the position of the business.

The income statement, statement of changes in equity and balance sheet are as follows:

SDB: CONSOLIDATED INCOME STATEMENT FOR THE YEAR ENDED 31 JULY 20X6

	20X6 $'000	20X5 $'000
Revenue	25,200	25,300
Cost of sales	(18,400)	(18,000)
Gross profit	6,800	7,300
Distribution costs	(970)	(1,030)
Administrative expenses	(1,750)	(1,720)
Finance costs	(1,220)	(1,140)
Share of losses of joint venture	(1,670)	–
Profit before tax	1,190	3,410
Income tax expense	(250)	(780)
Profit for the period	940	2,630
Attributable to		
Equity holders of the parent	810	2,230
Minority interest	130	400
	940	2,630

SDB: CONSOLIDATED STATEMENT OF CHANGES IN EQUITY FOR THE YEAR ENDED 31 JULY 20X6

	Share capital $'000	Other reserves $'000	Retained earnings $'000	Minority interest $'000	Total equity $'000
Balance at 1 August 20X5	4,000	–	18,600	540	23,140
Profit for the period			810	130	940
Dividends			(2,470)	(330)	(2,800)
Issue of share capital	1,600	2,000			3,600
Balance at 31 July 20X6	5,600	2,000	16,940	340	24,880

SDB: CONSOLIDATED BALANCE SHEET AT 31 JULY 20X6

	20X6 $'000	20X6 $'000	20X5 $'000	20X5 $'000
ASSETS				
Non-current assets				
Property, plant and equipment	19,900		17,800	
Investment in joint venture	7,500		–	
		27,400		17,800
Current assets				
Inventories	8,300		6,900	
Trade receivables	4,700		4,100	
Cash	3,100		13,000	
		16,100		24,000
		43,500		41,800

	20X6		20X5	
	$'000	$'000	$'000	$'000
EQUITY AND LIABILITIES				
Equity attributable to shareholders of the parent				
Called up share capital ($1 shares)	5,600		4,000	
Retained earnings	16,940		18,600	
Other reserves	2,000		–	
		24,540		22,600
Minority interest		340		540
Total equity		24,880		23,140
Non-current liabilities				
Long-term loans		13,600		13,600
Current liabilities				
Trade payables	4,770		4,280	
Income tax	250		780	
		5,020		5,060
		43,500		41,800

Your friend's queries are as follows.

(a) I've looked up IAS 31 *Interests in joint ventures*, which mentions proportionate consolidation and equity accounting as possible methods of accounting for joint ventures. I've not previously encountered joint ventures, or proportionate consolidation. Can you explain how IAS 31 affects these financial statements?

(b) The long-term loans are described in a note as 'repayable in three equal instalments in each of the years 20X8–20Y0'. What does this mean, and what are the implications for SDB's position?

(c) There is a note to the financial statements about a contingent liability of $10 million. Apparently, one of the models of house supplied by SDB has a tendency to collapse in adverse weather conditions, and $10 million is the amount claimed by litigants in a case that is due to be heard within the next 18 months. SDB's directors think it is possible that the entity will have to pay out. This seems a very large amount of money. How likely is it that the entity will have to pay out, and how bad would the effect be?

(d) I can see that the business's profitability has suffered during the year, but if anything, I'm more concerned about the fact that the cash balance has fallen by almost $10 million. I'd very much like to have your opinion on the entity's position.

Required

Write a report to your friend that:

(a) Explains the concept of a jointly controlled entity and the permitted approaches to accounting for it, identifying possible reasons for the selection of accounting method by SDB **(9 marks)**

(b) Analyses the financial statements of SDB, focusing as requested upon the entity's position, and including references to the queries about the long-term loans and the contingent liability **(16 marks)**
(Total = 25 marks)

15 Preparation question: Part disposal

Angel Co bought 70,000 shares in Shane Co (70% of Shane Co's share capital) for $120,000 on 1 January 20X6. At that date Shane Co's retained earnings stood at $10,000.

The balance sheets at 31 December 20X8, summarised income statements to that date and movement on retained earnings are given below:

31 DEC '8

	Angel Co $'000	Shane Co $'000
BALANCE SHEETS		
Non-current assets		
Property, plant and equipment	200	80
Investment in Shane Co	120	–
	320	80
Current assets	890	140
	1,210	220
Equity		
Share capital – $1 ordinary shares	500	100
Retained earnings	400	90
	900	190
Current liabilities	310	30
	1,210	220
SUMMARISED INCOME STATEMENTS		
Profit before interest and tax	110	30
Income tax expense	(40)	(12)
Profit for the period	70	18
STATEMENT OF CHANGES IN EQUITY		
Balance at 31.12.20X7	830	172
Profit for the period	70	18
Balance at 31.12.20X8	900	190

Angel Co sells 35,000 shares in Shane Co for $160,000 on 30 June 20X8, and the remaining holding is to be dealt with as an associate. This does not represent a discontinued operation.

No entries have been made in the accounts for the above transaction.

Disposal not accounted for – to the Bal sheet proceeds prob.t + removal + removal of means

Assume that profits accrue evenly throughout the year.

Required

Prepare the consolidated balance sheet, income statement and a statement of changes in equity (attributable to equity holders of the parent *only*) for the year ended 31 December 20X8.

Ignore income taxes. No impairment losses have been necessary to date.

Helping hands

1   Set out a proforma like the one below or use the one we have provided.
2   As 'no entries have been made in the accounts for the above transaction', adjust the balance sheet for the **parent** company gain.
3   Consolidate 100% Share Co's profit and income tax expense for the number of months Angel Co had control.

ANGEL GROUP
CONSOLIDATED BALANCE SHEET AS AT 31 DECEMBER 20X8

$'000

Non-current assets
Property, plant and equipment
Investment in Shane

_____

Current assets

_____

	$'000
Equity attributable to equity holders of the parent	
Share capital	
Retained earnings	
	___
	___
Current liabilities	
	___

CONSOLIDATED INCOME STATEMENT FOR THE YEAR ENDED 31 DECEMBER 20X8

	$'000
Profit before interest and tax	
Profit on disposal of shares in subsidiary	
Share of profit of associate	
Profit before tax	
Income tax expense	
Profit for the period	
Attributable to:	
Equity holders of the parent	
Minority interest	
	___

CONSOLIDATED STATEMENT OF CHANGES IN EQUITY (ATTRIBUTABLE TO EQUITY HOLDERS OF THE PARENT)

	$'000
Balance at 31 December 20X7	
Profit for the period	
Balance at 31 December 20X8	

16 Preparation question: 'D' shaped group balance sheet

Below are the balance sheets of three companies as at 31 December 20X9.

	Bauble Co $'000	Jewel Co $'000	Gem Co $'000
Non-current assets			
Property, plant and equipment	720	60	70
Investments in group companies	185	100	–
	905	160	70
Current assets	175	95	90
	1,080	255	160
Equity			
Share capital – $1 ordinary shares	400	100	50
Retained earnings	560	90	65
	960	190	115
Current liabilities	120	65	45
	1,080	255	160

You are also given the following information:

1   Bauble Co acquired 60% of the share capital of Jewel Co on 1 January 20X2 and 10% of Gem on 1 January 20X3. The cost of the combinations were $142,000 and $43,000 respectively. Jewel Co acquired 70% of the share capital of Gem Co on 1 January 20X3.

2   The retained earnings balances of Jewel Co and Gem Co were:

	1 January 20X2 $'000	1 January 20X3 $'000
Jewel Co	45	60
Gem Co	30	40

3   No impairment loss adjustments have been necessary to date.

Required

Prepare the consolidated balance sheet for Bauble Co and its subsidiaries as at 31 December 20X9.

> **Helping hands**
>
> 1   Use the proforma below as a guide to the layout needed and figures required.
> 2   Using the information in note 1, draw the group structure (as a 'D').
> 3   Consolidate together 100% the three balances for property, plant and equipment as there is control.
> 4   Determine the date when the group gained control of Gem Co. Using the information in note 2 you can then establish the pre-acquisition reserves figure.

BAUBLE GROUP – CONSOLIDATED BALANCE SHEET AS AT 31 DECEMBER 20X9

	$'000
Non-current assets	
Property, plant and equipment	
Goodwill	___
	___
Current assets	___
	___
Equity attributable to equity holders of the parent	
Share capital – $1 ordinary shares	
Retained earnings	___
	___
Minority interest	___
	___
Current liabilities	___
	___

17 Preparation question: 'D' shaped group income statement

Upper Co owns 75% of the ordinary shares of Middle Co and 20% of Lower.

Middle Co owns 60% of the ordinary shares of Lower Co.

The summarised income statements for the year ended 31 December 20X9 are as follows:

	Upper Co	Middle Co	Lower Co
	$'000	$'000	$'000
Profit before tax	1,500	750	150
Income tax expense	500	250	50
Profit for the period	1,000	500	100
Dividends declared during the period	300	100	40

Dividends have not been accounted for in the books of the recipient companies although they were declared before the year end.

Required

Prepare the summarised consolidated income statement for the year ended 31 December 20X9 for Upper Co.

> **Helping hand**
>
> Use the proforma below as a guide to the layout needed and figures required.

$'000

Profit before tax
Income tax expense
Profit for the period

Attributable to:
  Equity holders of the parent
  Minority interest

18 Big Group

54 mins

The balance sheets of Big, Small and Tiny at 30 September 20X9 (the accounting date for all three entities) are given below.

	Big		Small		Tiny	
	$'000	$'000	$'000	$'000	$'000	$'000
Non-current assets						
Property, plant and equipment	56,000		66,000		56,000	
Investments (Notes 1-3)	104,000		29,000		–	
		160,000		95,000		56,000
Current assets						
Inventories (Note 5)	45,000		44,000		25,000	
Trade receivables (Note 6)	40,000		30,000		16,000	
Cash in hand	8,000		6,000		3,000	
		93,000		80,000		44,000
		253,000		175,000		100,000
Equity						
Share capital (Notes 2 and 3)		90,000		80,000		32,000
Retained earnings		69,000		59,000		19,000
		159,000		139,000		51,000
Long-term loans		50,000				25,000
Current liabilities						
Trade payables (Note 5)	25,000		20,000		11,000	
Tax payable	7,000		6,000		4,000	
Bank overdraft	12,000		10,000		9,000	
		44,000		36,000		24,000
		253,000		175,000		100,000

Notes to the financial statements

1 On 1 October 20X3, when the retained earnings of Small showed a balance of $22 million, Big purchased 64 million of Small's $1 equity shares for a consideration of $91.5 million, payable in cash. On 1 October 20X3, a large property owned by Small had a balance sheet value of $7 million and a fair value to Big of $11 million. With the exception of this property, the fair values of all the identifiable net assets of Small were the same as their carrying values in the balance sheet of Small. The property that had a fair value of $11 million on 1 October 20X3 was sold by Small on 30 June 20X7.

2 On 1 April 20X5, when the retained earnings of Tiny stood at $10m, Big purchased 8 million of Tiny's $1 equity shares for a cash consideration of $12.5 million. A fair-value exercise was carried out but all of the net identifiable assets of Tiny at 1 April 20X5 had a fair value that was the same as their carrying values in the balance sheet of Tiny.

3 On 1 April 20X9, Small purchased 16 million of Tiny's $1 equity shares for a cash consideration of $29 million. A fair-value exercise was carried out but all of the net identifiable assets of Tiny at 1 April 20X9 had a fair value that was the same as their carrying values in the balance sheet of Tiny. During the year ended September 20X9, Tiny made a profit after taxation of $8 million and paid no dividends. This profit accrued evenly over the year.

4   A key reason behind the purchase of shares in Tiny by Big and Small was that Tiny supplied a component that was used by both entities. Until 1 April 20X9, the component was supplied by Tiny at cost plus a mark-up of 30 per cent. From 1 April 20X9, the mark-up changed to 20 per cent. On 30 September 20X9, the inventories purchased from Tiny (all purchases since 1 April) were as follows.

- In Big's books, $9 million
- In Small's books, $7.8 million

5   The trade payables of Big and Small show amounts of $6 million and $5 million respectively as being payable to Tiny, and these balances have been agreed. There was no other inter-group trading.

You are the management accountant responsible for the consolidation of the Big group. Your assistant is aware of the basic principles and procedures to be followed in preparing consolidated financial statements. She is clear on what is required to consolidate Small but is much less sure of what to do with Tiny. She is particularly puzzled by the fact that both Big and Small made investments in Tiny and that one of these investments took place in the financial year.

Required

Prepare the consolidated balance sheet of the Big group at 30 September 20X9.   **(30 marks)**

BPP note. This question is included as it is comprehensive. In the exam, questions will be worth no more than 25 marks.

19 Port (FR, 11/01, amended)   45 mins

International Accounting Standards make it clear that the treatment in consolidated financial statements of investments in other entities is dependent on the extent of the control or influence the investing entity is able to exercise over the other entity. Port has investments in three other entities.

(i)   On 15 May 20W0, Port purchased 40 million 50c equity shares in Harbor. The issued equity share capital of Harbor on 15 May 20W0 was 50 million 50c equity shares.

(ii)   On 15 June 20W1, Port purchased 30 million $1 equity shares in Inlet. The issued equity share capital of Inlet on 15 June 20W1 was 75 million $1 equity shares. The remaining equity shares in Inlet are held by a large number of investors – none with more than 5 million equity shares.

(iii)   On 15 July 20W2, Port purchased 25 million 50c equity shares in Bay. The issued equity share capital of Bay on 15 July 20W2 as 80 million 50c equity shares. Another investor owns 50 million equity shares in Bay. This investor takes an active interest in directing the operating and financial decisions of Bay. On a number of occasions the investor has required Bay to follow policies that do not meet with the approval of Port.

Equity shares in all of the entities carry one vote per share at general meetings. No party can control or influence the composition of the board of directors of any of the entities other than through its ownership of equity shares. There have been no instances where shareholders in any of the entities have acted together to increase their control or influence. All of the entities has issued any additional equity shares since Port purchased its interests. All of the entities are separate legal entities.

Extracts from the income statements of the four entities for their year ended 30 June 20X1 are given below:

	Port $'000	Harbor $'000	Inlet $'000	Bay $'000
Revenue	65,000	45,000	48,000	40,000
Cost of sales	(35,000)	(25,000)	(26,000)	(19,000)
Gross profit	30,000	20,000	22,000	21,000

Note 1

Port manufactures a product that is used by Harbor and Inlet. During the year ended 30 June 20X1, sales of the product to Harbor and Inlet were:

- To Harbor – $8 million.
- To Inlet – $7.5 million.

Opening and closing inventories of this product in the financial statements of Harbor and Inlet (all purchased from Port at cost plus 25% mark up, unchanged during the year) were as follows.

Entity	Closing inventory $'000	Opening inventory $'000
Harbor	3,000	2,400
Inlet	2,500	Nil

At 30 June 20X1, there were no amounts payable by Harbor and Inlet in respect of inventories purchased from Port before 30 June 20X1.

Note 2

There was no other trading between the entities other than the payment of dividends.

Required

(a) State the alternative treatments of investments in consolidated financial statements that are set out in International Accounting Standards. **(11 marks)**

(b) Identify the correct treatment of the investments in Harbor, Inlet and Bay in the consolidated financial statements of Port. **(5 marks)**

(c) Compute the consolidated revenue, cost of sales and gross profit of the Port group for the year ended 30 June 20X1. You should ensure that your computations are fully supported by relevant workings. **(4 marks)**

(d) Compute the adjustments that need to be made In respect of the transactions described in *Note 1* above when preparing the consolidated balance sheet of Port at 30 June 20X1. You should explain the rationale behind each adjustment you make. **(5 marks)**

(Total = 25 marks)

20 AZ (5/06)   45 mins

The balance sheets of AZ and two entities in which it holds substantial investments at 31 March 20X6 are shown below:

BALANCE SHEETS AS AT 31 MARCH 20X6

	AZ $'000	AZ $'000	BY $'000	BY $'000	CX $'000	CX $'000
Non-current assets						
Property, plant and equipment	10,750		5,830		3,300	
Investments	7,650		–		–	
		18,400		5,830		3,300
Current assets						
Inventories	2,030		1,210		1,180	
Trade receivables	2,380		1,300		1,320	
Cash	1,380		50		140	
		5,790		2,560		2,640
		24,190		8,390		5,940
Equity						
Called up share capital ($1 shares)		8,000		2,300		2,600
Preferred share capital		–		1,000		–
Reserves		10,750		3,370		2,140
		18,750		6,670		4,740
Current liabilities						
Trade payables	3,770		1,550		1,080	
Income tax	420		170		120	
Suspense account	1,250		–		–	
		5,440		1,720		1,200
		24,190		8,390		5,940

Notes

1   *Investments by AZ in BY*

Several years ago AZ purchased 80% of BY's ordinary share capital for $3,660,000 when the reserves of BY were $1,950,000. In accordance with the group's policy goodwill was recorded at cost, and there has been no subsequent impairment.

At the same time as the purchase of the ordinary share capital, AZ purchased 40% of BY's preferred share capital at par. The remainder of the preferred shares are held by several private investors.

2   *Investment by AZ in CX*

Several years ago AZ purchased 60% of CX's ordinary share capital for $2,730,000 when the reserves of CX were $1,300,000. Goodwill was recorded at cost and there has been no subsequent impairment.

On 1 October 20X5, AZ disposed of 520,000 ordinary shares in CX, thus losing control of CX's operations. However, AZ retains a significant influence over the entity's operations and policies. The proceeds of disposal, $1,250,000, were debited to cash and credited to a suspense account. No other accounting entries have been made in respect of the disposal. An investment gains tax of 30% of the profit on disposal will become payable by AZ within the twelve months following the balance sheet date of 31 March 20X6, and this liability should be accrued.

CX's reserves at 1 April 20X5 were $1,970,000. The entity's profits accrued evenly throughout the year.

3   *Additional information*

No fair value adjustments were required in respect of assets or liabilities upon either of the acquisitions of ordinary shares. The called up share capital of both BY and CX has remained the same since the acquisitions were made.

4   *Intra-group trading*

During the year ended 31 March 20X6, BY started production of a special line of goods for supply to AZ. BY charges a mark-up of 20% on the cost of such goods sold to AZ. At 31 March 20X6, AZ's inventories included goods at a cost of $180,000 that had been supplied by BY.

Required

(a)   Calculate the profit or loss on disposal after tax of the investment in CX that will be disclosed in

    (i)   AZ's own financial statements

    (ii)   The AZ group's consolidated financial statements   **(6 marks)**

(b)   Calculate the consolidated reserves of the AZ group at 31 March 20X6.   **(5 marks)**

(c)   Prepare the consolidated balance sheet of the AZ group at 31 March 20X6.   **(14 marks)**

Full workings should be shown.   **(Total = 25 marks)**

21 RW (5/05)   18 mins

RW held on 1 Jan 20X4 80% of the 1,000,000 ordinary shares of its subsidiary, SX. Summarised income statements of both entities for the year ended 31 December 20X4 are shown below.

	RW	SX
	$'000	$'000
Revenue	6,000	2,500
Operating costs	(4,500)	(1,700)
Profit before tax	1,500	800
Income tax expense	(300)	(250)
Profit for the period	1,200	550

RW purchased 800,000 of SX's $1 shares in 20X3 for $3.2 million, when SX's reserves were $2.4 million. Goodwill has been carried at cost since acquisition and there has been no subsequent impairment.

On 1 July 20X4, RW disposed of 200,000 shares in SX for $1 million. SX's reserves at 1 January 20X4 were $2.9 million, and its profits accrued evenly throughout the year. RW is liable to income tax at 30% on any accounting profits made on the disposal of investments.

The effects of the disposal are not reflected in the income statements shown above.

Required

Prepare the summarised consolidated income statement for RW for the year ended 31 December 20X4.

(10 marks)

22 AD (11/06)   45 mins

The balance sheets of three entities, AD, BE and CF at 30 June 20X6, the year end of all three entities, are shown below.

	AD		BE		CF	
	$'000	$'000	$'000	$'000	$'000	$'000
ASSETS						
Non-current assets						
Property, plant and equipment		1,900		680		174
Financial assets						
Investments in equity shares		880		104		–
Other (Note 3)		980		–		–
		3,760		784		174
Current assets						
Inventories	223		127		60	
Trade receivables	204		93		72	
Other financial asset (Note 4)	25		–		–	
Cash	72		28		12	
		524		248		144
		4,284		1,032		318
EQUITY AND LIABILITIES						
Equity						
Called up share capital ($1 shares)		1,000		300		100
Reserves		2,300		557		122
		3,300		857		222
Non-current liabilities		600		–		–
Current liabilities						
Trade payables	247		113		84	
Income tax	137		62		12	
		384		175		96
		4,284		1,032		318

Notes

1   *Investment by AD in BE*

AD acquired 80% of the ordinary shares of BE on 1 July 20X3 for $880,000 when BE's reserves were $350,000. Goodwill on acquisition continues to be unimpaired.

2   *Investment by BE in CF*

BE acquired 40% of the ordinary shares of CF on 1 January 20X6 for $104,000. BE appoints one of CF's directors and, since the acquisition, has been able to exert significant influence over CF's activities. CF's reserves at the date of acquisition were $102,000.

3   *Non-current financial asset*

AD's other non-current financial asset is a debenture with a fixed interest rate of 5%. AD invested $1 million in the debenture at par on its issue date, 1 July 20X4. The debenture is redeemable at a premium on 30 June 20X8; the applicable effective interest rate over the life of the debenture is 8%. The full annual interest amount was received and recorded by AD in June 20X5 and June 20X6, and the appropriate finance charge was recognised in the financial year ended 30 June 20X5. However, no finance charge has yet been calculated or recognised in respect of the financial year ended 30 June 20X6.

4   *Current financial asset*

The current financial asset of $25,000 in AD represents a holding of shares in a major listed company. AD maintains a portfolio of shares held for trading. At 30 June 20X6, the only holding in the portfolio was 4,000 shares in DG, a major listed company with 2.4 million ordinary shares in issue. The investment was recognised on its date of purchase, 13 May 20X6, at a cost of 625c per share. At 30 June 20X6, the fair value of the shares had risen to 670c per share.

5   *Intra-group trading*

BE supplies goods to both AD and CF. On 30 June 20X6, CF held inventories at a cost of $10,000 that had been supplied to it by BE. BE's profit margin on the selling price of these goods is 30%.

On 30 June 20X6, AD's inventories included no items supplied by BE. However, BE's receivables on 30 June 20X6 included $5,000 in respect of an intra-group balance relating to the supply of goods to AD. No equivalent balance was included in AD's payables because it had made a payment of $5,000 on 27 June 20X6, which was not received and recorded by BE until after the year end.

Required

(a)   Explain the accounting treatment in the balance sheet and income statement for the financial assets described in Notes 3 and 4 above, as required by IAS 39 *Financial Instruments: recognition and Measurement*.   **(5 marks)**

(b)   Prepare the consolidated balance sheet for the AD Group at 30 June 20X6.   **(20 marks)**

(Total = 25 marks)

23 AX (11/07)   45 mins

AX, a listed entity, is planning to acquire several smaller entities. In order to raise the cash for its programme of acquisitions, it has recently sold part of its stake in a subsidiary, CY, and has raised $10 million in a bond issue.

Summarised balance sheets for AX, CY and the other member of the group, EZ, at 31 October 20X7 are given below:

	AX	CY	EZ
	$'000	$'000	$'000
Non-current assets:			
Property, plant and equipment	20,000	8,900	5,000
Investment in subsidiaries (notes 1 & 2)	15,500	–	–
	35,500	8,900	5,000
Current assets	34,500	9,500	4,700
	70,000	18,400	9,700

	AX $'000	CY $'000	EZ $'000
Equity:			
Called up share capital ($1 shares)	20,000	4,000	3,000
Retained earnings	18,000	7,000	3,000
	38,000	11,000	6,000
Non-current liabilities	–	2,400	1,000
Current liabilities	18,000	5,000	2,700
Suspense account (notes 1 & 3)	14,000	–	–
	70,000	18,400	9,700

Notes

1 The investment in 80% of CY's ordinary share capital was purchased several years ago for $8 million when CY's retained earnings were $3.5 million. There has been no change since then in the amount of CY's share capital, and goodwill has remained unimpaired. No adjustments to fair value of CY's net assets were made either at acquisition or subsequently.

On 31 October 20X7 AX sold one quarter of its shareholding in CY to an unconnected party for $4 million. This amount has been debited to cash and credited to the suspense account. It is estimated that a tax liability of $400,000 will arise in respect of the profit on disposal of the investment; no provision for this liability has been made in the balance sheet above.

2 The investment in 100% of EZ's ordinary share capital was purchased on 30 April 20X5 for $7.5 million when EZ's retained earnings were $1.5 million. Goodwill has remained unimpaired since the date of acquisition.

Upon acquisition a revaluation exercise was carried out. Plant and equipment in EZ with a book value of $1 million was revalued to $1.5 million. There were no other adjustments in respect of fair value. The revaluation is treated as a consolidation adjustment only: EZ continues to recognise non-current assets at depreciated historic cost. The remaining useful life of the plant and equipment at 30 April 20X5 was estimated to be five years, of which thirty months had elapsed by 31 October 20X7.

3 AX issued $10 million of 5% convertible bonds on 31 October 20X7. The bonds were issued in units of $1,000 and are repayable on 31 October 20Y0. However, each bond is convertible into 250 ordinary shares at any time until maturity at the option of the bondholder. The market rate for similar, non-convertible, bonds is 7%. It can be assumed that there were no issue costs. The $10 million raised by the issue was debited to cash and credited to the suspense account.

Required

(a) Explain the appropriate accounting treatment to record the issue of convertible bonds, discussing the reasons for the approach that is adopted by International Financial Reporting Standards for this type of financial instrument. **(5 marks)**

(b) Prepare the consolidated balance sheet for the AX group at 31 October 20X7. **(20 marks)**

(Total = 25 marks)

24 Preparation question: Foreign operations

Standard Co acquired 80% of Odense SA for $520,000 on 1 January 20X4 when the reserves of Odense were 2,100,000 Danish Krone.

An impairment test conducted at the year end revealed impairment losses of 168,000 Danish Krone relating to Odense's recognised goodwill. No impairment losses had previously been recognised.

Required

Prepare the consolidated balance sheet, income statement and statement of changes in equity (attributable to equity holders of the parent *only*) for the Standard Group for the year ended 31 December 20X6.

Helping hand

Fill in the blanks in the proformas below.

BALANCE SHEETS AS AT 31 DECEMBER 20X6

	S $'000	O Kr'000	Rate	O $'000	Consol $'000
Property, plant and equipment	1,285	4,400	8.1	543	
Investment in Odense	520	–		–	
Goodwill	–	–		–	
	1,805	4,400		543	
Current assets	410	2,000	8.1	247	
	2,215	6,400		790	
Share capital	500	1,000	9.4	106	
Retained reserves	1,115				
Pre-acquisition		2,100	9.4	224	
Post-acquisition	–	2,200	Bal	324	
	1,615	5,300		654	
Minority interest					
Loans	200	300	8.1	37	
Current liabilities	400	800	8.1	99	
	600	1,100		136	
	2,215	6,400		790	

Exchange rates were as follows:

	Kr to $1
1 January 20X4	9.4
31 December 20X5	8.8
31 December 20X6	8.1
Average 20X6	8.4

INCOME STATEMENTS FOR YEAR ENDED 31 DECEMBER 20X6

	S $'000	O Kr'000	Rate	O $'000	Consol $'000
Revenue	1,125	5,200	8.4	619	
Cost of sales	(410)	(2,300)	8.4	(274)	
Gross profit	715	2,900		345	
Other expenses	(180)	(910)	8.4	(108)	
Impairment loss	–	–		–	
Dividend received from Odense	40				
Profit before tax	575	1,990		237	
Income tax expense	(180)	(640)	8.4	(76)	
Profit for the period	395	1,350		161	

Attributable to:
  Equity holders of the parent
  Minority interest

STATEMENTS OF CHANGES IN EQUITY FOR THE YEAR

	S $'000	O Kr'000
Balance at 31 December 20X5	1,415	4,355
Profit for the period	395	1,350
Total recognised income and expense for the period	395	1,350
Dividends paid	(195)	(405)
Balance at 31 December 20X6	1,615	5,300

CONSOLIDATED STATEMENT OF CHANGES IN EQUITY (ATTRIBUTABLE TO EQUITY HOLDERS OF THE PARENT)
FOR THE YEAR ENDED 31 DECEMBER 20X6

	$'000
Balance at 31 December 20X5	
Exchange differences on translating foreign operations	——
Net income recognised directly in equity	
Profit for the period	——
Total recognised income and expense for the period	
Dividends paid	——
Balance at 31 December 20X6	

25 Little (Pilot paper)   45 mins

Little was incorporated over twenty years ago, operating as an independent entity for fifteen years until 20X1 when it was taken over by Large. Large's directors decided that the local expertise of Little's management should be utilised as far as possible, and since the takeover they have allowed the subsidiary to operate independently, maintaining its existing supplier and customer bases. Large exercises 'arm's length' strategic control, but takes no part in day-to-day operational decisions.

The balance sheets of Large and Little at 31 March 20X7 are given below. The balance sheet of Little is prepared in francos (F), its reporting currency.

	Large $'000	Large $'000	Little F'000	Little F'000
Non-current assets				
Property, plant and equipment	63,000		80,000	
Investments	12,000		–	
		75,000		80,000
Current assets				
Inventories	25,000		30,000	
Trade receivables	20,000		28,000	
Cash	6,000		5,000	
		51,000		63,000
		126,000		143,000
Equity				
Share capital (50c/1 Franco shares)		30,000		40,000
Revaluation reserve				6,000
Retained earnings		35,000		34,000
		65,000		80,000
Non-current liabilities				
Long-term borrowings	20,000		25,000	
Deferred tax	6,000		10,000	
		26,000		35,000
Current liabilities				
Trade payables	25,000		20,000	
Tax	7,000		8,000	
Bank overdraft	3,000		–	
		35,000		28,000
		126,000		143,000

NOTES TO THE BALANCE SHEETS

Note 1 – Investment by Large in Little

On 1 April 20X1 Large purchased 36,000 shares in Little for 72 million francos. The accumulated profits of Little at that date were 26 million francos. There was no impairment of goodwill.

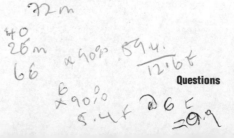

Note 2 – Intra-group trading

Little sells goods to Large, charging a mark-up of one-third on production cost. At 31 March 20X7, Large held $1 million (at cost to Large) of goods purchased from Little in its inventories. The goods were purchased during March 20X7 and were recorded by Large using an exchange rate of $1 = 5 francos. (There were minimal fluctuations between the two currencies during March 20X7.) At 31 March 20X6, Large's inventories included no goods purchased from Little. On 29 March 20X7, Large sent Little a cheque for $1 million to clear the intra-group payable. Little received and recorded this cash on 3 April 20X7.

Note 3 – Accounting policies

The accounting policies of the two companies are the same, except that the directors of Little have decided to adopt a policy of revaluation of property, whereas Large includes all property in its balance sheet at a depreciated historical cost. Until 1 April 20X6, Little operated from rented warehouse premises. On that date, the entity purchased a leasehold building for 25 million francos, taking out a long-term loan to finance the purchase. The building's estimated useful life at 1 April 20X6 was 25 years, with an estimated residual value of nil, and the directors decided to adopt a policy of straight-line depreciation. The building was professionally revalued at 30 million francos on 31 March 20X7, and the directors have included the revalued amount in the balance sheet. No other property was owned by Little during the year.

Note 4 – Exchange rates

Date	Exchange rate (francos to $1)
1 April 20X1	6.0
31 March 20X6	5.5
31 March 20X7	5.0
Weighted average for the year to 31 March 20X7	5.2
Weighted average for the dates of acquisition of closing inventory	5.1

Required

(a) Explain (with reference to relevant accounting standards to support your argument) how the financial statements (balance sheet and income statement) of Little should be translated into $s for the consolidation of Large and Little.

(5 marks)

(b) Translate the balance sheet of Little at 31 March 20X7 into $s and prepare the consolidated balance sheet of the Large group at 31 March 20X7.

(20 marks)

Note. Ignore any deferred tax implications of the property revaluation and the intra-group trading.

(Total = 25 marks)

26 Small (FR, 5/03, amended)   45 mins

Small was incorporated 18 years ago and prior to its acquisition by Big had built up its own customer base and local supplier network. This was not disturbed when Small became a subsidiary of Big as the directors of Big were anxious that the local expertise of the management of Small should be utilised as much as possible. Therefore all the day-to-day operational decisions regarding Small continued to be made by the existing management, with the directors of Big exercising 'arm's length' strategic control.

The balance sheets of Big and Small at 31 March 20X9 are given below. The balance sheet of Small is prepared in florins, the reporting currency for Small.

	Big		Small	
	$000	$000	Fl'000	Fl'000
Non-current assets				
Property, plant and equipment	60,000		80,000	
Investments	9,500		–	
		69,500		80,000
Current assets				
Inventories	30,000		40,000	
Trade receivables	25,000		32,000	
Cash	3,000		4,000	
		58,000		76,000
		127,500		156,000
Equity				
Share capital (50 cents/1/2 florin shares)		30,000		40,000
Revaluation reserve		15,000		–
Retained earnings		34,500		44,000
		79,500		84,000
Non-current liabilities				
Long-term borrowings	15,000		30,000	
Deferred tax	5,000		9,000	
		20,000		39,000
Current liabilities				
Trade payables	12,000		15,000	
Tax	16,000		18,000	
		28,000		33,000
		127,500		156,000

NOTES TO THE BALANCE SHEETS

Note 1 – Investment by Big in Small

On 1 April 20X3, Big purchased 60 million shares in Small for 57 million florins. The retained earnings of Small showed a balance of 20 million florins at that date. The accounting policies of Small are the same as those of Big except that Big revalues its land, whereas Small carries its land at historical cost. Small's land had been purchased on 1 April 20X0. On 1 April 20X3, the fair value of the land of Small was 6 million florins higher than its carrying value in the individual financial statements of that enterprise. By 31 March 20X9, the difference between fair value and carrying value had risen to 11 million florins. Apart from this accounting policy difference, no other fair value adjustments were necessary when initially consolidating Small as a subsidiary.

Note 2 – Intra-group trading

On 6 March 20X9, Big sold goods to Small at an invoiced price of $6,000,000, making a profit of 25% on cost. Small recorded these goods in inventory and payables using an exchange rate of 5 florins to $1 (there were minimal fluctuations between the two currencies in the month of March 20X9). The goods remained in the inventory of Small at 31 March 20X9 but on 29 March 20X9 Small sent Big a cheque for 30 million florins to clear its payable. Big received and recorded this cash on 3 April 20X9.

Note 3 – Exchange rates

Date	Exchange rate (florins to $1)
1 April 20X0	7
1 April 20X3	6
31 March 20X8	5·5
31 March 20X9	5
Weighted average for the year to 31 March 20X9	5·2
Weighted average for the dates of acquisition of closing inventory	5·1

Required

Translate the balance sheet of Small at 31 March 20X9 into $s and prepare the consolidated balance sheet of the Big group at 31 March 20X9.

(25 marks)

27 Home group (11/06)   18 mins

The income statements for Home and its wholly owned subsidiary Foreign for the year ended 31 July 20X6 are shown below.

	Home	Foreign
	$'000	Crowns '000
Revenue	3,000	650
Cost of sales	(2,400)	(550)
Gross profit	600	100
Distribution costs	(32)	(41)
Administrative expenses	(168)	(87)
Finance costs	(15)	(10)
Profit (loss) before tax	385	(38)
Income tax	(102)	10
Profit (loss) for the period	283	(28)

Notes

(a)   The presentation currency of the group is the $ and Foreign's functional currency is the Crown.

(b)   Home acquired 100% of the ordinary share capital of Foreign on 1 August 20X4 for 204,000 Crowns. Foreign's share capital at that date comprised 1,000 ordinary shares of 1 Crown each, and its reserves were 180,000 Crowns. In view of its subsidiary's losses, Home's directors conducted an impairment review of the goodwill at 31 July 20X6. They concluded that the goodwill had lost 20% of its value during the year (before taking exchange differences into account). The impairment should be reflected in the consolidated financial statements for the year ended 31 July 20X6.

(c)   On 1 June 20X6, Home purchased an item of plant for 32,000 Florins. At the year end, the payable amount had not yet been settled. No exchange gain or loss in respect of this item is reflected in Home's income statement above.

(d)   Exchange rates are as follows:

On 1 August 20X4:	1.7 Crowns = $1
On 31 July 20X5:	2.2 Crowns = $1
Average rate for year ended 31 July 20X6:	2.4 Crowns = $1
On 1 June 20X6:	1.5 Florins = $1
On 31 July 20X6:	1.6 Florins = $1

(e)   During the year, Foreign made sales of 50,000 Crowns to Home. None of the items remained in inventory at the year end.

Required

Prepare the consolidated income statement for the Home group for the year ended 31 July 20X6. (Work to the nearest $100)

(10 marks)

28 Preparation question: Consolidated cash flow statement

On 1 September 20X5 Swing Co acquired 70% of Slide Co for $5,000,000 comprising $1,000,000 cash and 1,500,000 $1 shares.

The balance sheet of Slide Co at acquisition was as follows:

	$'000
Property, plant and equipment	2,700
Inventories	1,600
Trade receivables	600
Cash	400
Trade payables	(300)
Income tax payable	(200)
	4,800

The consolidated balance sheet of Swing Co as at 31 December 20X5 was as follows:

	20X5	20X4
Non-current assets	$'000	$'000
Property, plant and equipment	35,000	25,000
Goodwill	1,400	–
	36,400	25,000
Current assets		
Inventories	16,000	10,000
Trade receivables	9,800	7,500
Cash	2,400	1,500
	28,200	19,000
	64,600	44,000
Equity attributable to equity holders of the parent		
Share capital	12,300	10,000
Share premium	5,800	2,000
Retained earnings	32,100	21,900
	50,200	33,900
Minority interest	1,600	–
	51,800	33,900
Current liabilities		
Trade payables	7,600	6,100
Income tax payable	5,200	4,000
	12,800	10,100
	64,600	44,000

The consolidated income statement of Swing Co for the year ended 31 December 20X5 was as follows:

	20X5
	$'000
Profit before tax	16,500
Income tax expense	(5,200)
Profit for the period	11,300
Attributable to:	
Equity holders of the parent	11,100
Minority interest	200
	11,300

Notes

(1) Depreciation charged for the year was $5,800,000. The group made no disposals of property, plant and equipment.

(2) Dividends paid by Swing Co amounted to $900,000.

Required

Prepare the consolidated cash flow statement of Swing Co for the year ended 31 December 20X5.

No notes to the cash flow statement are required.

SWING GROUP – CASH FLOW STATEMENT FOR THE YEAR ENDED 31 DECEMBER 20X5

	$'000	$'000
Cash flows from operating activities		
Profit before tax		
Adjustments for:		
Depreciation		
Impairment losses	_____	
Increase in trade receivables		
Increase in inventories		
Increase in trade payables	_____	
Cash generated from operations		
Income taxes paid (W4)	_____	
Net cash from operating activities		
Cash flows from investing activities		
Acquisition of subsidiary, net of cash acquired		
Purchase of property, plant & equipment (W1)	_____	
Net cash used in investing activities		
Cash flows from financing activities		
Proceeds from issue of share capital		
Dividends paid		
Dividends paid to minority interest (W3)	_____	
Net cash used in financing activities		_____
Net increase in cash and cash equivalents		
Cash and cash equivalents at the beginning of the period		_____
Cash and cash equivalents at the end of the period		_____

Workings

1   *Additions to property, plant and equipment*

PROPERTY, PLANT AND EQUIPMENT

$'000 $'000

2   *Goodwill impairment losses*

GOODWILL

$'000 $'000

3 *Dividends paid to minority interest*

MINORITY INTEREST

	$'000		$'000

4 Income taxes paid

INCOME TAX PAYABLE

	$'000		$'000

consolection
cash 1.5m
shares 3000k mkt price at dote 06
1.5m x2 issue.
= 4.5m.

29 Oscar   **45 mins**

On 1.10.X4 Oscar Co acquired 90% of Halina Co by issuing 1.5m shares at an agreed value of $2 per share and $1.5m in cash. At that time the balance sheet of Halina Co was as follows.

	$'000	$'000
Assets		
Non-current assets		2,850
Current assets		
Inventories	1,050	
Receivables	450	
Cash	150	
		1,650
Total assets		4,500
Liabilities		
Current liabilities: Trade payables		600

Net assets aquired = 3900 → goodwill

The consolidated balance sheets of Oscar Co as at 31 December were as follows.

Subsidiary not included

	20X4		20X3	
	$'000	$'000	$'000	$'000
Assets				
Non-current assets *includes Sub.*				
Tangible		37,500		34,500
Intangible: goodwill *c/d →*		990		
		38,940		
Current assets				
Inventories	21,750		18,000	
Receivables	20,550		16,500	
Cash	1,200		750	
		43,500		35,250
Total assets		81,990		69,750

	20X4		20X3	
	$'000	$'000	$'000	$'000
Equity and liabilities				
Equity attributable to equity holders of the parent				
Share capital: $1 shares	17,000		15,000	
Share premium account	10,000		7,500	
Retained earnings	26,865		22,950	
		53,865		45,450
Minority interest		525		
Total equity		54,390		45,450
Current liabilities				
Trade payables	25,350		22,800	
Income tax	2,250		1,500	
Total liabilities		27,600		24,300
Total equity and liabilities		81,990		69,750

The consolidated income statement for the year ended 31 December 20X4 was as follows.

	$'000
Revenue	150,000
Cost of sales	112,500
Gross profit	37,500
Administrative expenses	31,200
Profit before tax	6,300
Income tax expense	2,250
Profit for the period	4,050
Attributable to	
Equity holders of the parent	3,915
Minority interest	135
	4,050

Statement of consolidated reserves as at 31 December 20X4:

	$'000
Reserves at 1.1.20X4	22,950
Profit for the period attributable to equity holders of the parent	3,915
	26,865

You are also given the following information.

(a) All other subsidiaries are wholly owned.
(b) Depreciation charged to the consolidated income statement amounted to $3.15m. *odd ball*
(c) Wages and salaries amounted to $15m. *used in direct method only so ignore*

Required

Prepare a cash flow statement for the year ended 31 December 20X4 using the indirect method. **(25 marks)**

30 AH Group (11/05)   45 mins

Extracts form the consolidated financial statements of the AH group for the year ended 30 June 20X5 are given below.

AH GROUP: CONSOLIDATED INCOME STATEMENT FOR THE YEAR ENDED 30 JUNE 20X5

	2005 $'000
Revenue	85,000
Cost of sales	59,750
Gross profit	25,250
Operating expenses	5,650
Profit from operations	19,600
Finance cost	1,400
Profit before disposal of property	18,200
Disposal of property (note 2)	1,250
Profit before tax	19,450
Income tax	6,250
Profit for the period	13,200
Attributable to	
Minority interest	655
Group profit for the year	12,545
	13,200

AH GROUP: EXTRACTS FROM STATEMENT OF CHANGES IN EQUITY FOR THE YEAR ENDED 30 JUNE 20X5

	Share capital $'000	Share premium $'000	Consolidated retained earnings $'000
Opening balance	18,000	10,000	18,340
Issue of share capital	2,000	2,000	
Profit for period			12,545
Dividends			(6,000)
Closing balance	20,000	12,000	24,885

AH GROUP: BALANCE SHEET, WITH COMPARATIVES, AT 30 JUNE 20X5

	20X5 $'000	20X5 $'000	20X4 $'000	20X4 $'000
Assets				
Non current assets				
Property, plant and equipment	50,600		44,050	
Intangible assets *(note 3)*	6,410		4,160	
		57,010		48,210
Current assets				
Inventories	33,500		28,750	
Trade receivables	27,130		26,300	
Cash	1,870		3,900	
		62,500		58,950
		119,510		107,160

	20X5		20X4	
	$'000	$'000	$'000	$'000
Equity and liabilities				
Equity				
Share capital	20,000		18,000	
Share premium	12,000		10,000	
Consolidated retained earnings	24,885		18,340	
		56,885		46,340
Minority interest		3,625		1,920
Non current liabilities				
Interest-bearing borrowings		18,200		19,200
Current liabilities				
Trade payables	33,340		32,810	
Interest payable	1,360		1,440	
Tax	6,100		5,450	
		40,800		39,700
		119,510		107,160

Notes

1   Several years ago, AH acquired 80% of the issued ordinary shares of its subsidiary, BI. On 1 January 20X5, AH acquired 75% of the issued ordinary shares of CJ in exchange for a fresh issue of 2 million of its own $1 ordinary shares (issued at a premium of $1 each) and $2 million in cash. The net assets of CJ at the date of acquisition were assessed as having the following fair values.

	$'000
Property, plant and equipment	4,200
Inventories	1,650
Receivables	1,300
Cash	50
Trade payables	(1,950)
Tax	(250)
	5,000

2   During the year, AH disposed of a non-current asset of property for proceeds of $2,250,000. The carrying value of the asset at the date of disposal was $1,000,000. There were no other disposals of non-current assets. Depreciation of $7,950,000 was charged against consolidated profits for the year.

3   Intangible assets comprise goodwill on acquisition of BI and CJ (20X4: BI only). Goodwill has remained unimpaired since acquisition.

Required

Prepare the consolidated cash flow statement of the AH Group for the financial year ended 30 June 20X5 in the form required by IAS 7 *Cash flow statements,* and using the indirect method. Notes to the cash flow statement are **not** required, but full workings should be shown. **(25 marks)**

31 EAG Group (5/08)

45 mins

Extracts from the consolidated financial statements of the EAG Group for the year ended 30 April 2008 are as follows:

EAG GROUP: CONSOLIDATED INCOME STATEMENT FOR THE YEAR ENDED 30 APRIL 2008

	$ million
Revenue	30,750.0
Cost of sales	(26,447.5)
Gross profit	4,302.5
Distribution costs	(523.0)
Administrative expenses	(669.4)
Finance cost	(510.9)
Share of profit of associate	1.6
Profit on disposal of associate	3.4
Profit before tax	2,604.2
Income tax	(723.9)
Profit for the period	1,880.3
Attributable to	
Equity holders of the parent	1,652.3
Minority interests	228.0
	1,880.3

EAG GROUP: BALANCE SHEET AT 30 APRIL 2008

	2008		2007	
	$ million	$ million	$ million	$ million
ASSETS				
Non-current assets				
Property, plant and equipment	22,225.1		19,332.8.	
Goodwill		1,662.7		1,865.3
Intangible assets	306.5		372.4	
Investment in associate	-		13.8	
		24,194.3		21,584.3
Current assets				
Inventories	5,217.0		4,881.0	
Trade receivables	4,633.6		4,670.0	
Cash	62.5		88.3	
		9,913.1		9,639.3
		34,107.4		31,223.6
EQUITY AND LIABILITIES				
Equity				
Share capital	4,300.0		3,600.0	
Retained earnings	14,643.7		12,991.4	
		18,943.7		16,591.4
Minority interest		2,010.5		1,870.5
Non-current liabilities				
Long-term borrowings		6,133.9		6,013.0
Current liabilities				
Trade payables	5,579.3		5,356.3	
Short-term borrowings	662.4		507.7	
Income tax	777.6		884.7	
		7,019.3		6,748.7
		34,107.4		31,223.6

Notes

1 Depreciation of $2,024·7 million was charged in respect of property, plant and equipment in the year ended 30 April 2008.

2 On 1 January 2008 EAG disposed of the investment in associate for $18 million. The share of profit in the income statement relates to the period from 1 May 2007 to 31 December 2007. A dividend was received from the associate on 1 June 2007. There were no other disposals, and no acquisitions, of investments in the accounting period.

3 Goodwill in one of the group's subsidiaries suffered an impairment during the year. The amount of the impairment was included in cost of sales.

4 The long-term borrowings are measured at amortised cost. The borrowing was taken out on 1 May 2006, and proceeds of $6,000 million less issue costs of $100,000 were received on that date. Interest of 5% of the principal is paid in arrears each year, and the borrowings will be redeemed on 30 April 2011 for $6·55 million. All interest obligations have been met on the due dates. The effective interest rate applicable to the borrowings is 7%. The finance cost in the income statement includes interest in respect of both the long-term and the short-term borrowing. Short-term borrowing comprises overdrafts repayable on demand.

5 Amortisation of 25% of the opening balance of intangibles was charged to cost of sales. A manufacturing patent was acquired for a cash payment on 30 April 2008.

6 An issue of share capital at par was made for cash during the year.

7 Dividends were paid to minority interests during the year, but no dividend was paid to the equity holders of the parent entity.

Required

Prepare the consolidated cash flow statement of the EAG Group for the financial year ended 30 April 2008. The cash flow statement should be presented in accordance with the requirements of IAS 7 *Cash Flow Statements*, and using the indirect method. Notes to the financial statement are NOT required, but full workings should be shown.

(25 marks)

MEASUREMENT OF INCOME AND CAPITAL

Questions 32 to 47 cover measurement of income and capital, the subject of Part C of the BPP Study Text for Paper 8.

32 Section A questions: Accounting standards   36 mins

1   On 1 January 20X2 A purchased 40% of the equity share capital of B for $60,000. At this date the reserves of B stood at $30,000. During the year ended 31 December 20X4 A sold goods to B for $10,000 and these goods were still in inventory at the year end. A makes a gross profit margin of 25% on intra-group sales.

The balance sheet of B at 31 December 20X4 showed the following:

	$'000
Net assets	320
Share capital	100
Reserves	220
	320

At what amount should A's interest in B be stated in its consolidated balance sheet at 31 December 20X4?

(2 marks)

2   On 1 January 20X2 C purchased 60% of the equity share capital of E for a total cash price of $50 million. The total net assets of E were $60 million. However, the net assets of E were believed to have a fair value to the C Group of $65 million in total. The directors of C considered that a group re-organisation would be necessary because of the acquisition of E and that the cost of this would be $5 million. This reorganisation was completed by 31 August 20X2.

What is the amount of goodwill to be recognised on consolidation?   (2 marks)

3   On 1 January 20X5 Lion purchased 75% of the equity share capital of Unicorn for $5 million. The summarised assets and liabilities of Unicorn at that date are shown below.

	$'000
Tangible non-current assets	6,300
Current assets less current liabilities	260
	6,560
Non-current liabilities: Loan	(1,600)
	4,960

At 1 January 20X5 the net replacement cost (market value) of the tangible non-current assets was $6.6 million and their economic value (value in use) was $7.2 million. The loan carries a rate of interest of 10% per annum and is redeemable at par on 31 December 20X6. The interest cost is representative of current market rates.

The goodwill on consolidation in the consolidated balance sheet of Lion is:

A $396,500
B $605,000
C $846,500
D $1,055,000   (2 marks)

4   Street purchased goods for E450,000 from an overseas supplier on 30 November 20X6. Street paid for the goods on 31 January 20X7. They were not sold to third parties until February 20X7.

Exchange rates were:

	E=$1
30 November 20X6	1.5
31 December 20X6	1.45
31 January 20X7	1.55

What is the exchange difference that should be reported in the income statement for the year ended 31 December 20X6 and at what amount should the goods be included in inventory in the balance sheet at that date?

	Exchange difference	Inventory
A	$9,677 gain	$290,323
B	$9,677 gain	$300,000
C	$10,345 loss	$300,000
D	$10,345 loss	$310,345

(2 marks)

5   The following information appears in the consolidated balance sheet of the Queen group at 31 December 20X8:

	20X8	20X7
	$'000	$'000
Property, plant and equipment	720	515
Revaluation reserve	50	–

The depreciation charge for the year was $60,000. On 1 July 20X8 Queen acquired a subsidiary which had tangible non-current assets of $90,000. There were no disposals of property, plant and equipment during the year.

What was cash paid to acquire property, plant and equipment during the year ended 31 December 20X8?

A $65,000
B $125,000
C $175,000
D $215,000

(2 marks)

6   On 1 January 20X5 Plane acquired 60% of the equity share capital of Sycamore. Goodwill of $100,000 arose on the acquisition.

Sycamore's performance for the years ended 31 December 20X5 and 31 December 20X6 slightly exceeded budget. However, in the year ended 31 December 20X7 it made substantial losses that had not been forecast.

The goodwill arising on the acquisition of Sycamore should be reviewed for impairment:

A   Annually
B   In 20X5
C   In 20X7
D   In 20X5 and in 20X7

(2 marks)

7   Foresight operates a pension plan. The employees pay a fixed percentage of their gross salary into the plan. The entity also makes a contribution to the plan each month on behalf of the employees. The plan rules state that when an employee retires he or she will receive an annual pension of two thirds of their average salary during their last five years of service. This is a:

A   Defined benefit plan
B   Defined contribution plan
C   Past service cost
D   Termination benefit plan

(2 marks)

8   On 1 June 20X9 Realistic entered into an agreement with a factor. Each month 80% of the value of the receivables arising from credit sales during the month were sold to the factor, who assumed legal title and responsibility for collection of all debts. Upon receipt of the cash by the factor, the remaining 20% was paid to Realistic.

Any debtor who did not pay the factor within three months of the debt being factored was transferred back to Realistic. The factor recovers the cash from the amounts previously advanced to Realistic. In practice, bad debts are deducted from cash paid to Realistic by the factor because the factor can only recover bad debts from the proceeds of other receivables previously assigned to it.

If credit sales for the month of June 20X9 are $150,000 and no cash has yet been recovered by the factor, how should this transaction be reported in the financial statements of Realistic for the year ended 30 June 20X9?

A   Recognise a loan of $120,000.

B   Remove $120,000 from trade receivables and recognise a loan of $120,000.

C   Deduct the proceeds of $120,000 from the gross amount of trade receivables, showing the gross and the net amount separately on the face of the balance sheet.

D   Remove $150,000 from trade receivables and recognise a sundry receivable of $30,000.   **(2 marks)**

---

9   On 1 January 20X4, Sherry, a wine merchant, purchased for $20 million a large quantity of fine wine for eventual resale. The wine must be stored in carefully controlled conditions for at least five years from the date of purchase, otherwise it will not mature properly.

On 1 April 20X4, Sherry sold the wine to Madeira Bank for £25 million. Sherry physically retained the wine in its cellars, to that the maturing process could continue. Sherry agreed to re-purchase the wine from Madeira Bank for $33.47 million on 31 March 20X9.

How should this transaction be reported in the financial statements of Sherry for the year ended 31 March 20X5?

	Income statement/ *Statement of changes in equity*	*Inventories*	*Liabilities*
A	Interest charge of $1.5 million	$20 million	$26.5 million
B	Interest charge of $1.694 million	$20 million	$26.694 million
C	Profit on sale $5 million	Nil	Nil
D	Revaluation on gain $5 million	$25 million	$25 million

(2 marks)

---

10   The directors of Clean are finalising the financial statements for the year ended 31 December 20X3.

(1)   For many years, Clean has operated a chemical plant which contaminates the surrounding countryside. The entity sets performance targets relating to a number of social and ethical criteria including cleaning up environmental damage caused by its activities. These have been published in its award winning environmental report. However, Clean is not required by law to clean up environmental damage.

(2)   On 15 January 20X4 there was an accident at one of the entity's factories. This accident resulted in pollution affecting a nearby wildlife sanctuary. The Chairman of Clean has promised that the entity will reverse the damage caused by the accident as far as possible and this promise has been widely reported in the local and national press.

In the financial statements for the year ended 31 December 20X3, Clean should recognise a provision for the best estimate of costs in respect of:

A   Neither (1) nor (2)
B   (1) only
C   (2) only
D   Both (1) and (2)   **(2 marks)**

(Total = 20 marks)

33 Preparation question: Suggested alternatives

Two suggested alternatives to historical cost accounting are:

(i)   Current purchasing power accounting

(ii)   Current cost accounting

Required

(a)   Indicate the basis on which each of the two methods values the shareholders' equity of a limited liability company as at the end of a financial year.

(b)   Evaluate critically the two methods of computation of annual profit and retained earnings for the year, as shown by each of the two methods mentioned in (a) above.

Helping hands

1   Examination questions on this topic are as likely to be written ones as numerical ones. In any case, you should understand the topic sufficiently to give good definitions and descriptions of these two methods.

2   It would probably help to make an answer plan to part (b). Mark off the points in order of importance.

3   If you are still having problems with this topic, it is worth revising it in your BPP Study Text.

---

34 Leisure (FR, 5/01, amended)   45 mins

(a)   There are several measurement systems which can be used in accounting. The most important single characteristic which distinguishes them is whether they are based on historical cost or current value. A further related issue is that of general price changes which affect the significance of reported profits and the ownership interest. It is often stated that a measurement system based on current values is superior to one based on historical cost and that accounting practice should develop by greater utilisation of current values. Current value accounting can utilise replacement cost accounting and net realisable value techniques, which use entry and exit values respectively. If general inflation is a problem, it is possible to eliminate the effect by producing a 'real terms' measure of total gains and losses, where a current value system of accounting is adjusted for the effects of changes in General Purchasing Power (GPP).

Required

Describe the problems associated with replacement cost accounting and net realisable value accounting techniques.   **(7 marks)**

(b)   You are the management accountant of Leisure. On 1 January 20X0, the entity set up a subsidiary in Urep – a country whose currency is orbits. The investment by Leisure was 50 million orbits. The foreign subsidiary invested all the initial capital in a hotel complex and this complex is effectively the sole asset of the subsidiary. The hotel complex is not being depreciated by the subsidiary. Relevant exchange rates at 1 January 20X0 and 31 December 20X2 – the accounting date for Leisure and its subsidiary – were as follows.

Date	Number of orbits per $
1 January 20X0	25
31 December 20X2	220

The retail price index in Urep was 100 on 1 January 20X0 and 1,000 on 31 December 20X2.

Required

(i)   Discuss the effects that hyper-inflation can have on the usefulness of financial statements, and explain how entities with subsidiaries that are located in hyper-inflationary economies should reflect this fact in their consolidated financial statements. You should restrict your discussion to financial statements that have been prepared under the historical cost convention.   **(10 marks)**

(ii)   Compute the carrying value of the hotel complex in the consolidated financial statements of Leisure at 31 December 20X2:

- Assuming the economy of Urep is not a hyper-inflationary economy
- Assuming the economy of Urep is a hyper-inflationary economy

Critically evaluate the results you have obtained. **(8 marks)**

(Total = 25 marks)

35 Extract (FR, 5/01, amended)   18 mins

Extract prepares its financial statements to 31 December each year. During the years ended 31 December 20X2 and 31 December 20X3, the following events occurred.

(a)   Extract is involved in extracting minerals in a number of different countries. The process typically involves some contamination of the site from which the minerals are extracted. Extract makes good this contamination only where legally required to do so by legislation passed in the relevant country.

(b)   The entity has been extracting minerals in Copperland since January 20X0 and expects its site to produce output until 31 December 20X7. On 23 December 20X2, it came to the attention of the directors of Extract that the government of Copperland was virtually certain to pass legislation requiring the making good of mineral extraction sites. The legislation was duly passed on 15 March 20X3. The directors of Extract estimate that the cost of making good the site in Copperland will be $2 million. This estimate is of the actual cash expenditure that will be incurred on 31 December 20X7.

Required

Following the principles of IAS 37 *Provisions, contingents, liabilities and contingent assets*, compute the effect of the estimated cost of making good the site on the financial statements of Extract for *both* of the years ended 31 December 20X2 and 20X3. Give full explanations of the figures you compute.

The annual discount rate to be used in any relevant calculations is 10%.   **(10 marks)**

36 Clean (FR, 11/01, amended)   45 mins

Clean prepares its financial statements in accordance with International Accounting Standards. On 25 June 20X0, Clean made a public announcement of a decision to reduce the level of emissions of harmful chemicals from its factories. The average useful lives of the factories on 30 June 20X0 (the accounting reference date) was 20 years. The depreciation of the factories is computed on a straight-line basis and charged to cost of sales. The directors formulated the proposals for emission reduction following agreement in principle earlier in the year.

The directors prepared detailed estimates of the costs of their proposals and these showed that the following expenditure would be required.

- $30 million on 30 June 20X1
- $30 million on 30 June 20X2
- $40 million on 30 June 20X3

All estimates were for the actual anticipated cash payments. No contracts were entered into until after 1 July 20X0. The estimate proved accurate as far as the expenditure due on 30 June 20X1 was concerned. When the directors decided to proceed with this project, they used discounted cash flow techniques to appraise the proposed investment. The annual discount rate they used was 8%. The entity has a reputation of fulfilling its financial commitments after it has publicly announced them. Clean included a provision for the expected costs of its proposal in its financial statements for the year ended 30 June 20X0.

Required

(a)   Explain the decision of the directors of Clean to recognise the provision in the balance sheet at 30 June 20X0. You should refer to the provisions of relevant International Accounting Standards.   **(6 marks)**

(b)   Compute the appropriate provision in the balance sheets in respect of the proposed expenditure at 30 June 20X0 AND 30 June 20X1.   **(4 marks)**

(c)   Compute the two components of the charge to the income statement in respect of the proposal for the year ended 30 June 20X1. You should explain how each component arises and identify where in the income statement each component is reported.

(6 marks)

(d)   Evaluate the extent to which financial statements prepared in accordance with International Accounting Standards give useful information regarding the environmental policies of the reporting entity.   **(4 marks)**

(e)   On 31 January 20X3 it was announced that the entity was raising $14m before expenses by the issue of shares for cash of $7.00 each. The issue took place on 31 July 20X3 at market share price.

State your view of the appropriate treatment in the accounts to 30 June 20X1, giving your reasons. Draft an appropriate note and/or state the adjustment to be made.   **(5 marks)**

(Total = 25 marks)

37 Preparation question: Balance sheet valuations

(a)   Graben Co purchases a bond for $441,014 on 1 January 20X1. It will be redeemed on 31 December 20X4 for $600,000. The bond will be held to maturity and carries no coupon.

Required

Calculate the balance sheet valuation of the bond as at 31 December 20X1 and the finance income for 20X1 shown in the income statement.

Compound sum of $1: $(1 + r)^n$

Year	2%	4%	6%	8%	10%	12%	14%
1	1.0200	1.0400	1.0600	1.0800	1.1000	1.1200	1.1400
2	1.0404	1.0816	1.1236	1.1664	1.2100	1.2544	1.2996
3	1.0612	1.1249	1.1910	1.2597	1.3310	1.4049	1.4815
4	1.0824	1.1699	1.2625	1.3605	1.4641	1.5735	1.6890
5	1.1041	1.2167	1.3382	1.4693	1.6105	1.7623	1.9254

(b)   Baldie Co issues 4,000 convertible bonds on 1 January 20X2 at par. The bond is redeemable 3 years later at its par value of $500 per bond, which is its nominal value.

The bonds pay interest annually in arrears at an interest rate (based on nominal value) of 5%. Each bond can be converted at the maturity date into 30 $1 shares.

The prevailing market interest rate for three year bonds that have no right of conversion is 9%.

Required

Show the balance sheet valuation at 1 January 20X2.

Cumulative 3 year annuity factors:

- 5%   2.723
- 9%   2.531

38 Tall

45 mins

(a)   Three standards have been published by the IASB to deal with the complex area of financial instruments.

(i)   IAS 32 *Financial instruments: presentation*
(ii)   IFRS 7 *Financial instruments: disclosures*
(iii)   IAS 39 *Financial instruments: recognition and measurement*

Required

Describe the problems with the way that financial instruments have been accounted for in the past that these standards were issued to correct.   **(7 marks)**

(b) You are the management accountant of Tall. The entity is planning a number of acquisitions in 20Y0 and so you are aware that additional funding will be needed. Today's date is 30 November 20X9. The balance sheet of the company at 30 September 20X9 (the financial year-end of Tall) showed the following balances.

	$m
Equity share capital	100.0
Share premium account	35.8
Revenue reserve	89.7
	225.5
Net assets	225.5

On 1 October 20X9 Tall raised additional funding as follows:

- Tall issued 15 million $1 bonds at par. The bonds pay no interest but are redeemable on 1 October 20Y4 at $1.61 – the total payable on redemption being $24.15m. As an alternative to redemption, bondholders can elect to convert their holdings into $1 equity shares on the basis of one equity share for every bond held. The current price of a $1 share is $1.40 and it is reckonable that this will grow by at least 5 percent per annum for the next five years.

- Tall issued 10 million $1 preferred shares at $1.20 per share, incurring costs of $100,000. The preferred shares carry no dividend and are redeemable on 1 October 20Y5 at $2.35 per share – the total payable on redemption being $23.5m.

Your assistant is unsure how to reflect the additional funding in the financial statements of Tall. He expresses the opinion that both the new financial instruments should logically be reflected in the capital and reserves section of the balance sheet. He justifies this as follows.

- The preferred shares are legally shares and so capital and reserves is the appropriate place to present them.

- The bonds and the preferred shares seem to have similar terms of issue and is quite likely that the bonds will *become* shares in five years' time, given the projected growth in the equity share price.

He has no idea how to show the finance costs of the financial instruments in the income statement. He is aware that IAS 39 *Financial Instruments: Recognition and Measurement* has recently been issued, but is unaware of the details.

Required

(i) Write a memorandum to your assistant which evaluates the comments he has made regarding the presentation of the financial instruments and explains the correct treatment where necessary. Your memorandum should refer to the provisions of relevant accounting standards. **(7 marks)**

(ii) Explain and evaluate the relevant positions of IAS 39 regarding the computation of the finance cost of financial instruments such as bonds and preferred shares. You are **not** required to compute the finance costs for either of the instruments mentioned in this question. **(11 marks)**

(Total = 25 marks)

39 QRS (Pilot paper)   18 mins

The directors of QRS, a listed entity, have met to discuss the business's medium to long term financing requirements. Several possibilities were discussed, including the issue of more shares using a rights issue. In many respects this would be the most desirable option because the entity is already quite highly geared. However, the directors are aware of several recent cases where rights issues have not been successful because share prices are currently quite low and many investors are averse to any kind of investment in shares.

Therefore, the directors have turned their attention to other options. The finance director is on sick leave, and so you, her assistant, have been given the task of responding to the following note from the Chief Executive:

'Now that we've had a chance to discuss possible financing arrangements the directors are in agreement that we should structure our issue of financial instruments in order to be able to classify them as equity rather than debt. Any increase in the gearing ratio would be unacceptable. Therefore, we have provisionally decided to make two issues of financial instruments as follows.

(a)   An issue of non-redeemable preferred shares to raise $4 million. These shares will carry a fixed interest rate of 6%, and because they are shares they can be classified as equity.

(b)   An issue of 6% convertible bonds, issued at par value, to raise $6 million. These bonds will carry a fixed date for conversion in four years' time. Each $100 of debt will be convertible at the holder's option into 120 $1 shares. In our opinion, these bonds can actually be classified as equity immediately, because they are convertible within five years on terms that are favourable to the holder.

Please confirm that these instruments will not increase our gearing ratio should they be issued.'

Note You determine that the market rate available for similar non-convertible bonds is currently 8%.

Required

Explain to the directors the accounting treatment, in respect of debt/equity classification, required by IAS 32 *Financial instruments: presentation* for each of the proposed issues, advising them on the acceptability of classifying the instruments as equity.

Your explanation should be accompanied by calculations where appropriate.   **(10 marks)**

40 PX (5/05)   18 mins

During its financial year ended 31 December 20X4, an entity, PX, entered into the transactions described below.

In November 20X4, having surplus cash available, PX made an investment in the securities of a listed entity. The directors intend to realise the investment in March or April 20X5, in order to fund the planned expansion of PX's principal warehouse.

PX lent one of its customers, DB, $3,000,000 at a variable interest rate pegged to average bank lending rates. The loan is scheduled for repayment in 20X9, and PX has provided an undertaking to DB that it will not assign the loan to a third party.

PX added to its portfolio of relatively small investments in the securities of listed entities. PX does not plan to dispose of these investments in the short term.

Required

In accordance with IAS 39 *Financial instruments: recognition and measurement:*

(a)   Identify the appropriate classification of these three categories of financial asset and briefly explain the reason for each classification.   **(6 marks)**

(b)   Explain how the financial assets should be measured in the financial statements of PX at 31 December 20X4.
                                                                                                   (4 marks)

                                                                                        (Total = 10 marks)

41 AZG (5/08)   18 mins

On 1 February 2007, the directors of AZG decided to enter into a forward foreign exchange contract to buy 6 million florins at a rate of $1 = 3 florins, on 31 January 2010. AZG's year end is 31 March.

Relevant exchange rates were as follows:

    1 February 2007 $1 = 3 florins
    31 March 2007 $1 = 2·9 florins
    31 March 2008 $1 = 2·8 florins

(a)   Identify the three characteristics of a derivative financial instrument as defined in IAS 39 *Financial Instruments: Recognition and Measurement.*   **(3 marks)**

(b)   Describe the requirements of IAS 39 in respect of the recognition and measurement of derivative financial instruments.   **(2 marks)**

(c)   Prepare relevant extracts from AZG's income statement and balance sheet to reflect the forward foreign exchange contract at 31 March 2008, with comparatives. (Note: ignore discounting when measuring the derivative).   **(5 marks)**

(Total = 10 marks)

42 Preparation question: Defined benefit scheme

Brutus Co operates a defined benefit pension plan for its employees conditional on a minimum employment period of 6 years. The present value of the future benefit obligations and the fair value of its plan assets on 1 January 20X1 were $110 million and $150 million respectively.

In the financial statements for the year ended 31.12.X0, there were unrecognised actuarial gains of $43 million. (Brutus Co's accounting policy is to use the 10% corridor approach to recognition of actuarial gains and losses).

The pension plan received contributions of $7m and paid pensions to former employees of $10m during the year.

Extracts from the most recent actuary's report show the following:

	31.12.20X1
Present value of pension plan obligation	$116m
Market value of plan assets	$140m
Present cost of pensions earned in the period	$13m
Yield on high quality corporate bonds for the period	10%
Long term expected return on scheme assets for the period	12%

On 31 December 20X1, the rules of the pension plan were changed to improve benefits for plan members, vesting immediately. The actuary has advised that this will cost $20 million in total.

The average remaining working life of plan members at 31.12.X1 is 7 years. This tends to remain static as people leave and join.

Required

Produce the extracts for the financial statements for the year ended 31.12.X1.

Assume contributions and benefits were paid on 31 December.

Helping hand

Use the proformas below as a guidance to the work required.

INCOME STATEMENT NOTE

Defined benefit expense recognised in profit or loss

$'m

Current service cost
Interest cost
Expected return on plan assets
Net actuarial (gains)/losses recognised
Past service cost

BALANCE SHEET NOTES

Net defined benefit liability recognised in the balance sheet

$'m

Present value of defined benefit obligation
Fair value of plan assets

—————

Unrecognised actuarial gains

—————

Changes in the present value of the defined benefit obligation

$'m

Opening defined benefit obligation

Changes in the fair value of plan assets

$'m

Opening fair value of plan assets

—————

Working

Recognised/unrecognised actuarial gains and losses

$'m

43 Accounting for retirement benefits

45 mins

(a)   Accounting for retirement benefits remains one of the most challenging areas in financial reporting. The values being reported are significant, and the estimation of these values is complex and subjective. Standard setters and preparers of financial statements find it difficult to achieve a measure of consensus on the appropriate way to deal with the assets and costs involved. IAS 19 *Employee benefits* formerly focused on the income statement, viewing employee benefits as an operating expense. However, the revised Standard concentrates on the balance sheet and the valuation of the pension fund. The philosophy and rationale of the two statements are fundamentally different.

Required

(i)   Describe four key issues in the determination of the method of accounting for retirement benefits in respect of defined benefit plans; **(6 marks)**

(ii)   Discuss how IAS 19 *Employee benefits* deals with these key issues and to what extent it provides solutions to the problems of accounting for retirement benefits. **(8 marks)**

(b)   A, a public limited company, operates a defined benefit plan. A full actuarial valuation by an independent actuary revealed that the value of the liability at 31 May 20X0 was $1,500 million. This was updated to 31 May 20X1 by the actuary and the value of the liability at that date was $2,000 million. The scheme assets comprised mainly bonds and equities and the fair value of these assets was as follows:

	31 May 20X0 £m	31 May 20X1 £m
Fixed interest and index linked bonds	380	600
Equities	1,300	1,900
Other investments	290	450
	1,970	2,950

The scheme had been altered during the year with improved benefits arising for the employees and this had been taken into account by the actuaries. The increase in the actuarial liability in respect of employee service in prior periods was $25 million (past service cost). The increase in the actuarial liability resulting from employee service in the current period was $70 million (current service cost). The company had not recognised any net actuarial gain or loss in the income statement to date.

The company had paid contributions of $60 million to the scheme during the period. The company expects its return on the scheme assets at 31 May 20X1 to be $295 million and the interest on pension liabilities to be $230 million.

The average expected remaining working lives of the employees is 10 years and the net cumulative unrecognised gains at 1 June 20X0 were $247 million.

Required

Calculate the amount which will be shown as the net plan asset/plan reserve in the balance sheet of A as at 31 May 20X1, showing a reconciliation of the movement in the plan surplus during the year and a statement of those amounts which would be charged to operating profit. (Candidates should utilise IAS 19 *Employee benefits* in answering the question.) **(11 marks)**

(Total = 25 marks)

44 CBA (11/06)   18 mins

CBA is a listed entity that runs a defined benefit pension scheme on behalf of its employees. In the financial year ended 30 September 20X6, the scheme suffered an actuarial loss of $7.2 million. The entity's directors are aware that the relevant Accounting Standard, IAS 19 *Employee benefits*, was amended recently. They have asked you, the financial controller, to write a short briefing paper, setting out an outline of the options for accounting for the actuarial loss in accordance with the amended version of the Standard.

Required

Prepare the briefing paper explaining the options and identifying, as far as possible from the information given, the potential impact on the financial statements of CBA of the two alternative accounting treatments.

(10 marks)

45 BGA (11/07)

The following information relates to the defined benefits pension scheme of BGA, a listed entity:

The present value of the scheme obligations at 1 November 20X6 was $18,360,000, while the fair value of the scheme assets at that date was $17,770,000. During the financial year ended 31 October 20X7, a total of $997,000 was paid into the scheme in contributions. Current service cost for the year was calculated at $1,655,000, and actual benefits paid were $1,860,300. The applicable interest cost for the year was 6.5% and the expected return on plan assets was 9.4%.

The present value of the scheme obligations at 31 October 20X7 was calculated as $18,655,500, and the fair value of scheme assets at that date was $18,417,180.

BGA adopts the '10% corridor' criterion in IAS 19 *Employee benefits* for determining the extent of recognition of actuarial gains and losses. The average remaining service life of the employees was 10 years. Net unrecognised actuarial losses on 1 November 20X6 were $802,000.

Required

(a) Calculate the actuarial gain or loss on BGA's pension scheme assets and liabilities for the year ended 31 October 20X7.   **(8 marks)**

(b) Calculate the extent to which, if at all, actuarial gains or losses should be recognised in BGA's income statement for the year ended 31 October 20X7, using the '10% corridor' criterion.   **(2 marks)**

(Total = 10 marks)

46 Tree   45 mins

You are the management accountant of Tree, a listed limited liability company that prepares consolidated financial statements. Your Managing Director, who is not an accountant, has recently attended a seminar at which key financial reporting issues were discussed. She remembers being told the following.

- Financial statements of an entity should reflect the substance of its transactions;
- Revenue from the 'sale' of goods should only be recognised when certain conditions have been satisfied. Transfer of legal title to the goods is not necessarily sufficient for an entity to recognise revenue from their 'sale'.

The year end of Tree is 31 August. In the year to 31 August 20X1, the company entered into the following transactions.

Transaction 1

On 1 March 20X1, Tree sold a property to a bank for $5 million. The market value of the property at the date of the sale was $10 million. Tree continues to occupy the property rent-free. Tree has the option to buy the property back from the bank at the end of every month from 31 March 20X1 until 28 February 20X6. Tree has not yet exercised this option. The repurchase price will be $5 million plus $50,000 for every complete month that has elapsed from the date of sale to the date of repurchase. The bank cannot require Tree to repurchase the property and the facility lapses after 28 February 20X6. The directors of Tree expect property prices to rise at around 5% each year for the foreseeable future.

Transaction 2

On 1 September 20X0, Tree sold one of its branches to Vehicle for $8 million. The net assets of the branch in the financial statements of Tree immediately before the sale were $7 million. Vehicle is a subsidiary of a bank and was specifically incorporated to carry out the purchase – it has no other business operations. Vehicle received the $8 million to finance this project from its parent in the form of a loan.

Tree continues to control the operations of the branch and receives an annual operating fee from Vehicle. The annual fee is the operating profit of the branch for the 12 months to the previous 31 August less the interest payable on the loan taken out by Vehicle for the 12 months to the previous 31 August. If this amount is negative, then Tree must pay the negative amount to Vehicle.

Any payments to or by Tree must be made by 30 September following the end of the relevant period. In the year to 31 August 20X1, the branch made an operating profit of $2,000,000. Interest payable by Vehicle on the loan for this period was $800,000.

Required

(a) Explain the conditions that need to be satisfied before revenue can be recognised from the sale of goods. You should support your answer with reference to International Financial Reporting Standards as appropriate. **(4 marks)**

(b) Explain how the transactions described above will be dealt with in the consolidated financial statements (balance sheet and income statement) of Tree for the year ended 31 August 20X1.

(9 marks are allocated to transaction 1 and 7 marks to transaction 2) **(16 marks)**

(c) Show extracts from the published financial statements in respect of transactions 1 and 2, including any notes. **(5 marks)**

(Total = 25 marks)

47 LMN (5/06)   18 mins

LMN trades in motor vehicles, which are manufactured and supplied by their manufacturer, IJK. Trading between the two entities is subject to a contractual agreement, the principal terms of which are as follows.

(a) LMN is entitled to hold on its premises at any one time up to 80 vehicles supplied by IJK. LMN is free to specify the ranges and models of vehicle supplied to it. IJK retains legal title to the vehicles until such time as they are sold to a third party by LMN.

(b) While the vehicles remain on its premises, LMN is required to insure them against loss or damage.

(c) The price at which vehicles are supplied is determined at the time of delivery; it is not subject to any subsequent alteration.

(d) When LMN sells a vehicle to a third party, it is required to inform IJK within three working days. IJK submits an invoice to LMN at the originally agreed price; the invoice is payable by LMN within 30 days.

(e) LMN is entitled to use any of the vehicles supplied to it for demonstration purposes and road testing. However, if more than a specified number of kilometres are driven in a vehicle, LMN is required to pay IJK a rental charge.

(f) LMN has the right to return any vehicle to IJK at any time without incurring a penalty, except for any rental charge incurred in respect of excess kilometres driven.

Required

Discuss the economic substance of the contractual arrangement between the two entities in respect of the recognition of inventory and of sales. Refer, where appropriate, to IAS 18 *Revenue*. **(10 marks)**

48 Section A questions: Interpretation of accounts   36 mins

1   FG holds several properties under operating leases. Many financial reporting experts believe that operating leases should be treated in exactly the same way as finance leases.

What would be the immediate effect of this change on the entity's key performance measures?

	Return on capital employed	Gearing
A	Decrease	Decrease
B	Decrease	Increase
C	Increase	Decrease
D	Increase	Increase

(2 marks)

2   An entity owns several freehold properties, which it measures at current value, rather than historic cost. During the year ended 31 December 20X5 the market value of the properties has fallen significantly and an impairment loss has been recognised in the financial statements. In all cases, the recoverable amount of the properties is greater than depreciated historic cost.

What is the immediate effect of the impairment on the company's key performance measures?

	Return on capital employed	Gearing
A	Decrease	Decrease
B	Decrease	Increase
C	Increase	Decrease
D	Increase	Increase

(2 marks)

3   The return on capital employed of A is 80% of that of B. The operating profit margin of A is 64% of that of B.

What is A's asset turnover expressed as a percentage of B's?   (1 mark)

4   The Northern Bank has provided a long term loan to Norwood, a small business. Which of the following pairs of ratios is most likely to provide the bank with relevant information?

A   Asset turnover and expenses to sales
B   Gearing and interest cover
C   Return on capital employed and gross profit margin
D   Return on shareholders' equity and earnings per share   (2 marks)

5   The following information relates to M at 31 December 20X3:

	$'000
Trade receivables	80
Current asset investments (cash on deposit)	10
Trade payables	75
Bank overdraft	100

The entity has decided to take the following steps to reduce the overdraft.

(1)   Inventory with a book value of $8,000 will be sold at a loss of $2,000.

(2)   Debtors will be offered a cash discount of 10% for immediate payment. Debtors with a book value of $20,000 are expected to take advantage of this offer.

In return, the entity's bankers have agreed to make a loan of $40,000, which will be used immediately to purchase new machinery. The loan will be repayable in five equal instalments, the first of which falls due on 31 December 20X4.

Assuming that all the above transactions take place on 31 December 20X3, what is the revised quick (acid test) ratio on that date? **(3 marks)**

---

6   Z has a current ratio of 1.5, a quick ratio of 0.4 and a positive cash balance. If it purchases inventory on credit, what is the effect on these ratios?

	Current ratio	Quick ratio
A	Decrease	Decrease
B	Decrease	Increase
C	Increase	Decrease
D	Increase	Increase

(2 marks)

---

7   HJ has an asset turnover of 2.0 and an operating profit margin of 10%. The entity is about to launch a new product which is expected to generate additional sales of $1.6 million and additional profit of $120,000 in its first year. To manufacture the new product HJ will need to purchase additional assets of $500,000.

Assuming that the current operations continue to produce the same level of results, what will be the effect of the new product on the following ratios of HJ?

	Operating profit margin	Return on capital employed
A	Decrease	Decrease
B	Decrease	Increase
C	Increase	Decrease
D	Increase	Increase

(2 marks)

---

8   KL has the following capital and reserves at 31 December 20X9:

	$'000
Ordinary shares of 50c each	300
8% preferred shares of $1 each	100
Retained earnings	150
	550

KL also had $200,000 10% loan notes in issue throughout the year. Retained profit for the year was $20,000 after paying the preferred dividend and an ordinary dividend of $7,500.

What was the return on equity capital employed for the year ended 31 December 20X9? **(2 marks)**

---

9   The accounting ratios of ABC are very similar to the average ratios for the industry in which it operates. ABC has an average operating profit margin of 24% and an average asset turnover of 0.9.

This entity is likely to be:

A   An architect
B   A food retailer
C   An insurance broker
D   A manufacturer

(2 marks)

---

10   An entity has the following capital structure.

	$'000
$1 ordinary shares	100,000
10% $1 preferred shares	50,000
Retained earnings	80,000
	230,000
12% loan notes	100,000
	330,000

What is the most appropriate measure of the gearing ratio for a potential equity investor?

A   30.3%
B   43.5%
C   45.4%
D   83.3%

(2 marks)

(Total = 20 marks)

49 Preparation question: Financial analysis

The following five year summary relates to Wandafood Products Co, and is based on financial statements prepared under the historical cost convention.

			20X5	20X4	20X3	20X2	20X1
Financial ratios							
Profitability							
Margin	$\dfrac{\text{Trading profit}}{\text{Revenue}}$	%	7.8	7.5	7.0	7.2	7.3
Return on assets	$\dfrac{\text{Trading profit}}{\text{Net operating assets}}$	%	16.3	17.6	16.2	18.2	18.3
Interest and dividend cover							
Interest cover	$\dfrac{\text{Trading profit}}{\text{Net finance charges}}$	times	2.9	4.8	5.1	6.5	3.6
Dividend cover	$\dfrac{\text{Earnings per ord share}}{\text{Div per ord share}}$	times	2.7	2.6	2.1	2.5	3.1
Debt to equity ratios							
	$\dfrac{\text{Net borrowings}}{\text{Shareholder's funds}}$	%	65.9	61.3	48.3	10.8	36.5
	$\dfrac{\text{Net borrowings}}{\text{Shareholder's funds} + \text{minority interests}}$	%	59.3	55.5	44.0	10.1	33.9
Liquidity ratios							
Quick ratio	$\dfrac{\text{Current assets less inventory}}{\text{Current liabilities}}$	%	74.3	73.3	78.8	113.8	93.4
Current ratio	$\dfrac{\text{Current assets}}{\text{Current liabilities}}$	%	133.6	130.3	142.2	178.9	174.7
Asset ratios							
Operating asset turnover	$\dfrac{\text{Revenue}}{\text{Net operating assets}}$	times	2.1	2.4	2.3	2.5	2.5
Working capital turnover	$\dfrac{\text{Revenue}}{\text{Working capital}}$	times	8.6	8.0	7.0	7.4	6.2
Per share							
Earnings per share	– pre-tax basis	c	23.62	21.25	17.96	17.72	15.06
	– normal basis	c	15.65	13.60	10.98	11.32	12.18
Dividends per share		c	5.90	5.40	4.90	4.60	4.10
Net assets per share		c	102.10	89.22	85.95	85.79	78.11

Net opening assets include tangible non-current assets, inventory, receivables and payables. They exclude borrowings, taxation and dividends.

Prepare a report clearly interpreting and evaluating the information given. Include comments on possible effects of price changes which may limit the quality of the report.

Helping hands

1   You must get used to questions where a load of information is thrown at you.

2   You should read the information once carefully and then skim through it again, marking off the important points.

3   Produce an answer plan first, otherwise your answer will lack structure.

---

50 OPQ (11/05)   45 mins

You are assistant to the Finance Director (FD) of OPQ, a well known retailer of music, video and games products. OPQ's profit margins are under increasing pressure because of the entry of online retailers into the market. As part of their response to this challenge, OPQ's directors have decided to invest in entities in the supply chain of their most popular products. They are currently considering the acquisition of the business that supplies some of its best-selling computer games, PJ Gamewriters (PJ). The FD has asked you, as a preliminary step, to examine the most recent financial statements of the entity.

PJ was established in 20X0 by twin brothers, Paul and James, who had recently graduated in computing. Their first business success was a simulated empire building game; this has continued to being in a large proportion of PJ's revenue. However, they have also been successful in a range of other games types such as combat simulations, golf and football management games. The business has grown rapidly from year to year, and by 20X5 it employed ten full-time games writers. Manufacture and distribution of the software in various formats is outsourced, and the business operated from office premises in a city centre. PJ bought the freehold of the office premises in 20X2, and its estimated market value is now $900,000, nearly $350,000 in excess of the price paid in 20X2. Apart from the freehold building, the business owns few non-current assets.

The equity shares in PJ are owned principally by Paul, James and their parents, who provided the initial start-up capital. Paul and James are the sole directors of the business. A small proportion of the shares (around 8%) is owned by five of the senior software writers. PJ is now up for sale as the principal shareholders wish to realise the bulk of their investment in order to pursue other business interests. It is likely that about 90% of the shares will be for sale. The copyrights of the games are owned by PJ, but no value is attributed to them in the financial statements.

PJ's income statement and summarised statement of changes in equity for the year ended 31 July 20X5, and balance sheet at that date (all with comparatives) are as follows:

PJ: INCOME STATEMENT FOR THE YEAR ENDED 31 JULY 20X5

	20X5	20X4
	$'000	$'000
Revenue	2,793	2,208
Cost of sales (see note below)	(1,270)	(1,040)
Gross profit	1,523	1,168
Operating expenses	(415)	(310)
Profit from operations	1,108	858
Interest receivable	7	2
Profit before tax	1,115	860
Income tax expense	(331)	(290)
Profit for the period	784	570

Note. Cost of sales comprises the following:

Games writers' employment costs	700	550
Production costs	215	160
Directors' remuneration	200	200
Other costs	155	130
	1,270	1,040

PJ: SUMMARISED STATEMENT OF CHANGES IN EQUITY FOR THE YEAR ENDED 31 JULY 20X5

	20X5	20X4
	$'000	$'000
Opening balance	703	483
Profit for the period	784	570
Dividends	(500)	(350)
Closing balance	987	703

PJ: BALANCE SHEET AT 31 JULY 20X5

	20X5		20X4	
	$'000	$'000	$'000	$'000
Non-current assets				
Property, plant and equipment		610		620
Current assets				
Inventories	68		59	
Trade receivables	460		324	
Cash	216		20	
		744		403
		1,354		1,023
Equity				
Share capital	60		60	
Retained earnings	927		643	
		987		703
Current liabilities				
Trade and other payables	36		30	
Income tax	331		290	
		367		320
		1,354		1,023

Required

(a) Prepare a report on the financial performance and position of PJ Gameswriters, calculating and interpreting any relevant accounting ratios.
(17 marks)

(b) Explain the limitations of your analysis, identifying any supplementary items of information that would be useful.
(8 marks)

(Total = 25 marks)

51 Phoenix
45 mins

(a) There has been widespread debate for several years concerning the declining value of traditional methods of measuring corporate performance and the ability to predict corporate failure. Earnings per share, return on capital employed and other investment ratios are seemingly out of step with the needs of investors. The analysis of financial ratios is to a large extent concerned with the efficiency and effectiveness of management's use of resources and also with the financial stability of the entity.

However, many analysts feel that financial statements require several adjustments before any meaningful evaluation of corporate performance can be made. Analysts often make amendments to corporate profit and net assets before calculating even the most basic ratios because of their disapproval of certain generally accepted accounting principles and in an attempt to obtain comparability.

Required

Evaluate the usefulness of traditional accounting ratios, calculated by reference to published financial statements, in providing adequate information for analysts and investors.
(8 marks)

(b) Phoenix has carried on business for a number of years as a retailer of a wide variety of consumer products. The entity operates from a number of stores around the United Kingdom. In recent years the entity has found it necessary to provide credit facilities to its customers in order to maintain growth in revenue. As a result of this decision the liability to its bankers has increased substantially. The statutory financial statements for the year ended 30 June 20X9 have recently been published and extracts are provided below, together with comparative figures for the previous two years.

INCOME STATEMENTS FOR THE YEARS ENDED 30 JUNE

	20X7	20X8	20X9
	$m	$m	$m
Revenue	1,850	2,200	2,500
Cost of sales	(1,250)	(1,500)	(1,750)
Gross profit	600	700	750
Other operating costs	(550)	(640)	(700)
Profit from operations	50	60	50
Interest from credit sales	45	60	90
Interest payable	(25)	(60)	(110)
Profit before taxation	70	60	30
Income tax expense	(23)	(20)	(10)
Profit for the year	47	40	20

BALANCE SHEETS AT 30 JUNE

	20X7	20X8	20X9
	$m	$m	$m
Property, plant and equipment	278	290	322
Inventories	400	540	620
Trade receivables	492	550	633
Cash	12	12	15
	1,182	1,392	1,590
Share capital	90	90	90
Reserves	282	292	282
	372	382	372
Bank loans	320	520	610
Other interest bearing borrowings	200	200	320
Trade payables	270	270	280
Tax payable	20	20	8
	1,182	1,392	1,590

Other information

- Depreciation charged for the three years in question was as follows.

Year ended 30 June	20X7	20X8	20X9
	$m	$m	$m
	55	60	70

- The other interest bearing borrowings are secured by a floating charge over the assets of Phoenix. Their repayment is due on 30 June 20Y9.

- The bank loans are unsecured. The maximum lending facility the bank will provide is $630m.

- Over the past three years the level of credit sales has been:

Year ended 30 June	20X7	20X8	20X9
	$m	$m	$m
	300	400	600

The entity offers extended credit terms for certain products to maintain market share in a highly competitive environment.

Given the steady increase in the level of bank loans which has taken place in recent years, the entity has recently written to its bankers to request an increase in the lending facility. The request was received by the bank on 15 October 20X9, two weeks after the financial statements were published. The bank is concerned at the steep escalation in the level of the loans and has asked for a report on the financial performance of Phoenix for the last three years.

Required

As a consultant management accountant employed by the bankers of Phoenix, prepare a report to the bank which analyses the financial performance of Phoenix for the period covered by the financial statements. Your report may take any form you wish, but you are aware of the particular concern of the bank regarding the rapidly increasing level of lending. Therefore it may be appropriate to include aspects of prior performance that could have contributed to the increase in the level of bank lending. **(17 marks)**

(Total = 25 marks)

52 Grow by acquisition (FR, 5/02, amended)   45 mins

You are the management accountant of Expand – a large group that seeks to grow by acquisition. The directors of Expand have identified two potential target entities (A and B) and obtained copies of their financial statements. Extracts from these financial statements, together with notes providing additional information, are given below.

INCOME STATEMENTS
YEAR ENDED 31 DECEMBER 20X1

	A	B
	$'000	$'000
Revenue	68,000	66,000
Cost of sales	(42,000)	(45,950)
Gross profit	26,000	20,050
Other operating expenses	(18,000)	(14,000)
Profit before interest and tax	8,000	6,050
Finance cost	(3,000)	(4,000)
Profit before tax	5,000	2,050
Income tax expense	(1,500)	(1,000)
Net profit for the period	3,500	1,050

STATEMENTS OF CHANGES IN EQUITY
YEAR ENDED 31 DECEMBER 20X1

	A	B
	$'000	$'000
Balance at 1 January 20X1	22,000	16,000
Surplus on revaluation of properties	NIL	6,000
Net profit for the period	3,500	1,050
Dividends paid	(2,000)	(1,000)
Balance at 31 December 20X1	23,500	22,050

BALANCE SHEETS AT 31 DECEMBER 20X1

	A		B	
	$'000	$'000	$'000	$'000
Non-current assets				
Property, plant and equipment	32,000		35,050	
		32,000		35,050
Current assets				
Inventories	6,000		7,000	
Trade receivables	12,000		10,000	
		18,000		17,000
		50,000		52,050

	A		B	
	$'000	$'000	$'000	$'000
Equity				
Share capital ($1 shares)		16,000		12,000
Revaluation reserve		Nil		5,000
Retained earnings		7,500		5,050
		23,500		22,050
Non-current liabilities				
Long-term borrowings		16,000		18,000
Current liabilities				
Trade payables	5,000		5,000	
Income tax	1,500		1,000	
Short-term borrowings	4,000		6,000	
		10,500		12,000
		50,000		52,050

Notes

1   *Sale by A to X*

On 31 December 20X1, A supplied goods, at the normal selling price of $2.4 million, to another entity, X. A's normal selling price is at a mark up of 60% on cost. X paid for the goods in cash on the same day. The terms of the selling agreement were that A repurchase these goods on 30 June 20X2 for $2.5 million. A has accounted for the transaction as a sale.

2   *Revaluation of non-current assets by B*

B revalued its non-current assets for the first time on 1 January 20X1. The non-current assets of A are very similar in age and type to the non-current assets of B. However, A has a policy of maintaining all its non-current assets at depreciated historical cost. Both enterprises charge depreciation of non-current assets to cost of sales. B has transferred the excess depreciation on the revalued assets from the revaluation reserve to retained earnings as permitted in IAS 16 *Property, plant and equipment*.

Expand uses ratio analysis to appraise potential investment opportunities. It is normal practice to base the appraisal on four key ratios.

- Return on capital employed
- Gross profit margin
- Turnover of capital employed
- Leverage

For the purposes of the ratio analysis, Expand computes:

(i)   Capital employed as capital and retained earnings (equity) plus borrowings
(ii)   Borrowings as interest –bearing borrowings plus short-term borrowings

Your assistant has computed the four key ratios for the two entities from the financial statements provided and the results are summarised below.

Ratio	A	B
Return on capital employed	18.4%	13.1%
Gross profit margin	38.2%	30.4%
Turnover of capital employed	1.6	1.4
Leverage	46.0%	52.1%

Your assistant has informed you that, on the basis of the ratios calculated, the performance of A is superior to that of B in all respects. Therefore, Expand should carry out a more detailed review of A with a view to making a bid to acquire it. However, you are unsure whether this is necessarily the correct conclusion given the information provided in Notes 1 and 2.

Required

(a) Explain and compute the adjustments that would be appropriate in respect of Notes 1 and 2 so as to make the financial statements of A and B comparable for analysis. **(10 marks)**

(b) Recalculate the four key ratios mentioned in the question for both A and B after making the adjustments you have recommended in your answer to part (a). You should provide appropriate workings to support your calculations. **(4 marks)**

(c) In the light of the work that you have carried out in answer to parts (a) and (b), evaluate your assistant's conclusion that a more detailed review of A should be carried out, with a view to making a bid to acquire it. **(6 marks)**

(d) Identify the strengths and weaknesses of using a historical cost system of measurement for assets and liabilities. **(5 marks)**

(Total = 25 marks)

53 WXY (Pilot paper) 45 mins

You are a senior member of the finance team at WXY Products, a well established listed entity. The finance director has asked you to examine the most recent financial statements of a competitor, TUV.

TUV was established five years ago. It commenced trading in mobile phone accessories but has recently expanded its operations into the provision of fashion goods aimed at the 16-25 age group. Two years ago it obtained a listing on a secondary share trading market. There has been a recent report in the financial press speculating that, under the leadership of the recently appointed chief executive officer (CEO), TUV will seek a full listing on the primary market as soon as possible.

TUV's income statement, balance sheet and statement of changes in equity for the year ended 31 December 20X3 are as follows.

TUV
INCOME STATEMENT FOR THE YEAR ENDED 31 DECEMBER 20X3

	20X3 $m	20X2 $m
Revenue	325.4	261.2
Cost of sales	(248.5)	(201.3)
Gross profit	76.9	59.9
Distribution costs	(18.3)	(16.7)
Administrative expenses	(29.4)	(23.5)
Finance cost	(14.2)	(11.2)
Profit before tax	15.0	8.5
Income tax expense	(4.2)	(3.7)
Net profit for the period	10.8	4.8

TUV
STATEMENT OF CHANGES IN EQUITY FOR THE YEAR ENDED 31 DECEMBER 20X3

	Share capital $m	Revaluation surplus $m	Retained earnings $m	Total $m
Balance at 31 December 20X2	24.2	21.8	32.5	78.5
Surplus on revaluation of properties		58.3		58.3
Share capital: share options	2.3			2.3
Net profit for period			10.8	10.8
Dividends			(3.0)	(3.0)
Balance at 31 December 20X3	26.5	80.1	40.3	146.9

TUV
BALANCE SHEET AT 31 DECEMBER 20X3

	20X3		20X2	
	$m	$m	$m	$m
Non current assets				
Property, plant and equipment	338.5 ↑ investment		193.3	
Manufacturing licences	75.2 ↓		82.7	
		413.7		276.0
Current assets				
Inventories	48.7 ↑ stock		32.6	
Trade receivables	27.4 better credit control?		26.5	
Cash	no cash. –		6.2	
		76.1		65.3
		489.8		341.3
Equity				
Issued share capital	24.2		24.2	
Shares reserved for issue	2.3			
Revaluation surplus	80.1 ↑↑		21.8	
Retained earnings	40.3 ↑		32.5	
		146.9		78.5
Non current liabilities				
Long-term borrowings	244.1 ↑		219.6	
Deferred tax	26.7 ↑ future liab.		8.2	
		270.8		227.8
Current liabilities				
Trade payables	59.9 ↑		32.4	
Short-term borrowings	12.2 ↑		2.6	
		72.1		35.0
		489.8		341.3

Handwritten notes in right margin: Decrease in mfg licences trade ↑ in fashion on goods.

Handwritten note: not examinable

Notes to the financial statements include the following information.

(a) At the beginning of 20X3, TUV introduced a share option scheme for directors and senior staff. The directors had to adopt the provisions of IFRS 2 *Share based payment* in these financial statements.

(b) TUV has a policy of revaluation of property since its incorporation. During the year all of the entity's properties were revalued by a professionally qualified valuer on an open market basis.

In addition, you ascertain that WXY Products' current price/earnings (P/E) ratio is 37.4. The average P/E in the sector in which both WXY and TUV operate is 23.4 and TUV's P/E currently stands at 13.5 (based on earnings to 31 December 20X3).

Required

The finance director has asked you to prepare a report on the performance, position and prospects of TUV based on the financial statements and supplementary information shown above. In addition, he has requested a brief supplementary note for the directors' consideration about share-based payment.

(a) Prepare the report, which should be supported by relevant accounting ratios. **(20 marks)**

(b) Explain, in a supplementary note to the report, the principles and accounting adjustments required by IFRS 2 *Share based payment*, in accounting for share-based payment. Identify the effect on TUV's financial statements. **(5 marks)**

(Total = 25 marks)

54 EFG (Pilot paper)

You are a management accountant at EFG, an entity that has recently embarked upon an aggressive programme of acquisitions in order to grow its market share as rapidly as possible. EFG has targeted J, a well-established entity operating in the same sector, but with a significant level of export sales.

In order to be able to respond to opportunities quickly, EFG has established a basic set of four key financial ratios to assess the performance and position of target businesses. If a business's ratios fall within the set criteria, more detailed analysis will follow, prior to the launch of a formal bid.

The four key ratios and the criteria are as follows.

Gross profit margin	Should exceed 25%
Operating profit margin	Should exceed 13%
Return on total capital employed	Should exceed 25%
Gearing (long-term liabilities/shareholders' funds)	Should not exceed 25%

J's most recent financial statements are as follows.

J
INCOME STATEMENT FOR THE YEAR ENDED 31 JANUARY 20X4

	$'000
Revenue	1,810
Cost of sales	(1,381)
Gross profit	429
Operating expenses	(236)
Profit before interest and tax	193
Finance costs	(9)
Profit before tax	184
Income tax expense	(50)
Profit for the period	134

J
STATEMENT OF CHANGES IN EQUITY FOR THE YEAR ENDED 31 JANUARY 20X4

	Share capital $'000	Revaluation reserve $'000	Retained earnings $'000	Total $'000
Balance at 1 February 20X3	350	210	96	656
Transfer to realised profits		(10)	10	
Profit for period			134	134
Dividends			(21)	(21)
Balance at 31 January 20X4	350	200	219	769

J
BALANCE SHEET AT 31 JANUARY 20X4

	$'000	$'000
Non-current assets		
Property, plant and equipment		707
Current assets		
Inventories	201	
Trade receivables	247	
Cash	18	
		466
		1,173

	$'000	$'000
Equity		
Share capital	350	
Revaluation reserve	200	
Retained earnings	219	
		769
Non current liabilities		
Interest-bearing borrowings		248
Current liabilities		
Trade payables	142	
Income tax	14	
		156
		1,173

J's directors, who each hold a significant percentage of the ordinary share capital in the entity, are interested in EFG's potential bid, and they have co-operated fully in providing information. On a recent visit to the entity, EFG's finance director has ascertained that, in many respects, the financial and operating policies of the two businesses are very similar.

However, there are some differences, summarised as follows.

(a) J has a policy of revaluation of property, but EFG's key ratios are set on the assumption of valuation at depreciated historical cost. J owns one property, a warehouse building that was revalued five years ago. At that time, the revaluation surplus was $250,000, and the estimated useful life of the property was 25 years, assuming a residual value of nil. J depreciates the property on the straight-line basis.

(b) J employs a highly skilled team of sales representatives who are paid a substantial profit-related bonus at the end of each year. For the year ended 31 January 20X4, the total bonus paid was $96,000, included operating expenses. EFG's operating policy does not include the payment of bonuses to staff; the directors prefer to reward staff by a fixed salary. The financial controller estimates that EFG's operating policy would involve payment of additional fixed salaries of $50,000 instead of the bonus.

(c) The issued share capital of J includes $50,000 of 4% preferred shares. The directors of EFG believe that this should be classified as a non-current liability.

(d) J values inventories using an average cost basis, whereas EFG's valuation policy is first in, first out (FIFO). J's accountants have estimated that the valuation of their opening and closing inventories on a FIFO basis would be:

At 1 February 20X3 $208,000
At 31 January 20X4 $218,000

J's opening inventories at average cost were $197,000.

Required

(a) Calculate the four key financial ratios for J before making any adjustments in respect of changes required by EFG's financial and operating policies. **(2 marks)**

(b) Calculate the four key financial ratios for J after making adjustments in respect of changes required by EFG's financial and operating policies. (For this purpose, assume that the alternative in respect of the remuneration of sales representatives would take effect from 1 February 20X3.) Using EFG's criteria, advise the directors on whether or not they should pursue the potential acquisition of J. **(16 marks)**

(c) Discuss the principal advantages and limitations of EFG's approach to the initial appraisal of acquisition opportunities, identifying any specific weakness in the appraisal of J. **(7 marks)**

(Total = 25 marks)

55 DM (5/05)

45 mins

DM, a listed entity, has just published its financial statements for the year ended 31 December 20X4. DM operates a chain of 42 supermarkets in one of the six major provinces of its country of operation. During 20X4, there has been speculation in the financial press that the entity was likely to be a takeover target for one of the larger national chains of supermarkets that is currently under-represented in DM's province. A recent newspaper report has suggested that DM's directors are unlikely to resist a takeover. The six board members are all nearing retirement, and all own significant minority shareholdings in the business.

You have been approached by a private shareholder in DM. She is concerned that the directors have a conflict of interests and that the financial statements for 20X4 may have been manipulated.

The income statement and summarised statement of changes in equity of DM, with comparatives, for the year ended 31 December 20X4, and a balance sheet, with comparatives at that date are as follows:

DM: INCOME STATEMENT FOR THE YEAR ENDED 31 DECEMBER 20X4

	20X4 $m	20X3 $m
Revenue, net of sales tax	1,255	1,220
Cost of sales	(1,177)	(1,145)
Gross profit	78	75
Operating expenses	(21)	(29)
Profit from operations	57	46
Finance cost	(10)	(10)
Profit before tax	47	36
Income tax expense	(14)	(13)
Profit for the period	33	23

DM: SUMMARISE STATEMENT OF CHANGES IN EQUITY FOR THE YEAR ENDED 31 DECEMBER 20X4

	20X4 $m	20X3 $m
Opening balance	276	261
Profit for the period	33	23
Dividends	(8)	(8)
Closing balance	301	276

DM: BALANCE SHEET AT 31 DECEMBER 20X4

	20X4 $m	20X4 $m	20X3 $m	20X3 $m
Non current assets				
Property, plant and equipment	580		575	
Goodwill	100		100	
		680		675
Current assets				
Inventories	47		46	
Trade receivables	12		13	
Cash	46		12	
		105		71
		785		746

	20X4		20X3	
	$m	$m	$m	$m
Equity				
Share capital	150		150	
Retained earnings	151		126	
		301		276
Non current liabilities				
Interest-bearing borrowings	142		140	
Deferred tax	25		21	
		167		161
Current liabilities				
Trade and other payables	297		273	
Short-term borrowings	20		36	
		317		309
		785		746

Notes

1   DM's directors have undertaken a reassessment of the useful lives of property, plant and equipment during the year. In most cases, they estimate that the useful lives have increased and the depreciation charges in 20X4 have been adjusted accordingly.

2   Six new stores have been opened during 20X4, bringing the total to 42.

3   Four key ratios for the supermarket sector (based on the latest available financial statements of twelve listed entities in the sector) are as follows:

   (i)   Annual sales per store: $27.6m
   (ii)   Gross profit margin: 5.9%
   (iii)   Net profit margin: 3.9%
   (iv)   Non-current asset turnover (including both tangible and intangible non-current assets): 1.93

Required

(a)   Prepare a report, addressed to the investor, analysing the performance and position of DM based on the financial statements and supplementary information provided above. The report should also include comparisons with the key sector ratios, and it should address the investor's concerns about the possible manipulation of the 20X4 financial statements.   **(20 marks)**

(b)   Explain the limitations of the use of sector comparatives in financial analysis.   **(5 marks)**

(Total = 25 marks)

56 BZJ (5/06)   45 mins

You advise a private investor who holds a portfolio of investments in smaller listed companies. Recently, she has received the annual report of the BZJ Group for the financial year ended 31 December 20X5. In accordance with her usual practice, the investor has read the chairman's statement, but has not looked in detail at the figures. Relevant extracts from the chairman's statement are as follows.

> 'Following the replacement of many of the directors, which took place in early March 20X5, your new board has worked to expand the group's manufacturing facilities and to replace non-current assets that have reached the end of their useful lives. A new line of storage solutions was designed during the second quarter and was put into production at the beginning of September. Sales efforts have been concentrated on increasing our market share in respect of storage products, and in leading the expansion into Middle Eastern markets.
>
> The growth in the business has been financed by a combination of loan capital and the issue of additional shares. The issue of 300,000 new $1 shares was fully taken up on 1 November 20X5, reflecting, we believe, market confidence in the group's new management. Dividends have been reduced in 20X5 in order to increase profit retention to fund the further growth planned for 20X6. The directors believe that the

implementation of their medium– to long-term strategies will result in increased returns to investors within the next two to three years.'

The group's principal activity is the manufacture and sale of domestic and office furniture. Approximately 40% of the product range is bought in from manufacturers in other countries.

Extracts from the annual report of the BZJ Group are as follows:

BZJ GROUP
CONSOLIDATED INCOME STATEMENT FOR THE YEAR ENDED 31 DECEMBER 20X5

	20X5	20X4
	$'000	$'000
Revenue	120,366	121,351
Cost of sales	(103,024)	(102,286)
Gross profit	17,342	19,065
Operating expenses	(11,965)	(12,448)
Profit from operations	5,377	6,617
Interest payable	(1,469)	(906)
Profit before tax	3,908	5,711
Income tax expense	(1,125)	(1,594)
Profit for the period	2,783	4,117
Attributable to		
Equity holders of the parent	2,460	3,676
Minority interest	323	441
	2,783	4,117

BZJ GROUP
SUMMARISED CONSOLIDATED STATEMENT OF CHANGES IN EQUITY
FOR THE YEAR ENDED 31 DECEMBER 20X5 (ATTRIBUTABLE TO EQUITY HOLDERS OF THE PARENT)

	Retained earnings	Share capital	Share premium	Reval. reserve	Total 20X5	Total 20X4
	$'000	$'000	$'000	$'000	$'000	$'000
Opening balance	18,823	2,800	3,000		24,623	21,311
Surplus on revaluation of properties				2,000	2,000	
Profit for the period	2,460				2,460	3,676
Issue of share capital		300	1,200		1,500	–
Dividends paid 31/12	(155)				(155)	(364)
Closing balance	21,128	3,100	4,200	2,000	30,428	24,623

BZJ GROUP
CONSOLIDATED BALANCE SHEET AS AT 31 DECEMBER

	20X5		20X4	
	$'000	$'000	$'000	$'000
Non-current assets				
Property, plant and equipment	40,643		21,322	
Goodwill	1,928		1,928	
Trademarks and patents	1,004		1,070	
		43,575		24,320
Current assets				
Inventories	37,108		27,260	
Trade receivables	14,922		17,521	
Cash	–		170	
		52,030		44,951
		95,605		69,271

BPP
LEARNING MEDIA

	20X5		20X4	
	$'000	$'000	$'000	$'000
Equity				
Share capital ($1 shares)	3,100		2,800	
Share premium	4,200		3,000	
Revaluation reserve	2,000		–	
Relative earnings	21,128		18,823	
		30,428		24,623
Minority interest		2,270		1,947
Non-current liabilities				
Interest bearing borrowings		26,700		16,700
Current liabilities				
Trade and other payables	31,420		24,407	
Income tax	1,125		1,594	
Short-term borrowings	3,662		–	
		36,207		26,001
		95,605		69,271

Required

(a) Calculate the earnings per share figure for the BZJ Group for the years ended 31 December 20X5 and 20X4, assuming that there was no change in the number of ordinary shares in issue during 20X4. **(3 marks)**

(b) Produce a report for the investor that:

    (i) Analyses and interprets the financial statements of the BZJ Group, commenting upon the group's performance and position **(17 marks)**

    (ii) Discusses the extent to which the chairman's comments about the potential for improved future performance are supported by the financial statement information for the year ended 31 December 20X5 **(5 marks)**

(Total = 25 marks)

57 ABC (5/06)   45 mins

You are the assistant to the Chief Financial Officer (CFO) of ABC, a light engineering business based in Bolandia. ABC, a listed entity, has expanded over the last few years with the successful introduction of innovative new products. In order to further expand its product range and to increase market share, it has taken over several small, unlisted, entities within its own country.

ABC's directors have recently decided to expand its markets by taking over entities based in neighbouring countries. As the first step in the appraisal of available investment opportunities the CFO has asked you to prepare a brief report on the position and performance of three possible takeover targets: entity W based in Winlandia, entity Y based in Yolandia and entity Z based in Zeelandia. These three countries share a common currency with Bolandia, and all three target entities identify their principal activity as being the provision of light engineering products and services. The report is to comprise a one page summary of key data and a brief written report providing an initial assessment of the targets. The format of the summary is to be based upon the one generally used by ABC for its first-stage assessment of takeover targets, but with the addition of

(a) Price/earnings ratio information (because all three target entities are listed in their own countries)
(b) Some relevant country-specific information

You have produced the one-page summary of key data, given below, together with comparative information for ABC itself, based on its financial statements for the year ended 31 March 20X6.

	ABC	W	Y	Z
Country of operation	Bolandia	Winlandia	Yolandia	Zeelandia
Date of most recent	31 March	31 January	30 June	30 June
annual report	20X6	20X6	20X5	20X5
Financial statements prepared			Yolandian	
in compliance with:	IFRS	IFRS	GAAP	IFRS
Revenue	$263.4m	$28.2m	$24.7m	$26.3m
Gross profit margin	19.7%	16.8%	17.3%	21.4%
Operating profit margin	9.2%	6.3%	4.7%	8.3%
Return on total capital employed	11.3%	7.1%	6.6%	12.3%
Equity	$197.8m	$13.6m	$14.7m	$16.7m
Long-term borrowings	$10.4m	$6.2m	$1.3m	$0.6m
Average interest rate applicable to long-term borrowings by listed entities	7.5%	6%	8%	10%
Income tax rate	30%	28%	31%	38%
Inventories turnover	47 days	68 days	52 days	60 days
Receivables turnover	44 days	42 days	46 days	47 days
Payables turnover	46 days	50 days	59 days	73 days
Current ratio	1.4 : 1	0.7 : 1	1.1 : 1	0.9 : 1
P/E ratio	18.6	12.6	18.3	15.2

ABC has a cash surplus and would seek to purchase outright between 90% and 100% of the share capital of one of the three entities. The directors of ABC do not intend to increase the gearing of the group above its existing level. Upon acquisition they would, as far as possible, retain the acquired entity's management and its existing product range. However, they would also seek to extend market share by introducing ABC's own products.

Required

Prepare a report to accompany the summary of key data. The report should:

(a) Analyse the key data, comparing and contrasting the potential takeover targets with each other and with ABC itself. **(13 marks)**

(b) Discuss the extent to which the entities can be validly compared with each other, identifying the limitations of inter-firm and international comparisons. **(12 marks)**

(Total = 25 marks)

58 AXZ (11/06) 45 mins

AXZ is a rapidly expanding entity that manufactures and distributes hair care and other beauty products. Its directors are currently considering expansion into foreign countries by means of acquisitions of similar entities. Two acquisition possibilities are to be considered at the next board meeting: DCB, an entity operating in Lowland, and GFE which operates in Highland. The target acquisitions are of similar size, and operate within similar economic parameters and the same currency, although their tax regimes differ substantially. Neither entity is listed. Neither Lowland nor Highland requires unlisted entities to comply with IFRS, and consequently both entities comply with local GAAP. Local GAAP in both countries is, in most respects, similar to IFRS but there are some differences that must be taken into account when making comparisons between financial statements produced in the two countries. AXZ is listed, and complies with IFRS.

The directors of both DCB and GFE have co-operated fully in providing detailed information about their businesses. Provided that a reasonable price is offered for the shares, takeover is unlikely to be resisted by either entity. AXZ can afford to fund one acquisition but not both.

The most recent income statements of the three entities are provided below, together with some relevant balance sheet totals.

INCOME STATEMENTS FOR THE YEAR ENDED 30 SEPTEMBER 20X6

	AXZ $'000	DCB $'000	GFE $'000
Revenue	8,300	1,900	2,200
Cost of sales	(5,600)	(1,300)	(1,400)
Gross profit	2,700	600	800
Distribution costs	(252)	(60)	(65)
Administrative expenses	(882)	(180)	(250)
Finance costs	(105)	(25)	(65)
Profit before tax	1,461	335	420
Income tax expense	(366)	(134)	(105)
Profit for the period	1,095	201	315

EXTRACTS FROM BALANCE SHEETS AT 30 SEPTEMBER 20X6

	AXZ $'000	DCB $'000	GFE $'000
Total equity	4,820	1,350	1,931
Non-current liabilities (borrowings)	1,500	500	650
Non-current assets	9,950	1,680	2,400

Notes

1   It is customary for entities complying with local GAAP in Lowland to adopt the rates of depreciation used by the tax authorities. Tax depreciation is calculated on the straight-line basis in all cases, at a rate of 12.5% each year on all non-current assets. DCB's non-current assets have been held, on average, for three years, and none are fully depreciated. The age profile of non-current assets held by AXZ and GFE is very similar to that of DCB, but both entities charge an average of 10% straight line depreciation each year.

     All depreciation in all three entities has been charged to cost of sales.

2   Accounting for financial instruments is similar under Lowland GAAP and IFRS. However, Highland's GAAP takes a less prescriptive approach. GFE has $100,000 of 5% non-participating shares included in equity. Under IFRS, these shares would be classified as non-current liabilities. The 5% fixed charge on these shares has been reflected in the statement of changes in equity; under IFRS it would be shown as part of finance costs. This charge would not, however, be allowable against income tax in Highland.

3   The directors of AXZ plan to finance the acquisition through a combination of equity and debt that will be similar, proportionately, to the existing capital structure. When assessing possible takeover targets the following key accounting ratios are of especial interest:

     Gross profit margin
     Profit before tax as a percentage of sales
     Return on equity
     Return on total capital employed
     Non-current asset turnover
     Gearing (long-term debt as a percentage of equity)

     Their policy is to consider targets for takeover only if the above ratios for the combined group would not be adversely affected to any material extent.

Required

(a)   Calculate and tabulate for each entity the key ratios listed in Note 3, both before and after taking the information in Notes 1 and 2 above into account.   **(15 marks)**

(b)   Write a concise report for the directors of AXZ, which analyses the financial statement information and interprets the ratios calculated in your answer to part (a). You should also include in your analysis any additional ratios that are likely to be useful to the directors of AXZ in making their decision.   **(10 marks)**

(Total = 25 marks)

59 DPC (11/07)

45 mins

The directors of DPC, a listed entity, have been approached by three out of the five shareholders of PPS, an unlisted competitor. The PPS shareholders are nearing retirement age, and would like to realise their investment in the business. The two remaining shareholders do not object, but would like to retain between them at least a significant influence over the business.

The directors of DPC are currently concerned about the threat of a takeover bid for DPC itself. Although they would like to acquire an interest in PPS as it would help them to increase DPC's market share, they do not want to take any action that would adversely affect their financial statements and certain key accounting ratios (EPS, gearing [calculated as debt/equity], and non-current asset turnover).

There are two possibilities for consideration:

1 DPC could purchase 40% of the ordinary shares of PPS, giving it significant influence, but not control. The cost of this would be $3.5 million, to be settled in cash. DPC would pay $1 million out of its cash resources and would increase its existing long-term borrowings for the balance.

2 DPC could purchase 60% of the ordinary shares of PPS, giving it control. The cost of this would be $6 million, to be settled in cash. DPC would pay $3 million out of its cash resources, and would increase its existing long-term borrowings for the balance.

The purchase would take place on the first day of the new financial year, 1 January 20X8. Projected summary income statements for the 20X8 financial year, and projected summary balance sheets at 31 December 20X8 are shown below. The DPC figures are consolidated to include its existing 100% held subsidiaries (it currently holds no interests in associates). The projected financial statements for PPS are for that entity alone.

SUMMARY PROJECTED INCOME STATEMENTS FOR THE YEAR ENDED 31 DECEMBER 20X8

	DPC consolidated Projected: 20X8	PPS entity Projected: 20X8
	$'000	$'000
Revenue	60,300	10,200
All expenses including income tax	(55,300)	(9,500)
Profit for the period attributable to equity holders	5,000	700

SUMMARY PROJECTED BALANCE SHEETS AT 31 DECEMBER 20X8

	DPC consolidated Projected: 20X8	PPS entity Projected: 20X8	Notes
	$'000	$'000	
Non-current assets	50,400	9,800	2
Current assets	82,000	16,000	
	132,400	25,800	
Equity	31,400	4,000	3 & 4
Long-term liabilities	10,000	9,300	
Current liabilities	91,000	12,500	
	132,400	25,800	

Notes

1 DPC's consolidated projected financial statements at 31 December 20X8 do not take into account the proposed acquisition of PPS.

2 DPC's non-current asset figure includes goodwill on acquisition of various subsidiaries.

3 PPS's equity comprises 100,000 ordinary shares of $1 each, $3,200,000 of retained earnings brought forward on 1 January 20X8 and $700,000 profit for the period.

4 DPC will have 10 million ordinary shares of $1 each on 1 January 20X8. No issues of shares will be made during 20X8.

(a) Prepare draft projected financial statements for the DPC group for the year ending 31 December 20X8 under each of the following assumptions:

(i) DPC acquires 40% of the ordinary shares of PPS on 1 January 20X8;
(ii) DPC acquires 60% of the ordinary shares of PPS on 1 January 20X8.

It can be assumed that no impairment of either investment would have taken place by 31 December 20X8.

(14 marks)

(b) Calculate EPS, gearing and non-current asset turnover ratios based on the draft projected 31 December 20X8 financial statements for:

(i) DPC and its existing subsidiaries
(ii) DPC including the acquisition of an associate interest in PPS
(iii) DPC including the acquisition of a subsidiary interest in PPS

(6 marks)

(c) Discuss the differences in the accounting ratios under the different scenarios, identifying reasons for the most significant differences.

(5 marks)

(Total = 25 marks)

60 DAS (11/07)   45 mins

DAS, a listed entity, is engaged in house-building activities. It was listed a little over two years ago and it prepares its financial statements in compliance with International Financial Reporting Standards.

A business associate of yours is thinking about applying for a job as human resource manager at DAS. The job advertisement promises a 'great future in a rapidly expanding business'. She was made redundant when her last employer went into liquidation, and she is looking for a new role with a more stable and prosperous employer. She has obtained DAS's recently published financial statements for the year ended 31 August 20X7 and would like your advice on the entity's prospects for the future.

DAS provides several potentially useful voluntary disclosures about the nature of its business and its current work in progress. In the year ended 31 August 20X6 DAS sold 1,080 new houses. During the financial year ended 31 August 20X7, a major part of the entity's efforts were directed towards the development for housing on the site of a former hospital. This was DAS's largest project to date. By the year end most of the houses on site were nearly complete, and a few were ready for sale. The site contains 225 houses, which are expected to sell for between $425,000 and $600,000 each. DAS's directors consider that the development scheme has been successful; by the year end 100 of the available houses had been reserved by buyers who paid a 10% deposit. None of the hospital site house transactions had been completed by 31 August 20X7, although the Chief Executive's report noted that there were several completions during September and October 20X7. DAS sold 675 other houses during the year ended 31 August 20X7.

DAS's balance sheet at 31 August 20X7 and an income statement for the year then ended, together with comparatives, follow:

DAS: BALANCE SHEET AT 31 AUGUST 20X7

	20X7		20X6	
	$ million	$ million	$ million	$ million
Non-current assets:				
Property, plant and equipment		9.3		9.8
Current assets				
Inventories	270.5		275.0	
Trade and other receivables	3.2		3.7	
Cash	–		2.8	
		273.7		281.5
		283.0		291.3

	20X7		20X6	
	$ million	$ million	$ million	$ million
Equity				
Called up share capital ($1 shares)	8.2		8.2	
Other reserves	16.3		16.3	
Retained earnings	61.9		54.7	
		86.4		79.2
Non-current liabilities				
Long-term borrowings		114.7		112.0
Current liabilities				
Loans and borrowings	52.6		75.4	
Trade and other payables	29.3		24.7	
		81.9		100.1
		283.0		291.3

DAS: INCOME STATEMENT FOR THE YEAR ENDED 31 AUGUST 20X7

	20X7	20X6
	$ million	$ million
Revenue	157.9	243.0
Cost of sales	(126.5)	(192.7)
Gross profit	31.4	50.3
Expenses	(9.2)	(8.6)
Finance costs	(12.2)	(13.4)
Profit before tax	10.0	28.3
Income tax expense	(2.8)	(8.9)
Profit for the period	7.2	19.4

Notes

1   DAS's policy is to recognise revenue from the sale of houses upon legal completion of the transaction.

2   Most of the house-building work is undertaken by sub-contractors; DAS retains only a small direct labour force. Payments to sub-contractors are included as part of property under construction in inventories until such time as the houses are sold.

3   Inventories comprise the following:

	20X7	20X6
	$ million	$ million
Land held for development	130.0	210.0
Property under construction	140.5	65.0
	270.5	275.0

4   The statement of changes in equity (not given above) shows that no dividend was paid in the period of a little over two years since DAS was listed.

5   Deposits paid by buyers are included in trade and other payables.

6   Economic conditions are generally buoyant and house prices during 20X6 and 20X7 have risen at a rate significantly in excess of the general rate of inflation. Bank interest rates in respect of low risk lending have been running at between 5% and 6% throughout the two year period covered by the financial statements shown above.

Required:

Write a report to your business associate that analyses and interprets the information given above. The report should explain the extent to which DAS can be considered to meet her requirements for a 'stable and prosperous' employer.

Up to eight marks are available for the calculation and explanation of relevant accounting ratios.   **(25 marks)**

61 FJK (5/08)

45 mins

Several years ago, on leaving university, Fay, Jay and Kay set up a business, FJK, designing and manufacturing furniture for sale to retailers. When FJK was established, Fay and Jay each took 45% of the share capital, with Kay holding the remaining 10%. This arrangement has remained unchanged. Fay and Jay have always worked full-time in the business and remain its sole directors. Kay's role was initially part-time, but after the first two years she transferred to full-time work in her own consultancy business. Her contribution to FJK in recent years has been limited to occasionally providing advice. The relationship between the three shareholders has remained good, but all three are so busy that Kay rarely meets the others. FJK has been successful, and in February of each year, with the exception of 2008, has paid a substantial dividend to its three shareholders.

Kay's consultancy business has also been successful and she now employs 20 staff. You are Kay's financial adviser.

During 2006, the two directors decided to expand FJK's international sales, by establishing sales forces in two neighbouring countries. By early 2007, orders were starting to come in from the new countries. The expansion strategy has been very successful. Last week, Kay attended a meeting with Fay and Jay, to discuss the future of FJK. Fay and Jay explained that the business now requires more capital in order to fund further expansion, and the purpose of the meeting with Kay was to request her to inject capital of $250,000 into the business.

Kay was provided with a draft income statement for the year ended 31 March 2008 and a balance sheet at that date (given below). The draft statements are unaudited, but the figures are not expected to change, except for the income tax expense figure for 2008. FJK's accountant has not yet completed a tax calculation and so the 2007 figure of $164,000 has been used as an estimate. No statement of changes in equity has been provided, but the only movements on it would be in respect of a revaluation of property, plant and equipment that took place during the year, and the movement on retained earnings for profit for the period.

Kay, who has a reasonably good understanding of financial statements, is impressed by the revenue and profit growth. However, she has asked you, as her financial adviser, to look at the figures, in order to identify possible risks and problem areas.

FJK: DRAFT INCOME STATEMENT FOR THE YEAR ENDED 31 MARCH 2008

	2008	2007
	$'000	$'000
Revenue	5,973	3,886
Cost of sales	(4,318)	(2,868)
Gross profit	1,655	1,018
Distribution costs	(270)	(106)
Administrative expenses	(320)	(201)
Finance costs	(97)	(40)
Profit before tax	968	671
Income tax expense	(164)	(164)
Profit for the period	804	507

FJK: DRAFT BALANCE SHEET AT 31 MARCH 2008

	2008		2007	
	$'000	$'000	$'000	$'000
ASSETS				
Non-current assets				
Property, plant and equipment		3,413		1,586
Current assets				
Inventories	677		510	
Trade and other receivables	725		553	
Cash	–		12	
		1,402		1,075
		4,815		2,661

	2008		2007	
	$'000	$'000	$'000	$'000
EQUITY AND LIABILITIES				
Equity				
Called up share capital ($1 shares)	1		1	
Retained earnings	2,166		1,362	
Revaluation reserve	167		–	
		2,334		1,363
Non-current liabilities				
Long-term borrowings		763		453
Current liabilities				
Loans and borrowings	327		103	
Trade and other payables	1,227		578	
Income tax	164		164	
		1,718		845
		4,815		2,661

Required

Prepare a report for Kay that

(a)   analyses and interprets the draft financial statements and discusses FJK's performance and position.

(19 marks)

(b)   discusses possible risks and problem areas revealed by the financial statements, and the actions that the directors could take to address these risks and problems.   **(6 marks)**

(Up to 8 marks are available for the calculation of relevant accounting ratios.)

(Total = 25 marks)

62 BHG (5/08)   45 mins

BHG is a successful listed entity that designs and markets specialist business software. BHG's directors have decided to adopt a policy of expansion into overseas territories through the acquisition of similar software businesses possessing established shares of their domestic markets. BHG's aim is to obtain control, or at the minimum, significant influence (represented by at least 40% of issued share capital) of investee entities. Target investee entities are likely to be listed entities in their own countries, but the acquisition of unlisted entities is not ruled out.

You are a senior accountant in BHG, and you have been asked by the Chief Financial Officer (CFO) to establish a set of key accounting ratios for use in:

1   the initial appraisal of potential acquisitions;
2   on-going appraisal following acquisitions.

The ratios will be used as part of a suite of quantitative and non-quantitative measurements to compare businesses with each other. The CFO has suggested that it would be appropriate to identify no more than 5-7 key financial ratios.

One of your assistants has suggested a list of 5 key accounting ratios as suitable for both initial and on-going appraisal and comparison. She has provided reasons to support the case for their inclusion as key ratios.

1   Earnings per share: 'one of the most important investor ratios, widely used by all classes of investor to assess business performance'.
2   Dividend yield: 'this ratio provides a very useful measurement that allows comparison with yields from other equity and non-equity investments'.
3   Gearing: 'this is of critical importance in determining the level of risk of an equity investment'.

4   Gross profit margin: 'allows investors to assess business performance, and is of particular use over several accounting periods within the same organisation. It is also very useful for comparing performances between businesses'.

5   Asset turnover ratios: 'allow the investor to compare the intensity of asset usage between businesses, and over time'.

Required

(a)   Discuss the extent to which each of the 5 suggested accounting ratios is likely to be useful to BHG for both initial and on-going appraisal and comparison, and the extent to which your assistant's assessments of the value of the ratios are justified.   **(15 marks)**

(b)   Explain the problems and limitations of accounting ratio analysis in making inter-firm and international comparisons.   **(10 marks)**

(Total = 25 marks)

63 Preparation question: EPS

(a)   Fenton Co had 5,000,000 ordinary shares in issue on 1 January 20X1.

On 31 January 20X1, the company made a rights issue of 1 for 4 at $1.75. The cum rights price was $2 per share.

On 30 June 20X1, the company made an issue at full market price of 125,000 shares.

Finally, on 30 November 20X1, the company made a 1 for 10 bonus issue.

Profit for the year was $2,900,000.

The reported EPS for year ended 31 December 20X0 was 46.4c.

Required

What was the earnings per share figure for year ended 31 December 20X1 and the restated EPS for year ended 31 December 20X0?

(b)   (i)   Sinbad Co had the same 10 million ordinary shares in issue on both 1 January 20X1 and 31 December 20X1. On 1 January 20X1 the company issued 1,200,000 $1 units of 5% convertible loan stock. Each unit of stock is convertible into 4 ordinary shares on 1 January 20X9 at the option of the holder. The following is an extract from Sinbad Co's income statement for the year ended 31 December 20X1:

	$'000
Profit before interest and tax	980
Interest payable on 5% convertible loan stock	(60)
Profit before tax	920
Income tax expense (at 30%)	(276)
Profit for the period	644

Required

What was the basic and diluted earnings per share for the year ended 31 December 20X1?

(ii)   Talbot Co has in issue 5,000,000 50c ordinary shares throughout 20X3.

During 20X1 the company had given certain senior executives options over 400,000 shares exercisable at $1.10 at any time after 31 May 20X4. The average market value of one ordinary share during the period was $1.60. Talbot Co had made a profit after tax of $540,000 in 20X3.

Required

What is the basic and diluted earnings per share for the year ended 31 December 20X3?

(c)

Profit attributable to ordinary equity holders of the parent entity	$30 million
Profit attributable to discontinued operations attributable to the parent entity	$5 million
Ordinary shares outstanding	50 million
Average market value of one ordinary share during year	$7.50
Potential ordinary shares	
Options	12 million with exercise price of $6
Convertible preference shares	2 million entitled to a cumulative dividend of $1 per share.
	Each is convertible to two ordinary shares
2% Convertible bond	Nominal amount $100 million.
	Each $1,000 bond is convertible 100 ordinary shares. There is no amortisation of premium or discount affecting the determination of interest expense.
Tax rate	30%

Required

Calculate the basic and diluted EPS.

64 JKL (Pilot paper)   18 mins

JKL is a listed entity preparing financial statements to 31 August. At 1 September 20X3, JKL had 6,000,000 50c shares in issue. On 1 February 20X4, the entity made a rights issue of 1 for 4 at 125c per share; the issue was successful and all rights were taken up. The market share price of one share immediately prior to the issue was 145c per share. Earnings after tax for the year ended 31 August 20X4 were $2,763,000.

Several years ago, JKL issued a convertible loan of $2,000,000. The loan carries an interest rate of 7% and its terms of conversion (which are at the option of the stockholder) are as follows:

For each $100 of loan stock:

Conversion at 31 August 20X8:   105 shares
Conversion at 31 August 20X9:   103 shares

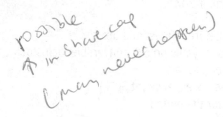

JKL is subject to an income tax rate of 32%.

Required

(a)   Calculate basic earnings per share and diluted earnings per share for the year ended 31 August 20X4.

(7 marks)

(b)   The IASB *Framework for the Preparation and Presentation of Financial Statements* states that the objective of financial statements is to provide information that is:

'useful to a wide range of users in making economic decisions'.

Explain to a holder of ordinary shares in JKL both the usefulness and limitations of the diluted earnings per share figure.

(3 marks)

(Total = 10 marks)

LEARNING MEDIA

65 CB (5/05)

18 mins

On 1 February 20X4, CB, a listed entity, had 3,000,000 ordinary shares in issue. On 1 March 20X4, CB made a rights issue of 1 for 4 at $6.50 per share. The issue was completely taken up by the shareholders.

Extracts from CB's financial statements for the year ended 31 January 20X5 are presented below.

CB: EXTRACTS FROM INCOME STATEMENT FOR THE YEAR ENDED 31 JANUARY 20X5

	$'000
Operating profit	1,380
Finance cost	(400)
Profit before tax	980
Income tax expense	(255)
Profit for the period	725

CB: EXTRACTS FROM SUMMARISED STATEMENT OF CHANGES IN EQUITY
FOR THE YEAR ENDED 31 JANUARY 20X5

	$'000
Balance at 1 February 20X4	7,860
Issue of share capital	4,875
Surplus on revaluation of properties	900
Profit for the period	725
Equity dividends	(300)
Balance at 31 January 20X5	14,060

Just before the rights issues, CB's share price was $7.50, rising to $8.25 immediately afterwards. The share price at close of business on 31 January 20X5 was $6.25.

At the beginning of February 20X5, the average price earnings (P/E) ratio in CB's business sector was 28.4, and the P/E of its principal competitor was 42.5.

Required

(a) Calculate the earnings per share for CB for the year ended 31 January 20X5, and its P/E ratio at that date.

(6 marks)

(b) Discuss the significance of P/E ratios to investors and CB's P/E ratio relative to those of its competitor and business sector.

(4 marks)

(Total = 10 marks)

66 EPS ratio (11/07)

18 mins

Earnings per share (EPS) is generally regarded as a key accounting ratio for use by investors and others. Like all accounting ratios, however, it has its limitations. You have been asked to make a brief presentation to CIMA students on the topic.

Required

(a) Explain why EPS is regarded as so important that the IASB has issued an accounting standard on its calculation.

(2 marks)

(b) Explain the general limitations of the EPS accounting ratio and its specific limitations for investors who are comparing the performance of different entities.

(8 marks)

(Total = 10 marks)

67 Preparation question: Operating segments

The Multitrade Group has three divisions, A, B and C. Details of their revenue, results and assets are given below.

	$'000
Division A	
Sales to B	304,928
Other sales (home)	57,223
Middle East export sales	406,082
Pacific fringe export sales	77,838
	846,071
Division B	
Sales to C	31,034
Export sales to Europe	195,915
	226,949
Division C	
Export sales to North America	127,003

	Head office $'000	Division A $'000	Division B $'000	Division C $'000
Operational profit/(loss) before tax		162,367	18,754	(8,303)
Re-allocated costs from				
Head office		48,362	24,181	24,181
Interest costs		3,459	6,042	527
Non-current assets	49,071	200,921	41,612	113,076
Current assets	47,800	121,832	39,044	92,338

Required

(a) Prepare a segmental report in accordance with IFRS 8 *Operating segments* for publication in Multitrade's group accounts in so far as the information permits.

(b) Comment on what the user of the accounts does and does not learn from this segmental report.

Helping hands

1   The calculations are very straightforward in this question, but be careful with your layout.

2   Make sure you show all the categories necessary for disclosure under IAS 14.

3   As with all financial information, you have to be able to put it to good use for it to have a value, which is the point in part (b). Your answer should be in point form.

---

68 Price (FR, 11/01, amended)   45 mins

(a)   Briefly state:

   (i)   The case for segment reporting
   (ii)   The case against segment reporting   **(5 marks)**

(b)   You are an investment analyst. A client of yours, Mr A, owns 3.5% of the share capital of Price. Price is a listed limited liability company and prepares financial statements in accordance with International Accounting Standards. The company supplies machinery to agricultural businesses. The year end of Price is 31 July and the financial statements for the year ended 31 July 20X1 were approved by the directors on 30 September 20X1. Following approval, copies of the financial statements were sent to all shareholders in readiness for the annual general meeting which is due to be held on 30 November 20X1. Extracts from these financial statements are given below.

INCOME STATEMENTS
YEAR ENDED 31 JULY

	20X1	20X0
	$'000	$'000
Revenue	54,000	51,000
Cost of sales	(42,000)	(40,000)
Gross profit	12,000	11,000
Other operating expenses	(6,300)	(6,000)
Profit from operations	5,700	5,000
Finance cost	(1,600)	(1,000)
Profit before tax	4,100	4,000
Income tax expense	(1,200)	(1,200)
Profit for the period	2,900	2,800

BALANCE SHEETS
AT 31 JULY

	20X1		20X0	
	$'000	$'000	$'000	$'000
Property, plant and equipment		44,200		32,000
Current assets				
Inventories	8,700		7,500	
Receivables	13,000		12,000	
Cash and cash equivalents	200		1,500	
		21,900		21,000
		66,100		53,000
Equity				
Share capital		20,000		20,000
Retained earnings		20,300		14,000
		40,300		34,000
Non-current liabilities		15,400		10,000
Current liabilities				
Trade payables	8,000		7,800	
Tax	1,200		1,200	
Bank overdraft	1,200		Nil	
		10,400		9,000
		66,100		53,000

STATEMENT OF CHANGES IN EQUITY

	Year ended 31 July 20X1
	$'000
Balance at 31 July 20X0	34,000
Surplus on revaluation of properties	5,000
Net profit for the period	2,900
Dividends	(1,600)
Balance at 31 July 20X1	40,300

EXTRACTS FROM NOTES TO THE FINANCIAL STATEMENTS

Finance cost – year ended 31 July

	20X1	20X0
	$'000	$'000
On 10% interest-bearing borrowings	1,000	1,000
On zero-rate bonds	400	Nil
On bank overdraft	200	Nil
	1,600	1,000

Non-current liabilities at 31 July	20X1	20X0
	$'000	$'000
10% borrowings repayable 31 July 20X6	10,000	10,000
Zero-rate bonds	5,400	Nil
	15,400	10,000

The zero-rate bonds were issued for proceeds of $5 million on 1 August 20X0. the lenders are not entitled to interest during their period of issue. The bonds are repayable on 31 July 20X4 for a total of $6,802,450. The bonds are quoted on a recognised stock exchange. However, the company intends to hold the bonds until they mature and then repay them.

Revaluation of properties

This is the first time the company has revalued any of its properties.

Depreciation of non-current assets

Depreciation of non-current assets for the year totalled $4 million (20X0 – $3 million).

Your client always attends the annual general meeting of the company and likes to put questions to the directors regarding the financial statements. However, he is not a financial specialist and does not wish to look foolish by asking inappropriate questions. Mr A intends to ask the following three questions and seeks your advice based on the information provided. The points he wishes to make are as follows.

Point 1:

Why, when the company has made almost the same profit as last year and has borrowed more money through a bond issue, has the company got a bank overdraft of $1.2 million at the end of the year when there was a positive balance of $1.5 million in the bank at the end of the previous year? This looks wrong to me.

Point 2:

The company has a revaluation surplus of $5 million included in the statement of changes in equity. I have never understood this statement. Surely surpluses are shown in the income statement. Perhaps our accountants are unaware of the correct accounting treatment?

Point 3:

I don't understand the treatment of the zero-rate bonds. The notes tell me that these were issued for $5 million and no interest was paid to the investors. The accounts show a finance cost of $400,000 and a balance owing of $5.4 million. Is this an error? On the other hand, perhaps the $5.4 million is the fair value of the bonds? I feel sure an International Accounting Standard has been issued that requires companies to value their borrowings at fair value.

Required

Prepare a reply to Mr A that evaluates the issues he has raised in the three points and provides appropriate advice. You should support your advice with references to International Accounting Standards.

The mark allocation is as follows:

Point 1 **(9 marks)**
Point 2 **(4 marks)**
Point 3 **(7 marks)**

(Total = 25 marks)

69 STV (11/05)   45 mins

One of your colleagues has recently inherited investments in several listed entities and she frequently asks for your advice on accounting issues. She has recently received the consolidated financial statements of STV, an entity that provides haulage and freight services in several countries. She has noticed that note 3 to the financial statements is headed 'Segment information'.

Note 3 explains that STV's primary segment reporting format is business segments of which there are three: in addition to road and air freight, the entity provides secure transportation services for smaller items of high value. STV's *Operating and Financial Review* provides further background information: the secure transport services segment was established only three years ago. This new operation required a sizeable investment in infrastructure which was principally funded through borrowing. However, the segment has experienced rapid revenue growth in that time, and has become a significant competitor in the industry sector.

Extracts from STV's segment report for the year ended 31 August 20X5 are as follows.

	Road haulage		Air freight		Secure transport		Group	
	20X5	20X4	20X5	20X4	20X5	20X4	20X5	20X4
	$m	$m	$m	$m	$m	$m	$m	$m
Revenue	653	642	208	199	98	63	959	904
Segment result	169	168	68	62	6	(16)	243	214
Unallocated corporate expenses							(35)	(37)
Operating profit							208	177
Interest expense							(22)	(21)
Share of profits of associates	16	12					16	12
Profit before tax							202	168
Income tax							(65)	(49)
Profit							137	119
Other information								
Segment assets	805	796	306	287	437	422	1,548	1,505
Investment in equity method associates	85	84					85	84
Unallocated corporate assets							573	522
Consolidated total assets							2,206	2,111
Segment liabilities	345	349	176	178	197	184	718	711
Unallocated corporate liabilities							37	12
Consolidated total liabilities							755	723

Your colleague finds several aspects of this note confusing:

'I thought I'd understood what you told me about consolidated financial statements; the idea of aggregating several pieces of information to provide an overall view of the activities of the group makes sense. But the segment report seems to be trying to disaggregate the information all over again. What is the point of doing this? Does this information actually tell me anything useful about STV? I know from talking to you previously that financial information does not always tell us everything we need to know. So, what are the limitations in this statement?'

Required

(a)   Explain the reasons for including disaggregated information about business segments in the notes to the consolidated financial statements.   **(5 marks)**

(b)   Analyse and interpret STV's segment disclosures for the benefit of your colleague, explaining findings in a brief report.   **(12 marks)**

(c)   Explain the general limitations of segment reporting, illustrating your answer where applicable with references to STV's segment report.   **(8 marks)**

(Total = 25 marks)

70 Glowball

The directors of Glowball, a public limited company, had discussed the study by the Institute of Environmental Management which indicated that over 35% of the world's largest 250 corporations are voluntarily releasing green reports to the public to promote corporate environmental performance and to attract customers and investors. They have heard that their main competitors are applying the 'Global Reporting Initiative' (GRI) in an effort to develop a worldwide format for corporate environmental reporting. However, the directors are unsure as to what this initiative actually means. Additionally they require advice as to the nature of any legislation or standards relating to environmental reporting, as they are worried that any environmental report produced by the company may not be of sufficient quality and may detract and not enhance their image if the report does not comply with recognised standards. Glowball has a reputation for ensuring the preservation of the environment in its business activities.

Further the directors have collected information in respect of a series of events which they consider to be important and worthy of note in the environmental report but are not sure as to how they would be incorporated in the environmental report or whether they should be included in the financial statements.

The events are as follows.

(a)   Glowball is a company that pipes gas from offshore gas installations to major consumers. The company purchased its main competitor during the year and found that there were environmental liabilities arising out of the restoration of many miles of farmland that had been affected by the laying of a pipeline. There was no legal obligation to carry out the work but the company felt that there would be a cost of around $150 million if the farmland was to be restored.

(b)   Most of the offshore gas installations are governed by operating licenses which specify limits to the substances which can be discharged to the air and water. These limits vary according to local legislation and tests are carried out by the regulatory authorities. During the year the company was prosecuted for infringements of an environmental law in the USA when toxic gas escaped into the atmosphere. In 20X2 the company was prosecuted five times and in 20X1 eleven times for infringement of the law. The final amount of the fine/costs to be imposed by the courts has not been determined but is expected to be around $5 million. The escape occurred over the seas and it was considered that there was little threat to human life.

(c)   The company produced statistics that measure their improvement in the handling of emissions of gases which may have an impact on the environment. The statistics deal with:

    (i)   Measurement of the release of gases with the potential to form acid rain. The emissions have been reduced by 84% over five years due to the closure of old plants.

    (ii)   Measurement of emissions of substances potentially hazardous to human health. The emissions are down by 51% on 20W8 levels.

    (iii)   Measurement of emissions to water that removes dissolved oxygen and substances that may have an adverse effect on aquatic life. Accurate measurement of these emissions is not possible but the company is planning to spend $70 million on research in this area.

(d)   The company tries to reduce the environmental impacts associated with the siting and construction of its gas installations. This is done in the way that minimises the impact on wild life and human beings. Additionally when the installations are at the end of their life, they are dismantled and are not sunk into the sea. The current provision for the decommissioning of these installations is $215 million and there are still decommissioning costs of $407 million to be provided as the company's policy is to build up the required provision over the life of the installation.

Required

Prepare a report suitable for presentation to the directors of Glowball in which you discuss the following elements:

(a)   Current reporting requirements and guidelines relating to environmental reporting.   **(10 marks)**

(b)   The nature of any disclosure which would be required in an environmental report and/or the financial statements for the events (a)-(d) above.   **(15 marks)**

(The mark allocation includes four marks for the style and layout of the report.)   **(Total = 25 marks)**

71 FW (5/05)

FW is a listed entity involved in the business of oil exploration, drilling and refining in three neighbouring countries. Aye, Bee and Cee. The business has been consistently profitable, creating high returns for its international shareholders. In recent years, however, there has been an increase in environmental lobbying in FW's three countries of operation. Two years ago, an environmental group based in Cee started lobbying the government to take action against FW for alleged destruction of valuable wildlife habitats in Cee's protected wetlands and the displacement of the local population. At the time, the directors of FW took legal advice on the basis of which they assessed the risk of liability at less than 50%. A contingent liability of $500 million was noted in the financial statements to cover possible legal costs, compensation to displaced persons and reinstatement of the habitats, as well as fines.

FW is currently preparing its financial statements for the year ended 28 February 20X5. Recent advice from the entity's legal advisors has assessed that the risk of a successful action against FW has increased, and must now be regarded as more likely than not to occur. The board of directors has met to discuss the issue. The directors accept that a provision of $500 million is required, but would like to be informed of the effects of the adjustment on certain key ratios that the entity headlines in its annual report. All of the directors are concerned about the potentially adverse effect on the share price, as FW is actively engaged in a takeover bid that would involve a substantial share exchange. In addition, they feel that the public's image of the entity is likely to be damaged. The chief executive makes the following suggestion:

> 'Many oil business now publish an environmental and social report, and I think It may be time for us to do so. It would give us the opportunity to set the record straight about what we do to reduce pollution, and could help to deflect some of the public attention from us over this law suit. In any case, it would be a good public relations opportunity; we can use it to tell people about our equal opportunities programme. I was reading about something called the Global Reporting Initiative [GRI]. I don't know much about it, but it might give us some help in structuring a report that will get the right message across. We could probably pull something together to go out with this year's annual report.'

The draft financial statements for the year ended 28 February 20X5 include the following information relevant for the calculation of key ratios. All figures are before taking into account the $500 million provision. The provision will be charged to operating expenses.

	$m
Net assets (before long-term loans) at 1 March 20X4	9,016
Net assets (before long-term loans) at 28 February 20X5	10,066
Long-term loans at 28 February 20X5	4,410
Share capital + reserves at 1 March 20X4	4,954
Share capital + reserves at 28 February 20X5	5,656
Revenue	20,392
Operating profit	2,080
Profit before tax	1,670
Profit for the period	1,002

The number of ordinary shares in issue throughout the years ended 29 February 20X4 and 28 February 20X5 were 6,000 million shares of 25c each.

FW's key financial ratios for 20X4 financial year (calculated using financial statements for the year ended 29 February 20X4) were:

Return on equity (using average equity):	24.7%
Return on net assets (using average net assets):	17.7%
Gearing (debt as a percentage of equity):	82%
Operating profit margin:	10.1%
Earnings per share:	12.2c per share

Required

In your position as assistant to FW's Chief Financial Officer produce a briefing paper that

(a) Analyses and interprets the effects of making the environmental provision on FW's key financial ratios. You should take into account the possible effects on the public perception of FW. **(12 marks)**

(b) Identifies the advantages and disadvantages to FW of adopting the Chief Executive's proposal to publish an environmental and social report. **(7 marks)**

(c) Describes the **three** principal sustainability dimensions covered by the GRI's framework of performance indicators. **(6 marks)**

(Total = 25 marks)

72 Widespread
18 mins

You are the management accountant of Widespread, an entity that is incorporated in the United Kingdom (using IFRS) and which has a number of subsidiaries located in various countries around the world. One of these subsidiaries is Dixie Inc, an entity based in the USA. Your managing director, who is not an accountant, has decided to take an interest in the preparation of the consolidated financial statements. Some time later he calls you into the office because he is confused by the reconciliation statement that the chief accountant of Dixie Inc has prepared. This statement is shown below.

	$'000
Profit before taxation per local accounts	56,000
Capitalisation of development costs net of related amortisation	7,000
Write-off capitalised interest net of related amortisation	(4,000)
Restatement of inventory on the FIFO basis from the LIFO basis	7,500
Profit before taxation for consolidation	66,500

The managing director does not really understand why this reconciliation statement is necessary. He is wondering whether the group should adopt international accounting standards in an effort to avoid having to prepare it.

Required

Write a report to your managing director that:

(a) Explains in general terms why the reconciliation statement is necessary. **(3 marks)**

(b) Identifies the accounting issue that underpins each of the three items in the statement. **(7 marks)**

(Total = 10 marks)

73 Nearby (FR, 11/01, amended)
18 mins

You are the chief accountant of Nearby. Nearby has a number of subsidiaries located in various parts of the world. One of these subsidiaries is Faraway. Faraway prepares its financial statements in accordance with local Accounting Standards. Nearby prepares its consolidated financial statements using International Accounting Standards. Whenever an International Accounting Standard has a benchmark treatment and an allowed alternative treatment, Nearby follows the benchmark treatment.

The accountant of Faraway has prepared the financial statements for the year ended 30 September 20X1 – also the accounting reference date of Nearby. The income statement and the statement of changes in equity for the year ended 30 September 20X1 (together with comparatives) drawn up in local currency (LC) were as shown below.

INCOME STATEMENTS
YEAR ENDED 30 SEPTEMBER

	20X1	20X0
	LC'000	LC'000
Revenue	56,000	53,000
Cost of sales	(34,000)	(32,000)
Gross profit	22,000	21,000
Other operating expenses	(10,000)	(9,800)
Profit from operations	12,000	11,200
Finance cost	(4,000)	(3,800)
Profit before tax	8,000	7,400
Income tax expense	(3,000)	(2,800)
Profit for the period	5,000	4,600

STATEMENTS OF CHANGES IN EQUITY

	20X1	20X0
Balance at 30 September 20X0 (30 September 20W9)	30,000	27,800
Net profit for the period	5,000	4,600
Dividends	(2,500)	(2,400)
Balance at 30 September 20X1 (30 September 20X0)	35,200	30,000

The local Accounting Standards that are used in preparing the financial statements of Faraway are the same as International Accounting Standards with the exception of the following.

1   Faraway values its inventories using the LIFO basis. This valuation is acceptable for local tax purposes. Relevant inventory values are as follows.

Date	Inventory value under LIFO	Inventory value under FIFO
30 September 20X1	9,500	10,000
30 September 20X0	7,700	8,000
30 September 20W9	8,600	9,000

The rate of local corporate tax is 36%.

2   On 1 October 20W3, Faraway acquired an unincorporated business for 50 million units of local currency. The fair value of the net assets of this business on 1 October 20W3 was 30 million units of local currency. The resulting goodwill was written off to the revenue reserve as permitted by local Accounting Standards.

The accountant of Faraway has sent the financial statements to you with a suggestion that consolidation would be much easier if all group companies used International Accounting Standards to prepare their individual financial statements.

Required

Restate the income statement and statement of changes in equity of Faraway in local currency (both the current year and the comparative) so as to comply with International Accounting Standards.   **(10 marks)**

74 Current issues (FR, 11/02, amended)   36 mins

You are the management accountant of Clean, an entity listed in a country that permits enterprises to publish financial statements in accordance with International Accounting Standards. Clean is considering seeking a listing on a US stock exchange in the near future. Your chief executive officer takes a keen interest in financial reporting but he is not a professionally-qualified accountant. He has recently sent you a memorandum that contains three issues relating to current financial reporting practice.

Issue (a)
I have heard that (following an agreement with the International Organisation of Securities Commissions), foreign entities like us, which wish to raise funds on the US capital markets, will soon be able to file financial statements that comply with International Accounting Standards rather than domestic US standards. Is this true? Even if it is I don't understand why this would be a significant benefit for us.

Issue (b)

My political contacts tell me that government ministers are very interested in extending the practice of environment reporting. What exactly does 'environmental reporting' mean and to what extent is it mandatory? Why does there seem to be a trend towards greater environmental reporting? You don't need to go into massive detail, just give me an outline of what is involved.

Issue (c)

One of the phrases I often hear is 'our employees are our most important asset'. I largely agree with this sentiment, but if it is true, then surely this should be reflected in some way on the balance sheet. I do not recall seeing such an asset in previous balance sheets and would be most grateful for your advice.

Required

Draft a reply to the issues the Chief Executive Officer has raised. You should refer to the provisions of International Accounting Standards, and any other relevant documents where you consider them to be of assistance in supporting your reply. However, you need not refer to the detailed provisions of any individual US standards.

The allocation of marks is

	(a)	**(7 marks)**
	(b)	**(7 marks)**
	(c)	**(6 marks)**

(Total = 20 marks)

75 Intellectual capital (11/06)   18 mins

In many industries there is a large gap between the market capitalisation of listed entities and the balance sheet value of their net assets. Some commentators have suggested that the gap comprises unrecognised intangible assets in the form of intellectual capital obtained through the employment of human resources, and that these assets should be capitalised.

Required

Identify the principal arguments for and against the proposal to capitalise intellectual capital.   **(10 marks)**

76 Convergence project (5/08)   18 mins

An important development in international accounting in recent years has been the convergence project between the IASB and the US standard setter, the Financial Accounting Standards Board (FASB).

Required

(a) Describe the objectives, and progress to date, of the convergence project, illustrating your response with examples of the work that has been successfully undertaken.   **(6 marks)**

(b) Identify four continuing, and significant, areas of difference that exist between IFRS and US GAAP.

(4 marks)

(Total = 10 marks)

77 Environmental disclosure (11/07)   18 mins

It is becoming increasingly common for listed entities to provide non-financial disclosures intended to inform stakeholders about the business's environmental policies, impacts and practices. Supporters of such voluntary disclosures argue that stakeholders have a right to be informed about environmental issues in this way. However, there are also arguments against this type of disclosure.

Required

Identify and explain the principal arguments **against** voluntary disclosures by businesses of their environmental policies, impacts and practices.   **(10 marks)**

SECTION A QUESTIONS: MIXED BANKS

Questions 78 to 86 give practice in Section A style questions, arranged in mixed topic banks.

78 Mixed bank (1)   36 mins

1   X's asset turnover is very low compared with that of its main competitor.

     What could be the reason for this?

     A   X carries its non-current assets at historic cost, while its competitor carries them at current value.
     B   X embarked on a major programme of capital investment towards the end of the previous year.
     C   X has a smaller proportion of productive assets than its competitor.
     D   X has recruited a number of additional production staff during the year.   **(2 marks)**

---

2   On 1 January 20X3 Beta had in issue 10 million ordinary shares of $1 each. On 31 March 20X3 it made a rights issue on a 1 for 2 basis for $1.25 per share. The cum rights price was $1.75 per share. On 30 September 20X3 it issued a further 5 million shares at full market price. These were the first share issues that Beta had made for many years.

     Beta's earnings for the year ended 31 December 20X2 were $1.8 million. Its earnings for the year ended 31 December 20X3 were $2.1 million.

     What was Beta's earnings per share for the years ended 31 December 20X3 and 31 December 20X2 as restated?

	20X3	20X2
A	13.12 cents	12.86 cents
B	13.75 cents	16.25 cents
C	13.75 cents	18.00 cents
D	14.23 cents	19.94 cents

     (2 marks)

---

3   Savoy owns 80% of Spring and 30% of White. Spring also owns 15% of White.

     Extracts from the income statements for the year ended 31 December 20X7:

	Savoy $'000	Spring $'000	White $'000
Gross profit	700	550	500

     What is group gross profit for the year ended 31 October 20X5?

     A $1,250,000
     B $1,365,000
     C $1,460,000
     D $1,475,000   **(2 marks)**

---

4   XYZ purchased an 80% interest in ABC on 1 July 20X0 for $2,360,000 when the fair value of ABC's net assets was $2,240,000.

     On 30 June 20X3 XYZ sold all its shares in ABC for $3,600,000. The net assets of ABC were $3,310,000 at the date of disposal.

     What is the profit on disposal of the shares in ABC that will be included in the consolidated income statement for the year ended 30 June 20X3?   **(2 marks)**

5   On 1 January 20X4, Geranium acquired 60% of the equity share capital of Rose for $5 million. At that date, the net assets of Rose were $8 million.

On 1 July 20X9 Geranium sold three quarters of its holding in Rose for $6.5 million.

The capital and reserves of Rose at 31 December 20X9 are shown below:

	$'000
Share capital ($1 ordinary shares)	5,000
Retained earnings at 1 January 20X9	6,500
Retained profit for the year ended 31 December 20X9	2,000
	13,500

What is the profit or loss on disposal of the shares in Rose?

A $675,000 profit
B $725,000 loss
C $725,000 profit
D $3,025,000 loss   (2 marks)

6   The consolidated accounts of Neroli show the following amounts in respect of minority interests.

	20X4 $'000	20X3 $'000
Minority interest (in the consolidated balance sheet)	275	260
Minority interest in profit for the year	35	

Neroli has one foreign operation of which it owns 80%. Exchange losses shown as a movement on consolidated reserves for the year ended 31 December 20X4 were $20,000.

Another subsidiary, which was owned 75%, revalued its property, resulting in a revaluation surplus of $40,000.

What amount should be shown as 'dividends paid to minority interests' in the consolidated cash flow statement for the year ended 31 December 20X4?   (2 marks)

7   On 1 January 20X3 Bartlett issued $450,000 loan notes. Issue costs were $200. The loan notes carry a coupon rate of interest at 3% (payable in arrears) and are redeemable on 31 December 20X4. The effective finance cost of the loan notes is 12%.

At what amount should the loan notes be reported in the balance sheet at 31 December 20X3?   (3 marks)

8   The following information relates to an entity.

	$'000
Credit sales for the year ended 31 December 20X6	5,600
Credit purchases for the year ended 31 December 20X6	4,500
Trade receivables at 31 December 20X6	690
Trade payables at 31 December 20X6	250

The entity's working capital cycle has been calculated at 105 days.

How much inventory did the entity hold at 31 December 20X6 (to the nearest thousand pounds)?

A $493,000
B $614,000
C $986,000
D $1,227,000   (2 marks)

9   On 30 September 20X5 Alpha made a 1 for 3 rights issue at $2.00 per share. At that date, the latest cum rights price was $2.50. Before making the rights issue, Alpha had 15 million $1 ordinary shares in issue.

after tax for the year ended 31 December 20X5 was $1.5 million.

Calculate earnings per share for the year ended 31 December 20X5.   **(2 marks)**

---

10   A owns 90% of the equity share capital of B and when B already owned 80% of the equity share capital of C. The summarised balance sheets of B and C at 31 December 20X5 are shown below.

	B	C
	$'000	$'000
Investment in C	900	–
Other net assets	6,100	5,000
	7,000	5,000
Share capital ($1 ordinary shares)	2,000	1,000
Reserves	5,000	4,000
	7,000	5,000

What is the minority interest in the consolidated balance sheet of the A Group at 31 December 20X5?

     (1 mark)

     (Total = 20 marks)

79 Mixed bank (2)   36 mins

1   Owen acquired 90% of the equity shares in Sassoon on 1 January 20X5 when the retained earnings of Sassoon and Thomas were $200,000 and $80,000 respectively. Sassoon had acquired 60% of the equity shares in Thomas on 1 January 20X4 when the retained earnings of Thomas were $40,000.

Extracts from the balance sheets at 31 March 20X8 are shown below:

	Owen	Sassoon	Thomas
	$'000	$'000	$'000
Investment in Sassoon and Thomas	400	100	
Other net assets	1,000	250	150
	1,400	350	150
Share capital	500	100	50
Retained earnings	900	250	100
	1,400	350	150

How much goodwill arose on consolidation?   **(2 marks)**

---

2   On 1 January 20X4, Geranium acquired 60% of the equity share capital of Rose for $5 million. At that date, the net assets of Rose were $8 million.

On 1 July 20X9 Geranium sold three quarters of its holding in Rose for $6.5 million.

The capital and reserves of Rose at 31 December 20X9 are shown below:

	$'000
Share capital ($1 ordinary shares)	5,000
Retained earnings at 1 January 20X9	6,500
Retained profit for the year ended 31 December 20X9	2,000
	13,500

At what amount should the investment in Rose be shown in the consolidated balance sheet of the Geranium group at 31 December 20X9?   **(2 marks)**

3   Parent has three overseas subsidiaries.

(1)   A is 80% owned. A does not normally enter into transactions with Parent, other than to pay dividends. It operates as a fairly autonomous entity on a day to day basis although Parent controls its long term strategy.

(2)   B is 100% owned and has been set up in order to assemble machines from materials provided by Parent. These are then sent to the UK where Parent sells them to third parties.

(3)   C is 75% owned and is located in France. It manufactures and sells its own range of products locally. It negotiates its own day to day financing needs with French banks.

Which of the subsidiaries are likely to have a different functional currency from Parent?

A   A and B
B   A and C
C   B and C
D   all three subsidiaries   **(2 marks)**

4   Rat acquired 75% of the equity share capital of Mole, a foreign operation, on 1 January 20X5, when its net assets were Units 720,000. Summarised balance sheets of the two entities at 31 December 20X6 are shown below:

	Rat	Mole
	$'000	Unit'000
Investment in Mole	350	–
Other net assets	2,550	960
	2,900	960
Share capital ($1/Unit1 ordinary shares)	1,000	500
Retained earnings	1,900	460
	2,900	960

Exchange rates were as follows:

	Unit=$1
1 January 20X5	2.0
31 December 20X6	2.5

What are consolidated retained earnings at 31 December 20X6?   **(2 marks)**

5   On 1 January 20X3 Deferred issued $600,000 loan notes. Issue costs were $200. The loan notes do not carry interest, but are redeemable at a premium of $152,389 on 31 December 20X4. The effective finance cost of the debentures is 12%.

What is the finance cost in respect of the loan notes for the year ended 31 December 20X4?

A $72,000
B $76,194
C $80,613
D $80,640   **(2 marks)**

6   TUV has a subsidiary in an overseas country where the local currency is Crowns. The principal assets of this subsidiary are a number of freehold properties. The value of these properties is $30 million Crowns. TUV regards the subsidiary as a foreign operation. No depreciation is charged on the properties as they are estimated to have indefinite useful lives. The following information is relevant:

	Exchange rate	Current price index
	Cr = $1	in overseas country
30 June 20X4	1.5	100
30 June 20X7	12.0	1,100

What is the value at which the properties should be included in the group financial statements of TUV at 30 June 20X7?   **(2 marks)**

7   Green operates a nuclear power station. The power station is due to be decommissioned on 31 December 20X8 but will be fully operational up to that date. It has been estimated that the cost of decommissioning the power station and cleaning up any environmental damage to the surrounding area, as required by legislation, will be $60 million. Green recognised a provision for this expenditure at 31 December 20X0. A suitable discount rate for evaluating investments of this nature (appropriately adjusted for risk) is 12%.

What is the charge to the income statement in respect of the provision for the year ended 31 December 20X1?

A $2,880,000
B $3,030,000
C $5,910,000
D $7,500,000   **(2 marks)**

---

8   Information from the balance sheet of MNO has been expressed as percentages of total assets less current liabilities:

	%
Land and property	78
Other non-current assets	19
Inventories and work in progress	–
Trade receivables	459
Cash/short term investments	89
	645
Bank overdraft	(5)
Trade payables	(540)
Total assets less current liabilities	100

In which of the following industries could MNO be operating?

A   Housebuilding
B   Insurance broking
C   Manufacturing
D   Retailing   **(2 marks)**

---

9   On 30 June 20X3, Sugar entered into an agreement with two other investors to establish a new entity, Spice. All three investors subscribed for one third of the equity shares in Spice and each share carries one vote. All three investors appointed two representatives to the six-member board of directors of Spice. All key policy decisions require the agreement of five of the six board members.

The following statements refer to the treatment of the investment in Spice in the consolidated financial statements of Sugar for the year ended 30 September 20X3.

(i)   Spice will be treated as a joint venture simply because the three investors hold one third of the shares each.

(ii)   Spice will be treated as a joint venture in this case, but only because of the requirement that key policy decisions require the consent of at least five of the directors.

(iii)   If Spice carries on a business that is distinct from that of its investors, then it will be consolidated using proportional consolidation.

(iv)   Spice is only a joint venture if the requirement that key policy decisions require the consent of five directors is established by contract.

Assuming the benchmark treatment set out in IAS 31 *Interests in joint ventures* is used, which of the above statements are true?

A   (i) and (iii) only
B   (i), (iii) and (iv) only
C   (ii) and (iii) only
D   (ii), (iii) and (iv) only   **(2 marks)**

10   On 1 July 20X0, Super acquired 75% of the ordinary shares in Man for $6 million. Goodwill of $1 million arose on the acquisition.

On 31 December 20X8, Super disposed of part of its shareholding in Man for $4 million, retaining a 40% interest. The net assets of Man on 1 July 20X8 were $8.5 million and Man made a profit of $800,000 in the year ended 30 June 20X9 (no dividends were paid or declared by Man in that year).

What is the profit on disposal that will be included in the consolidated income statement of Super for the year ended 30 June 20X9?

A $418,333
B $535,000
C $885,000
D $1,200,000   (2 marks)

(Total = 20 marks)

80 Mixed bank (3) (Pilot paper)   36 mins

1   The consolidated financial statements of P for the year ended 31 March 20X4 showed the following balances.

(i)   Minority interest in the consolidated balance sheet at 31 March 20X4 is $6 million ($3.6 million at 31 March 20X3).

(ii)   Minority interest in the consolidated income statement for the year ended 31 March 20X4 is $2 million.

During the year ended 31 March 20X4, the group acquired a new 75% subsidiary whose net assets at the date of acquisition were $6.4 million. On 31 March 20X4, the group revalued all its properties and the minority interest in the revaluation surplus was $1.5 million. There were no dividends payable to minority shareholders at the beginning or end of the year.

Required

What is the dividend paid to minority shareholders that will be shown in the consolidated cash flow statement of P for the year ended 31 March 20X4?   (3 marks)

2   D has owned 80% of the equity shares of E since 1 January 20X2. E has owned 60% of the equity shares of F since 1 January 20X0. The retained earnings of F at the latest balance sheet date (31 December 20X9) stood at $30 million. The retained earnings of F stood at $12 million on 1 January 20X0 and $14 million on 1 January 20X2.

Required

Ignoring goodwill, what will be included in the consolidated retained earnings of D at 31 December 20X9 in respect of F?   (3 marks)

3   The following statements refer to a situation where an investing entity (K) seeks to exert control or influence over another entity (L). Assume that K is required to prepare consolidated accounts because of other investments.

(i)   If K owns more than 20%, but less than 50% of the equity shares in L, then L is bound to be an associate of K.

(ii)   If K controls the operating and financial policies of L, then L cannot be an associate of K.

(iii) If L is an associate of K, then any amounts payable by L to K are not eliminated when preparing the consolidated balance sheet of K.

Which of the statements are true?

- A   (i) and (ii) only
- B   (ii) only
- C   (ii) and (iii) only
- D   (i) and (iii) only

(2 marks)

---

4   Q has a defined benefit pension plan and prepares financial statements to 31 August 20X2. The following additional information is relevant for the year ended 31 August 20X3.

The net pension liability at 31 August 20X3 is stated before making any adjustment in respect of actuarial gains or losses arising in the year.

No actuarial gains or losses were recognised in the income statement for the year.

The expected return on assets was $60 million.

The unwinding of the discount on the pension liability was $30 million.

The current service cost was $45 million.

The entity granted additional benefits to existing pensioners that vested immediately and that have a present value of $10 million. These were not allowed for in the original actuarial assumptions.

The entity paid pension contributions of $40 million.

The net pension liability are as follows:

31.8.20X3	31.8.20X2
$40m	$35m

Ignoring deferred tax, what is the actuarial gain or loss arising in the year ended 31 August 20X3?

- A   A loss of $5 million
- B   A loss of $10 million
- C   A loss of $20 million
- D   A gain of $20 million

(2 marks)

---

5   Current cost accounting adopts the principle of value to the business. State what the missing words are in the following sentences.

When considering replacement cost and recoverable amount, what is the value to the business?

What is recoverable amount? (2 marks)

---

6   Describe, in a maximum of 40 words, the principal requirements of IAS 29 *Financial reporting in hyper-inflationary economies*. (2 marks)

---

7   At 1 April 20X3, S held 80,000 of the 100,000 issued ordinary shares of T. The acquisition of T took place on 1 April 20X2, and goodwill on acquisition was recorded at $120,000. Goodwill was impaired; the amount of the impairment was $36,000. On 1 October 20X3, S disposes of 20,000 shares in T for $125,000. At that date, T's total net assets are $400,000.

Calculate the consolidated profit or loss before tax on disposal of the shares. (3 marks)

---

8   As well as its investment in T (see question 7), S held 25% of the shares of U, and exerts a significant influence over it. U sells goods to S. During the year ending 31 March 20X4, U sells goods to S for $100,000. The cost of the goods to U is $80,000. At the year end, S's inventories include $16,000 of goods purchased from U.

Calculate the adjustment required in respect of unrealised profit, and describe the accounting treatment of the adjustment in the consolidated income statement and the consolidated balance sheet. (3 marks)

(Total = 20 marks)

81 Mixed bank (4) (5/05)

1   The FG group of entities comprises FG and its subsidiaries, HI and JK.

    FG acquired 80% of HI's ordinary shares on 31 December 20X1, when the reserves of HI stood at $10,000,000, and the reserves of JK stood at $7,600,000.

    HI acquired 75% of JK's ordinary shares on 31 December 20X0, when the reserves of JK stood at $7,000,000.

    At 31 December 20X4, HI's reserves stood at $12,200,000, and JK's reserves stood at $10,600,000.

    There have been no other acquisitions and disposals in the group, and no impairments of goodwill or intra-group trading adjustments have been recorded.

    How much profit has been added to consolidated reserves in the FG group in respect of the investments in HI and JK between acquisition and 31 December 20X4?

    A $3,560,000
    B $3,920,000
    C $4,010,000
    D $4,460,000   **(2 marks)**

2   On 1 March 20X5, PB, a listed entity, acquired 80% of 3,000,000 issued ordinary shares of SV. The consideration for each share acquired comprised a cash payment of $1.20, plus two ordinary shares in PB. The market value of a $1 ordinary share in PB on 1 March 20X5 was $1.50, rising to $1.60 by the entity's year end on 31 March 20X5. Professional fees paid to PB's external accountants and legal advisers in respect of the acquisition were $400,000.

    What is the fair value of consideration in respect of this acquisition, for inclusion in PB's financial statements for the year ended 31 March 20X5?

    A $10,080,000
    B $10,480,000
    C $10,560,000
    D $10,960,000   **(2 marks)**

3   Where the purchase price of an acquisition is less than the aggregate fair value of the net assets acquired, which *one* of the following accounting treatments of the difference is required by IFRS 3 *Business combinations*?

    A   Deduction from goodwill in the consolidated balance sheet
    B   Immediate recognition as a gain in the statement of changes in equity
    C   Recognition in the income statement over its estimated useful life
    D   Immediate recognition as a gain in the income statement   **(2 marks)**

4   On March 20X4, NS acquired 30% of the shares of TP. The investment was accounted for as an associate in NS's consolidated financial statements. Both NS and TP have an accounting year end of 31 October. NS has no other investments in associates.

    Net profit for the year in TP's income statement for the year ended 31 October 20X4 was $230,000. It declared and paid a dividend of $100,000 on 1 July 20X4. No other dividends were paid in the year.

    What amount will be shown as an inflow in respect of earnings from the associate in the consolidated cash flow statement of NS for the year ended 31 October 20X4?

    A $20,000
    B $26,000
    C $30,000
    D $46,000   **(2 marks)**

5   Which of the following statements, in respect of foreign currency translation, are correct according to IAS 21 *The effects of changes in foreign exchange rates*?

   (i)   The functional currency of an entity is selected by management.
   (ii)   The presentation currency of an entity is selected by management.
   (iii)   The functional currency of an entity is identified by reference to circumstances of the business.
   (iv)   The presentation currency of an entity is identified by reference to circumstances of the business.

   A   (i) and (ii) only
   B   (iii) and (iv) only
   C   (i) and (iv) only
   D   (ii) and (iii) only   **(2 marks)**

---

6   During the financial year ended 28 February 20X5, MN issued the two financial instruments described below. For *each* of the instruments, identify whether it should be classified as debt or equity, **explaining in not more than 40 words each** the reason for your choice. In each case you should refer to the relevant International Accounting Standard or International Financial Reporting Standard.

   (i)   Redeemable preferred shares with a coupon rate 8%. The shares are redeemable on 28 February 20X9 at premium of 10%   **(2 marks)**

   (ii)   A grant of share options to senior executives. The options may be exercised from 28 February 20X8.   **(2 marks)**

---

7   The following statement contains a missing word:

   'Current purchasing power accounting is based upon the concept of _____ capital maintenance.'

   Which ONE of the following is the missing word?

   A   Real
   B   General
   C   Physical
   D   Cash-based   **(2 marks)**

---

8   On 1 February 20X4, BJ sold a freehold interest in land to a financing institution for $7.2 million. The contracted terms require that BJ repurchase the freehold on 31 January 20X7 for $8.82 million. BJ has the option to repurchase on 31 January 20X5 for $7.7 million, or on 31 January 20X6 for $8.24 million. Prior to the disposal, the land was recorded at its carrying value of $6 million in BJ's accounting records. The receipt of $7.2 million has been recorded with a corresponding credit to suspense account. No other accounting entries have been made in respect of this transaction.

   At 31 January 20X5, BJ's directors decide not to take up the option to repurchase.

   Briefly explain the substance of this transaction, and prepare journal entries to record it correctly in the accounting records of BJ for the year ended 31 January 20X5.

                                                                                                                   (4 marks)

                                                                                                          (Total = 20 marks)

82 Mixed bank (5) (11/05) 36 mins

1 FAL owns 75% of the issued ordinary share capital and 25% of the issued irredeemable preferred shares in PAL. The share capital and retained earnings of PAL at 31 March 20X5, the FAL group's year end, were:

	$
Ordinary share capital	60,000
7% preferred share capital	20,000
	80,000
Retained earnings	215,000
	295,000

[handwritten: this pref share only → Belongs with ord shares]

Upon acquisition of FAL's interests in PAL, which took place on 30 September 20X4, the fair values of PAL's net assets were the same as book values, with the exception of an item of plant. The carrying value of the plant at 30 September 20X4 was $10,200, and its fair value was $15,600. Its estimated remaining useful life at that date was 4 years. Depreciation is charged for each month of ownership. No adjustment was made in PAL's own accounting records for the increase in fair value.

[handwritten: Depn]

Required *[handwritten: 25%]*

Calculate the minority interest in PAL at 31 March 20X5 for inclusion in the group's consolidated balance sheet (to the nearest $). **(4 marks)**

---

2 AB owns a controlling interest in another entity, CD, and exerts significant influence over EF, an entity in which it holds 30% of the ordinary share capital.

During the financial year ended 30 April 20X5, EF sold goods to AB valued at $80,000. The cost of the goods to EF was $60,000. 25% of the goods remained in AB's inventory at 30 April 20X5.

What is the correct consolidation adjustment in respect of the inventory? **(3 marks)**

---

3 Which *one* of the following describes the method of accounting preferred by IAS 31 *Interests in joint ventures* for jointly controlled entities?

A Trade investment with disclosure of share of assets by way of note
B The equity method of consolidation
C Proportionate consolidation
D Acquisition accounting with deduction of a minority interest. **(2 marks)**

---

4 IAS 29 *Financial reporting in hyperinflationary economies* lists characteristics of the economic environment of a country which tend to indicate that hyperinflation is a problem.

Identify *two* of these characteristics. **(4 marks)**

---

5 On 1 January 20X5, an entity issued a debt instrument with a coupon rate of 3.5% at a par value of $6,000,000. The directly attributable costs of issue were $120,000. The debt instrument s repayable on 31 December 2011 at a premium of $1,100,000.

What is the total amount of the finance cost associated with the debt instrument?

A $1,470,000
B $1,590,000
C $2,570,000
D $2,690,000 **(2 marks)**

---

6 XYZ operates a defined benefit pension plan for its employees. The present value of the plan's obligations on 1 September 20X4 was $6,600,000, increasing to $7,200,000 by the entity's year end on 31 August 20X5. Benefits paid to members of the pension plan during the year were $650,000 and the current service cost for the financial year was $875,000. The increase in the present value of the pension plans liabilities for the year was $540,000.

What was the actuarial gain or loss in respect of the plan's obligations for the year ended 31 August 20X5?

A Gain of $165,000
B Loss of $285,000
C Gain of $1,465,000
D Loss of $1,585,000   (2 marks)

7   At its year end, 31 March 20X5, entity JBK held 60,000 shares in a listed entity, X. The shares were
    purchased on 11 February 20X5 at a price of 85c per share. The market value of the shares on 31 March
    20X5 was 87.5c. The investment is categorised as held-for-trading.

    Show the journal entries required in respect of both the initial acquisition of the investment and its
    subsequent remeasurement on 31 March 20X5.   (3 marks)

                                                                              (Total = 20 marks)

83 Mixed bank (6) (5/06)   36 mins

1   On 30 September 20X5, GHI purchased 80% of the ordinary share capital of JKL for $1.45 million. The book
    value of JKL's net assets at the date of acquisition was $1.35 million. A valuation exercise showed that the
    fair value of JKL's property, plant and equipment at that date was $100,000 greater than book value, and
    JKL immediately incorporated this revaluation into its own books. JKL's financial statements at 30
    September 20X5 contained notes referring to a contingent liability (with a fair value of $200,000).

    GHI acquired JKL with the intention of restructuring the latter's production facilities. The estimated costs of
    the restructuring plan totalled $115,000.

    Calculate goodwill on acquisition, and identify any of the above items that should be excluded from the
    calculation in accordance with IFRS 3 *Business combinations*.   (3 marks)

2   DA controls another entity, CB, owning 60% of its ordinary share capital. At the group's year end, 31
    December 20X5, CB included $6,000 in its receivables in respect of goods supplied to DA. However, the
    payables of DA included only $4,000 in respect of amounts due to CB. The difference arose because, on 31
    December 20X5, DA sent a cheque for $2,000, which was not received by CB until 3 January 20X6.

    Which *one* of the following sets of consolidation adjustments to current assets and current liabilities is
    correct?

    A Deduct $6,000 from both consolidated receivables and consolidated payables.
    B Deduct $3,600 from both consolidated receivables and consolidated payables.
    C Deduct $6,000 from consolidated receivables and $4,000 from consolidated payables, and include
       cash in transit of $2,000.
    D Deduct $6,000 from consolidated receivables and $4,000 from consolidated payables, and include
       inventory in transit of $2,000.   (2 marks)

3   PQR holds several investments in subsidiaries. In December 20X5, it acquired 100% of the ordinary share
    capital of STU. PQR intends to exclude STU from consolidation in its group financial statements for the year
    ended 28 February 20X6, on the grounds that it does not intend to retain the investment in the longer term.

    Explain, with reference to the relevant International Financial Reporting Standard, the conditions relating to
    exclusion of this type of investment from consolidation.   (2 marks)

4   BLX holds several investments in subsidiaries. One of these, CMY, is located abroad. CMY prepares its financial statements in its local currency, the crown.

Several years ago, when the exchange rate was 5 crowns = $1, CMY purchased land at a cost of 170,000 crowns. On 1 June 20X5, when the exchange rate was 6·5 crowns = $1 the land was revalued at a fair value of 600,000 crowns. The exchange rate at the group's year end, 31 December 20X5, was 7 crowns = $1.

In accordance with the requirements of IAS 21 *The effects of changes in foreign exchange rates*, at what value in $ should the land be recognised in BLX's group financial statements at 31 December 20X5?

A $85,714
B $90,440
C $100,154
D $120,000   (2 marks)

5   During its financial year ended 31 March 20X6, CDO acquired 100% of the issued share capital of DEP for €750,000. The purchase was partially financed by a loan for €600,000. The loan is designated by CDO as a hedging instrument. CDO's functional currency is the $.

Explain the accounting treatment required for gains and losses on the investment and its hedging instrument.   (2 marks)

6   On 1 January 20X1, EFG issued 10,000 5% convertible bonds at their par value of $50 each. The bonds will be redeemed on 1 January 20X6. Each bond is convertible at the option of the holder at any time during the five year period. Interest on the bond will be paid annually in arrears.

The prevailing market interest rate for similar debt without conversion options at the date of issue was 6%.

At what value should the equity element of the hybrid financial instrument be recognised in the financial statements of EFG at the date of issue?   (4 marks)

7   In the context of IAS 19 *Employee benefits*, explain how an experience gain or loss arises.   (3 marks)

8   During its financial year ended 31 January 20X6, TSQ issued share options to several of its senior employees. The options vest immediately upon issue.

Which *one* of the following describes the accounting entry that is required to recognise the options?

A   DEBIT the statement of changes in equity   CREDIT liabilities
B   DEBIT the statement of changes in equity   CREDIT equity
C   DEBIT the income statement   CREDIT liabilities
D   DEBIT the income statement   CREDIT equity   (2 marks)

(Total = 20 marks)

84 Mixed bank (7) (11/06)   36 mins

1   GPX's financial statements included an investment in associate at $6,600,000 in its consolidated balance sheet at 30 September 20X5. At 30 September 20X6, the investment in associate had increased to $6,750,000. GPX's pre-tax share of profit in the associate was $420,000, with a related tax charge of $180,000. The net amount of $240,000 was included in the consolidated income statement for the year ended 30 September 20X6.

There were no impairments to the investment in associate, or acquisitions or disposals of shares during the financial year.

What is the amount of the cash flow related to this investment for inclusion in the consolidated cash flow statement for the year ended 30 September 20X6?

A	$90,000
B	$240,000
C	$390,000
D	$420,000	(2 marks)

2   CXP owns 75% of the ordinary share capital of its subsidiary, DYQ. The shares were acquired on 1 November 20X5 when DYQ's reserves stood at $152,000. DYQ acquired a 65% investment in its subsidiary, EZR, on 1 May 20X5. EZR's reserves were $189,000 on 1 May 20X5, and $202,000 on 1 November 20X5.

Reserves for the three entities at 31 October 20X6, the entities' year end, were as follows:

CXP $266,000
DYQ $178,000
EZR $214,000

There had been no impairment of goodwill in respect of either investment since acquisition.

Calculate the balance of consolidated reserves for inclusion in the consolidated balance sheet of the CXP group at 31 October 20X6.   (3 marks)

3   AMY, an entity with a 30 September year end, holds several investments in subsidiaries. On 1 April 20X6, it disposed of 10,000 of its 40,000 $1 shares in its subsidiary BNZ for $95,000. AMY had acquired the shares, which represented 80% of BNZ's ordinary share capital, on 1 April 20X4 for $250,000, when BNZ's reserves totalled $186,000. BNZ's net assets at the date of disposal were $275,000. Since acquisition, there has been no impairment to goodwill.

Calculate the consolidated profit or loss on disposal of the shares for inclusion in AMY's financial statements for the year ended 30 September 20X6.   (4 marks)

4   BJS, a listed entity, had a weighted average of 27 million ordinary shares in issue during its financial year ended 31 August 20X6. It was also financed throughout the year by an issue of 12% convertible bonds with a par value of $50 million. The bonds are convertible at the option of the holders at the rate of 12 new ordinary shares for every $100 of bonds at par value. The tax rate applicable to BJS was 30% during the financial year. The profit attributable to ordinary shareholders for the year ended 31 August 20X6 was $100 million.

Calculate earnings per share, and diluted earnings per share, for BJS for the year ended 31 August 20X6.
                                                                                                          (4 marks)

5   On 1 January 20X6, an entity, ABC, issued bonds with a nominal value of $5 million, incurring $150,000 in issue costs. The coupon rate of the bonds is 2.5%. They are redeemable on 1 January 20Y6 at a premium of $1.75 million.

Calculate the total amount of finance cost associated with the bonds.   (3 marks)

6   ST, UV and WX are listed entities operating in the same business sector. At 31 October 20X6, their P/E ratios were reported as follows:

ST   16.2
UV   12.7
WX   8.4

Which one of the following statements about these P/E ratios is correct?

The P/E ratios suggest that:

A   ST is regarded by the market as the riskiest of the three entities.

B   ST has the highest earnings per share of the three entities.

C   UV represents the safest investment because its P/E lies approximately midway between the other two.

D   WX's share price may be relatively lower than that of ST and UV because of an adverse effect such as a profit warning.

(2 marks)

7   The asset backing of an investment in shares is calculated by dividing the book value of equity by the number of shares in issue.

Identify **two** reasons why a comparison of this ratio between two or more entities may be invalid.

(2 marks)

(Total = 20 marks)

85 Mixed bank (8) (11/07)

36 mins

1   GPT regularly sells goods to its subsidiary in which it owns 60% of the ordinary share capital. During the group's financial year ended 31 August 20X7, GPT sold goods to its subsidiary valued at $100,000 (selling price) upon which it makes a margin of 20%. By the group's year end all of the goods had been sold to parties outside the group.

What is the correct consolidation adjustment in respect of these sales for the year ended 31 August 20X7?

A   No adjustment required

B   DR Revenue $60,000; CR Cost of sales $60,000

C   DR Revenue $80,000; CR Cost of sales $80,000

D   DR Revenue $100,000; CR Cost of sales $100,000.

(2 marks)

2   Which ONE of the following is a valid reason for excluding a subsidiary from consolidation under current International Financial Reporting Standards?

A   The subsidiary has been acquired exclusively with a view to its subsequent disposal

B   The activities of the subsidiary are so dissimilar from those of the rest of the group that it would be misleading to include it in the consolidation

C   A formally documented decision has been made by the directors to wind down the activities of the subsidiary

D   The subsidiary operates in a hyperinflationary environment

(2 marks)

3   On 31 July 20X7, AGR acquired 80% of the ordinary share capital of its subsidiary BLK. The book value of BLK's net assets at the date of acquisition was $1,300,000. This value included $300,000 in respect of certain specialised items of plant, which were bought on 31 July 20X4. The plant is being depreciated on a straight line basis over six years with an assumption of nil residual value. No estimate of market value at the date of acquisition is available, but it would cost $700,000 to replace the plant at current prices.

Since 20X5, BLK has been developing a specialised industrial process. Following registration of the patent and some coverage in the trade press, BLK received an offer for the patent of $150,000 in April 20X7. The offer was rejected. BLK does not recognise the patent as an asset. AGR's directors think it probable that other processes developed by BLK have a market value, and they have made a broad estimate of $75,000 to cover such items which have not been capitalised by BLK.

Shortly before the acquisition of BLK took place, its directors had started a programme to rationalise production. The estimated cost of the programme was $250,000, but no provision for it was recognised in the entity's financial statements at 31 July 20X7. The programme has continued and is now (November 20X7) substantially complete.

Calculate the fair value of BLK's net assets that would be included in the consolidated balance sheet of AGR at 31 July 20X7, assuming that there are no relevant issues other than those given above. If appropriate, explain your reasons for excluding any of the possible adjustments to fair value. **(4 marks)**

---

4   LPD buys goods from its 75% owned subsidiary QPR. QPR earns a mark-up of 25% on such transactions. At the group's year end, 30 June 20X7, LPD had not yet taken delivery of goods, at a sales value of $100,000, which were despatched by QPR on 29 June 20X7.

At what amount would the goods in transit appear in the consolidated balance sheet of the LPD group at 30 June 20X7?

    A $60,000
    B $75,000
    C $80,000
    D $100,000   **(2 marks)**

---

5   The initial measurement of financial liabilities should be at fair value. Explain the general valuation rule in IAS 39 *Financial instruments: recognition and measurement* that should be applied to the subsequent measurement of financial liabilities, other than those specifically mentioned as exceptions.   **(2 marks)**

---

6   On 1 September 20X6, BLT held 60% of the ordinary share capital of its only subsidiary CMU. The consolidated equity of the group at that date was $576,600, of which $127,000 was attributable to the minority interest.

On 28 February 20X7, exactly halfway through the financial year, BLT bought a further 20% of the ordinary share capital of CMU. In the year ended 31 August 20X7 BLT's profits for the period were $98,970 and CMU's were $30,000. BLT paid a dividend of $40,000 on 1 July 20X7. There were no other movements in equity. It can be assumed that profits accrue evenly throughout the year.

Prepare a consolidated statement of changes in equity for the BLT group for the year ended 31 August 20X7.

(4 marks)

---

7   STB is preparing its consolidated cash flow statement for the year ended 31 October 20X7. Its consolidated opening balance at net book value for property, plant and equipment was $207,000. During the year the STB group disposed of plant for proceeds of $8,500 that had cost $62,000 several years ago and which was fully written down at 1 November 20X6. There were no other disposals. The depreciation charge for the year ended 31 October 20X7 was $32,000. The consolidated closing book value for property, plant and equipment was $228,000.

What was the cash outflow in respect of purchases of property, plant and equipment for inclusion in the consolidated cash flow statement of STB group for the year ended 31 October 20X7?

    A $11,000
    B $44,500
    C $53,000
    D $115,000   **(2 marks)**

---

8   Identify TWO conditions which must exist in order for hedge accounting to be permitted under IAS 39 *Financial instruments: Recognition and Measurement.*   **(2 marks)**

(Total = 20 marks)

86 Mixed bank (9) (5/08)

36 mins

1   AB owns 60% of the issued ordinary share capital of CD. CD owns 60% of the issued ordinary share capital of EF. Which ONE of the following statements is correct?

The effective interest of AB in EF is

A   20%
B   24%
C   36%
D   60%

(2 marks)

2   SG acquired a controlling interest in TH on 1 April 20X7, paying 3 million shillings (TH's functional currency) for 700,000 of TH's issued share capital of 1,000,000 1 shilling ordinary shares. TH's reserves at the date of acquisition were 1,500,000 shillings.

Rates of exchange were:

1 April 2007 1$ = 5 shillings
31 March 2008 1$ = 4·7 shillings

Calculate goodwill on acquisition (assuming no impairment has taken place) in respect of the TH acquisition for inclusion in the SG group's balance sheet at 31 March 20X8.   **(2 marks)**

3   On 31 December 20X7, LMN set up a joint venture entity, OPQ, with two partners. Each partner owns exactly one third of the issued share capital of OPQ and all business decisions are taken jointly.

Throughout its financial year ended 31 March 20X8, LMN held 80% of the share capital of its subsidiary RST.

Revenue for the period ended 31 March 20X8 recorded in the books of the three entities was as follows:

	$
LMN	21,500
OPQ	5,400
RST	12,600

LMN's directors have decided to adopt the proportionate method of consolidation where permitted by IFRS. During the year, RST supplied LMN with goods with a sales value of $1,400. The cost to RST of these goods was $1,200.

What is the amount of consolidated revenue for inclusion in LMN's group income statement for the year ended 31 March 20X8?

A $31,980
B $33,150
C $34,500
D $34,700

(2 marks)

4   The current cost accounting (CCA) method of accounting for changing price levels requires a series of adjustments to historical cost operating profit.

Describe the purpose and nature of the cost of sales adjustment (CoSA).   **(2 marks)**

5   CDP made an issue of 5% cumulative preference shares during its financial year ended 31 January 20X8. The shares have no fixed redemption date. (Under the terms of the issue CDP does not have to pay the 5% distribution in a given year, but if it fails to do so, the obligation is carried forward to a future year).

Categorise the financial instrument as either equity or liability, and give the reason for your categorisation.

(2 marks)

6   HXB is a manufacturer of machinery. On 30 September 20X7, it sold a machine to its 100% subsidiary, IYC, for $200,000. The cost to HXB of the machine was $150,000. IYC recorded the asset in its own books at the initial cost of $200,000. IYC's policy is to depreciate machinery at 2% per full month of ownership, on the straight line basis.

       Calculate the consolidation adjustment, and prepare the appropriate consolidation journal entry, in respect of this asset for the consolidated financial statements of the HXB group for the year ended 31 March 20X8.

          (3 marks)

---

7   On 1 March 2007, XPR acquired control of YQS, purchasing 60% of its issued ordinary share capital. YQS is located in a country where compliance with most, but not all, IFRS is required by law. For example, there is no requirement to discount liabilities. No material fair value adjustments were identified at the date of acquisition of YQS, except in respect of a deferred liability to a supplier which will fall due on 1 March 20X9. The amount payable on that date will be $300,000. The discount rate relevant to the liability is 8%.

       YQS's profit for the period ended 29 February 20X8 was $67,600 before taking into account any unwinding of the discount in respect of the liability referred to above.

       Calculate the share of profit for the period attributable to equity shareholders of the parent, after taking into account any adjustment required in respect of the liability.   **(3 marks)**

---

8   NST runs a defined benefit pension scheme for its employees. NST uses the 'corridor'' approach for the recognition of actuarial gains and losses permitted by IAS 19 *Employee Benefits*. At 30 April 20X8, the present value of the pension obligation was $18·6 million. Unrecognised actuarial gains at that date were $0·7 million and the fair value of plan assets was $16·9 million.

       Calculate the net plan asset or liability for inclusion in NST's balance sheet at 30 April 20X8.   **(2 marks)**

---

9   Describe the appropriate accounting treatment, as required by IAS 39 *Financial Instruments: Recognition and Measurement* for gains or losses on financial assets classified as 'held-for-trading'.   **(2 marks)**

          (Total = 20 marks)

Answers

Extra guidance

Remember you can find additional guidance on a number of questions in this kit on BPP's website: www.bpp.com/cima/extra-question-guidance

1 Preparation question: Prescriptive standards

Accounting policies and practices have been increasingly regulated by the introduction of IFRSs. It has, however, always been recognised that **financial reporting** involves the **exercise** of **judgement** as the overriding requirement for each entity is to present a **true and fair view** to its shareholders.

The statement attacks the wide variety of policies and practices, 20 years or so after the first IAS was introduced. Is it fair to do so?

Variety of acceptable policies and practices

(a) **Why does the variety exist?**

The statement is correct to the extent that a wide variety does still exist in the few areas where there is still **no accounting standard** on an issue, or where accounting standards have become **outdated**. For example, IAS 18 Revenue sets out broad principles for revenue recognition but does not specifically cover many of the more sophisticated types of transaction that have been developed recently. Entities are left to **interpret imprecise accounting requirements** and a variety of solutions have emerged.

(b) **What action is the IASB taking?**

Until relatively recently many differences existed in areas where standards have been introduced. However, the IASB is **committed to reducing the number of permitted alternatives** and has just completed a major project to improve several of the IASs introduced by its predecessor body. For example, the revised version of IAS 8 no longer allows a change in accounting policy to be dealt with either retrospectively or in the current period; all changes must be accounted for retrospectively. To date the IASB's IFRSs have taken the same approach. For example, IFRS 3 Business combinations has prohibited pooling of interests accounting; all combinations must now be treated as acquisitions.

(c) **Where can choices still be made?**

There are still **some areas where choices can be made** and where these have a significant effect on an entity's results and financial position. For example, when measuring most non-current assets, an entity can choose whether to apply the cost model (historic cost) or to apply the revaluation model (fair value). Generally, where an accounting standard permits a choice there is a good reason for it. In this case, the IASB wishes to encourage the use of fair values, as these provide more relevant information, but accepts that there are many cases in which the practical problems of using fair value would outweigh the benefits.

Wrong to assume any significant degree of comparability

This feeling flows logically out of the assertion in the first sentence. Clearly, it has some merit given the lack of standardisation of some areas. On the other hand, it is perhaps too sweeping.

Most of the more contentious accounting areas apply to more complicated groups of public companies. They are very aware of the **impression** their **published accounts give** and therefore are keen to find choices that reflect their business well. Comparability is therefore diminished.

Smaller, owner-managed companies, however, often have few contentious accounting policy areas to address and **no real incentive** to spend too long **dressing things up**. Consequently it is possible to see reasonable comparability between their accounts.

Overall though, for most public-interest companies only a skilled reader of accounts and accounting policies is able to make effective comparisons.

Should more prescriptive standards be introduced?

This can be interpreted in two ways – should more standards be introduced and should they be more prescriptive.

(a) Certainly it is uncontroversial to argue that more grey areas should be tackled in order to bring in standards where they are currently lacking. The IASB is moving into these areas with discussion papers and by continuing to work on the *Framework*. There are too many material areas where no real guidance exists, eg discounting.

(b)   Whether these new standards should be more prescriptive is more difficult. **Two distinct views exist**.

   (i)   There are those who **lament** the ever decreasing amount of judgement preparers and auditors are able to use.

   (ii)   There is also an argument that prescriptive standards can encourage creative accounting, because rules can be circumvented. Others, however, **welcome** the moves towards standardisation taken by the IASB.

The key to resolving the debate is to **clarify what users want**. In many cases, the more prescriptive approach being taken by the IASB is being increasingly widely appreciated. There will always be a trade-off between comparability and flexibility. My feeling is that most users do not have the time or the expertise to worry about nuances of treatment and disclosure and prefer the increased confidence given by increasing comparability.

Conclusion

In conclusion, much has been done to cut down on some of the variety of options available. A lot still remains to be done, however, and the mood is that more prescriptive standards rather than less will best meet users' needs. In the meantime making effective comparisons between the accounts of large quoted companies remains a challenging task.

2 MNO

> **Text reference**. The OFR is covered in Chapter 1.
>
> **Top tips**. This is a very straightforward question, for which the structure is given to you. In the absence of any indication to the contrary, you can assume that the three parts of the question carry an equal weighting.
>
> **Easy marks**. Don't forget to present your answer as a briefing paper. Even if you are shaky on the details of the OFR, you can pick up a couple of marks for doing this.

Briefing paper to the directors of MNO: Operating and Financial Review (OFR)

(a)   **Relevant regulatory requirements of an OFR**

Increasingly international companies are including a form of Operating and Financial Review (OFR) within their annual financial statements. However, there is currently **no formal regulatory requirement**, either internationally or nationally, to prepare an OFR.

IAS 1 *Presentation of financial statements* encourages the preparation and presentation of a management review in the financial statements that would be likely to cover many of the areas typically covered by an OFR. However, this is not mandatory therefore any disclosure is voluntary. In October 2005 the IASB issued a **discussion paper** on 'Management Commentary' but as yet no exposure draft has been published on the topic.

In the UK there is **no legal requirement** for companies to produce an OFR but for those that do the ASB issued in January 2006 a *Reporting Statement: Operating and Financial Review* but this has no status except as **a source of guidance**.

(b)   **Purpose and typical content of an OFR**

The overall purpose of an OFR is that it is to provide **forward-looking information**, addressed to and aimed at shareholders in the company, in order to help them to assess the strategies adopted by the company and the potential for those strategies to succeed. The OFR should both **complement and supplement the financial statements**, it should be comprehensive and understandable, balanced and neutral and comparable over time.

The **key elements** of an OFR will tend to be:

   (i)   The nature of the business, including a description of the market, competitive and regulatory environment in which the business operates

(ii)   The business's objectives and strategies

(iii)   The development and performance of the business both in the current financial year and in the future

(iv)   The resources, principal risks and uncertainties and relationships that may affect the business's long-term value

(v)   The position of the business including a description of the capital structure, treasury policies and objectives and liquidity of the business both currently and in the future

The OFR should also **include information** about:

(i)   Environmental matters

(ii)   The employees

(iii)   Social and community issues

(iv)   Details of persons with which the business has contractual arrangements which are essential to the business

(v)   Receipts from and returns to shareholders

(c)   Advantages and drawbacks of an OFR

There are a number of **advantages** to MNO of producing an OFR:

(i)   The production of an OFR is often viewed favourably by shareholders as a further means of communication and transparency.

(ii)   The investment community could perceive MNO as a progressive and forward looking company.

(iii)   If a compulsory OFR were to be introduced at some future date by the IASB then MNO would already have the structures and systems in place to report the necessary information.

There are, however, **drawbacks** to producing an OFR.

(i)   If a genuinely useful OFR is to be produced then it is likely to require a large amount of management time and therefore be costly to the business.

(ii)   There is a risk that users of the financial statements may concentrate only on the rather more user-friendly OFR in preference to the financial statements themselves and therefore not have a clear picture of the position and results of the business.

3 Section A questions: Group accounts (1)

1   L and M are subsidiaries of K. Through them K controls 45% of N and 50% of O. To give control, the parent's holding must be *greater than* 50%.

2   65%. Only voting equity shareholdings give control, so only the 25c ordinary shares are considered here.

3   B   Consul cannot exercise significant influence over Warrior because it is controlled by another company. However, it has the largest shareholdings and a board seat, so exercising significant influence, over Admiral. Sultan is not so clear. As another entity also has significant influence over it is likely that Consul does too.

4   D   X controls Y and A. Therefore X controls 55% of Z.

5   UV is not consolidated. The civil war means that the parents is no longer able to exercise control over the subsidiary; consequently the definition of the subsidiary is not met. WX continues to be consolidated but is classified as 'held for sale' under IFRS 5. Exclusion by different activities is not permitted under IFRS because adequate information should be available from IAS 14 *Segment reporting*.

6 The answer is $54m

	$m
Falcon	58
Kestrel (80% × 25 – 20)	4
Less impairment of goodwill	(8)
	54

Goodwill:	
Cost of investment	24
Net assets acquired (80% × 20)	(16)
	8

7 C

	$'000
Cost of investment	400
Net assets acquired (90% × 350)	(315)
	85

8

	$'000	$'000
Net assets acquired:		
Ordinary shares of 50c each	300	
Retained earnings at 1 January 20X1	80	
Retained profit for the 9 months ended 30 September 20X1		
(9/12 × 40)	30	
	410	
Group share (80%)		328
Add goodwill		20
		348

9 A The provision for unrealised profit is $5,000 (30,000 × 20/120).

The subsidiary has sold to the parent, therefore the unrealised profit has arisen in the accounts of the subsidiary and must be allocated between the group and the minority interest.

10

	$'000
XY	160
PQ	90
Inventory in transit	10
Provision for unrealised profit (20 + 10 × 30%)	(9)
	251

4 Section A questions: Group accounts (2)

1

	$
X	60,000
Y (20% × 30,000)	6,000
Z (25% × 20,000)	5,000
	71,000

2 D Revenue is reduced by the full amount of intra-group sales. ✓

3 B Gross profit is reduced by the element of unrealised profit, which is 10,000 × 25/125.

4

	$
Pumpkin	100,000
Squash	80,000
	180,000
Less intra-group sales	(8,000)
Add provision for unrealised profit (8,000 – 5,000)	3,000
	175,000

5   C

	$'000
Subsidiary	55,000
Less provision for unrealised profit (15,000 × 20/120 × ½)	(1,250)
	53,750
MI share (20%)	10,750

6

	$'000
Profit after tax (900 + 400)	1,300
Less minority interest	
Preferred shares (70% × 1,000 × 10%)	(70)
Ordinary shares (20% × (400 – 100)	(60)
	1,170

(handwritten annotations: "take out amt paid pret share. for pref shares" and "← ?")

7

	$'000
Consolidated balance sheet	445
Strachey	(420)
	25
Add provision for unrealised profit (60 × 20/120)	10
	35

8

	$
Consolidated balance sheet	230,000
Woolf	(202,000)
	28,000
Add provision for unrealised profit (5,000 × 80%)	4,000
Group share of Stephen	32,000
Retained earnings of Stephen (100/80)	40,000

9   The answer is $13.5m

	$m
Cost of investment	12.0
Group share of post-acquisition reserves (30% × 5)	1.5
	13.5

Alternative working

	$m
Group share of net assets at 31 December 20X7 (30% × $35 million)	10.5
Goodwill	3.0
	13.5

Goodwill	
Cost of investment	12
Net assets acquired (30% × (25 + 5)	(9)
	3

5 Develop

The main principles behind the preparation of consolidated financial statements are the concepts of **control** and **significant influence**.

Treatment of subsidiaries

If a parent has a **subsidiary** then this means that the parent **controls the subsidiary** usually through holding 50% or more of the shares. The concept of control means that the assets and liabilities of the subsidiary are being used as the parent wishes them to be used and are almost an extension of the assets and liabilities of the parent itself. For this reason all of the assets and liabilities of the subsidiary are added into those of the parent to show the shareholders the total assets and liabilities that are under the control of the parent.

However, **although the parent controls the subsidiary it may not own all of the shares of the subsidiary and therefore the ownership interest must be recognised**. This is done by including in the minority interest figure the minority shareholders' share of the net assets that have been included in the balance sheet.

In the **income statement** it is again recognised that due to the parent's control of the subsidiary **all of the profits** of the subsidiary are **available for use by the parent** and therefore all are included in the income statement. However again the ownership interest is recognised by showing the minority's share of those profits in the minority interest figure.

In summary, consolidated financial statements reflect economic substance by presenting the financial performance and position of the **group as a single entity**.

Treatment of associates

The position with an **associate** is however **different**. In essence an associate is an entity in which the parent owns between 20% and 50% of the shares. The associate is **not controlled** by the parent. Therefore in the consolidated financial statements the **assets and liabilities are not added into** those of the parent as they are for a subsidiary.

However, the parent does have a significant influence over the operating and policy decisions of the associate and therefore to simply show the associate at cost in the balance sheet would not be giving the parent's shareholders enough information. Therefore in the balance sheet the associate balance is shown as the **cost of the associate plus the parent's share of the post acquisition profits of the associate**. This figure can also be calculated as the group share of the net assets of the associate.

To mirror the treatment of the associate in the balance sheet the consolidated income statement includes just the **group share of the profits of the associate** for the year.

Treatment of trade investments

A **trade investment** is one in which the parent has **neither significant influence nor control**. The holding of a trade investment is simply a share holding which will entitle the owner of the shares to a part of the dividend each year. Therefore the treatment of the trade investment is to show it at **cost in the balance sheet** and to include any dividend income from the shares in the income statement. This provides the shareholders of the parent with the information that they need regarding this simple investment.

6 Fair values

When a parent purchases shares in a subsidiary then in most cases the amount that is paid for those shares is not the same as the value of the net assets that have been purchased. The **difference** is known as **goodwill**. Goodwill is found by comparing the cost of the investment to the net assets acquired and the goodwill is then **capitalised** on the balance sheet.

Therefore in order to find the true value of the goodwill on the purchase the **purchase consideration must be compared to the true value of the net assets acquired**. If the value of the net assets is lower than their true value then the figure recorded for goodwill will be too high. Conversely if the book value of the net assets is too high then too small a value will be recorded for goodwill. Therefore it is necessary in order to find the true value of goodwill to compare the fair value of the purchase consideration to the fair value of the net assets acquired.

The **fair value exercise** must take place on the net assets of the subsidiary **at the date of acquisition** so that the true value of the goodwill can be found.

There is a further reason for stating the net assets of a subsidiary at fair value. Because consolidated financial statements show the group as a single economic entity, they must measure assets at their **cost to the group**, not at their cost to the subsidiary as an individual entity. The cost to the group is the amount paid by the group, in other words, fair value.

7 Preparation question: Simple consolidation

P GROUP
CONSOLIDATED INCOME STATEMENT FOR THE YEAR ENDED 31 DECEMBER 20X7

	$'000
Revenue (200,000 + 150,000 – 1,500)	348,500
Cost of sales (120,000 + 90,000 – 1,500 + (W2) 125 + (W3) 120)	(208,745)
Gross profit	139,755
Other expenses (30,000 + 30,000 + 800)	(60,800)
Share of profit of associate [(6,000 × 30%) – (W2) 60]	1,740
Profit before tax	80,695
Income tax expense (20,000 + 10,500)	(30,500)
Profit for the period	50,195
Attributable to:	
Equity holders of the parent	46,344
Minority interest [(19,500 – (W2) 125 – (W3) 120) × 20%]	3,851
	50,195

CONSOLIDATED STATEMENT OF CHANGES IN EQUITY FOR THE YEAR ENDED 31 DECEMBER 20X7

	Equity attributable to equity holders of the parent	Minority interest	Total equity
	$'000	$'000	$'000
Balance at 31.12.20X6 (2,900 + (W6) 55,372) / (W7)	58,272	4,268	62,540
Profit for the period	46,344	3,851	50,195
Balance at 31.12.20X7 (2,900 + (W4) 101,716) / (W5)	104,616	8,119	112,735

Workings

1   *Group structure*

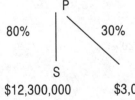

P

80%   30%

S   A

$12,300,000 $3,000,000 Pre-acq'n retained earnings

2 PUP adjustments

	$'000
S ⇒ P (1,500 – 1,000) × ¼	125
A ⇒ P (700 – 500) × 30%	60

3 Fair value adjustment

	Difference at acquisition	Movement*	Difference at B/S date
	$'000	$'000	$'000
Property, plant and equipment	1,200	(480)	720
	1,200	(480)	720

* Additional depreciation = $\frac{1,200}{10}$ = 120 per annum × 4 years = 480

4 Retained earnings at 31.12.20X7

	P	S	A
	$'000	$'000	$'000
Per Q	78,200	38,500	16,000
Less: PUP (W2)	(60)	(125)	
Less: Fair value adjustment (W3)		(480)	
Less: Pre-acquisition retained earnings		(12,300)	(3,000)
	78,140	25,595	13,800
Share of post acquisition retained earnings			
S (25,595 × 80%)	20,476		
A (13,000 × 30%)	3,900		
Goodwill impairment losses to date (S)	(800)		
	101,716		

5 Minority interest at 31.12.20X7

		$'000
Net assets/equity per question		40,000
Less: PUP (W2)		(125)
Add: Fair value adjustment (W3)		720
		40,595
MI share	20%	8,119

6 Retained earnings at 31.12.20X6

	P	S	A
	$'000	$'000	$'000
Per Q at 31.12.20X7	78,200	38,500	16,000
Profit for 20X7	(30,000)	(19,500)	(6,000)
Less: Fair value adjustment (3 × (W3) 120)		(360)	
Less: Pre-acquisition retained earnings		(12,300)	(3,000)
	48,200	6,340	7,000
Share of post acquisition retained earnings			
S (6,340 × 80%)	5,072		
A (7,000 × 30%)	2,100		
	55,372		

7 Minority interest at 31.12.20X6

		$'000
Net assets/equity per question		20,500
Add: Fair value adjustment at 31.12.X6 (W3) (720 + 120)		840
		21,340
MI share	20%	4,268

8 XYZ

(a) *Consolidated goodwill*

		$'000
AB (W1)		9,300
CD (W2)		1,860
		11,160

Workings

1 *Goodwill on acquisition of AB*

	$'000	$'000
Purchase consideration		14,700
Less: Net fair value of identifiable assets and liabilities acquired:		
Net tangible assets (1,000 + 2,850)	3,850	
Brand name	2,900	
	6,750	
80%		(5,400)
Goodwill on acquisition		9,300

2 *Goodwill on acquisition of CD*

	$'000
Purchase consideration (39.6 × 60,000)	2,376
Net assets acquired at 1 April 20X3	
(60% × (100 + (700 + (80 × 9/12)))	(516)
Goodwill on acquisition	1,860

(b) Following IFRS 3 *Business combinations* the goodwill is carried at cost and an annual impairment review carried out with any impairment losses being deducted from the carrying amount of the goodwill in the balance sheet.

Much of the purchase price of both AB and CD is for goodwill which is to be expected in a service industry such as recruitment. However, both of the subsidiaries acquired are successful and it is likely that there has been no impairment in the value of their goodwill. Thus there will be no impact on retained earnings at this stage, although the situation may change.

9 AAY

AAY Group: Consolidated statement of changes in equity for the year ended 31 March 20X8

	Equity attributable to equity holders of the parent	Minority interest	Total
	$000	$000	$000
Balance b/d (W3)/(143,700 − 400 PUP) × 20%	690,780	28,660	719,440
Profit for the year (W2)	99,140	4,360	103,500
Dividend paid (6,000 × 20%)	(18,000)	(1,200)	(19,200)
Balance c/d (W4 & 5 proof)	771,920	31,820	803,740

Workings

1 *Adjustment for intra-group trading*

	$000
Unrealised profit in opening inventory 25/125 × $2m	400
Unrealised profit in closing inventory 25/125 × $3m	600
Increase in provision required	200

2 *Profit for the year*

	$000
Consolidated profit (81,700 + (22,000 + 400 − 600)	103,500
Attributable to:	
Equity holders of the parent (bal)	99,140
Minority interest (22,000 + 400 − 600) × 20%	4,360
	103,500

3 *Group equity b/d*

	AAY	BBZ
	$000	$'000
Per question	662,300	143,700
Unrealised profit (W1)		(400)
Pre-acquisition equity		(107,700)
		35,600
BBZ – Group share (35,600 × 80%)	28,480	
	690,780	

4 *Group equity c/d (proof)*

	AAY	BBZ
	$000	$'000
Per question	726,000	159,700
Dividend (6,000 × 80%))	4,800	
Unrealised profit (W1)		(600)
Pre-acquisition equity		(107,700)
		51,400
BBZ – Group share (51,400 × 80%)	41,120	
	771,920	

5 *Minority interest c/d (proof)*

	AAY	
	$000	
BBZ	159,700	
Less unrealised profit	(600)	
	159,100	
× 20%		31,820

10 Preparation question: Joint venture

TOP GROUP: CONSOLIDATED BALANCE SHEET

	$'000
Non-current assets	
Property, plant and equipment (70,000 + (45,000 × 25%))	81,250
Goodwill (W2)	2,000
	83,250
Current assets (93,000 + (52,000 × 25%))	106,000
	189,250

	$'000
Equity	
Share capital	50,000
Retained earnings (W3)	81,500
	131,500
Current liabilities (51,000 + (27,000 × 25%))	57,750
	189,250

Workings

1 *Group structure*

Top

| 6 years ago

25% |

| Pre-acq'n r/e $35,000,000

Notch

2 *Goodwill*

	$'000	$'000
Cost of combination		12,000
Net assets acquired		
Share capital	5,000	
Retained earnings	35,000	
25%	40,000	10,000
		2,000

3 *Retained earnings*

	Top Co	Notch Co
	$'000	$'000
Per Q	74,000	65,000
Pre-acquisition retained earnings		(35,000)
	74,000	30,000
Notch – share of post acquisition ret'd earnings (30,000 × 25%)	7,500	
	81,500	

11 Textures

(a) (i) IAS 28 *Investments in associates* requires the use of the **equity method unless** the investment is **classified as held for sale** in accordance with IFRS 5 *Non-current assets held for sale and discontinued operations*.

Advantages

(1) The consolidated income statement shows profits attributable to the group not income received or receivable, reflecting the reality of the significant influence situation.

(2) The consolidated balance sheet figure for investments in associates will increase by the group share of retained profits.

Disadvantages

(1) The correct debt/equity ratio is not revealed because the level of gearing in the associate's accounts is not shown in the consolidated balance sheet. This effectively means that an opportunity for off balance sheet financing exists.

(2) The composition of the assets and liabilities of the associate is not revealed (an extension of the previous point).

(ii) **Proportionate consolidation** differs from normal consolidation in that **only** the **group share of assets, liabilities and profits are brought into account**. There is therefore **no minority interest**. The investor's share of its joint activity assets and liabilities is included under each formal heading, not just as net amounts.

IAS 31 also allows equity accounting to be used to account for joint ventures as an alternative to proportionate consolidation.

Advantages

(1) This method clearly shows the **size** of an **investor's interest** in a joint venture and any related liabilities. The **financing** and **structure** of the **venture** is **also shown**, in relation to the rest of the group. All this information helps users to **judge past performance** and **assess future prospects**.

(2) This method treats the investment as if the investor had **direct control** of its **share of the assets and results** of the joint venture, which is very close to the reality of the situation, even though in fact it shares control of the entire venture.

(3) Proportionate consolidation is used for joint ventures which consist of a **sharing of facilities** and so other joint ventures should use this method for consistency.

Disadvantages

(1) It may **not** be made **clear** (and it may not be possible to make clear) **which assets** and **liabilities** are **controlled** (directly or indirectly) by the group and those which are not. This will **muddy** the **waters** around the group results and confuse users of accounts. In particular, group figures which include consolidated and proportionately consolidated figures might be seen as meaningless.

(2) What does 50% of a piece of machinery mean? Taking **fractions** of items and adding them into the group accounts **may** only **confuse users**.

(b) (i) **Textures and Pills joint venture**

In this case there is an agreement to jointly fund and control the assets in the Asian marketing office. The assets are dedicated to the activities of the joint venture and are intended to produce benefits for each venturer. Each party has contracted to remain responsible for the debts of the joint venture in the event of default by the other.

This would **appear** to be a **jointly controlled entity** and IAS 31 suggests that the **benchmark treatment** adopted should be **proportionate consolidation**.

Therefore each venturer will account for:

	$
50% of non-current assets	150,000
50% of current assets	15,000
	165,000

in the consolidated balance sheet.

The consolidated income statement of each venturer will include 50% of the office expenses incurred ($46,000).

(ii) *Eurohelp: retained profit b/f*

	$'000
As at 1 December 20X5	
Net assets	6,750
Capital introduced (100/30 × 750)	(2,500)
Profit b/f at 1 December 20X5	4,250
Group share (30%)	1,275

(c) **MEMORANDUM**

To: Non Executive Director
From: Finance Director
Date: 20.11.X6
Re: *Afrohelp*

(i) **Conditions to be satisfied if Afrohelp is to avoid being treated as a quasi subsidiary (special purpose entity) at 30.11.X6.**

IAS 27 deals with the treatment of investments in subsidiaries in consolidated financial statements and it was introduced to deal with situations where the substance of an investment is one of control. **Subsidiaries** are now defined by reference to the **ability** to **control** rather than simply the ownership rights acquired.

In the case of Afrohelp there appears to be a **genuine 50:50 situation** where **risks** are **shared**. Without the input from Computer Control, Afrohelp could not trade; whereas if Computer Control was merely providing finance, then the **substance of the investment** would be that **Textures controls Afrohelp** through the **direction of operating policies**. Therefore it would seem that the present accounting treatment is correct subject to confirmation of the following points.

(1) Is there any evidence that Textures or Computer Control **actually exercise dominant influence** over Afrohelp?

(2) Does any particular class of shareholder enjoy **preferential voting rights**? (It appears not from the situation described.)

(3) Do the shareholders of Textures and Computer Control **jointly share** the **risks** and **rewards** from the investment?

(4) Does the **profit sharing** arrangement operate in a **true 50:50 split** with no payments or management charges being extracted so as to give each investor more of the profits (or losses) earned?

(ii) **Treatment as a quasi subsidiary (special purpose entity)**

The Afrohelp results would be consolidated, with the following effects on the consolidated figures.

	$
Reduce revenue by	162,000
Reduce cost of sales by	110,000
Reduce inventory by	52,000

Treatment as an associate

The net unrealised gain of 50% × $(162,000 – 110,000) = $26,000 will be deducted from the share of the associate's net assets shown in the balance sheet. The gain attributable to the joint venture partner can be treated as realised.

12 AJ

(a)   AJ owns 80% of the share capital of BK and as such this would imply that BK was a **subsidiary** of AJ. The deciding factor on subsidiary status is whether the parent has control of the subsidiary and there is nothing to imply here that AJ does not control BK. Therefore BK will be **consolidated using the acquisition method**.

The investment in CL of 40% of the share capital would normally indicate that CL is an **associate** of AJ. This will be the case if AJ has **significant influence, rather than control**, of CL. The fact that AJ has the right to appoint one of the five directors and that the remaining 60% of the shares are owned principally by three other investors implies that AJ does have significant influence. Therefore CL will be treated as an **associate** and **accounted for using the equity method**.

(b)   AJ GROUP
CONSOLIDATED BALANCE SHEET AT 31 MARCH 20X5

	$'000
Non-current assets	
Property, plant and equipment (12,500 + 4,700 + 195 (W3))	17,395
Goodwill (W4)	1,700
Investment in associate (W5)	4,560
Other financial assets (18,000 – 7,500 – 4,400 – 2,000 intragroup loan)	4,100
	27,755
Current assets	
Inventories (7,200 + 8,000 – 200 (W2))	15,000
Trade receivables (6,300 + 4,300)	10,600
Cash	800
	26,400
	54,155
Equity attributable to equity holders of the parent	
Share capital	10,000
Reserves (W6)	13,156
	23,156
Minority interest (W7)	1,199
	24,355
Non-current liabilities	
Loan notes (10,000 + 3,000 – 2,000 intragroup)	11,000
Current liabilities	
Trade payables (8,900 + 6,700)	15,600
Income tax (1,300 + 100)	1,400
Short term borrowings (600 + 1,200)	1,800
	18,800
	54,155

Workings

1   *Group structure*

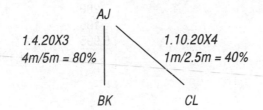

AJ

1.4.20X3
4m/5m = 80%

1.10.20X4
1m/2.5m = 40%

BK   CL

2   *Intragroup trading*

Unrealised profit (BK → AJ) 1,000,000 × 25/125   200,000

Dr Retained reserves (BK)	200,000
Cr Group inventories	200,000

3   *Fair value adjustments (BK)*

	At acquisition 1.4.20X3 $'000	Movement $'000	At B/S date 31.5.20X5 $'000
Land (1,115 – 920)	195	–	195

4   *Goodwill (BK)*

	$'000	$'000
Cost of combination		7,500
Net assets acquired:		
Share capital	5,000	
Ret'd reserves at acquisition	1,500	
Fair value adjustment (W3)	195	
	6,695	
Group share	80%	(5,356)
		2,144
Impairment losses to date		(444)
At balance sheet date		1,700

5   *Investment in associate (CL)*

	$'000
Cost of associate	4,400
Share of post-acquisition retained reserves ((4,300 – 3,900) × 40%)	160
	4,560

6   *Consolidated retained reserves*

	AJ $'000	BK $'000	CL $'000
Per question	14,000	1,000	4,300
PUP (W2)		(200)	
Fair value movement (W3)			
Retained reserves at acquisition		(1,500)	(3,900)
		(700)	400
Group share			
BK ((700) × 80%)	(560)		
CL (400 × 40%)	160		
Impairment losses to date	(444)		
	13,156		

7   *Minority interest (BK)*

	$'000	$'000
Net assets	6,000	
PUP (W2)	(200)	
Fair value adjustment (W3)	195	
	5,995	
Minority share	20%	1,199

13 ST

Text reference. Joint ventures are covered in Chapter 6.

Top tips. This is a fairly straightforward consolidation with the addition of the treatment of WX as a joint venture using proportionate consolidation. This basically means including just 50% of each income statement figure for WX. However this is complicated by the intra group sale from WX to ST. As ST is only consolidating 50% of WX's figures then adjustments for the intra group sale and unrealised profit are only 50% of the total figures.

Easy marks. Easy marks are available for setting out the proforma and adding across. Also, remember to split out the profit into parent and minority interests.

ST GROUP
CONSOLIDATED INCOME STATEMENT FOR THE YEAR ENDED 31 JANUARY 20X6

	$'000
Revenue (W1)	3,490
Cost of sales (W2)	(2,266)
Gross profit	1,224
Operating expenses (450 + 375 + 74 × 50%)	(862)
Profit from operations	362
Finance cost (16 + (12 – 6))	(22)
Profit before tax	340
Income tax expense (45 + 53 + 26 × 50%)	(111)
Profit for the period	229

Attributable to

Equity holders of the parent (bal fig)	196
Minority interest (110 × 30% (UV))	33
	229

Workings

1   *Revenue*

		$'000
ST		1,800
UV		1,400
WX (600 × 50%)	300	
Less intra-group trading 20 × 50%	(10)	
		290
		3,490

2   *Cost of sales*

	$'000
ST	1,200
UV	850
Less intra-group trading (20 × 50%)	(10)
WX (450/2)	225
Add unrealised profit (20 × 20% × ½) × 50%	1
	2,266

14 SDB

REPORT

To: Mr X
From: Management Accountant
Date:
Subject: SDB

(a)   **The concept of a jointly controlled entity**

A **jointly controlled entity** is one where two or more parties have a contractual agreement to undertake an economic activity which is under joint control.

IAS 31 allows **two methods** of accounting for jointly controlled entities – the **equity method** and **proportionate consolidation**.

Equity method of accounting

Under the **equity method of accounting** the venture is included in the balance sheet in **one line** at a figure which is the cost of the venture plus the group's share of the post acquisition profits or less the group's share of the post acquisition losses. The income statement also shows the group's share of the profits after tax of the joint venture.

Proportionate consolidation

Proportionate consolidation is where the group's share of each of the assets, liabilities, income and expenses of the joint venture are included in the balance sheet and income statement. This can be done in one of **two ways**.

(i)   Combining the group's share of the joint venture's assets, liabilities, income and expenses with those of the group on a line by line basis

(ii)   Showing a separate figure for joint venture assets, liabilities, income and expenses on a line by line basis.

SDB's method

The method that has been chosen by **SDB** is the **equity method** as there is just a single figure for the joint venture in both the balance sheet and the income statement. The equity method **does not disclose as much information** about the details of the joint venture as proportionate consolidation and indeed the equity method can be criticised for allowing **liquidity problems** or **gearing problems to be hidden**. Therefore if there were some aspects of the joint venture financial statements that SDB does not wish to disclose to its shareholders the equity method would be the obvious choice.

(b)   There are a number of key factors regarding the financial statements and position of SDB which I will address in turn. These are:

•   Profitability levels
•   Joint venture

- Cash flow position
- Future prospects

Profitability levels

If the loss from the joint venture is excluded then the group has only been slightly less profitable in 20X6 than in 20X5 with its profit before tax as a percentage of revenue reduced from 13.4% to 11.3% (see working). Obviously the **large loss from the joint venture impacts quite dramatically on the financial statements**. However, as the **underlying profitability has not decreased too much** there is hope for the future.

Joint venture

The joint venture was clearly entered into during the year and it is entirely possible that the loss was anticipated by the directors in the early stages of the venture and it will probably be expected to **improve its performance** as it becomes more established.

Cash flow position

You have commented on the cash position of the business which clearly is **of some concern**. There has been expenditure during the year of over $2 million on non-current assets and $9.17 million (7,500 + 1,670) on the joint venture. There have been **increases in inventory** levels and **receivables levels which tie up cash** but also an increase in trade payables levels which would slightly alleviate any problems. Most significantly there has been a very **large dividend payment** during the year which is almost three times the size of the profit for the year. The only significant receipt other than those from trading has been $3.6 million from an issue of shares. Therefore there has been a very **significant net cash outflow** during the year which has resulted in the noted $10 million decrease in cash balances.

Future prospects

As noted above it is hoped that a **reasonable level of profitability** in the core business will continue and that the joint **venture will turn around** and become a profit making rather than loss making venture. However, there are **concerns** for the future.

(i)   The long term loans are due for repayment starting in 2 years time. This means that in each year from 20X8 to 20Y0 the group will need to find just over $4.5 million in cash in order to repay each instalment as it falls due. It is possible that the directors have negotiated further loans to replace these but that we cannot tell from the financial statements. If not then the cash must be found otherwise the creditor could put the company into liquidation.

(ii) The other concerning possible future event is the **possible litigation costs** of $10 million. These have been **disclosed** in the financial statements as a **contingent liability** as the directors think that it is only possible that the claim will succeed. If the directors and auditors had thought that it was probable then the amount would have been provided for in the balance sheet and charged in the income statement. This indicates that there is less than a 50% chance that the costs will be incurred, as if it had been more than 50% a provision would have had to be made. However, given the state of the group's cash flows an outgoing of $10 million would be hard to sustain.

Conclusion

On balance the group **does not look to be in a good position**. Profitability has declined although not too dramatically and there are definite cash outflows due in two years for the loans and a potentially devastating cash outflow in a slightly shorter time scale if the litigation goes against SDB. The hope is that the joint venture will become established and produce income and cash for the business but without that the prospects look fairly bleak.

Signed: Management Accountant

Working

	20X6	20X5
PBT excluding joint venture	$\dfrac{1,190 + 1,670}{25,200}$	$\dfrac{3,410}{25,300}$
PBT as % of revenue	11.3%	13.5%

15 Preparation question: Part disposal

ANGEL GROUP
CONSOLIDATED BALANCE SHEET AS AT 31 DECEMBER 20X8

	$'000
Non-current assets	
Property, plant and equipment	200
Investment in Shane (W3)	88
	288
Current assets (890 + 160)	1,050
	1,338
Equity attributable to equity holders of the parent	
Share capital	500
Retained earnings (W4)	528
	1,028
Current liabilities	310
	1,338

CONSOLIDATED INCOME STATEMENT FOR THE YEAR ENDED 31 DECEMBER 20X8

	$'000
Profit before interest and tax [110 + (30 × 6/12)]	125.00
Profit on disposal of shares in subsidiary (W6)	75.15
Share of profit of associate (18 × 6/12 × 35%)	3.15
Profit before tax	203.30
Income tax expense [40 + (12 × 6/12)]	(46.00)
Profit for the period	157.30
Attributable to:	
Equity holders of the parent	154.60
Minority interest (18 × 6/12 × 30%)	2.70
	157.30

CONSOLIDATED STATEMENT OF CHANGES IN EQUITY (ATTRIBUTABLE TO EQUITY HOLDERS OF THE PARENT)

	$'000
Balance at 31 December 20X7 [500 + (W7) 373.4]	873.4
Profit for the period	154.6
Balance at 31 December 20X8 (per balance sheet)	1,028.0

Workings

1   *Timeline*

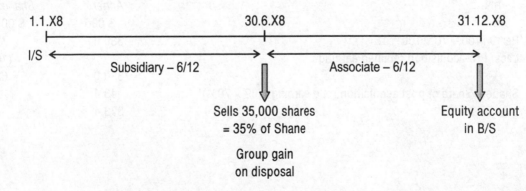

2   *Profit on disposal of Shane in Angel's separate financial statements*

	$'000
Sale proceeds	160
Less: cost of Shane (120 × 35%/70%)	(60)
	100

3   *Investment in associate (Shane)*

	$'000
Cost of associate (120 × 35%/70%)	60
Share of post acquisition retained reserves [(90 − 10) × 35%]	28
	88

4   *Goodwill - Shane*

	$'000	$'000
Cost of combination		120
Less:		
Share capital	100	
Retained earnings	10	
	110	
Group share (110 × 70%)		(77)
		43

35%/70% = ½ sold	35%/70% = ½ retained
21.5	21.5
	included in
	(120 × ½) in
	associate valuation

5   *Retained earnings*

	Angel	Shane
	$'000	$'000
Per Q	400	90
Add: profit on disposal (W2)	100	
Less: Pre-acquisition retained earnings		(10)
	500	80
Shane – Share of post acquisition ret'd earnings (80 × 35%)	28	
	528	

6   *Group profit on disposal*

	$'000	$'000
Sale proceeds		160
Less: net assets disposed of [(190 − (18 × 6/12)) × 35%)]	63.35	
goodwill (W4)	21.50	
		(84.85)
		75.15

7   *Retained earnings b/f*

	Angel	Shane
	$'000	$'000
Per Q (400 − 70)/(100 − 18)	330.0	72
Less: Pre-acquisition retained earnings		(10)
	330.0	62
Shane – Share of post acquisition ret'd earnings (62 × 70%)	43.4	
	373.4	

16 Preparation question: 'D' shaped group balance sheet

BAUBLE GROUP – CONSOLIDATED BALANCE SHEET AS AT 31 DECEMBER 20X9

	$'000
Non-current assets	
Property, plant and equipment (720 + 60 + 70)	850
Goodwill (W2)	126
	976
Current assets (175 + 95 + 90)	360
	1,336
Equity attributable to equity holders of the parent	
Share capital – $1 ordinary shares	400
Retained earnings (W3)	600
	1,000
Minority interest (W4)	106
	1,106
Current liabilities (120 + 65 + 45)	230
	1,336

Workings

1   Group Structure

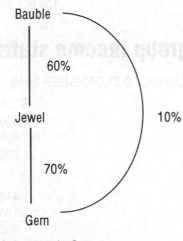

Bauble interest in Gem

– direct	10%
– indirect (60% × 70%)	42%
	52%
Minority interest in Gem	48%

2   *Goodwill*

	B in J		B in G		J in G	
	$'000	$'000	$'000	$'000	$'000	$'000
Cost of combination		142		43		100
Share of net assets acquired as represented by						
Share capital	100		50		50	
Ret'd earnings	45		40		40	
	145		90		90	
Group share	60%		10%		70%	
		87		9		63
Goodwill		55		34		37

Total goodwill = $126,000

3 Consolidated retained earnings

	B $'000	J $'000	G $'000
Per Q	560	90	65
Less: pre-acquisition ret'd earnings		(45)	(40)
		45	25
J – share of post acquisition ret'd earnings (45 × 60%)	27		
G – share of post acquisition ret'd earnings (25 × 52%)	13		
	600		

4 Minority interest

	Jewel $'000	Gem $'000
Net assets per question	190	115
Goodwill (W2)	37	
Less: cost of investment in Gamma	(100)	
	127	115
Minority share	× 40%	× 48%
	50.8	55.2
	106.0	

17 Preparation question: 'D' shaped group income statement

UPPER GROUP – CONSOLIDATED INCOME STATEMENT FOR THE YEAR ENDED 31 DECEMBER 20X9

	$'000
Profit before tax (1,500 + 750 + 150)	2,400
Income tax expense (500 + 250 + 50)	800
Profit for the period	1,600
Attributable to:	
Equity holders of the parent	1,440
Minority interest (W)	160
	1,600

Working

Group structure

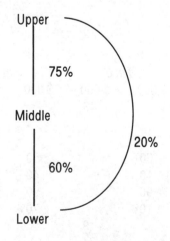

Minority interest in Lower	
Direct	20%
Indirect (25% × 60%)	15%
	35%

Minority interest in profit for the year

	$'000
Middle (500 × 25%)	125
Lower (100 × 35%)	35
	160

18 Big group

Text reference. Multi-entity structures are covered in Chapter 7.

Top tips. Do not panic at the amount of information thrown at you. Work through the information logically. Set up a proforma balance sheet and slot the figures in as you can. Do not forget to detail your workings for items such as goodwill and reserves. Bear in mind that this question is longer than you would get in an exam.

At the beginning of the year, Big had a 25% holding in Tiny. This gives Big a significant influence over Tiny but not control. Tiny is an associate of Big. Tiny's results for the first six months of the year will be treated as an associate under the rules of IAS 28 (the equity method).

A further purchase of shares was made by Small on 1 April 20X9. This is therefore a 'piecemeal' acquisition so goodwill must be calculated separately for each purchase of Tiny. The group structure is now as follows:

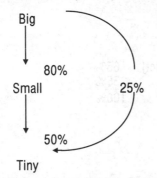

Big now owns 65% of Tiny (25% directly + (80% × 50%) via Small). So for the second six months of the year, Big **controls** Tiny and it is treated as a **subsidiary.** Tiny's results for the second six months of the year will, therefore, be consolidated on a line by line basis under IAS 27 in the income statement.

BIG GROUP
CONSOLIDATED BALANCE SHEET AS AT 30 SEPTEMBER 20X9

	$'000
Non-current assets	
Property, plant and equipment (56,000 + 66,000 + 56,000)	178,000
Goodwill (W4)	14,200
	192,200
Current assets	
Inventories (45,000 + 44,000 + 25,000 − (W2) 2,800)	111,200
Trade receivables (40,000 + 30,000 + 16,000 − 6,000 − 5,000 intragroup)	75,000
Cash in hand (8,000 + 6,000 + 3,000)	17,000
	203,200
	395,400

	$'000
Equity attributable to equity holders of the parent	
Share capital	90,000
Retained earnings (W5)	97,430
	187,430
Minority Interest (W6)	39,970
	227,400
Non-current liabilities	
Long-term loans (50,000 + 25,000)	75,000
Current liabilities	
Trade payables (25,000 + 20,000 + 11,000 – 6,000 – 5,000 intragroup)	45,000
Tax payable (7,000 + 6,000 + 4,000)	17,000
Bank overdraft (12,000 + 10,000 + 9,000)	31,000
	93,000
	395,400

Workings

1   *Group structure*

Big's effective interest in Tiny [(80% x50%) indirect +25% direct]	65%
∴ Minority interest	35%
	100%

2   *Provision for unrealised profit*

	$'000
Big $\left(\dfrac{9,000}{120} \times 20\right)$	1,500
Small $\left(\dfrac{7,800}{120} \times 20\right)$	1,300
	2,800

3   *Fair value adjustment – Small*

	Difference at acquisition $'000	Movement $'000	Difference at B/S date $'000
Property (11,000 – 7,000)	4,000	(4,000)	0
	4,000	(4,000)	0

4 Goodwill

	Big in Small		Small in Tiny		Big in Tiny	
	$'000	$'000	$'000	$'000	$'000	$'000
Cost of combination		91,500		29,000		12,500
Fair value of NA acquired:						
Share capital	80,000		32,000		32,000	
Retained earnings	22,000		15,000 *Note*		10,000	
Fair value adjustment (W3)	4,000		-		-	
	106,000		47,000		42,000	
Group share	80%		50%		25%	
		(84,800)		(23,500)		(10,500)
		6,700		5,500		2,000

Note

	$'000
Retained earnings at 30.9.X9	19,000
Less: profits after tax for period since acquisition (8,000,000 × 6/12)	(4,000)
Retained earnings at 1.4.X9	15,000

Consolidated goodwill 6,700 + 5,500 + 2,000 = 14,200

5 Retained earnings

	Big	Small	Tiny 25%	Tiny 40%
	$'000	$'000	$'000	$'000
Retained earnings per question	69,000	59,000	19,000	19,000
Less: Unrealised profit (W2)			(2,800)	(2,800)
Fair value movement (W3)		(4,000)	-	-
Pre-acquisition retained earnings		(22,000)	(10,000)	(15,000)
		33,000	6,200	1,200

Small: (33,000× 80%)	26,400
Tiny: (6,200 × 25%)	1,550
(1,200 × 40%)	480
	97,430

6 Minority interest

	Small	Tiny
	$'000	$'000
Net assets per question	139,000	51,000
Less: unrealised profit (W2)		(2,800)
Goodwill (W4)	5,500	
Less: cost of investment in Tiny	(29,000)	*W4*
	115,500	48,200
Minority share	× 20%	× 35%
	23,100	16,870
		39,970

19 Port

Text reference. This topic is covered mainly in Chapter 6 but some aspects of this question are covered in Chapters 2 to 6.

Top tips. Watch the treatment of the various investments. In the exam, many students treated Bay as an associate despite lack of control. Many students also did badly in parts (b) and (c). Make sure you know how to deal with unrealised profit.

(a) International Financial Reporting Standards (IFRSs) set out **four alternative ways** in which investments can be treated.

(i) Where the **investor controls the investee**, the controlling entity (the parent) and the controlled entity (the subsidiary) form a group. **Consolidated financial statements** are prepared for the group. The gains, losses, assets, liabilities and cash flows of the parent and the subsidiary are aggregated in order to present the financial performance and position of the group as a **single economic entity**. This treatment is required by IFRS 3 *Business combinations* and IAS 27 *Consolidated and separate financial statements*.

(ii) Where the **investor does not have control but exerts significant influence** over the investee's operating and financial policies the investee is an associate and **the equity method is used**, as required by IAS 28 *Investments in associates*. The investor's share of the results and net assets of the investee are not combined with the investor's own activities and resources, but are brought into its financial statements on a single line in the income statement and balance sheet respectively. This treatment recognises the investor's share of the results and net assets, but does not misrepresent the extent of its influence over the investee.

(iii) Where the investor **shares control over the investee** with others the investee is a joint venture and is **proportionately consolidated**, as required by IAS 31 *Financial reporting of interests in joint ventures*. The investor's share of each of the assets, liabilities, income and expenses of a jointly controlled entity is combined with similar items in the investor's own financial statements. The **equity method may also be used**. Like the equity method, proportionate consolidation recognises the investor's share of the results and net assets, but does not misrepresent the extent of its influence over the investee.

(iv) Where the investor **does not exercise control, joint control or significant influence**, the only amounts recognised in the consolidated financial statements are the **investment at cost** (as required by IAS 39 *Financial instruments: Recognition and Measurement*) and **any investment income**.

(b) **Harbor**

Port owns 80% of the equity share capital of Harbor. Therefore Port clearly **controls** Harbor and Harbor is a **subsidiary**.

Inlet

Port owns 40% of the equity share capital of Inlet. This is **not sufficient to control** Inlet, but the fact that there are no other major shareholdings indicates that Port **can exercise significant influence** over the policies adopted by Inlet. Therefore Inlet is **an associate** of Port.

Bay

Port owns 31.25% of the equity share capital of Bay. Where an investor holds 20% or more of the voting rights normally it is normally presumed that the investor can exercise significant influence (and therefore has an associate). However, **another investor holds 62.5% of the equity share capital and clearly exercises control in practice** (by making Bay adopt policies that do not meet with the approval of Port). Therefore Bay is a simple **non-current asset investment**.

(c)

	Port	Harbor	Adjustments	Consolidated
	$'000	$'000	$'000	$'000
Revenue (W1)	65,000	45,000	(8,000)	102,000
Cost of sales (W1)	(35,000)	(25,000)	8,000	
(W2)			(120)	(52,120)
Gross profit	30,000	20,000	(120)	49,880

Workings

1	*Intra-group sales*		$'000	$'000
	DEBIT	Revenue	8,000	
	CREDIT	Cost of sales		8,000

Elimination of the sales made by Port to Harbor

2   *Provision for unrealised profit*

Inventory relating to intra-group sales have increased by $600,000 (3,000 – 2,400)
Provision for unrealised profit is $120,000 (600 × 25/125).

(d) **Adjustments to the consolidated balance sheet**

(i)

		$'000	$'000
DEBIT	Consolidated retained earnings	600	
CREDIT	Inventories		600

Unrealised profit eliminated from the inventory of Harbor Ltd (3,000 × 25/125).

This adjustment is needed because the consolidated financial statements must present the activities of the group as a **single economic entity**. Port has made a profit of 25% of cost on its sales to Harbor. Harbor has not yet sold all these goods to third parties and so part of the profit made by Port plc has **not yet been realised by the group** and must be eliminated from the consolidated financial statements.

(ii)

		$'000	$'000
DEBIT	Consolidated retained earnings	200	
CREDIT	Investment in associate		200

Group share of unrealised profit eliminated from the net assets of Inlet (40% × 2,500 × 25/125).

The rationale behind this adjustment is similar to the rationale behind adjustment (i). Some of the goods sold by Port to Inlet remain in inventory and therefore the inventory of Inlet must be **adjusted to eliminate the unrealised profit**. Because Inlet is an associate rather than a subsidiary, the consolidated balance sheet does not include the individual assets and liabilities of Inlet. Instead the cost of the investment and the group share of retained earnings of Inlet are reported in a single line within non-current assets. **Therefore only the group share of the unrealised profit is eliminated**.

20 AZ

Text reference. Disposals are covered in Chapter 8.

Top tips. This is a fairly straightforward disposal and consolidated balance sheet question which leads you through the processes step by step. Take care in Part (a) that you use the correct percentages for the disposal particularly when dealing with the goodwill relating to the disposal which is 1/3 of the original goodwill.

Easy marks. Most of the 25 marks are for preparing the consolidated balance sheet. Even if you got the calculations wrong in Part (a) and (b), you will get the marks for carrying your figures over correctly into Part (c).

(a) Shareholding in CX originally = 60% × 2,600,000 shares = 1,560,000 shares

Sale of 520,000 shares leaves remaining shareholding of 1,040,000 shares = 40%

(i) Profit on disposal in AZ's own financial statements

	$'000
Proceeds	1,250
Less cost (2,730 × 20/60)	(910)
	340
Less tax (340 × 30%)	(102)
Profit after tax	238

(ii) **Profit on disposal in AZ's consolidated financial statements**

	$'000
Proceeds	1,250
Less share of net assets disposed of (20% × 4,655 (W2))	(931)
Less unimpaired goodwill relating to disposal (20/60 × 390 (W3))	(130)
Profit on disposal before tax	189
Less tax (part (i))	(102)
Consolidated profit on disposal	87

Workings

1 *Group structure*

Originally

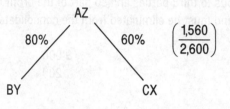

After the disposal of shares in CX on 1 October 20X5, AZ owns 1,040,000 shares. The remaining holding of 40%, and the fact that AZ has retained 'significant influence' mean that CX will be treated as an associate as from 1 October 20X5.

2 *Net assets disposed of*

	$'000
Share capital	2,600
Reserves at 1 April 20X5	1,970
Profit to 1 October 20X5 (2,140 – 1,970 × 6/12)	85
Net assets at date of disposal	4,655

3 *Goodwill*

	$'000	$'000
Cost of investment		2,730
Less net assets acquired		
Share capital	2,600	
Reserves	1,300	
	3,900	
Group share 60%		2,340
Goodwill on acquisition		390

(b) **Consolidated reserves at 31 March 20X6**

	AZ	BY	CX
	$'000	$'000	$'000
Per question	10,750	3,370	2,140
Profit on disposal (Part (a)(i))	238		
Provision for unrealised profit (180,000 × 20/120)		(30)	
	10,988		
Less pre-acquisition		(1,950)	(1,300)
		1,390	840
Share of BY: 80% × 1,390	1,112		
Share of CX: 40% × 840	336		
	12,436		

(c) AZ GROUP
     CONSOLIDATED BALANCE SHEET AS AT 31 MARCH 20X6

	$'000	$'000
Non-current assets		
Property, plant and equipment (10,750 + 5,830)		16,580
Goodwill (W1)		260
Investment in associate (W2)		2,156
Other investments (W3)		860
		19,856
Current assets		
Inventory (2,030 + 1,210 − (180 × 20/120))	3,210	
Trade receivables (2,380 + 1,300)	3,680	
Cash (1,380 + 50)	1,430	
		8,320
		28,176
Equity		
Share capital		8,000
Consolidated reserves (Part (b))		12,436
		20,436
Minority interest (W4)		1,728
Current liabilities		
Trade payables (3,770 + 1,550)	5,320	
Income tax (420 + 170 + 102 (Part a))	692	
		6,012
		28,176

Workings

1   Goodwill

	$'000	$'000
Cost of ordinary shares of BY		3,660
Less net assets acquired		
Share capital	2,300	
Reserves	1,950	
	4,250	
Group share (80% × 4,250)		3,400
Goodwill on acquisition		260

Note. The group share of preferred shares is separately cancelled out, leaving only the minority share.

2   *Investment in associate*

	$'000
Investment at cost (40/60 × 2,730)	1,820
Share of post acquisition profits (40% × (2,140 − 1,300))	336
	2,156

Or

	$'000
Share of net assets at balance sheet date 40% × 4,740	1,896
Add goodwill (390 × 40/60)	260
	2,156

3   *Other investments*

	$'000
Investments per balance sheet	7,650
Less investment in BY	(3,660)
Less investment in BY preference shares	(400)
Less investment in CX	(2,730)
Other investments	860

4   *Minority interest*

	$'000	$'000
In BY's preferred shares (60% × 1,000)		600
In BY's other net assets		
Per question (6,670 – 1,000)	5,670	
Less provision for unrealised profit	(30)	
	5,640	
× 20%		1,128
		1,728

21 RW

Text reference. Changes in the composition of a group are covered in Chapter 8.

Top tips. This question involves a partial disposal where a subsidiary is retained and the preparation of a consolidated income statement. A good approach might be as follows.

Step 1   Draw a time line to identify the changes over the year.

Step 2   Set up the income statement proforma and insert the basic figures for the group and minority interest.

Step 3   Calculate the goodwill on consolidation.

Step 4   Calculate the gain on disposal and transfer this to the proforma income statement. Ensure you include the unimpaired goodwill relating to the disposal in the disposal profit and loss calculation.

Step 5   Complete the income statement.

Easy marks. The obvious easy marks in this question are for setting out the proforma and adding things together. Otherwise the marks are fairly evenly distributed between goodwill, tax, share of net assets at disposal, preparation of income statement (including profit on disposal) and minority interest.

Examiner's comment. The most common error in this question was to consolidate only a proportion of SX's revenue and costs. Even after the sale of 200,000 shares SX is a still a subsidiary of RW and therefore will be consolidated for the entire year. Adjustments must then be made for the profit on sale and for the minority interest. Even if candidates could not correctly deal with the disposal aspects of the question they could pick up marks for calculations such as goodwill and minority interest.

RW GROUP: CONSOLIDATED INCOME STATEMENT FOR THE YEAR ENDING 31 DECEMBER 20X4

	$'000
Revenue (6,000 + 2,500)	8,500
Operating costs (4,500 + 1,700)	(6,200)
Profit on partial disposal of subsidiary (W3)	45
Profit before tax	2,345
Income tax expense (300 + 250 + 60 (W4))	(610)
Profit for the period	1,735
Attributable to:	
Equity holders of the parent	1,570
Minority interest ((550 × 6/12 × 20%) + (550 × 6/12 × 40%))	165
	1,735

Workings

1   *Group structure*

RW

|

        80% reduced to 60% on 1/7/20X4

SX

Time line

1.1.X4	1.7.X4	31.12.X4

I/S ← — Subsidiary – all year — →

20% MI × 6/12   40% NIC × 6/12

Held
800,000 shares
= 80% of SX

Sells
200,000 shares
= 20% of SX
Calculate gain/loss
on disposal at this date

2   *Goodwill*

	$'000	$'000
Cost of combination		3,200
Share of net assets acquired:		
Share capital	1,000	
Pre-acquisition reserves	2,400	
	3,400	
Group share	80%	(2,720)
		480

3   *Consolidated profit on disposal*

	$'000
Sale proceeds	1,000
Less: Share of net assets at date of disposal	(835)
$[1,000 + (2,900 + (550 \times 6/12))] \times 20\%$	
Less goodwill disposed (480 (W2) × 20/80)	(120)
	45

4   *Tax on profit on disposal*

Parent company profit (1,000 − (3,200 × 20/80))	200
Tax at 30%	(60)

22 AD

Text reference. Financial instruments are covered in Chapter 13.

Top tips. Do not spend too long working out the figures in part (a). You will gain marks for explaining the treatment. In part (b), it helps if you learn our layout for reserves and minority interest workings.

Easy marks. Setting out the proforma and having workings in place will earn you marks, even if you slip up on the unrealised profit and other details. There will be marks available for the basic consolidation of parent and direct subsidiary. As for the indirectly held associate, there will be basic marks for not treating it as a subsidiary and for showing an understanding of equity accounting.

Examiner's comments. Candidates generally found it more difficult to deal with the non-current financial asset than the current financial asset.

(a) **Non-current financial asset – Note 3**

The non-current financial asset is an investment in a **debenture**. The accounting treatment of this investment will depend upon how it is **classified**. If AD intends to hold the debenture until maturity it will be classified as a **'held-to-maturity'** investment and accounted for at **amortised cost**. This means that each year the effective interest is credited to the income statement and added to the value of the investment. The actual interest income of $50,000 is deducted from the investment value.

In the year ending June 20X5 the asset would have been valued at $1,030,000 (see working) and it would appear that in the current year the interest received of $50,000 has been credited to the investment to give a balance sheet value of $980,000. At 30 June 20X6 this asset value will have increased by $8,000 to $106,000 and the income statement credited with this same amount.

Current financial asset – Note 4

The **current asset investment** in shares in DG would be classified as a financial asset at **fair value through profit or loss** as it is part of a portfolio held for trading and as such would be **revalued to fair value** at the balance sheet date. Therefore it would appear in the balance sheet at $26,800 (4,000 × $6.70) with the **gain** of $1,800 since acquisition taken to the **income statement**.

Working: Investment in debenture

	$'000
1.7.20X4 cost	1,000
Effective interest to 30.6.20X5	80
(1,000 × 8%)	
Coupon interest received 30.6.20X5	(50)
(1,000 × 5%)	
∴ b/f 1.7.20X5	1,030
Coupon interest received 30.6.20X6	(50)
Figure as per question	980
Effective interest to 30.6.20X6	
(1,030 × 8%) (see note)	82
	1,062

Note. The effective interest is calculated on the carrying value of $1,030,000 which stood throughout the year until the coupon interest was received on 30 June 20X6.

(b) AD GROUP – CONSOLIDATED BALANCE SHEET AS AT 30 JUNE 20X6

	$000	$000
ASSETS		
Non-current assets		
Goodwill (W2)		360.0
Property, plant and equipment (1,900 + 680)		2,580.0
Financial assets		
Investment in associate (W3)		110.8
Debenture (part a)		1,062.0
		4,112.8
Current assets		
Inventories (223 + 127)	350.0	
Trade receivables (204 + 93 – 5*)	292.0	
Other financial asset (part a)	26.8	
Cash (72 + 28 + 5*)	105.0	
		773.8
		4,886.6

*Cash in transit

EQUITY AND LIABILITIES

	$'000	$'000
Equity		
Called up share capital		1,000.0
Reserves (W4)		2,554.8
		3,554.8
Minority interest (W5)		172.8
		3,725.6
Non-current liabilities		600.0
Current liabilities		
Trade payables (247 + 113)	360.0	
Income tax (137 + 62)	199.0	
		559.0
		4,886.6

Workings

1   *Group structure*

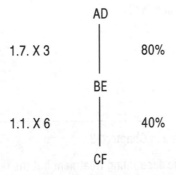

AD	
1.7. X 3	80%
BE	
1.1. X 6	40%
CF	

CF is a sub-associate. It will be equity accounted using the 40% held by BE (and thus controlled by AD) and added to the net assets of BE when the minority interest is calculated (see W4).

2   *Goodwill on purchase of BE*

	$'000	$'000
Cost of combination		880
Net assets acquired		
Share capital	300	
Reserves	350	
	650	
Group share 80% × 650		520
Goodwill		360

3   *Investment in associate*

	$000
Cost	104.0
Group share post acquisition profits	
40% × (122 – 102)	8.0
Less unrealised profit on inventory	
(10,000 × 30%) × 40%	(1.2)
	110.8

4 Consolidated reserves

	AD	BE
	$'000	$'000
Per question	2,300.0	537.0
Increase in fair value of asset	1.8	
Effective interest on debenture	82.0	
Post acquisition profits of CE		8.0
Less unrealised profit on inventory (W3)		(1.2)
Pre acquisition		(350.0)
Share of BE		213.8
80% × 213.8	171.0	
	2,554.8	

5 Minority interest

	$'000
Net assets at balance sheet date per question	857.0
Consolidated investment in sub-associate (W2)	110.8
Less cost of investment in sub-associate (W2)	(104.0)
	863.8
Minority share 20%	172.8

23 AX

> **Text reference.** The topics in this answer are covered in Chapter 13.
>
> **Top tips.** Part (a) requires not just a statement of the accounting treatment but the reasons for the approach adopted by the IASB.
>
> In addition, you would be expected to calculate the amounts to be attributed to debt and equity respectively as the required information is given in the question and the discount factors are given in the maths tables and formulae.
>
> **Easy marks.** Make sure you explain the accounting treatment even if you don't get the numbers right as this should help you gain most of the marks.
>
> To optimise the marks you receive in part (b) make sure you approach the consolidation methodically and show your workings.

(a) A convertible bond is a compound instrument consisting of liability and equity and according to IAS 32 *Financial Instruments: presentation* the components of the instruments should be classified and accounted for separately.

The approach of the IASB in IAS 32 follows the principle that in accounting for financial instruments we need to consider not only the legal form but also the substance of a contractual agreement.

By requiring split accounting IAS 32 ensures that the substance rather then the legal form of the contractual agreement is properly accounted. In addition the treatment ensures that financial liabilities and equity instruments are accounted for in a consistent manner irrespective of whether they are transacted separately or as a single instrument.

The liability component should be valued using current market interest rates. The equity component will be calculated as a residual by subtracting the liability element from the total value of the convertible bond which is $10 million. The market value of the bond is calculated as:

	$
Present value of principal:	
$10m payable at the end of the five years: $10m × 0.819	8,160,000
Present value of interest payable annually in arrears for three years	
$500,000 × 2.624	1,312,000
	9,472,000

The equity element is therefore $528,000 (= $10,000,000 − $9,472,000).

Note. For the purposes of Part (b) the liability element has been rounded to $9.5m and the residual equity element to $0.5m.

(b) AX GROUP
CONSOLIDATED BALANCE SHEET AS AT 31 DECEMBER 20X7

	$	$
Assets		
Property, plant and equipment (W6)		34,150,000
Goodwill (W2) 2,500,000 + 1,500,000		4,000,000
		38,150,000
Current assets: 34,500,000 + 9,500,000 4,700,000		48,700,000
		86,850,000
Equity and liabilities		
Equity		
Share capital: $20m + $0.5m	20,500,000	
Retained earnings (W3)	22,950,000	
Minority interest (W2)	4,400,000	
		47,850
Liabilities		
Current liabilities $(18 + 5 + 2.7 + 0.4)m	26,100,000	
Non-current liabilities $(9.5 + 2.4 + 1)m	12,900,000	
		39,000
		86,850,000

Workings

Clearing the suspense account:

1   *Consolidation: Group structure*

AX

60%
(originally 80%)

100%

CY   EZ

2   *Goodwill*

Acquisition of EZ

	$	$
Cost of combination		7,500,000
Share of net assets acquired		
Share capital	3,000,000	
Revaluation	500,000	
Retained earnings	1,500,000	
	5,000,000	
Group share: 100%		5,000,000
		2,500,000

Acquisition of CY

	$	$
Cost of combinations		8,000,000
Share of net assets acquired		
Share capital	4,000,000	
Retained earnings	3,500,000	
	7,500,000	
Group share: 80%		6,000,000
		2,000,000

Sold: ¼   to CBS: ¾
= $500,000 $1,500,000

3   *Retained earnings*

	AX	CY	EZ
	$'000	$'000	$'000
Per question	18,000	7,000	3,000
Profit on disposal (W5(i))	1,600		
Additional deprecation on revaluation			(250)
		7,000	2,750
Pre-acquisition		(3,500)	(1,500)
		3,500	1,250
Share of CY: 60% × 3,500	2,100		
Share of EZ: 100% × 1,250	1,250		
	22,950		

4   *Minority interests*

This is 40% of the net assets of CY at 31 October 20X7.

40% × $11,000,000 = $4,400,000.

5   Clearing the suspense account:

(i)   *Disposal of one quarter of CY*

		$	$
DEBIT	Suspense account	4,000,000	
CREDIT	Investment		2,000,000
CREDIT	Profit on disposal		1,600,000
CREDIT	Tax liability		400,000

(ii)   *Issue of convertible bond*

		$	$
DEBIT	Suspense account	10,000,000	
CREDIT	Long-term liability		9,472,000
CREDIT	Equity		528,000

Rounded to $9,500,000 and $500,000 respectively.

6   *Fair value adjustment*

Fair value	Book value	Acq'n date	Movement	B/S date
$'000	$'000	$'000	$'000	$'000
1,500	1,000	500	(250)*	250
		↓	↓	↓
		Goodwill	Ret'd earnings of EZ	Minority interest

* (500/5 years) × 2½ years = (500/60 mths) × 30 mths = 250

24 Preparation question: Foreign operations

STANDARD GROUP
CONSOLIDATED BALANCE SHEET AS AT 31 DECEMBER 20X6

	S $'000	O Kr'000	Rate	O $'000	Consol $'000
Property, plant and equipment	1,285	4,400	8.1	543	1,828
Investment in Odense	520	–		–	–
Goodwill (W2)	–	–		–	277
	1,805	4,400		543	2,105
Current assets	410	2,000	8.1	247	657
	2,215	6,400		790	2,762
Share capital	500	1,000	9.4	106	500
Retained reserves (W3)	1,115				1,395
Pre-acq'n	–	2,100	9.4	224	–
Post-acq'n	–	2,200	Bal fig	324	–
	1,615	5,300		654	1,895
Minority interest (654 × 20%)					131
					2,026
Loans	200	300	8.1	37	237
Current liabilities	400	800	8.1	99	499
	600	1,100		136	736
	2,215	6,400		790	2,762

CONSOLIDATED INCOME STATEMENT FOR THE YEAR ENDED 31 DECEMBER 20X6

	S $'000	O Kr'000	Rate	O $'000	Consol $'000
Revenue	1,125	5,200	8.4	619	1,744
Cost of sales	(410)	(2,300)	8.4	(274)	(684)
Gross profit	715	2,900		345	1,060
Other expenses	(180)	(910)	8.4	(108)	(288)
Impairment loss (W2)					(21)
Dividend received from Odense	40				–
Profit before tax	575	1,990		237	751
Income tax expense	(180)	(640)	8.4	(76)	(256)
Profit for the period	395	1,350		161	495

Attributable to:	
Equity holders of the parent	463
Minority interest (161 × 20%)	32
	495

CONSOLIDATED STATEMENT OF CHANGES IN EQUITY (ATTRIBUTABLE TO EQUITY HOLDERS OF THE PARENT)
FOR THE YEAR ENDED 31 DECEMBER 20X6

	$'000
Balance at 31/12/X5 (500 + (W5) 1,065)	1,565
Exchange differences on translating foreign operations (W4)	62
Net income recognised directly in equity	62
Profit for the period	463
Total recognised income and expense	525
Dividends paid (Standard)	(195)
Balance at 31/12/X6 (per B/S)	1,895

Workings

1   *Group structure*

Standard

1.1.X4 | 80%

Odense

Pre-acquisition ret'd reserves 2,100,000 Krone

2   *Goodwill*

	Kr'000	Kr'000	Rate	$'000
Cost of combination ($520,000 × 9.4)		4,888		
Share capital	1,000			
Retained earnings	2,100			
	3,100			
Group share (80%)		(2,480)		
		2,408	9.4	256
Exchange differences 20X4-20X5		–	β	18
At 31.12.X5		2,408	8.8	274
Impairment losses 20X6		(168)	8.1	(21)
Exchange differences 20X6		–	β	24
At 31.12.X6		2,240	8.1	277

3   *Consolidated retained reserves carried forward*

	Standard $'000	Odense $'000
Per question (O: 224 + 324)	1,115	548
Pre-acquisition		(224)
		324
Group share (324 × 80%)	259	
	1,374	
Less: Goodwill impairment losses (W2)	(21)	
Add: Goodwill exchange differences ((W2) 18 + 24))	42	
	1,395	

4   *Exchange differences in period*

	$'000	$'000
On translation of net assets (gross)		
Closing NA @ CR	654	
Opening NA @ OR (4,355 @ 8.8)	(495)	
Less retained profit as translated		
(161 – 50) (from I/S & B/S working)	(111)	
Exchange gain	48	
Group share (80%)		38
On goodwill (W2)		24
		62

5   *Consolidated retained reserves b/f proof*

	Standard $'000	Odense $'000
Per question (per question)/[224 + 324 – 161 + 50 – (W4) 48)]	915	389
Pre-acquisition		(224)
		165
Group share (165 × 80%)	132	
	1,047	
Less: Goodwill impairment losses (W2)	(0)	
Add: Goodwill exchange differences (W2)	18	
	1,065	

25 Little

(a)   From the information in the question it is clear that Little operates on a largely independent basis from Large with its own supplier and customer bases and no day to day part being played by Large in operational decisions. Therefore the cash flows of Little will not have a day to day impact on those of Large. As such IAS 21 *The effects of changes in foreign exchange rates* requires that the financial statements of Little for consolidation purposes should be translated using the **presentation currency** or **closing rate** or **net investment method**. Under this method the balance sheet assets and liabilities are translated at the **spot rate** of exchange on the **balance sheet date** and the income statement is translated at a **weighted average rate** of exchange for the year. Any exchange differences are not reported in the income statement, as they have no impact on the cash flows of the group, but instead are reported as a **movement on equity**.

(b)   *Translation of Little balance sheet into $*

	F000	Rate	$'000
Non-current assets			
Property, plant and equipment			
(80,000 – 6,000 revaluation adjustment)	74,000	5	14,800
Current assets			
Inventories	30,000	5	6,000
Trade receivables	28,000	5	5,600
Cash	5,000	5	1,000
	137,000		27,400

	F000	Rate	$'000
Equity			
Share capital	40,000	6	6,667
Revaluation surplus (6,000 – 6,000)			
Pre acquisition retained reserves	26,000	6	4,333
Post acquisition retained reserves (34,000 – 26,000)	8,000	Bal	3,800
	74,000		14,800
Non-current liabilities			
Long-term borrowings	25,000	5	5,000
Deferred tax	10,000	5	2,000
Current liabilities			
Trade payables	20,000	5	4,000
Tax	8,000	5	1,600
	137,000		27,400

CONSOLIDATED BALANCE SHEET AS AT 31 MARCH 20X7

	$'000	$'000
Non-current assets		
Goodwill (W5)		2,520
Property, plant and equipment (63,000 + 14,800)		77,800
Current assets		
Inventories (25,000 + 6,000 – (1,000 × 25%))	30,750	
Trade receivables (20,000 + 5,600 – 1,000)	24,600	
Cash (6,000 + 1,000 + 1,000 cash in transit)	8,000	
		63,350
		143,670
Equity		
Called up share capital		30,000
Retained reserves (W4)		38,615
Minority interest (W6)		1,455
		70,070
Non-current liabilities		
Long-term borrowings (20,000 + 5,000)	25,000	
Deferred tax (6,000 + 2,000)	8,000	
		33,000
Current liabilities		
Trade payables (25,000 + 4,000)	29,000	
Tax (7,000 + 1,600)	8,600	
Bank overdraft	3,000	
		40,600
		143,670

Large

I.4.XI

$\dfrac{36,000}{40,000}$ 90%

Little

Pre-acquisition retained earnings 26m francos

Workings

1   *Group structure*

Investment in Little = 36,000/40,000 = 90%

2 Goodwill

	F000	F000	Rate	$'000
Cost of combination (12,000 × 6)		72,000		
Less				
Share capital	40,000			
Pre acquisition ret'd earnings	26,000			
	66,000 ×90%	(59,400)		
At 1.4.20X1		12,600	6	2,100
Foreign exchange gain		–	Bal	420
At 31.3.20X7		12,600	5	2,520

3 Retained reserves

	$'000
Large	35,000
Little – post acquisition (3,800 × 90%)	3,420
Unrealised profit (90% × 250)	(225)
Foreign exchange gain on goodwill (W5)	420
	38,615

4 Minority interest

	$'000
Minority share of net assets ($14,800 × 10%)	1,480
Less unrealised profit (250 × 10%)	(25)
	1,455

26 Small

Text reference. Foreign currency translation is covered in Chapter 9.

Top tips. This is a fairly straightforward question on producing a consolidated balance sheet, including a foreign currency translation.

You are required to carry out the translating and prepare the consolidated balance sheet. **Do not forget to adjust for the accounting policy difference** before doing the translation. Remember to eliminate intra-group balances and unrealised profits before consolidating. The final step is to calculate the capital and retained earnings.

Adjustment to net assets for change in accounting policy

	Adjusted figure at acquisition	Adjusted figure at balance sheet date
	Fl'000	Fl'000
Share capital (½ Fl shares)	40,000	40,000
Revaluation reserve	6,000	11,000
Retained earnings	20,000	44,000
	66,000	95,000

Top tips. You are not told the share capital at acquisition and you are not told that there have been any movements in the share capital since acquisition. Therefore assume that the share capital of Small at acquisition was Fl 40m. This equates to 80m shares. As Big purchased 60m shares, this is a 75% shareholding (60/80).

Translation of Small's balance sheet

	Fl'000	Rate	$'000
Property, plant and equipment (80 + 11)	91,000	5	18,200
Inventories	40,000	5	8,000
Trade receivables	32,000	5	6,400
Cash	4,000	5	800
	167,000		33,400

	FI'000	Rate	$'000
Share capital	40,000	6	6,667
Revaluation reserve: pre-acquisition	6,000	6	1,000
post-acquisition (11 – 6)	5,000	5	1,000
Retained earnings: pre-acquisition	20,000	6	3,333
post acquisition (44 – 20)	24,000	(balance)	7,000
	95,000		19,000
Long term borrowings	30,000	5	6,000
Deferred tax	9,000	5	1,800
Trade payables	15,000	5	3,000
Current tax	18,000	5	3,600
	167,000		33,400

Consolidated balance sheet

BIG GROUP
CONSOLIDATED BALANCE SHEET
AS AT 31 MARCH 20X9

	$'000	$'000
Non-current assets		
Property, plant and equipment (60 + 18.2)		78,200
Intangible assets (W2)		1,500
		79,700
Current assets		
Inventory (30 + 8 – 1.2 (W3))	36,800	
Trade receivables (25 + 6.4 – 6 (W4))	25,400	
Cash (3 + 0.8 + 6 (W4))	9,800	
		72,000
		151,700
Equity attributable to equity holders of the parent		
Share capital (Big only)		30,000
Revaluation reserve (15 + 75% × 1)		15,750
Retained earnings (W5)		38,800
		84,550
Minority interest (W6)		4,750
		89,300
Non-current liabilities		
Long term borrowings (15 + 6)	21,000	
Deferred tax (5 + 1.8)	6,800	
		27,800
Current liabilities		
Trade payables (12 + 3)	15,000	
Tax (16 + 3.6)	19,600	
		34,600
		151,700

Workings

1   Group structure

2   Unrealised profit

Sales from Big to Small: $6m × $\dfrac{25}{125}$ = $1,200,000

3	Goodwill on consolidation		
		Fl'000	Fl'000
	Consideration		57,000
	Net assets acquired at fair value		
	Share capital	40,000	
	Revaluation reserve	6,000	
	Retained earnings	20,000	
		66,000	
	Group share: 75%		49,500
			7,500
	Translated at closing rate (7,500 ÷ 5)		1,500
	Translated at acquisition (7,500 ÷ 6)		1,250

4	Trade receivables and cash		
		Receivables	Cash
		$'000	$'000
	Big	25,000	3,000
	Small	6,400	800
	Cash in transit	(6,000)	6,000
		25,400	9,800

5	Retained earnings		
		Big	Small
		$'000	$'000
	Per question/part (b)(ii)	34,500	7,000
	Unrealised profit (W3)	(1,200)	
		33,300	
	Share of Small's post-acquisition reserves		
	75% × $7,000,000	5,250	
	Exchange gain on retranslation of goodwill (W2)	250	
		38,800	

6	Minority interest	
		$'000
	25% × $19m	4,750

27 Home group

Text reference. This topic is covered in Chapter 5.

Top tips. Make sure you use the average rate to translate the income statement. Do not spend too long on the impairment of goodwill.

Easy marks. These are available for setting out the proforma, translating and adding together.

Examiner's comments. Although the question was generally well answered, some candidates thought that no adjustment was required for intra-group sales on the grounds that the inventory purchased had been sold to third parties outside the group.

HOME GROUP – CONSOLIDATED INCOME STATEMENT FOR YEAR ENDED 31 JULY 20X6

	$'000
Revenue (3,000 + 270.8 (W1) – (50/2.4))	3,250.0
Cost of sales (2,400 + 229.2 (W1) – (50/2.4))	(2,608.4)
Gross profit	641.6
Distribution costs (32 + 17.1) (W1)	(49.1)
Administrative expenses (168 + 36.3) (W1)	(204.3)
Impairment of goodwill (W2)	(1.9)
Exchange difference (W3)	1.3
Finance costs (15 + 4.2) (W1)	(19.2)
Profit before tax	368.4
Income tax (102 – 4.2) (W1)	(97.8)
Profit for period	270.6

Workings

1   *Translation of Foreign*

	Foreign Crowns 000	Exchange rate	Foreign $'000
Revenue	650	2.4	270.8
Cost of sales	550	2.4	229.2
Distribution costs	41	2.4	17.1
Administrative exp	87	2.4	36.3
Finance costs	10	2.4	4.2
Income tax (credit)	10	2.4	4.2

2   *Goodwill*

	Crowns	Crowns	Rate	$
Cost of combination		204,000		
Less fair value of net assets acquired				
Share capital	1,000			
Reserves	180,000			
	181,000			
Group share: 100%		181,000	1.7	
		23,000	1.7	13,529
Impairment loss: 20%		(4,600)	2.4	(1,917)
Exchange difference			balance	(112)
At 31 July 20X6		18,400	1.6	11,500

3   *Exchange difference on plant*

	$
Purchase price 32,000 florins /1.5	21,333
Year end re-translation 32,000 florins/1.6	20,000
Exchange gain	1,333

28 Preparation question: Consolidated cash flow statement

SWING GROUP – CASH FLOW STATEMENT FOR THE YEAR ENDED 31 DECEMBER 20X5

	$'000	$'000
Cash flows from operating activities		
Profit before tax	16,500	
Adjustments for:		
Depreciation	5,800	
Impairment losses (W2)	240	
	22,540	
Increase in trade receivables (9,800 – 7,500 – 600)	(1,700)	
Increase in inventories (16,000 – 10,000 – 1,600)	(4,400)	
Increase in trade payables (7,600 – 6,100 – 300)	1,200	
Cash generated from operations	17,640	
Income taxes paid (W1)	(4,200)	
Net cash from operating activities		13,440
Cash flows from investing activities		
Acquisition of subsidiary net of cash acquired (1,000 – 400)	(600)	
Purchase of property, plant and equipment (W2)	(13,100)	
Net cash used in investing activities		(13,700)
Cash flows from financing activities		
Proceeds from issue of share capital		
(12,300 + 5,800 – 10,000 – 2,000 – (5,000 – 1,000))	2,100	
Dividends paid	(900)	
Dividends paid to minority interest (W3)	(40)	
Net cash used in investing activities		1,160
Net increase in cash and cash equivalents		900
Cash and cash equivalents at the beginning of the period		1,500
Cash and cash equivalents at the end of the period		2,400

Workings

1 Additions to property, plant and equipment

PROPERTY, PLANT AND EQUIPMENT

	$'000		$'000
b/d	25,000		
On acquisition	2,700	Depreciation	5,800
∴ Additions	13,100	c/d	35,000
	40,800		40,800

2 Goodwill impairment losses

GOODWILL

	$'000		$'000
b/d	0	∴ Impairment loss	240
On acquisition			
(5,000 – (4,800 × 70%))	1,640	c/d	1,400
	1,640		1,640

3   *Dividends paid to minority interest*

MINORITY INTEREST

	$'000		$'000
		b/d	0
∴ Dividends paid	40	Acquisition (4,800 × 30%)	1,440
c/d	1,600	I/S	200
	1,640		1,640

4   *Income taxes paid*

INCOME TAX PAYABLE

	$'000		$'000
		b/d	4,000
∴ Income taxes paid	4,200	Acquisition	200
c/d	5,200	I/S	5,200
	9,400		9,400

29 Oscar

> **Text reference.** Consolidated cash flow statements are covered in Chapter 10.
>
> **Top tips.** By far the trickiest part is the note for the purchase of subsidiary. Bear in mind that the purchase consideration is in cash as well as shares.
>
> **Easy marks.** The reconciliation of profit from operations to cash generated from operations is very straightforward. You need to remember to exclude the figures for the subsidiary. Easy marks are also available for the proforma, and for calculating tax paid.

CASH FLOW STATEMENT FOR THE YEAR ENDED 31 DECEMBER 20X4

	Notes	$'000	$'000
Cash flows from operating activities			
Profit before tax		6,300	
Adjustment for:			
Depreciation		3,150	
		9,450	
Increase in receivables (20,550 – 16,500 – 450)		(3,600)	
Increase in inventories (21,750 – 18,000 – 1,050)		(2,700)	
Increase in trade payables (25,350 – 22,800 – 600)		1,950	
Cash generated from operations		5,100	
Income taxes paid (W3)		(1,500)	
Net cash from operating activities			3,600
Cash flows from investing activities			
Purchase of property, plant and equipment (W1)		(3,300)	
Purchase of subsidiary (net of cash and			
cash equivalents acquired) (1,500 – 150)	1	(1,350)	
Net cash used in investing activities			(4,650)
Cash flows from financing activities			
Proceeds from issues of share			
(27,000 – 22,500 – 3,000 (non cash))		1,500	
Net cash used in financing activities			1,500
Increase in cash and cash equivalents			450
Cash and cash equivalents at beginning of year			750
Cash and cash equivalents at end of year			1,200

Workings

1   *Purchase of property, plant and equipment*

PROPERTY, PLANT AND EQUIPMENT

	$'000		$'000
Balance b/f	34,500	Depreciation	3,150
Halina Co property, plant and equipment	2,850		
Additions	3,300	Receivables balance c/f	37,500
	40,650		40,650

2   GOODWILL

	$'000		$'000
Balance b/f	–		
On acquisition of Halina	990*	Balance c/f	990
	990		990

* Goodwill arising on acquisition		$'000
Cost of combination		
Shares (1.5m @ $2)		3,000
Cash		1,500
		4,500
Less net assets acquired		
(4,500 – 600) × 90%		(3,510)
		990

3   *Tax paid in year*

INCOME TAX EXPENSE

	$'000		$'000
Cash paid	1,500	Balance b/f	1,500
Balance c/f	2,250	Income statement	2,250
	3,750		3,750

4   MINORITY INTEREST

	$'000		$'000
		Balance b/f	–
		*On acquisition of Halina	390
Balance c/f	525	Income statement	135
	525		525

*Net assets at acquisition		$0'000
(4,500 – 600)		3,900
MI 10%		390

30 AH Group

AH GROUP CONSOLIDATED CASH FLOW STATEMENT FOR THE YEAR ENDED 30 JUNE 20X5

	$'000	$'000
Cash flows from operating activities		
Profit before taxation	19,450	
Adjustment for		
Depreciation	7,950	
Profit on disposal of property	(1,250)	
Interest expense	1,400	
	27,550	
Decrease in trade receivables (27,130 – 26,300 – 1,300)	470	
Increase in inventories (33,500 – 28,750 – 1,650)	(3,100)	
Decrease in trade payables (33,340 – 32,810 – 1,950)	(1,420)	
Cash generated from operations	23,500	
Interest paid (W3)	(1,480)	
Income taxes paid (W4)	(5,850)	
Net cash from operating activities		16,170
Cash flows from investing activities		
Acquisition of subsidiary, net of cash acquired (2,000 – 50)	(1,950)	
Purchase of property, plant and equipment (W1)	(11,300)	
Proceeds from sale of property	2,250	
Net cash used in investing activities		(11,000)
Cash flows from financing activities		
Repayment of interest-bearing borrowings	(1,000)	
Dividends paid (6,000 + (W2) 200)	(6,200)	
Net cash used in financing activities		(7,200)
Net decrease in cash and cash equivalents		(2,030)
Cash and cash equivalents at beginning of period		3,900
Cash and cash equivalents at end of period		1,870

Note. Dividends paid could also be shown under financing activities and dividends paid to minority interest could also be shown under either operating activities or under financing activities.

Workings

1   *Acquisition of property, plant and equipment*

PROPERTY, PLANT AND EQUIPMENT

	$'000		$'000
Opening balance	44,050	Depreciation	7,950
Subsidiary balance	4,200	Disposal	1,000
Acquisitions (bal fig)	11,300	Closing balance	50,600
	59,550		59,550

2   *Dividends paid to minority interest*

MINORITY INTEREST

	$'000		$'000
Cash paid (bal fig)	200	Opening balance	1,920
		On acquisition (5,000 × 25%)	1,250
Closing balance	3,625	Income statement	655
	3,825		3,825

3   *Interest paid*

INTEREST PAYABLE

	$'000		$'000
Cash paid (bal fig)	1,480	Opening balance	1,440
Closing balance	1,360	Income statement	1,400
	2,840		2,840

4   *Income taxes paid*

INCOME TAXES PAYABLE

	$'000		$'000
Cash paid (bal fig)	5,850	Opening balance	5,450
		Subsidiary balance	250
Closing balance	6,100	Income statement	6,250
	11,950		11,950

31 EAG Group

EAG GROUP: CONSOLIDATED CASH FLOW STATEMENT FOR THE YEAR ENDED 30 APRIL 2008

	$m	$m	Ref to workings
Cash flows from operating activities			
Profit before taxation		2,604.2	
Adjustments for:			
Depreciation	2,024.7		
Impairment of goodwill	202.6		2
Amortisation of intangibles	93.1		
Interest expense	510.9		
Profit on disposal of associate	(3.4)		
Share of profit of associate	(1.6)		
		2,826.3	
		5,430.5	
Increase in inventories (5,217.0 – 4,881.0)		(336.0)	
Decrease in receivables (4,670.0 – 4,633.6)		36.4	
Increase in payables (5,579.3 – 5,356.3)		223.0	
Cash generated from operations		5,353.9	
Interest paid		(390.0)	7
Income taxes		(831.0)	6
Net cash from operating activities		4,132.9	
Cash flows from investing activities			
Purchase of property, plant & equipment	(4,917.0)		1
Purchase of intangibles	(27.2)		3
Proceeds from sale of associate	18.0		
Dividend received from associate	0.8		4
Net cash used in investing activities		(4,925.4)	
		(792.5)	
Cash flows from financing activities			
Proceeds from issue of share capital			
(4,300.0 – 3,600.0)	700.0		
Dividends paid to minority interest	(88.0)		5
Net cash used in financing activities		612.0	
Net decrease in cash and cash equivalents		(180.5)	
Cash at the beginning of the period (88.3 – 507.7)		(419.4)	
Cash at the end of the period (62.5 – 662.4)		(599.9)	

Workings

1   *Additions to PPE*

Property, plant and equipment (NBV)

	$m		$m
NBV b/fwd	19,332.8	Depreciation charge	2,024.7
Additions		NBV c/fwd	22,225.10
(balancing fig.)	4,917.0		
	24,249.8		24,249.8

2   *Goodwill impairment losses*

Goodwill

	$m		$m
b/d	1,865.3	Impairment loss	
		(balancing figure)	202.6
		c/d	1,662.7
	1,865.3		1,865.3

3   *Purchase of intangibles*

Intangibles

	$m		$m
Balance b f/wd	372.4	Amortisation	
Purchase of patent		($372.4m × 25%)	93.1
(balancing fig.)	27.2	Bal c/fwd	306.5
	399.6		399.6

4   *Dividend from associate*

Investment in associate

	$m		$m
Balance b/fwd	13.8	Disposal proceeds	18.0
Share of profit to		Dividend received	
31.12.X7	1.6	1.6.X7 (balancing	
Profit on disposal	3.4	fig.)	0.8
	18.8		18.8

5   *Dividend paid to minority interest*

Minority interest

	$m		$m
Dividend paid		Bal c/d	1,870.5
(balancing fig.)	88.0	Profit attributable	
Balance c/fwd	2,010.5	to minority	228.0
	2,098.5		2,098.5

6   *Income taxes paid*

Income taxes

	$m		$m
Paid (balancing		Balance b/fwd	884.7
fig.)	831.0	Income statement:	
Balance c/fwd	777.6	provision	723.9
	1,608.6		1,608.6

7   *Interest paid*

	$m
Long-term borrowing	
1.5.X6 (6,000 – 100)	5,900.0
Effective interest @ 7%	413.0
Cash paid (5% × 6,000)	(300.0)
30.4.X7	6,013.0
Effective interest @ 7%	420.9
Cash paid	(300.0)
	6,133.9
Total finance cost in income statement	510.9
Less interest on long-term borrowings	(420.9)
Balance = Interest on short-term borrowings	90.0

Total cash outflow in respect of interest: $90.0m + $300.0m = $390.0m

32 Section A questions: Accounting standards

1

	$'000
Cost of investment	60
Group share of post-acquisition reserves (40% × 220 − 30)	76
Unrealised intra-group profit (40% × 10 × 25%)	(1)
	135

2

	$m
Cost of investment	50
Net assets acquired (60% × 65)	(39)
	11

The provision for reorganisation costs cannot be included in the goodwill calculation because it reflects the acquirer's intentions, rather than an actual liability of E at the date of acquisition (IFRS 3 and IAS 37).

3   D

	$'000
Cost of investment	5,000
Net assets acquired (75% × 5,260)	(3,945)
	1,055

Net assets acquired:	$'000
Tangible non-current assets (net replacement cost)	6,600
Net current assets	260
Loan	(1,600)
	5,260

The fair value of the long term loan (ie, the amount expected to be paid) is the same as its carrying value, because interest of 10% will be paid until the loan matures.

4   C

	$
1 November 20X6 (450,000 @ 1.5)	300,000
31 December 20X6 (450,000 @ 1.45)	(310,345)
	(10,345)

The inventory is a non-monetary asset. It is translated at the date of the original transaction and remains in the balance sheet at that amount.

5   B

PROPERTY, PLANT AND EQUIPMENT (NET BOOK VALUE)

	$'000		$'000
Balance b/f	515	Depreciation	60
Subsidiary	90		
Revaluation	50		
Cash paid (balancing figure)	125	Balance c/f	720
	780		780

6   A

IFRS 3 states that goodwill acquired in a business combination should be reviewed for impairment annually.

7   A

See the definitions in IAS 19.

8   A

The substance of the arrangement is that the factor has made a loan to Realistic. Realistic still bears the risk of bad debts and therefore it has not disposed of its trade receivables.

9   A   The substance of the transaction is a financing arrangement, rather than a sale. Therefore the inventories are retained in the balance sheet and a liability is recognised for the cash received of $25 million

The premium of $8.47 million on payment of the loan is effectively interest, and the loan should be measured at amortised cost. The effective interest rate is 6% (from tables: 25/33.47 = 0.747) and therefore interest of £1.5 million is charged to the income statement and added to the carrying amount of the loan.

10   B   In both cases, Clean has a constructive obligation to clean up environmental damage. However, the pollution caused by the accident in (2) did not occur until after the year end and therefore there was no obligation at the balance sheet date. (Clean should treat the accident as a non-adjusting event after the balance sheet date under IAS 10.)

33 Preparation question: Suggested alternatives

(a)   **CPP accounting**

Shareholders' equity (= net assets) is valued as the purchasing power, stated in year-end dollars, invested by the shareholders in the net assets of the entity. Non-monetary items therefore have their cost, less depreciation, indexed up from the date of acquisition to the balance sheet date. Monetary assets and liabilities are automatically already stated in year-end dollars, so no adjustment is required for them.

CCA

Shareholders' equity is valued as the aggregate of the deprival values of the net assets of the business. Non-monetary items are therefore quoted at the lower of net replacement cost and recoverable amount (recoverable amount being defined as the higher of net realisable value and economic value). Monetary assets and liabilities are automatically already stated at their balance sheet date deprival value, so no adjustment is required for them.

(b)   **CPP accounting**

The reported profit is the amount available for distribution to the shareholders after maintaining the purchasing power of shareholders' equity. This profit can be determined either via the CPP income statement or via a determination of net asset values. In the income statement both sales and cost of sales must be revalued to year-end dollars from dollars at the date of each transaction. If sales and purchases occur evenly through a year, it is convenient to restate each to year-end dollars from average dollars for the year. Depreciation charged will be the amount of the year-end balance sheet value of the non-current assets consumed in the period, and there will also be a gain/loss recognised in holding net monetary liabilities/assets in the period.

Via the balance sheet the CPP net profit can be determined by the following.

$P = D + (E_1 - E_0)$

Where   P   is the CPP accounting profit;

         D   is the distributions made to shareholders, restated in terms of year-end dollars;

         E_0 is the shareholders' equity at the start of the year, restated in terms of dollars at the end of the year;

         E_1 is the shareholders' equity at the end of the year, expressed in terms of dollars at the end of the year.

The retained earnings for the year will be the excess of P over D above. CPP is generally regarded as being more useful than straight historical cost accounting, but suffers from the weakness that the balance sheet amounts are difficult to interpret.

Current cost accounting

CCA profits are obtained by applying current cost adjustments to historical cost figures.

An illustrative CCA income statement follows.

	$	$
Historical cost profit before interest and taxation		X
Less current cost operating adjustments		
COSA	X	
ADA	X	
MWCA	X	
Others	X	
		(X)
Current cost operating profit		X
Gearing adjustment	X	
Net interest payable	(X)	
		X
Current cost PBT		X
Tax (HC charge)		(X)
Current cost profit attributable		
to shareholders		X
Dividends (HC amount)		(X)
Current cost retained profit		X

The current cost operating profit is therefore the amount of profits that the entity has generated, after sufficient retentions have been made to maintain the operating capability of the business (maintain the non-current assets, inventory and level of monetary working capital).

The main problems with CCA have been a general lack of understanding of what the method is trying to achieve, coupled with a lack of enthusiasm for any seemingly complicated set of adjustments, at a period of time when inflation levels are generally low.

34 Leisure

Text reference. Changes in price levels are covered in Chapter 11.

Top tips. This question illustrates quite well the principal difficulties associated with the production of financial statements adjusted for price level changes (the complexity of the calculations and the problem of explaining the results to the management of an entity). It is unlikely that you would get a full 25 mark question on inflation in the exam.

Easy marks. Part (a) contains easy marks for just listing out material from your Study Text. Likewise Part (b) (i).

(a) **Disadvantages of replacement cost accounting**

    (i)   The indices used to value assets can be unreliable or inappropriate.

    (ii)   The asset values used may relate to new types of assets (not those currently in use) and hence the balance sheet values may not reflect the technology actually in use.

    (iii)   RCA does not take into account changes in general price levels nor gains or losses arising from holding monetary liabilities or assets.

    (iv)   The term 'replacement cost' is imprecise, it could mean the cost of an equivalent asset for example.

Disadvantages of net realisable value accounting

    (i)   It is only relevant if the asset is expected to be sold in an active market. Net realisable values may not be readily available for specialist items with no alternative uses.

    (ii)   Net realisable values have little relevance if the asset is expected to continue to be used by an entity.

    (iii)   There is a real problem in valuing intangible assets such as goodwill and also liabilities.

(iv)   If a firm is not a going concern additional liabilities may emerge which can be very difficult to value such as closure costs. Should liabilities be included at contractual amounts or the amounts required to settle the liabilities?

(v)   The use of the NRV method implies that a business may not be a going concern, this can give an unfortunate appearance for an entity's financial statements.

(vi)   NRV does not account for general price level changes.

(b)   (i)   **The effects of hyperinflation on the financial statements**

Hyperinflation can reduce the usefulness of financial statements in the following ways:

(1)   The amounts at which assets are stated in the balance sheet are unlikely to reflect their current values.

(2)   The level of profit for the year may be misleading. Income appears to increase rapidly, while expenses such as depreciation may be based on out of date costs and are artificially low.

(3)   It is therefore difficult to make any meaningful assessment of an entity's performance as assets are understated and profits are overstated.

These are well known disadvantages of basing financial statements on historic cost and they affect most entities. However, where there is hyperinflation these problems are exacerbated. In addition, where an entity's financial statements are translated into dollars, hyperinflation often gives rise to significant exchange differences which may absorb reserves.

How hyperinflation should be dealt with in the financial statements

IAS 29 does not provide a definition of hyperinflation. However, it does include guidance as to characteristics of an economic environment of a country in which hyperinflation may be present. These include, but are not limited to, the following.

(1)   The general population prefers to keep its wealth in non-monetary assets or in a relatively stable foreign currency

(2)   Interest rates, wages and prices are linked to a price index

(3)   The cumulative inflation rate over three years is approaching, or exceeds, 100%

IAS 29 states that the financial statements of an entity that reports in the currency of a hyperinflationary economy should be restated in terms of the measuring unit current at the balance sheet date. This involves remeasuring assets and liabilities by applying a general price index. The gain or loss on the net monetary position is included in net income and separately disclosed. The fact that the financial statements have been restated should also be disclosed, together with details of the index used.

IAS 21 *The effects of changes in foreign exchange rates* states that where there is hyperinflation, the financial statements of a foreign operation should be restated in accordance with the requirements of IAS 29 before they are translated into the currency of the reporting entity. In this way users are made aware of the effect of hyperinflation on the results and net assets of the entity.

(ii)   **Carrying value of hotel complex at 31 December 20X2**

Assuming the economy of Urep is not a hyperinflationary economy

The closing rate is used. This produces a value of:

50 million ÷ 220 = $227,273

Use of the closing rate without adjustments produces an amount based on the original cost. Because the exchange rate has increased from 25 to 220 over the life of the complex, there is a cumulative exchange loss of $1,772,727 (50 million ÷ 25 – 227,273). The hotel complex appears to be worth much less at 31 December 20X0 than when it was first acquired.

Assuming the economy of Urep is a hyperinflationary economy

Before the cost of the hotel complex is translated into dollars it is restated using the retail price index. This produces a value of:

$$50 \text{ million} \times 1000/100 \div 220 = \$2,272,727$$

This method adjusts the value of the complex to reflect the effect of ten-fold inflation over the two year period. In this way the 'disappearing assets' problem is overcome. In fact the asset now appears to be worth more than when it was first acquired.

35 Extract

> **Text reference.** IAS 37 is covered in Chapter 14.
>
> **Top tips.** A good knowledge of IAS 37 is needed in this question. Do not disregard the discounting aspects, these calculations are quite straightforward as you are given the formulae in the exam.

Extract should recognise a provision for the estimated costs of making good the site because:

(a)   It has a present obligation to incur the expenditure as a result of a past event. In this case the obligating event occurred when it became virtually certain that the legislation would be passed. Therefore the obligation existed at 31 December 20X2

(b)   An outflow of resources embodying economic benefits is probable

(c)   It is possible to make a reliable estimate of the amount

Effect on the financial statements

For the year ended 31 December 20X2:

(a)   A provision of $1,242,000 (2,000,000 × 0.621) is reported as a liability under provisions.

(b)   A non-current asset of $1,242,000 is also recognised. The provision results in a corresponding asset because the expenditure gives the entity access to future economic benefits; there is no effect on the income statement for the year.

For the year ended 31 December 20X3:

(a)   Depreciation of $248,400 (1,242,000 × 20%) is charged to the income statement. The non-current asset is depreciated over its remaining useful economic life of 5 years from 31 December 20X2 (the site will cease to produce output on 31 December 20X7).

(b)   Therefore at 31 December 20X3 the net book value of the non-current asset will be $993,600 (1,242,000 – 248,400).

(c)   At 31 December 20X3 the provision will be $1,366,000 (2,000,000 × 0.683).

(d)   The increase in the provision of $124,000 (1,366,000 – 1,242,000) is recognised in the income statement as a finance cost. This arises due to the unwinding of the discount.

Note. This answer takes the view that the obligation to make good the site gives rise to future economic benefits because the company could not continue to generate income from the site without incurring the expenditure. For this reason an asset is recognised at the same time as the provision. Unlike the equivalent UK standard, IAS 37 does not deal with this issue. An alternative answer would be possible:

For the year ended 31 December 20X2:

(a)   A provision of $1,242,000 (2,000,000 × 0.621) is reported as a liability under provisions.

(b)   There is a corresponding charge of $1,242,000 to the income statement. If this is material it is disclosed separately as required by IAS 8.

For the year ended 31 December 20X3:

(a)   At 31 December 20X3 the provision will be $1,366,000 (2,000,000 × 0.683).

(b)   The increase in the provision of $124,000 (1,366,000 – 1,242,000) is recognised in the income statement as a finance cost. This arises due to the unwinding of the discount.

36 Clean

(a) IAS 37 *Provisions, contingent liabilities and contingent assets* states that a provision should be recognised if all the following conditions are met.

   (i) There is a **present obligation** to **transfer economic benefits** as a result of a past transaction or event.
   (ii) It is **probable** that a transfer of economic benefits will be required to settle the obligation.
   (iii) A **reliable estimate** can be made of the amount of the obligation.

   Two of the three conditions are very clearly met. Clean will **incur expenditure** (transfer of economic benefits is virtually certain) and the directors have prepared **detailed estimates** of the amount.

   Although Clean is not legally obliged to carry out the project, it appears that it has a **constructive obligation** to do so. IAS 37 states that an entity has a constructive obligation if both of the following apply.

   (i) It has **indicated to other parties** that it will accept certain responsibilities (by an **established pattern** of past practice or published policies).
   (ii) As a result, it has created a **valid expectation** on the part of those other parties that it will discharge those responsibilities.

   Clean has a reputation of fulfilling its financial commitments once they have been publicly announced. Therefore the obligating event is the announcement of the proposal on 25 June 20X0, the obligation exists at 30 June 20X0 (the balance sheet date) and Clean is **required to recognise a provision**.

(b) Provision at 30 June 20X0:

		$'000
Expenditure on:		
30 June 20X1	30,000 × 0.926	27,780
30 June 20X2	30,000 × 0.857	25,710
30 June 20X3	40,000 × 0.794	31,760
		85,250

Provision at 30 June 20X1:

		£'000
Expenditure on:		
30 June 20X2	30,000 × 0.926	27,780
30 June 20X3	40,000 × 0.857	34,280
		62,060

(c) The charge to the income statement for the year ended 30 June 20X1 consists of:

   (i) Depreciation (85,250,000 ÷ 20) $ 4,262,500

   This is reported in cost of sales.

   The provision of $85,250,000 also represents an **asset** as it gives rise to future economic benefits (it enhances the performance of the factories). This is **capitalised and depreciated over 20 years** (the average useful economic life of the factories).

   (ii) Unwinding of the discount (see working) $ 6,810,000

   This is reported as a **finance cost**.

Working

	$'000
Provision at 1 July 20X0	85,250
Expenditure on 30 June 20X1	(30,000)
Unwinding of discount (balancing figure)	6,810
Provision at 30 June 20X1	62,060

Alternative calculation

	$'000
Expenditure on:	
30 June 20X1 (30,000 – 27,780)	2,220
30 June 20X2 (27,780 – 25,710)	2,070
30 June 20X3 (34,280 – 31,760)	2,520
	6,810

(d) International Financial Reporting Standards (IFRS) **do not contain any specific requirement to disclose** any information about an entity's **environmental policies**.

Because disclosure is **voluntary**, entities can disclose as much or as little information as they wish in whatever way that they wish. There is nothing to prevent an entity from making disclosures in **such a general way** that they are **meaningless**, or from presenting information **selectively**. Disclosure is normally made in the Financial Review or the Directors' Report and **does not have to be audited**.

Entities are required to disclose information about **provisions and contingent liabilities** relating to environmental matters, such as the **cost of rectifying damage, decommissioning costs and claims for damages**. They are also required to disclose information about large and unusual items recognised in the income statement. Therefore **any significant expenditure and the reason for it should be apparent**. It may be possible to deduce some information about environmental policies from these disclosures.

In practice, an increasing number of large entities **choose to make extensive and extremely informative reports** detailing their environmental policies and their performance in implementing them. This information is often audited. However, these disclosures normally take the form of a completely separate '**environmental report**', and are not included in the published financial statements themselves.

(e) **Share issue**

(i) *Accounting treatment*

This is an event after the balance sheet date which is **non-adjusting** (per IAS 10) because, although the announcement was made before the year end, the conditions for receipt of the funds did not exist at the balance sheet date. Nor did the entitlement to receive the funds exist at the year end, as the intention to issue the shares might not eventually have been carried out.

(ii) *Required adjustment/disclosure*

Disclosure should be by note, because of the **materiality** of the issue, giving the date of issue, the number of shares issued ($14m/$7.00 = 2m shares), the price at which they were issued ($7.00) and the total funds raised ($14m). The percentage increase in the company's share capital should be noted and the use for which the funds were raised.

37 Preparation question: Balance sheet valuations

(a) **Income statement** $

Finance income

   (441,014 × (W) 8%)   35,281

Balance sheet

Non-current assets

   Financial asset (441,014 + 35,281)   476,295

Working

Effective interest rate

$$\frac{600,000}{441,014} = 1.3605$$

∴ From tables interest rate is 8%

(b)

(b) **Compound instrument**

Presentation

	$
Non-current liabilities	
Financial liability component of convertible bond (Working)	1,797,467
Equity	
Equity component of convertible bond (2,000,000 – (Working) 1,797,467)	202,533

Working

Fair value of equivalent non-convertible debt

	$
Present value of principal payable at end of 3 years	1,544,367
$(4,000 \times \$500 = \$2m \times \dfrac{1}{(1.09)^3}$	
Present value of interest annuity payable annually in arrears for 3 years [(5% × $2m) × 2.531]	253,100
	1,797,467

38 Tall

Text reference. Financial instruments are covered in Chapter 13.

Top tips. Once again a memorandum answer is required in part (b). Do ensure that you write your answer in the correct format or you will lose marks. This is a difficult question on the provisions of IAS 39, a highly controversial standard.

(a) The international financial community was **concerned over the way that financial instruments in general, and derivatives in particular, were reported in financial statements**. In summary, the concerns were that financial instruments could rapidly transform the risk profile of an entity in a way that was not apparent under previous reporting practices. For example, a derivative, acquired for nil cost (and hence, under previous requirements, not recognised in the balance sheet), can be used to convert a dollar floating rate liability into a sterling fixed rate one. A derivative may be used to 'hedge' the risk that sales expected to occur next year in dollars may be worth less when converted into sterling because sterling may strengthen in the meantime. In both cases, the value of the derivative can change very significantly so that it represents a substantial asset or liability by the year end. This would not have been apparent to the reader under previous accounting standards (ie before IAS 39).

Furthermore, in some cases derivatives and other financial instruments have been used unwisely, **exposing entities to potentially large losses**. Such gains and losses were often not reported as they arose but were deferred until realised. Among other things, this gave rise to abuse through 'cherry picking' (eg in a bad year selling instruments with an unrealised gain so as to boost reported profits).

MEMORANDUM

To: Assistant management accountant
From: Management accountant
Date: 30 November 20X9
Subject: **Funding**

(i)   1   Presentation of financial instruments

1.1   Your suggestion that both the preference shares and bonds should be included in the shareholders' funds section is incorrect.

1.2   IAS 32 governs the presentation of financial instruments.

1.3   Under IAS 32 there is a distinction made between debt and equity. This depends on whether the issuer is required contractually to issue cash or another financial asset to the holder of the financial instrument.

1.4   Since the bonds must be redeemed on the maturity date, they contain a debt element. The instrument must, under IAS 32, be split into its debt and equity components. The debt component is reported under non-current liabilities and the equity component is reported in the equity section of the balance sheet.

1.5   The preference share are legally shares but, under IAS 32, they are treated as long-term liabilities. The reason is because there is an obligation to pay dividends **and to redeem the shares on the maturity date**.

(ii) 2   **IAS 39 requirements**

2.1   Most financial instruments are held at amortised cost.

2.2   Both the debt elements of the convertible bonds and the preferred shares will be held at amortised cost.

2.3   Amortisation of the redemption premium will be recognised as a finance cost in the income statement using the internal rate at return of the instrument to apportion it between accounting periods.

2.4   Certain financial instruments can be held at fair value. However, these are restricted to:

(1)   Financial instruments classified as 'fair value through profit or loss', that is instruments held for trading purposes or derivatives

(2)   Available for sale

39 QRS

> **Text reference**. Financial instruments are covered in Chapter 13.
>
> **Top tips.** Questions on financial instruments are unlikely to be more complicated than this, if this question and the one on the May 2005 paper are anything to go by. The main point to grasp is that the non-redeemable preferred shares are a liability and the convertible bonds are a hybrid instrument. For the latter, once the debt element has been valued, the equity element comes out as a balancing figure.
>
> **Easy marks.** These are available for classifying the instruments. The valuation calculation for the convertible bonds may look fiddly, but if you set it out as we do, showing clearly that you know that the equity element is a balancing figure, you would get some easy marks even if you got the present value calculations wrong.

IAS 32 *Financial instruments: presentation* requires that any financial instruments that have the characteristics of a liability should be classified as such in the balance sheet.

Non-redeemable preferred shares

Although the **non-redeemable preferred shares** are permanent and are described as shares they also have a dividend which is effectively a fixed amount of interest which is payable for each period. As such they are **long-term liabilities despite their name** and should be classified as such in the balance sheet rather than as equity.

Convertible bonds

The **convertible bonds** are slightly different as according to IAS 32 they would be classified as **hybrid or compound financial instruments**. Convertible bonds are argued to have some debt characteristics, annual payment of a fixed amount of interest, and some equity characteristics in that they are likely to be converted into equity shares in the future. IAS 32 therefore requires convertibles to be **partially presented** as **debt and partially presented as equity**. The valuation of the debt and equity elements is not easy but one method identified by IAS 32 involves valuation of the debt element by reference to an equivalent market rate of interest for non-convertible bonds with the equity element being the residual figure.

If the market rate of 8% for similar non-convertible bonds together with present value tables is used then the following valuations can be calculated:

	$
Present value of the capital element of the bond	
$6,000,000 \times 0.735$ (Note 1)	4,410,000
Present value of interest element	
$6,000,000 \times 6\% \times 3.312$ (Note 2)	1,192,320
Debt element valuation	5,602,320
Total valuation	6,000,000
Equity element valuation	397,680

Notes

1   This is the discount factor at 8% for four years time when the convertibles would be converted.
2   This is the accumulated discount factor for the four payments of interest at 8% until the date of redemption.

Therefore the two proposals for issues of financial instruments would result in the vast majority of the $10 million being raised being classified as debt finance with a consequently significant increase in the gearing of the company. The alternative is to reconsider a rights issue which would of course be classified as equity.

40 PX

Text reference. Financial instruments are covered in Chapter 13.

Top tips. The main points to be made are the correct classification for each type of financial asset; the fact that fair value measurement is an option for any financial asset; that held-for-trading and available for sale assets are to be measured at fair value and held-to-maturity are to be measured at amortised cost.

Easy marks. As you can see, 6 out of the 10 available marks are for correct classification, which is straightforward memory work.

Examiner's comment. This question was not answered by many candidates and answered very badly by most of those who did attempt it. The examiner is making it quite clear that the requirements of IAS 39 will be examined and therefore should be studied.

(a)   The **investment in the securities of a listed entity** would be classified according to IAS 39 as a **financial asset at fair value through profit and loss**. This is an asset that is held for trading as the directors acquired the investment with the intention of realising it in the short term.

   The **loan to DB** is a **financial asset** and falls into the category **loans and receivables** for classification and measurement purposes.

The additional **small investments in listed securities** would be classified as **available-for-sale investments** as they do not fall into any of IAS 39's other classifications for financial assets.

(b) The **investment in securities of a listed company**, as a financial asset at fair value through profit and loss, should be measured at **fair value and any increase or decrease in fair value taken to the income statement**.

The **loan**, as with all loans and receivables not held for trading purposes, is measured at **amortised cost**.

The **small investments**, as available-for-sale investments, are measured at **fair value**.

41 AZG

(a) According to IAS 39, a financial instrument or other contract is a derivative if it has the following three characteristics.

   (i) Its value changes in response to the change in a specified interest or exchange rate, or in response to the change in a price, rating, index or other variable.

   (ii) It requires no initial net investment or a very small net investment compared to the net investment that other types of contract would require in order to have the same response to changes in the value of the underlying instrument.

   (iii) It is settled at a future date.

   The futures contract meets all three characteristics and it is therefore a derivative.

(b) IAS 39 requires that derivative financial instruments should be recognised as either assets or liabilities. They should be measured at fair value both upon initial recognition and subsequently on the balance sheet, and changes in their fair value should be recognised in profit or loss unless they qualify for hedge accounting treatment as effective hedging instruments, or when the underlying instrument is an unquoted equity instrument.

(c) **AZG: extract from income statement for the year ended 31 March 20X7**

	20X7	20X6
Gain on derivative	$73,891	$68,966

AZG: EXTRACT FROM BALANCE SHEET AT 31 MARCH 20X7

	20X7	20X6
Derivative asset	$142,857	$68,966

Workings

The dollar fair value of the forward foreign exchange contract at the relevant dates will be:

27 February 20X6	Fair value: Fl 6,000,000/3	= $2,000,000
31 March 20X6	Fair value: Fl 6,000,000/2.9	= $2,068,966
31 March 20X7	Fair value: Fl 6,000,000/2.8	= $2,142,857

		$
Gain recognised in year ended 31 March 20X6: $2,068,966 − $2,000,000 =		68,966
Gain recognised in year ended 31 March 20X7: $2,142,857 − $2,068,966 =		73,891
Derivative asset at fair value at 31 March 20X7: $68,966 + $73,891	=	142,857

42 Preparation question: Defined benefit scheme

INCOME STATEMENT NOTE

Defined benefit expense recognised in profit or loss

	$'m
Current service cost	13
Interest cost (10% × 110)	11
Expected return on plan assets (12% × 150)	(18)
Recognised actuarial gains (Working)	(4)
Past service cost	20
	22

BALANCE SHEET NOTES

Net defined benefit liability recognised in the balance sheet

	$'m
Present value of pension obligation	116
Fair value of plan assets	(140)
	(24)
Unrecognised actuarial gains/(losses) (Working)	42
	18

Changes in the present value of the defined benefit obligation

	$'m
Opening defined benefit obligation	110
Interest cost (10% × 110)	11
Current service cost	13
Benefits paid	(10)
Past service cost	20
Actuarial gain (balancing figure)	(28)
Closing defined benefit obligation	116

Changes in the fair value of plan assets

	$'m
Opening fair value of plan assets	150
Expected return on plan assets (12% × 150)	18
Contributions	7
Benefits paid	(10)
Actuarial loss (balancing figure)	(25)
Closing fair value of plan assets	140

WORKING

Recognised/unrecognised actuarial gains and losses

	$'m	$'m
Corridor limits, greater of:		
10% of pension obligation b/d (10% × 110)	11	
10% of plan assets b/d (10% × 150)	15	
⇒ Corridor limit	15	
Unrecognised gains b/d		43
Gain recognised in I/S [(43 – 15)/7]		(4)
Gain on obligation in the year		28
Loss on assets in the year		(25)
Unrecognised gains c/d		42

43 Accounting for retirement benefits

(a)   (i)   There are many key issues in determining how accounting for retirement benefits in respect of a defined benefit plan is carried out:

         (1)   The two main alternative approaches are what might be called the **income statement approach** or the **balance sheet approach**. Under the income statement approach the pension cost is seen as an operating cost and under the accruals or matching concept the attempt is made to spread the total pension cost over the service lives of the employees. The balance sheet approach however concentrates on the valuation of the assets and liabilities of the plan and the cost to the income statement is the change in value of the plan net assets or liabilities.

         (2)   Regarding the assets of the defined benefit plan there are two issues, **whether or not they should be included** on the balance sheet of the company and **how** they would be **valued**. Alternative valuation methods such as cost, market value and fair value are available.

         (3)   How should scheme liabilities be valued? Should they be valued using an **actuarial valuation or a market value**? Usually actuarial techniques will have to be used as there is no market value for such liabilities but then there is an issue over which actuarial method should be used – accrued benefits or prospective benefits.

         (4)   Should **discounting** be used when valuing the scheme liabilities in order to take account of the time value of money?

Additional points

You would also have scored marks if you identified any of the following points.

(1)   If **actuarial gains and losses** occur where should they be **recognised** – in the incomes statement or in a secondary statement? Should such gains and losses be recognised immediately or spread over the remaining service lives of the employees? Or should the actuarial gains and losses only be recognised in the income statement if they exceed a predetermined amount? The problem that faces standard setters is how to deal with the volatility of actuarial gains and losses.

(2)   **How often** should **actuarial valuations** take place? In theory they should take place at each year end but the costs and practicalities of this makes it difficult and onerous.

(3)   If there are **changes to the defined benefit plan** such as improvement of benefits or addition of new benefits in relation to past service how should these be accounted for? The alternatives are to recognise the cost immediately in the income statement, spread it over the remaining service lives of employees or to offset it against any surplus in the scheme.

   (ii)   IAS 19 *Employee benefits* follows a **balance sheet approach** to accounting for defined benefit schemes. The assets of the scheme are to be valued on an actuarial basis using the **projected unit credit method** and the liabilities should be discounted to reflect the time value of money and the particular characteristics of the liability. The discount rate to be used is the rate of return on high quality corporate bonds of equivalent currency and term as the scheme liabilities being valued.

         The net amount of the fair value of the assets and the discounted value of the liabilities appears in the balance sheet as a **surplus or a deficit**. Actuarial valuations should take place with sufficient regularity to ensure that the financial statement amounts do not differ materially from the amounts that would be determined at the balance sheet date.

The balance sheet asset cannot exceed the **net total** of:

(1) any unrecognised actuarial losses and past service cost

(2) the present value of any available funds from the plan or reduction in future contributions to the plan

Gains and losses are measured at the year end and recognised in the subsequent year. Any net gain or loss is amortised in the income statement if it is **in excess of 10% of the greater of the defined benefit obligation or the fair value** of the **plan** assets. The period of amortisation must not exceed the average remaining service period.

Past service costs for active employees are recognised in the income statement on **a straight line basis** over the average remaining vesting period.

IAS 19 offers a choice of treatments of how to deal with profits or losses not recognised in the income statement. Actuarial gains or losses can be deferred if the cumulative amount remains within the 10% limit or corridor and any amount outside the corridor can be amortised over any period shorter than the working lives of the employees or even written off to the income statement immediately. Alternatively all actuarial gains and losses can be recognised in the income statement provided that the treatment is consistent.

(b) **Net plan asset as at 31 May 20X1**

	$m
Fair value of plan assets	2,950
Actuarial valuation of liabilities	(2,000)
Pension scheme surplus	950
Unrecognised actuarial gains (W1)	(692)
Net plan asset	258

A test must be carried out to ensure that the net plan asset does not exceed the future economic benefit that it represents for the company.

Charge to operating profit

	$m
Current service cost	70
Past service cost	25
Interest on liabilities	230
Actuarial gain recognised (W4)	(5)
Return on scheme assets	(295)
	25

Changes in present value of the defined benefit obligation

	$m
Opening defined benefit obligation	1,500
Interest cost	230
Current service cost	70
Past service cost	25
Actuarial loss (balance figure)	175
	2,000

Changes in the fair value of plan assets

	$m
Opening fair value of plan assets	1,970
Return on plan assets	295
Contributions	60
Actuarial gain (balance figure)	625
	2,950

Workings

1   *Unrecognised actuarial gains*

	$m
Unrecognised actuarial gains at 1 June 20X0	247
Actuarial loss on obligation (W2)	(175)
Actuarial gain on plan assets (W3)	625
	697
Actuarial gain recognised (W4)	(5)
Unrecognised actuarial gain at 31 May 20X1	692

2   *Present value of obligation*

	$m
Present value of obligation at 1 June 20X0	1,500
Interest cost	230
Current service cost	70
Past service cost	25
	1,825
Actuarial loss (balancing figure)	175
Present value of obligation at 31 May 20X1	2,000

3   *Fair value of plan assets*

	$m
Fair value of plan assets at 1 June 20X0	1,970
Return on plan assets	295
Contributions	60
	2,325
Actuarial gain (balancing figure)	625
Fair value of plan assets at 31 May 20X1	2,950

4   *Actuarial gain recognised in income statement*

The 10% limits will be the greater of 10% of $1,500m and 10% of $1,970m.

	$m
Net unrecognised gain	247
10% corridor (10% × $1,970)	(197)
	50
Amortisation over 10 years (50/10)	5

44 CBA

Text reference. Employee benefits are covered in Chapter 12.

Top tips. Explain the treatment allowed before the amendment, then go on to say what the alternative is.

Easy marks. Even if you don't know what the amendment says, you should be able to pick up something for commenting on the treatment allowed before the alternative was available.

Examiner's comments. There was a lack of basic knowledge with some candidates referring to the 'corridor' criterion without explaining how this should be applied.

IAS 19 *Employee benefits* deals with, amongst other employee benefit matters, the accounting requirements for defined benefit pension schemes. One of the accounting areas dealt with are those of actuarial gains and losses.

Actuarial gains and losses are the effects of **differences between the previous actuarial assumptions and what actually occurred** (experience adjustments) and the effects of changes in actuarial assumptions. The IAS specifies that if the accumulated unrecognised actuarial gains and losses exceed 10% of the greater of the defined benefit obligation or the fair value of the plan assets then the **excess amount should be recognised**.

Pre December 2004

Before the amendment of IAS 19 in December 2004, the method of recognition was to divide this actuarial gain or loss **by the expected average remaining working lives** of the participating employees and then recognise it in the income statement.

Post December 2004

The **amendment** in 2004 (following from the treatment of actuarial gains and losses in the UK's FRS 17) allows companies a **further option**. This option is to **recognise the actuarial gains or losses in full in the period** in which they occur but not in the income statement. Instead, they are recognised in a **statement of recognised income and expense**.

Position for CBA

As far as our company is concerned, we have an actuarial loss of $7.2 million. The three options that face us in accounting terms are:

(a) **Spread the actuarial loss over the remaining working lives** of the employees and charge the current year's portion to the income statement as an expense.

(b) **Recognise the full loss** in the statement of recognised income and expense.

(c) Recognise the **full loss directly in retained earnings** in the period in which they occur (in the statement of recognised income and expense, which then becomes compulsory).

The impact of these options is that if the loss is shown in the income statement then this will **affect reported profit and earnings per share** which may impact on our share price. However, if the full loss is reported in the statement of recognised income and expense or in retained earnings there is no effect on reported profit or earnings per share.

45 BGA

Text reference. These topics are covered in Chapter 12.

Top tips. Accounting for defined benefit pension schemes under IAS 19 *Employee benefits* is one of the most complex areas of financial reporting.

Make sure you follow a careful step by step approach. First set out the gain or loss on the **obligation**, calculating the actuarial gain or loss on the obligation as a balancing figure. Then set out the gain or loss on **plan assets**, again calculating the actuarial gain or loss on the plan assets as a balancing figure.

Consider the corridor limit to determine the amount to be recognised in the income statements.

Easy marks. You will gain a substantial proportion of the marks for setting out correctly the constituent elements of the gain or loss on the obligation and the constituent elements of the gain or loss on the plan assets. Show your workings and identify the balancing figure to ensure you gain the remaining two marks.

Gains or loss on obligation

	$
Present value of obligation at start of year	18,360,000
Interest cost (6.5% × $18,360,000)	1,193,400
Current service cost	1,655,000
Benefits paid	(1,860,300)
Actuarial gain on obligation (balancing figure)	(692,600)
Present value of obligation at the end of the year	18,655,500

Gains or loss on plan assets

	$
Fair value of plan assets at start of year	17,770,000
Expected return on plan assets (9.4% × $17,770,000)	1,670,380
Contributions	997,000
Benefits paid	(1,860,300)
Actuarial loss on obligation (balancing figure)	(159,900)
Fair value of plan assets at the end of the year	18,417,180

(a)   The **actuarial loss** for the year ended 31 October 20X7 on BGA's assets is $159,900 and $692,600 on the **defined benefit obligation**.

(b)   At the start of the year, ie on 1 November 20X6, the net cumulative unrecognised actuarial gains were $802,000.

This means that the amount of **actuarial gains** and **losses** to be recognised in the income statement for year ended 31 October 20X7 will be calculated through the steps set out below. First we need to consider the corridor limits.

Do the **net cumulative unrecognised actuarial gains and losses** exceed 10% of the greater of:

–   The present value of the obligation before deducting plan assets
        10% × 18,360,000 = $1,836,000

–   The fair value of the plan assets
        10% × 17,770,000 = $1,777,000

As the **net cumulative unrecognised actuarial gains** at the start of the year of $802,000 were less than 10 per cent of the greater of:

•   The **present value** of the **obligation** before deducting **plan assets**
•   The **fair value** of any **plan assets**

No actuarial gains and losses will be recognised in the income statement during the year ending 31 October 20X7.

46 Tree

Text reference. This topic is covered in Chapter 16.

Top tips. This question tests your ability to apply the *Framework* and IAS 18. Part (c) asks for the effects of disclosure in the financial statements.

For Transaction 1 the key issue is whether Tree has retained the risks of owning the property. The detailed reasoning behind this needs to be explained. Make sure you use the information given in the question.

In Transaction 2, remember that the $1 million profit on disposal and operating fee of $1,200,000 are cancelled as intra group transactions.

(a)   IAS 18 *Revenue* states that the following conditions must be satisfied before revenue from the sale of goods can be recognised.

(i)   The entity **has transferred to the buyer the significant risks and rewards** of ownership of the goods. In most cases, transfer of the risks and rewards of ownership coincides with the transfer of legal title or the passing of possession to the buyer, but **this is not always the case**. If the entity retains significant risk of ownership, the transaction is not a sale and revenue cannot be recognised. For example, the entity might retain an obligation for unsatisfactory performance not covered by normal warranty provisions. However, if the risk retained is insignificant, the transaction is a sale and revenue is recognised. For example, a retail sale is recognised where a refund is offered if the customer is not satisfied, provided that the seller can reliably estimate future returns and recognises a liability based on previous experience and other relevant factors.

(ii)   The **entity** retains **neither continuing managerial involvement** to the degree usually associated with ownership **nor effective control** over the goods sold.

(iii) The amount of revenue can be **measured reliably**.

(iv)   It is **probable** that the economic benefits associated with the transaction will flow to the **entity**. For example, it may be uncertain that a foreign government will grant permission to remit consideration from a sale in a foreign country. Revenue cannot be recognised until the uncertainty is removed.

(v)   The costs incurred or to be incurred in respect of the transaction can be **measured reliably**.

(b)   **Transaction 1**

The key issue here is whether Tree has retained the risks inherent in owning the property. This depends on whether Tree is likely to exercise its option to repurchase the property in practice.

(i)   Tree can repurchase the property at any time until 28 February 20X6, but the bank cannot require repurchase. This means that Tree is **protected against any fall in the value of the property** below $5 million. This suggests that **some risk** has been **transferred to the bank**.

(ii)   In practice, the value of the property is expected to rise by 5% each year for the foreseeable future. Therefore it is **extremely unlikely** that the value of the property will fall below $5 million.

(iii) Tree **can benefit from the expected rise** in the value of the property by buying it back at a price that is well below its anticipated market value.

In conclusion, Tree is **likely to exercise the option** and therefore has **retained the risk of changes** in the property's market value. Other important aspects of the transaction are:

(i)   The 'sale' price of the property was **only 50% of its market value**.

(ii)   Tree occupies the **property rent-free** (a reward of ownership).

(iii) The repurchase price depends on the **length of time that elapses** between the date of the agreement and the date of repurchase, **rather than on the market value** of the property.

Therefore, the transaction is essentially a **loan secured on the property**, rather than an outright sale. The $50,000 payable for each month that the bank holds the property is **interest** on the loan.

The property **remains in the consolidated balance sheet** at its cost or market value (depending on the accounting policy adopted by Tree). The **loan** of $5 million and **accrued interest** of $300,000 (6 × 50,000) are reported under **non-current liabilities**. Interest of $300,000 is recognised in the consolidated income statement.

Transaction 2

> **Top tips.** The key issue is that Tree retains a source of risks and benefits, even after the disposal.

The key issue is whether Tree **retains the risks associated** with the ownership of the branch.

Tree **continues to control the operations** of the branch and the amount that it receives from Vehicle is the operating profit of the branch less the interest payable on the loan. Tree also suffers the effect of any operating losses made by the branch. Therefore the **position is essentially the same as before** the 'sale'.

Although Vehicle is not a subsidiary of Tree plc as defined by IAS 27 *Consolidated and separate financial statements,* it is a special purpose entity (**quasi-subsidiary**). It gives rise to benefits for Tree that are in substance no different from those that would arise if it were a subsidiary. Its assets, liabilities, income and expenses **must be included** in the consolidated financial statements.

The assets and liabilities of Vehicle are included in the consolidated balance sheet at $7 million (their original value to the group). The loan of $8 million is recognised as a non-current liability. The profit on disposal of $1 million and the operating fee of $1,200,000 are cancelled as intra-group transactions. The operating profit of $2,000,000 is included in the consolidated income statement as is the loan interest of $800,000.

(c)   **Transaction 1**

	$'000
Non current assets	
Property, plant and equipment	NBV
Non-current liabilities	
Loan	5,000
Accrued interest	300

Notes to accounts

The loan is secured on property with a market value of $10m at 1 March 20X1.

Transaction 2

Accounted for under the normal consolidated accounting rules (see (b) above). No additional disclosure required.

47 LMN

The question of the **commercial substance** of the arrangement between LMN and IJK regarding the recognition of inventory and of sales is dependent upon **which party receives the benefits and bears the risks involved** in the agreement. It is the entity which receives the benefits and bears the risks which should recognise the vehicles as inventory.

LMN receives the following **benefits**:

(a)   It is free to specify the type of inventory, ie ranges and models, which it holds.

(b)   If there is an increase in price between the date of delivery and the time of sale LMN still only has to pay this price determined at the time of delivery.

(c)   It is free to use the cars for demonstrations and road testing.

(d)   It has the right to return any vehicle to IJK without incurring a penalty.

LMN also bears the following **risks**:

(a)   It must insure the vehicles.

(b)   If there is a decrease in price between the date of delivery and the time of sales LMN cannot benefit from this as the original agreed price must be paid.

(c)   Although LMN can use the vehicles for demonstration purposes a charge may become payable.

IJK receives the **benefit of retaining** legal title of the vehicles until they are sold to a third party.

However, **IJK** also bears **two significant risks**:

(a)   It bears the substantial risk of slow-moving or obsolete vehicles as LMN can return vehicles at any time without incurring a penalty.

(b)   It bears the significant financial risk of financing the inventory as IJK is not paid for the vehicles until 33 days after LMN has sold the vehicles to a third party.

Therefore the situation is not clear cut but **on balance** given the significant risks that remain with IJK it is likely that **IJK should recognise the vehicles as inventory** rather than LMN.

Regarding the recognition of sales revenue IAS 18 *Revenue* requires that a sale should be recognised when the seller transfers to the buyer the significant risks and rewards of ownership of the goods. In this case these risks and rewards are only transferred by IJK when a sale is made to a third party by LMN. Therefore it would appear that IJK should only recognise its sales revenue on the vehicles when a sale is made to a third party by LMN.

48 Section A questions: Interpretation of accounts

1   B   Assets and therefore capital employed would increase, while there would probably be relatively little impact on earnings (depreciation charges would replace lease rentals). Obligations under finance leases and therefore debt would increase, but there would be little effect on shareholders' funds.

2   D   Non-current assets and therefore capital employed decrease while profit increases due to the lower depreciation charge. Because the recoverable amount of the properties is above depreciated historic cost, the impairment loss is recognised in the statement of changes in equity and does not affect reported profit.

Gearing increases because capital employed decreases but there is no effect on debt.

3   The relationship between the three ratios is: operating profit margin × asset turnover = ROCE or ROCE ÷ operating profit margin = asset turnover.

Therefore: 64% × 125% = 80% or 80% ÷ 64% = 125%.

4   B   Although all these ratios could be of interest to the bank, as a long term loan creditor the bank will be particularly interested in factors that affect the company's ability to pay interest. These include: whether it is getting into further debt or improving its situation; and the level of profit in relation to interest expense.

5   Quick ratio: $\dfrac{70,000}{159,000} = 0.44:1$

	$'000
Assets as stated (80 + 10)	90
Less debtors taking advantage of discount	(20)
	70

	$'000
Liabilities as stated (75 + 100)	175
Cash received from sale of inventory (8 – 2)	(6)
Cash received from trade receivables (20 × 90%)	(18)
Current portion of new loan (40 ÷ 5)	8
	159

6   A   Example: suppose the entity purchases inventory worth $300,000:

	Current ratio	Quick ratio
Before	$\dfrac{1,500}{1,000} = 1.5$	$\dfrac{400}{1,000} = 0.4$
After	$\dfrac{1,800}{1,300} = 1.4$	$\dfrac{400}{1,300} = 0.3$

7   B   Calculate the ratios relating to the new product:

Operating profit margin: $\frac{120}{1,600}$ = 7.5% (less than existing margin of 10%)

ROCE: $\frac{120}{500}$ = 24% (greater than existing ROCE of 20%)

Existing ROCE is 10% × 2 = 20%.

8     $\frac{\text{Profit available to equity shareholders}}{\text{Shareholders' equity}}$

$\frac{20 + 7.5}{300 + 150}$ = 6.1%

9   D   ABC has a relatively high operating profit and a relatively low asset turnover. This suggests that it is capital intensive. A and C would not normally have high levels of non-current assets. B is more likely to have significant non-current assets, but this type of business normally has low operating profit share margins. Therefore option D is the most likely option.

10   C $\frac{\text{Loan notes and preferred shares}}{\text{Total capital employed}} = \frac{100 + 50}{330}$ = 45.4%

49 Preparation question: Financial analysis

Text reference. Financial analysis is covered in Chapter 17.

Top tips. This is a straightforward question on interpretation of accounts, of a manageable size and providing you with all the ratios you need. You should, as with all interpretation questions, spend some time *thinking* about the ratios before you start writing. Mark what you think are the significant trends shown in the question and make brief notes which will serve as an answer plan. Then proceed to discuss each area, using sensible headings to break your report up, and including a brief introduction and conclusion.

WANDAFOOD PRODUCTS
FIVE YEAR SUMMARY: 20X1 TO 20X5

Prepared by: An Accountant
Date: 28 February 20X6

1   Introduction

1.1   This report discusses the trends shown in the five year summary prepared from the published accounts for the five years ended 31 December 20X5. It also considers how price changes over that period may have limited the usefulness of the historical cost data provided.

2   Profitability

2.1   The net profit margin has remained fairly constant, although it dropped in 20X3. Operating asset turnover has decreased over the five years, pulling back a little in 20X4. Return on assets, the primary ratio produced by combining these two secondary ratios, has therefore decreased over the period but was at its lowest in 20X3.

2.2   These findings seem to indicate that assets are being used inefficiently and that this has caused the decrease in return on assets. Inflation may be responsible for increases in revenue which would mask even worse decreases in efficiency.

3   Interest and dividend cover

3.1   Interest cover improved markedly between 20X1 and 20X2, falling back a little in 20X3 and 20X4 but now below the 20X1 level, indicating increases in debt and/or interest rates. Dividend cover, however, after dropping below 20X1 levels, has now recovered some lost ground. In both cases cover was adequate, even at the lowest points. However, since there has been a substantial increase in gearing, interest cover ought to be watched carefully. Profits may be available to cover interest and dividends, but this must be matched by good cash flow.

4 Debt to equity

4.1 Debt to equity fell dramatically in 20X2 but has steadily increased until in 20X5 it was almost double its 20X1 level. Minority interests appear to have remained a relatively insignificant element in the group's funding. It is more likely that debt has increased than equity has decreased (for example, because of a purchase or redemption of own shares). Interest cover has fallen in line with this increase in borrowing as a proportion of long-term capital.

5 Liquidity

5.1 Both the current and the quick ratios have declined over the period, except for 20X2 when they both improved. However, they have been fairly constant between 20X3 and 20X5 and are quite high, although comments on the adequacy of these ratios are of very limited utility in the absence of information about the company's activities and industry averages.

5.2 The reduction may have been planned to reduce the costs involved in maintaining high levels of inventory and allowing generous credit to customers. From the differential between the quick and current ratios it would seem that inventory is a significant asset here. However, current liabilities must not be allowed to increase to the extent that current assets (and especially liquid assets) are insufficient to cover them, as this can lead to a liquidity crisis. Worsening liquidity ratios can be an indicator of overtrading; but this most often arises when expansion is funded from short-term borrowings, whereas new long-term debt appears to have been found in this case.

6 Assets

6.1 As working capital has fallen in size, it is now being used more efficiently, generating more revenue from a reduced base. It would seem likely, given the slight fall in operating asset turnover, that non-current asset turnover has worsened considerably and that the improvement in working capital turnover has compensated for this in calculating return on assets. It may be that long-term borrowings have financed capital expenditure which has not yet affected operations. (An increase in the amount of non-current assets would decrease non-current asset turnover if revenue did not increase correspondingly.)

7 Investors' ratios

7.1 Earnings, dividends and net assets per share have all increased over the period. There has, therefore, been no need to increase dividends regardless of fluctuations in earnings.

7.2 The increase in net assets per share seems to indicate either that retained profits and borrowings have been used to increase non-current asset expenditure or (less likely) that assets have been revalued each year.

8 Inflation

8.1 Historical cost accounts do not show the effect on the group's operating capacity of rising prices over a period. The modest increases in EPS and dividend do not suggest that profit has increased sufficiently to compensate for more than a very low level of inflation. It is also possible that the value of assets is understated, so that ROCE and asset turnover measures are all understated. The underlying trends in real terms may be very much worse than those shown in historical cost terms.

9 Conclusion

9.1 The group would appear, from this superficial analysis, to be a steady performer but not expanding fast. This may be an advantage in times of recession: debt is probably not so high as to cause liquidity problems nor have shareholders come to expect a high payout ratio. However, inflation may be eroding its profits. The possible recent expansion of non-current assets may help it to grow in future, as will its improved working capital management.

50 OPQ

(a)

REPORT

To: Financial Director, OPQ
From: Assistant
Date: November 20X5
Subject: PJ Gamewriters

Introduction

I have been asked to examine the most recent financial statements of PJ Gamewriters (PJ) as a preliminary step in consideration of the acquisition of the business. This report is based upon the financial statements of PJ for the year ended 31 July 20X5 together with comparative figures for the previous year. The analysis is based upon a number of relevant accounting ratios which are included in the Appendix to this report.

Financial performance

PJ appears to have **performed well** during 20X5. Revenue has increased by 26% but this has not been at the cost of profitability as its gross profit margin was high at 53% in 20X4 but has increased even further to 55% during the current year and its operating profit margin has increased from 39% to 40%. Overall the operating profit has increased by 29% between the two years indicating that costs are being well-controlled despite the increased turnover. Such **high margins are to be expected** given the 'intellectual' nature of their business.

Again as would be expected in a human capital business return on **capital employed is extremely high** at 112% although this has decreased from 122% in the previous year. Because of the increase in profitability, in theory this, is due to a worsening of the asset turnover. This indicates that the assets of the business are not being used as effectively in 20X5 as in 20X4. However, the ROCE figure for 20X5 would be decreased to about 83% (still high) if the market value of the office premises had been incorporated into the financial statements. Because the assets that are recognised in the balance sheet are not actually used to generate revenue, ROCE and asset turnover are only of limited significance.

We are also told that PJ owns the copyright to the games but these have not been included in the financial statements. If the fair value of these copyrights were to be included then the ROCE would be reduced to perhaps a more normal level.

Financial position

The **liquidity** position of the business has **improved significantly** largely due to a $200,000 increase in cash balances. This surplus cash is even after having paid a dividend of $500,000 for the year compared to just $350,000 in the previous year. This dividend payment is 64% of the profit for the period compared to 61% in the previous year. The cash would appear to have been invested in a bank account with an increase in interest receivable in the income statement but, even if it is assumed that the $200,000 has been invested for say only half of the year, this is still only giving a return of 7%.

In terms of control of the business it has **no debt finance and has a high level of retained earnings** which could perhaps be put to more profitable use. There would appear to be fairly good control of trade receivables with an average collection period of 60 days and low levels of inventory. The payables payment period is very low but as most of these costs are employment costs this is not too surprising.

Conclusion

PJ is clearly a **growing and profitable business**. Even if the property revaluation and the copyrights were included on the balance sheet it is likely that return on capital employed would still be healthy. There are no apparent liquidity problems and working capital appears to be fairly well managed. However, the excess of retained earnings, high cash balance and high dividend may indicate that the **best use of its resources is not being made**.

APPENDIX

Key accounting ratios

		20X5	20X4
Gross profit margin	1,523/2,793	55%	
	1,168/2,208		53%
Operating profit margin	1,108/2,793	40%	
	858/2,208		39%
Return on capital employed	1,108/987	112%	
	858/703		122%
Return on capital employed (using market value)	1,108/987+350		83%
Current ratio	744/367	2.04	
	403/320		1.26
Receivables payment period	460/2,793 × 365	60 days	
	324/2,208 × 365		54 days
Payables payment period	36/1,270 × 365	10 days	
	30/1,040 × 365		10 days
Dividends/profit for year	500/784	64%	
	350/570		61%

(b) The main limitations of the analysis of this business concern the **assets which are not on the balance sheet** and the nature of such an 'intellectual' or 'human asset' based business.

Assets not on the balance sheet

Although the market value of the office premises has not been included in the financial statements it is possible to make rough estimates of the effect this would have on return on capital employed given the fact that we have an estimated current market value. However, more problematic is the **value of the copyrights** to the games. This is likely to be a large intangible asset which if included in the balance sheet would not only reduce the return on capital employed to a more reasonable level but also give a better picture of the actual worth of the business. It would therefore be useful to have an estimate from the directors of PJ of the worth of these copyrights.

Nature of the business

PJ is a business which is heavily reliant on its small workforce. There are currently 10 games writers with average employment costs of $70,000 each and employment costs make up about 55% of the cost of sales figure. These **employees are key to the future of the business** and one must consider whether they would remain with the business if the current owners were to sell the business. In particular, information about the views and plans of the five senior software writers who hold shares in the company would be useful. In addition, the reason for the proposed sale is that Paul and James wish to pursue other interests. Any potential acquirer will need to consider what impact the loss of their technical skills will have on the success of the business.

Effect of outsourcing

PJ outsources its manufacturing and distribution operations. It is not clear how these arrangements work or how they have affected the figures in the financial statements. For example, inventory levels appear low. Is there consignment inventory and has this been correctly recorded? More details are needed, particularly about the way in which **revenue is recognised** and about the make up of the figures for inventories and receivables. In recent years, many software companies have adopted inappropriate revenue recognition policies and it is possible that revenue is overstated.

51 Phoenix

> **Text references**. OFR is covered in Chapter 1, financial analysis in Chapter 17 and off balance sheet finance in Chapter 16.
>
> **Top tips.** Remember that you may be asked to talk about ratios, rather than calculate them. Part (a) is a useful general review. Make sure you mention the impact of different accounting policies, inflation and the use of historical values for capital employed as well as other factors that may affect the usefulness of accounting ratios.

(a)   An evaluation of the **usefulness of accounting ratios** could include the following points.

(i)   Ratios calculated using historical cost accounts do not reflect current values or current costs and are of less use for predictive purposes.

(ii)   Differences in accounting policies can make comparisons difficult between companies even where adequate disclosures are made in accounts.

(iii)   Return on capital employed is a key ratio but the capital employed figure traditionally uses the historical value of capital employed. The real cost of shareholders investments is their opportunity cost (the amount lost by *not* selling shares at market price). The return to shareholders is based upon dividends received *not* future dividends expected.

(iv)   Recent accounting standards have improved the balance sheet presentation but some assets and liabilities may still be held off balance sheet (such as accounting for pension costs and operating leases).

(v)   There is still a trend for creative accounting (especially where management remuneration is linked to profits), however new accounting standards have reduced the scope for this.

(vi)   The business environment changes rapidly, traditional ratio analysis may not reflect this.

> **Top tips.** The question asks for a report and so you should set out your answer in the correct format. It is always advisable to show the ratios in a separate appendix for clarity.

(b)   **REPORT**

To: The bankers of Phoenix
From: Consultant management accountant
Subject: Financial performance 20X7 – 20X9
Date: 30 October 20X9

1   Introduction

1.1   In accordance with your instructions, I set out below a review of the entity's financial performance over the last three years.

1.2   The main focus of this report is on the reasons for the increase in the level of bank loans.

1.3   Appropriate accounting ratios are included in the attached appendix.

2   Bank lending

2.1   The main reason for the steep increase in bank lending is due to the entity not generating sufficient cash from its operating activities over the past three years.

2.2   For the year ended 30 June 20X8, the entity had a net cash deficiency on operating activities of $18m.

2.3 In addition, for at least the past two years, the cash generated from operating activities has not been sufficient to cover interest payable. Therefore those payments, together with tax and dividends, have had to be covered by borrowings.

2.4 As at 30 June 20X9, bank borrowings were $610m out of a total facility of $630m. Payment of the proposed dividends alone would increase the borrowings to the limit.

3 Operating review

3.1 Although revenue has been rising steadily over the period, operating profit has remained almost static.

3.2 Over this period the operating profit margin has risen, but not as much as would be expected. The cost of sales have risen in almost the same proportion as revenue. This may be due to increased costs of raw materials, as inventories have risen steeply; but the turnover of inventory has been falling or static over the same period.

3.3 There has also been a large increase in trade receivables. Both the increase in inventories and trade receivables have had to be financed out of operating activities leading to the present pressure on borrowings.

3.4 Although the number of days sales in trade receivables has fallen steadily over the period, the trade receivables at the end of June 20X9 still represent nearly a year's credit sales. This is excessive and seems to imply a poor credit control policy, even taking into account the extended credit terms being granted by the company.

4 Recommendations

4.1 The entity needs to undertake an urgent review of its credit terms in order to reduce the levels of trade receivables.

4.2 Inventory levels are also extremely high (representing over four months' sales) and should be reviewed.

4.3 Operating costs also need to be kept under control in order to generate more cash from sales.

Please contact me if you need any further information.

Signed: An Accountant

Appendix: Accounting ratios

		20X7	20X8	20X9
1	*Operating profit margin*			
	$\dfrac{\text{Profit before interest}}{\text{Revenue}} \times 100\%$	$\dfrac{(50+45)}{1,850} \times 100\%$	$\dfrac{(60+60)}{2,200} \times 100\%$	$\dfrac{(50+90)}{2,500} \times 100\%$
		= 5.1%	= 5.5%	= 5.6%
2	*Operating costs*			
	$\dfrac{\text{Other operating costs}}{\text{Revenue}} \times 100\%$	$\dfrac{550}{1,850} \times 100\%$	$\dfrac{640}{2,200} \times 100\%$	$\dfrac{700}{2,500} \times 100\%$
		= 29.7%	= 29.1%	= 28.0%
3	*Inventory turnover*			
	$\dfrac{\text{Cost of sales}}{\text{Inventory}}$	$\dfrac{1,250}{400}$	$\dfrac{1,500}{540}$	$\dfrac{1,750}{620}$
		= 3.1 times	= 2.8 times	= 2.8 times
4	*Trade receivables turnover*			
	$\dfrac{\text{Trade receivables}}{\text{Credit sales}} \times 365$	$\dfrac{492}{(300+45)} \times 365$	$\dfrac{550}{(400+60)} \times 365$	$\dfrac{633}{(600+90)} \times 365$
		= 521 days	= 436 days	= 335 days

(*Note.* Interest from credit sales has been added, as this is likely to be included in the trade receivables figure)

5	Cash generated from operations	20X8	20X9
		$m	$m
	Profit before interest	120	140
	Depreciation	60	70
	Increase in inventory	(140)	(80)
	Increase in trade receivables	(58)	(83)
	Increase in trade payables	–	10
		(18)	57

6 ROCE

	20X7	20X8	20X9
$\dfrac{\text{Profit before interest}}{\text{Net assets}+\text{borrowings}}\times 100\%$	$\dfrac{95}{(372+520)}\times100\%$	$\dfrac{120}{(382+720)}\times100\%$	$\dfrac{140}{(372+930)}\times100\%$
	= 10.7%	= 11.0%	= 10.8%

7 Interest cover

	20X7	20X8	20X9
$\dfrac{\text{Profit before interest}}{\text{Interest payable}}$	$\dfrac{95}{25}=3.8$	$\dfrac{120}{60}=2.0$	$\dfrac{140}{110}=1.3$

8 Gearing

$\dfrac{\text{Borrowings}}{\text{Net assets}+\text{borrowings}}$	$\dfrac{520}{892}=58.3\%$	$\dfrac{720}{1,102}=65.3\%$	$\dfrac{930}{1,302}=71.4\%$

9 Asset turnover

$\dfrac{\text{Revenue}}{\text{Net assets}+\text{borrowings}}$	$\dfrac{1,850}{892}=2.1$	$\dfrac{2,200}{1,102}=2.1$	$\dfrac{2,500}{1,302}=1.92$

52 Grow by acquisition

Text references. Off balance sheet finance is covered in Chapter 16. Changes in price levels are covered in Chapter 11.

Top tips. This question requires students to amend financial statements so that they are comparable for analysis. To obtain full marks in Part (a), you need to adjust the financial statements to give a common basis for accounting for non-current assets. In practice this involves reversing the effects of a revaluation carried out by Company B. Students also need to reverse out the effects of a 'window-dressing' type transaction that is carried out by Company A. Part (b) should be straightforward. In Part (c) you need to comment on the changes made in Parts (a) and (b). A key factor here is the potential effect on the investment choice following the adjustments. In Part (d) the key distinction between historical cost and other systems is that the historical system is based on verifiable transactions that have already occurred whilst other systems are based on estimates.

The change from the usual type of ratio question seemed to throw some candidates. Many students encountered problems in correctly computing the adjustments required in respect of the non-current asset valuation. Answers to Part (c) were particularly disappointing. Part (d) was well answered.

(a) **Note 1**

The substance of this transaction is that X has made a loan of $2.4m to A. All aspects of the 'sale' should be eliminated, as follows.

(i) Reduce revenue by $2,400,000.
(ii) Reduce cost of sales by $2,400,000 × 100/160 = $1,500,000.
(iii) Reduce gross profit by ($2,400,000 − $1,500,000) = $900,000.
(iv) Increase loans by $2,400,000.

Note 2

To be comparable, the non-current assets of A and B should either both be shown at cost or both at a revalued amount, with the revaluation done on the same basis. It is not feasible to 'revalue' A's non-current assets for purposes of comparison. However, B's non-current assets can be shown at cost by reversing out the revaluation, as follows.

(i)   Reduce non-current assets by $5,000,000.
(ii) Reduce the revaluation reserve to nil.
(iii) Reduce cost of sales by $1,000,000. This is the excess depreciation no longer required.
(iv) Increase gross profit by $1,000,000.

Summary

A

Item	Per original f/s	Adjustment	New figure
	$'000	$'000	$'000
Revenue	68,000	(2,400)	65,600
Cost of sales	42,000	(1,500)	40,500
Gross profit	26,000	(900)	25,100
Profit before interest and tax	8,000	(900)	7,100
Inventory	6,000	1,500	7,500
Short term borrowing	-	2,400	2,400
Total borrowings (4,000 + 16,000)	20,000	2,400	22,400
Shareholders' funds	23,500	900	22,600

B

Item	Per original f/s	Adjustment	New figure
Non-current assets	35,050	(5,000)	30,050
Revaluation reserve	5,000	(5,000)	Nil
Cost of sales	45,950	(1,000)	44,950
Gross profit	20,050	1,000	21,050
Profit before interest and tax	6,050	1,000	7,050
Shareholders' funds	22,050	(5,000)	17,050

(b)   All monetary amounts in $'000

Ratio	A	B
Return on capital employed	$\dfrac{7,100}{22,600 + 22,400} = 15.8\%$	$\dfrac{7,050}{17,050 + 6,000 + 18,000} = 17.2\%$
Gross profit margin	$\dfrac{25,100}{65,600} = 38.3\%$	$\dfrac{21,050}{66,000} = 31.9\%$
Turnover of capital employed	$\dfrac{65,600}{45,000} = 1.5$	$\dfrac{66,000}{41,050} = 1.6$
Leverage	$\dfrac{22,400}{45,000} = 49.8\%$	$\dfrac{24,000}{41,050} = 58.5\%$

BPP note. The effective loan of $2.4m could arguably be excluded from borrowings as it is short term. Candidates who took this approach were not penalised.

(c)   The adjustments carried out to make the financial statements of the two entities comparable make it **far less easy to decide** which entity to target. The ratios are now far more similar. **A** has a **higher gross profit and gross profit margin**. However, the **return on capital employed is lower.** The main reason for this is that A's other operating expenses are higher than B's. The revenue figures are now nearly identical due to the elimination of the 'sale' from the accounts of A. The turnover of capital employed, both before and after adjustments, do not show significant differences.

Where **A** has an **advantage** over B is in **the leverage (gearing) ratio**. Leverage of both entities has increased, but more so in the case of B. Whether this influences the directors' decision depends on whether they intend to change the financial structure of the company.

Overall it would appear that **B** would be a **better investment**. However, there is not a great deal to choose between the two entities, and this exercise shows the importance of adjusting financial statements to achieve uniform accounting policies when making this kind of decision. It is notable that the 'sale' by A was **incorrectly** accounted for, while B's revaluation is **permissible**.

(d) **Strengths of historical cost accounting**

(i)   It is easy to understand.

(ii)   It is objective – current value systems may be regarded as subjective.

(iii)   The historical cost of an element can be measured reliably, as it is generally the consideration given or received.

(iv)   Current value systems may mislead the user into thinking that the balance sheet indicates the value of the business as a going concern. This would not happen with historical cost accounting.

Weaknesses of historical cost accounting

(i)   Non-current asset values are unrealistic. Historical cost may bear little relation to market value or value to the business in terms of future economic benefits.

(ii)   Items which do not have a verifiable cost of creation cannot be measured.

(iii)   Depreciation is inadequate to finance the cost of replacing a non-current asset.

(iv)   Holding gains on inventory are included in profit in times of rising prices. Arguably this is not genuine profit.

53 WXY

Text reference. Financial analysis is covered in Chapter 17.

Top tips. Part (a), the main part of the report, is quite general in its requirements. But look at the three key words: performance, position and prospects – these suggest that a range of ratios need to be calculated, covering profitability, liquidity, gearing and investors. First decide which ratios you are going to calculate. Do not spend too long calculating them but get on with the analysis.

Easy marks. As always, with ratio questions, you will gain marks for any comments you can back up, so *you can always write something*. Easy marks are available, too, for getting the report format correct.

(a)   **REPORT**

To: Finance Director
From: Finance Team, Senior member
Subject: Financial Statements of TUV for the year ended 31 December 20X3

Introduction

This report considers the performance, position and prospects of TUV based upon the financial statements for the year ended 31 December 20X3. The financial ratios upon which the report is based are included in the Appendix to the report.

General overview

Before considering the financial ratios in detail there are a number of factors that become clear from a general overview of the financial statements.

- **Revenue** has **increased** by almost 25% between 20X2 and 20X3
- The company has **no cash balances** at the end of 20X3 and short term borrowings have significantly increased
- The **properties** have been **revalued** during the year leading to an increase in the figure for capital employed
- The effective rate of **interest** on long-term borrowings appears to have **increased** by about 0.7% between 20X2 and 20X3.

Review of financial ratios

The general factors noted above indicate that there has been a significant increase in activity for TUV and potentially a cash flow problem that might be related to this. The analysis of the financial ratios that follows will expand upon this.

Profitability

Both the gross and operating profit **margins have improved** over the period as has the return on capital employed. This indicates an improvement in profitability although the **return on capital employed** is still relatively **low**. A further problem is that the return on shareholders' funds has decreased indicating that the best use of debt finance is not possibly being made. Some of this however may be due to the revaluation of the properties which will have increased capital employed and reduced profit by larger depreciation charges.

Liquidity

The most obvious concern with liquidity is the **lack of cash** at the end of 20X3. This is also backed up by declining and dangerous looking current and acid test ratios. There would appear to be a distinct lack of liquidity within the company.

Turning to the details of working capital management this appears to complement the feeling of **lack of liquidity**. The trade receivables collection period, already quite short at 37 days in 20X2, has been reduced to 31 days for 20X3 indicating a fairly aggressive debt collection policy. In contrast the trade payables payment period has increased from 59 to 88 days indicating that the company is taking significantly more trade credit.

From review of the working capital and liquidity ratios it would appear that TUV are showing signs of **overtrading**. Their revenue has increased significantly with a small increase in profit but this has led to a significant increase in inventory holdings, which will tie up cash, a small rise in receivables and a significant increase in short term funding from creditors.

Gearing

The **levels of debt to equity** within the company are also **of concern** although they have decreased in the 20X3 financial statements to a debt level of 166% of equity compared to 279% in the previous year. It is entirely possible that the directors decision to revalue the properties was a move to improve the gearing levels as the amount of long term borrowing has increased in absolute terms despite the decrease in the gearing ratio due to the increase in the revaluation surplus. There is little doubt however that such high levels of gearing will be of concern to both the current lenders and any potential investors in TUV. This may be evidenced by the fact that the effective rate of interest charged during 20X3 is 0.7% higher than that in 20X2 which may be indicative of lenders requiring a higher return for this increasingly risky investment.

The increase in profitability of TUV has however reflected itself in an increase in interest cover although at only 2.1 times this is still low. Perhaps more worrying however is the fact that the company has no cash with which to service the debt.

Investor confidence

The price earnings ratio of TUV at 13.5 is significantly **lower** than both our own and the industry average figure of 23.4. This indicates a lack of investor confidence in the company and a view that the investment is fairly high risk. However, it must be said that in general terms most companies listed on a secondary share trading market are likely to have a lower P/E ratio than those listed on the primary market but having said that TUV's P/E ratio does seem particularly low.

Conclusion

TUV would appear to be showing fairly **classic signs of overtrading** with a large increase in revenue and fairly severe liquidity and working capital management problems. The company is also exceptionally **highly geared** which would appear to indicate that there would be little chance of any additional debt finance being available hence the need to find equity funding in the near future. However, there is a small **increase in profitability** which may continue but in the short term the lack of cash and high gearing levels may be a threat to the company's continued operations.

APPENDIX 1: RATIOS

Financial ratios

	20X3	20X2
Profitability		
Gross profit margin 76.9/325.4 × 100	23.6%	
59.9/261.2 × 100		22.9%
Operating profit margin 29.2/325.4 × 100	9.0%	
19.7/261.2 × 100		7.5%
Return on capital employed 29.2/403.2 (W1) × 100	7.2%	
19.7/300.7 (W1) × 100		6.6%
Return on shareholders' funds 15.0/146.9 × 100	10.2%	
8.5/78.5 × 100		10.8%
Liquidity		
Current ratio 76.1/72.1	1.06	
65.3/35.0		1.87
Acid test ratio 27.4/72.1	0.38	
32.7/35.0		0.93
Inventory turnover 48.7/248.5 × 365	72 days	
32.6/201.3 × 365		59 days
Trade receivables collection period 27.4/325.4 × 365	31 days	
26.5/261.2 × 365		37 days
Trade payables payment period 59.9/248.5 × 365	88 days	
32.4/201.3 × 365		59 days
Gearing ratios		
Gearing (long term debt/shareholders funds) 244.1/146.9 × 100	166%	
219.6/78.5 × 100		279%
Interest cover 29.2/14.2	2.1 times	
19.7/11.2		1.8 times

Working: capital employed

Capital employed = Shareholders funds + long term borrowings + short term borrowings

20X3   = 146.9 + 244.1 + 12.2 = 403.2
20X2   = 78.5 + 219.6 + 2.6 = 300.7

(b) **APPENDIX 2: ADOPTION OF IFRS 2**

IFRS 2 *Share based payment* was introduced to reflect the principle that entities rewarding staff and managers by means of share options or awards should recognise the effects of such transactions.

In the financial statements the transactions should be recognised at fair value, rather than cost, which, in the case of share options, can be negligible. IFRS 2 requires the calculation of additional charges, which must be set off against income. This reduces profitability compared with pre-IFRS 2 periods. There is a corresponding increase in equity where the transaction is to be settled eventually by the issue of more shares. Where the transaction is to be settled in cash, the increase is to be shown in liabilities.

The effect can be seen in the financial statements of TUV in the statement of changes in equity, where there is an amount of **$2.3m in respect of share options**. There will be a **related charge** in the **income statement**, probably in administrative expenses.

54 EFG

Text reference. These topics are covered in Chapter 17.

Top tips. This type of question is something of a favourite with the examiner. You are asked to calculate key ratios, then to adjust for changes in accounting policies, than to re-calculate the ratios. There is a fair amount of comment and explanation as well as calculation, so make sure you allow enough time for this.

Easy marks. Obviously part (a), the original ratio calculations get you two easy marks. However, don't forget that the same easy marks will be available for re-calculating the ratios if even, if you make a mistake with the adjustments.

(a) Gross profit margin $= \dfrac{429}{1,810} \times 100 = 23.7\%$

Operating profit margin $= \dfrac{193}{1,810} \times 100 = 10.7\%$

Return on total capital employed $= \dfrac{193}{769 + 248} = 19.0\%$

Gearing $= \dfrac{248}{769} \times 100 = 32.2\%$

(b) *Adjustments to financial statements*

INCOME STATEMENT

	$'000
Revenue	1,810
Cost of sales (1,381 – 10 (W1) – 6 (W4))	1,365
Gross profit	445
Operating expenses (236 – 46 (W2))	(190)
Profit before interest and tax	255
Finance cost	(9)
Profit before tax	246
Income tax expense	(50)
Net profit for the year	196

BALANCE SHEET

	$'000	$'000
Non-current assets		
Property, plant and equipment (707 – 200 (W1))		507
Current assets		
Inventories (201 + 17 (W4))	218	
Trade receivables	247	
Cash (18 + 46 (W2))	64	
		529
		1,036

	$'000	$'000
Equity		
Share capital (350 – 50 (W3))	300	
Revaluation surplus (200 – 200 (W1))		
Retained earnings (219 + 11 (W4) – 134 + 196 – 10)	282	
		582
Non-current liabilities		
Long-term borrowings (248 + 50 (W3))		298
Current liabilities		
Trade payables	142	
Income tax	14	
		156
		1,036

Financial ratios after adjustments

Gross profit margin $= \dfrac{445}{1,810} \times 100 = 24.6\%$

Operating profit margin $= \dfrac{255}{1,810} \times 100 = 14.1\%$

Return on total capital employed $= \dfrac{255}{582 + 298} \times 100 = 29.0\%$

Gearing $= \dfrac{298}{582} \times 100 = 51.2\%$

Advice to directors

According to EFG's criteria the initial screening of J, before adjustments, would have meant that none of the four criteria for the key ratios were met and therefore the assessment of J would have been abandoned at that stage.

After adjustments for operating and accounting policies the operating profit margin meets the criteria of exceeding 13% and the return on total capital employed meets the criteria of exceeding 25%. The gross profit margin at 24.6% only just fails the 25% criteria. However the gearing ratio, at 51.2%, is significantly higher than the level of 25% maximum set by EFG's criteria. Therefore on the face of it the potential investment in J should not be pursued further although it may be treated as a borderline case.

Workings

1   *Revaluation*

The balance on the revaluation account of $200,000 must be deducted from non-current assets in order to reduce the value to depreciated historical cost. The transfer from the revaluation surplus to retained earnings of $10,000 is the additional annual depreciation charge due to the revaluation. This must be added back in the income statement by reducing cost of sales by $10,000.

2   *Bonus*

To reflect EFG's policy of no bonus payments but higher salaries the $96,000 bonus must be deducted from operating expenses and additional charge of $50,000 made which requires a net deduction from operating expenses of $46,000. The bonus and the additional wages can be assumed to be cash expenses therefore there will be an increase in cash balance of $46,000.

3   *Preferred shares*

The $50,000 of preferred share capital must be deducted from share capital and added into non-current liabilities.

4   *Inventories*

Opening inventory for J must be increased by $11,000 and closing inventories increased by $17,000. This has the net effect of decreasing cost of sales by $6,000.

The opening adjustment of $11,000 is an increase in opening retained earnings and the closing adjustment is an increase in inventories in the balance sheet by $17,000.

(c)   **Advantage of EFG's approach**

The appraisal of potential acquisition targets is a task which requires a lot of senior management time. Therefore the principal advantage of EFG's approach, by assessing just four key ratios initially, is to be able to weed out any clearly unsuitable potential targets before any great amount of time and effort has been expended upon assessing them.

Limitation of EFG's approach

However the drawback to EFG's approach is that it could be regarded as overly simplistic. Only four financial ratios are initially considered and all four must satisfy the criteria before any further assessment of the company is made. This may mean that potentially attractive companies fail, perhaps one of the criteria, and are no longer considered. This might be particularly true of the low criteria set by EFG for the gearing level of potential acquisitions. Many very successful companies are highly geared as this is often a cheaper and more efficient method of financing than equity finance. Therefore some potentially good investment opportunities may be missed at this initial stage by strict adherence to all four criteria, such as J itself.

Specific weakness in the appraisal of J

This might be the adjustment for salaries. The bonus that J pays to its highly skilled team of sales representatives would be replaced by EFG by higher fixed salaries. However this means a net drop in income for the sales representative of $46,000 which may not be acceptable to them. If a number of these sales representatives leave J due to this policy then the current level of sales may not continue therefore decreasing the desirability of J as a potential target.

55 DM

> **Text reference**. Financial analysis is covered in Chapter 17.
>
> **Top tips.** You should start by calculating the relevant accounting ratios. However, since there are only five marks out of 25, you should not spend too long doing this. Next, you should comment on significant items in the ratios. There are eight marks for this. Comparing the results with the sector information gives you another three marks, and four are available for comment on the possible manipulation of the financial statements.
>
> **Easy marks.** With ratio questions *you can always say something.*. Marks are available for saying things like 'gross profit margin has remained the same'. However, to get a pass you will have to give some reasons why. They don't need to be deep, but they need to be there.
>
> **Examiner's comments**. The main criticism of the examiner for this question is that in many instances lots of ratios were calculated but very little analysis carried out. Start the answer by calculating some key ratios but only those that you think may be of use in your answer. Note that the question specifically refers to the possibility of creative accounting regarding the increase in asset lives and this must be alluded to in the answer.

(a)   **Report to investor**

Date: October 20X5

This report has been prepared at your request based upon the financial statements of DM for the last two years to 31 December 20X4. A number of ratios have been calculated and these, together with some supermarket sector comparatives, are included in the appendix to this report.

Profitability – revenue

During 20X4 DM has opened 6 new stores which is an expansion rate of 17% although this has led to an increase in revenue of only 3%. It has also led to a fall in annual sales per store although the **annual store sales** for DM are still considerably higher than the sector average. However this may simply be due to the fact that DM has larger stores than the average. The reduction in annual sales per store may also be due to the fact that not all of the new stores were fully operational for the entire year.

Profitability – gross profit margin

Gross profit margin has remained the same for the last two years and is marginally **higher than the industry average**. In contrast the operating profit margin has increased 18% over the two year period although we have no sector comparative to compare this to. However we are told that the directors have reviewed the useful lives of the non-current assets and in most cases have increased them. This in turn will reduce the annual depreciation charge and therefore increase operating profit although there has been no real improvement in operating performance.

Profitability – net profit margin

Net profit margin for DM has increased from 2.9% to 3.7% and is now approaching the sector average. As the interest cost and tax expense have largely remained constant between the two years then this increase in net profit margin is due to the increased operating margin which in turn may be due to the change in depreciation charges.

Asset utilisation – asset turnover

The overall non-current asset turnover has **increased slightly over last year** but is still lower than the sector average. This increase could be due to the new stores although the non-current asset figure has remained almost the same as last year which is surprising due to the opening of the new stores. However it is possible that most of the capital expenditure on the new stores was actually incurred last year before the stores were brought into operation.

Asset utilisation – current ratio

The **current ratio is low** in both years as would be expected in a supermarket but has improved. There is also a distinct increase in the amount of cash being held. The inventory turnover period has not changed although there has been a slight increase in the payables payment period which will have a positive effect on cash flow. Finally the level of gearing has remained fairly constant and would not appear to be a problem.

Conclusion

DM has been **expanding** in the last two year and has appeared to **maintain and indeed improve its profitability** during this period. Its gross profit margin compares well with the sector average as do sales per store although the net profit margin has not kept pace with the sector average. It is possible, however, that the increasing operating profit margin and therefore net profit margin have been **manipulated** by the directors by the **increase in useful lives of the non-current assets** and therefore reduction in depreciation charges, This may have been done in order to encourage a high offer in any takeover bid that might be made. The directors would of course benefit personally from the sale of their individual stakes in the company at a high price but from the evidence we have it is not possible to state conclusively that this is the case. Further information would be required.

APPENDIX – RATIOS

	20X4	20X3	Sector
Gross profit margin	78/1,255 × 100 = 6.2%	75/1,220 × 100 = 6.1%	5.9%
Operating profit margin	57/1,255 × 100 = 4.5%	46/1,220 × 100 = 3.8%	
Net profit margin	33/1,255 × 100 = 2.6%	23/1,220 × 100 = 1.9%	3.9%
Annual sales per store	1,255/42 = $29.9m	1,220/38 = $32.1m	$27.6m
Non-current asset turnover	1,255/680 = 1.85	1,220/675 = 1.81	1.93

	20X4	20X3	Sector
Current ratio	105/317 = 0.33	71/309 = 0.23	
Inventory turnover	47/1,177 × 365 = 14.6 days	46/1,145 × 365 = 14.7 days	
Payables payment period	297/1,177 × 365 = 92 days	273/1,145 × 365 = 87 days	

(b) Sector comparatives can provide useful information in ratio analysis but as with all comparisons there are both general and specific drawbacks. These include the following.

(i) The sector figures are an **average** figure for the sector and therefore can be easily **affected by** just a **few abnormal** results or figures.

(ii) The companies included in the sector figures may be of **different sizes** which may affect their sector results.

(iii) The companies included in the sector figures may have **different year ends** which may affect the balance sheet figures used in a variety of ratios particularly in the retail business.

(iv) As with all comparisons the different companies in the sector may have **different accounting policies** which may mean that their results and resulting ratios are not strictly comparable.

(v) There are a number of **different ways of calculating various key ratios** and if different companies in the sector calculate them in these different ways they will not be comparable.

(vi) The **sector information may not contain all of the ratios** that might be called upon for a full analysis. For example in this case information about the average operating profit margin and average gearing for the sector might be useful.

56 BZJ

Text reference. EPS is covered in Chapter 15.

Top tips. Part a) is a very straightforward EPS calculation . In Part (b) there is a lot of information, so start by calculating some of the most basic ratios covering profitability, liquidity and gearing. These will soon give you an idea of where you will be going with your narrative. Remember to comment on the EPS figures that you will have calculated for Part (a). Do allow yourself time to produce a decent report as the marks will be available for the analysis rather than the calculation of the ratios. Make sure in Part (c) that you relate the Chairman's statement to the evidence you find in the financial statements.

Easy marks. Keep writing, as you can always find something to say. Even if your conclusions are different from the examiner's or you make a mistake in your calculations, you will gain easy marks.

(a) *Earnings per share*

Year ended 31 December 20X4

$$\text{EPS} = \frac{\$3,676,000}{2,800,000}$$

$$= 131.3c$$

Year ended 31 December 20X5

$$\text{EPS} = \frac{\$2,460,000}{2,850,000}$$

$$= 86.3c$$

Working: number of shares 20X5

Date	Narrative	Shares	Time	Weighted Average
1.1.X5	b/f	2,800,000	$\times \frac{10}{12}$	2,333,333
1.11.X5	Issue at full market price	300,000		
		3,100,000	$\times \frac{2}{12}$	516,667
				2,850,000

(b)

REPORT

To: Investor
From: Advisor
Date: March 20X6
Subject: **BZJ Group financial statements year ended 31 December 20X5**

As requested I have considered the financial statements of the BZJ Group for the year ended 31 December 20X5 and have calculated various financial ratios for 20X5 and 20X4 which are included in an appendix to this report.

Profitability

There do appear to be some **concerns about the financial performance and profitability** of the group during 20X5. There has been no evidence of growth in performance and indeed a 0.8% **decrease in revenue** from last year despite the large investment in the group during 20X5. There has also been a significant decrease in return on total capital employed from 15.3% to 8.5% and in return on equity from 21.5% to 12.0%.

Reasons for fall in return

These decreases in overall return have been caused both by **decreases in operating profitability and reduced performance**. Both the gross profit margin and operating profit margin have shown significant decreases over the position in 20X4. It is possible that these reduced margins have been caused partly by increased depreciation charges due to the investment of approximately $18 million in additional property, plant and equipment. More worryingly, however, the fall in margins may be due to the new storage products or the Middle East market where margins may be lower. If this is the case, then it is possible that these lower profit margins will continue in the future.

Asset turnover

Both **asset turnover** and **non-current asset turnover** have shown **significant decreases** indicating that the additional investment in non-current assets and working capital have not resulted in increased turnover. However it should be borne in mind that the additional finance was only raised two months before the year end, and if the non-current asset additions were also made at the same time then they have had only a short period in which to be used effectively.

Liquidity

In overall terms the liquidity of the business certainly appears to be **less healthy** at 31 December 20X5 than it was a year earlier. The cash balances found a year ago have been replaced by substantial short term borrowings, and both the current ratio and acid test ratio have decreased significantly. Although there would appear to be no immediate liquidity crisis, there is a definite trend towards a lower level of liquidity in the group.

Inventory turnover

Inventory turnover at the end of 20X4 was already quite long at 97 days but this has **increased significantly** at the end of 20X5 to 131 days. This could be due to a build up of inventory prior to anticipated growth in turnover in 20X6 or alternatively may indicate that the new products are not selling as fast as was anticipated.

Receivables and payables

On the brighter side there has been an improvement in the trade receivables period meaning that money is being received more quickly from credit customers. However, the payables period of 111 days is very long (an increase from 87 days at the end of 20X4) although this could be partly due to the large amount of purchases from foreign countries.

Gearing

During the year, $10 million of loan finance has been raised together with over $3.5 million of short term borrowings. These increases have led to an already high debt/equity ratio of 62.9% at the end of 20X4 rising to 81.7% at the end of 20X5. The funds have clearly been used to fund part of the investment in additional property, plant and equipment and as noted above it may be that these assets are not yet being used to their full potential.

It must be noted, however, that the 300,000 shares issued in November 20X5 were fully subscribed for at a premium of $4 per share which would indicate that the market is not concerned about this **high level of gearing**.

Interest cost

The additional loan finance has obviously **affected** the **interest cost** in the income statement and interest cover has reduced from 7.3 times last year to 3.7 times at the end of 20X5. While this still gives the group a fairly reasonable margin of safety, if the interest charged in the income statement is compared to the short term and long term borrowings at the year end the average rate is only 5%. This indicates that the additional finance has not been in place for long and that therefore there is likely to be an increase in the interest charges in 20X6.

Investors

From an investor's point of view there has clearly been a **marked decrease in their returns**. Earnings per share has decreased from 131.3c to 86.3c and dividend per share has decreased from 13c to 5c. In line with the Chairman's comments, funds are clearly being retained within the business for expansion as dividend cover has increased from 10.1 times last year to 15.87 times this year.

Chairman's comments

The Chairman's statement indicates that the new management are investing in new products, new markets and new property, plant and equipment in order to expand and grow the business. It is clear that there is indeed a large investment in new non-current assets and in working capital but as yet this **investment has not fed through to improved performance** with all profitability measures in decline. However, the new product was not put into production until September 20X5 and the additional finance for the non-current asset investment was not raised until November 20X5, therefore it is likely that the 20X5 financial statements do not yet show the full extent of the results of this expansion programme. The reduced dividend indicates that funds are being retained within the business to fund the growth plans as the Chairman explains, and it is to be hoped that these plans will, as stated by the Chairman, lead to 'increased returns to investors within the next two to three years', although there is little evidence of this in the financial statements for 20X5.

Conclusion

There is concern about the profit margins in the group, the management of working capital and the uses to which the additional investment are being put. However, there would appear to be no immediate concerns about the position of the business and hope that management's **expansionary plans** may come to fruition in 20X6 and beyond.

		20X5	20X4
(i)	**Profitability**		

Gross profit margin
17,342/120,366 × 100   14.4%
19,065/121,351 × 100   15.7%

Operating profit margin
5,377/120,366 × 100   4.5%
6,617/121,315 × 100   5.5%

Return on total capital employed
5,377/30,428 + 2,270 + 26,700 + 3,662   8.5%
6,617/24,623 + 1,947 + 16,700   15.3%

Asset turnover
120,366/30,428 + 2,270 + 26,700 + 3,662   1.91
121,315/24,623 + 1,947 + 16,700   2.80

Non-current asset turnover
120,366/43,575   2.76
121,351/24,320   4.99

Return on equity
2,908/30,428 + 2,270   12.0%
5,711/24,623 + 1,947   21.5%

(ii) **Liquidity**

Current ratio
52,030/36,207   1.44
44,951/26,001   1.73

Acid test ratio
14,922/36,207   0.41
17,691/26,001   0.68

Inventory turnover
37,108/103,024 × 365   131 days
27,260/102,286 × 365   97 days

Receivables turnover
14,922/120,366 × 365   45 days
17,521/121,351 × 365   53 days

Payables turnover
31,420/103,024 × 365   111 days
24,407/102,286 × 365   87 days

(iii) **Gearing**

Debt/equity ratio
26,700/30,428 + 2,270 × 100   81.7%
16,700/24,623 + 1,947 × 100   62.9%

Interest cover
5,377/1,469   3.7
6,617/906   7.3

(iv)   **Investor ratios**

Dividend per share

155/3,100	5c	
364/2,800		13c

Dividend cover

2,460/155	15.87	
3,676/364		10.1

57 ABC

Text reference. Financial analysis is covered in Chapter 17.

Top tip. In Part (a) use the list of key data given as a structure for your comparison and make sure that you do use each of the key pieces of data given in your answer. In Part (b) do not limit yourself to a list of the standard limitations of ratio analysis but apply it to an international stage and apply it to the particular scenario given.

Easy marks. These may be obtained by making full use of the information given to you in the question. Do not be afraid to state the obvious, for example that the revenue and net assets are similar for all three companies.

REPORT

To: Directors of ABC
From: Assistant to CFO
Date: May 20X6
Subject: Possible takeover targets – W, Y and Z

As requested this report provides a comparison of the key data for the three potential takeover targets, W, Y and Z and our own similar data and also discussion of the validity of inter-firm and international comparisons.

(a)   **Comparison of company performance**

All three of the potential takeover targets have a **similar level of revenue and net assets**. In terms of both revenue and asset value they are all approximately **one tenth of the size of ABC**.

Profitability

Z appears to be clearly the **most profitable** with significantly higher gross profit margin, operating profit margin and return on total capital employed than the other two companies. Indeed its gross profit margin and return on total capital employed are both higher than those of ABC. However, these ratios are based upon pre-tax figures, and it should be noted that the income tax rate in Zeelandia is significantly higher than in Bolandia or the other two countries.

Assets and liabilities

All three companies have a significantly **lower current ratio than ABC**, with those of W and Z looking quite low indeed for a light engineering business. All three companies **hold their inventories for significantly longer than ABC** with the inventory turnover of W the highest at 68 days which may indicate slow-moving or obsolete inventory. **Receivables turnover** in all three companies is **similar** and also very similar to that of ABC probably reflecting the similar nature of the businesses and their customers. However, there is a much wider fluctuation in payables turnover periods with that of Z seeming high at 73 days. This may be a conscious policy, given Z's fairly low current ratio, or may be due to poor payables management.

Gearing

ABC's gearing level is very low with debt amounting to about 5% of equity and it is group policy that group gearing should not be increased. The level of gearing in Z is **even lower** than that of ABC which is possibly understandable given the higher level of interest rates in Zeelandia. However, **W** has a **much higher** level of gearing with debt being approximately 50% of equity, possibly due to the lower rate of interest in Winlandia.

This gearing would increase the group gearing to approximately 8% if W were acquired, but of course upon acquisition ABC could decide to reduce the borrowings of W if these were not acceptable.

P/E ratios

As would be expected of four companies in the same type of business the four **P/E ratios are within a fairly narrow band**. The P/E ratio of W is lowest at 12.6, possibly indicating that the shares are relatively undervalued, or that the investment is viewed as more risky due to its gearing or that the most recent earnings figures (January 20X6) have not yet been reflected in the share price.

Conclusion

There do not appear to be any major problems with any of the three companies. However, on the basis of this basic, preliminary analysis company Z would appear to be the superior company in terms of performance and of our requirements for a takeover company. Before any conclusions are drawn, a great deal of further information and analysis would be required.

(b) **Inter-firm and international comparisons**

There are always limitations to the validity of inter-firm comparisons and these can be exacerbated when the comparison is being made between companies in different countries.

Accounting standards

The figures that appear in the financial statements, and therefore the financial ratios that are calculated from these figures, will be affected by the accounting standards followed by each company. In this case ABC, W and Z all use IFRS but the financial statements of Y have been prepared according to Yolandian GAAP. There may be significant differences between Yolandian GAAP and IFRS.

Accounting policies

Even if the financial statements are prepared using IFRS there could still be significant differences between the accounting policies of the companies. For example, if some companies value their property, plant and equipment at depreciated cost whereas others use the valuation model, then this will significantly affect the financial statements and the financial ratios calculated from those statements such as return on total capital employed.

Size of companies

The size of a company can affect the figures and ratios. In this case all three potential target companies are approximately the same size but they are all about 10% of the size of ABC. This may affect comparison of figures between the companies and ABC as ABC may well benefit from economies of scale.

Type of business

Although all four companies are said to be in the same business, provision of light engineering products and services, it is likely in practice that there could be considerable differences between the detailed patterns of business which affect comparison of the figures. For example some companies may provide products through hire or leasing which would change the profile of their financial statements.

Single period comparison

As with all comparisons of financial indicators a single period set of figures gives no indication of the trend of figures and on its own may be misleading.

Accounting date

The comparison has been based upon financial statements for all three companies for periods ending before those of ABC. In particular, those of Y and Z are based on financial statements nine months before those of ABC. Obviously a lot can change in a company in that sort of time period, and it could be argued that the financial figures for Y and Z are too out of date to be particularly meaningful.

International economies

Each of the four companies is based in a different country, although they at least share a common currency. Each of these countries exhibits considerable differences in interest rates and tax rates and each is likely to differ in terms of economic state. The economic cycle and regulatory regime of the country can have a significant effect on the figures in the financial statements reducing the value of comparison. Similarly the size and nature of the stock market in each country could affect the P/E ratios that have been quoted. In a small, illiquid stock market, share prices and therefore P/E ratios will tend to be lower than those in a larger more liquid market.

58 AXZ

Text reference. Financial analysis is covered in Chapter 17. International issues are covered in Chapter 19.

Top tips. There are a lot of ratios to crunch through. Be methodical. Set out your adjustments to the financial statements clearly first, then if you make a mistake, the marker can still give you credit in your ratio calculations and report.

Easy marks. There are quite a few marks for mechanical number crunching.

Examiner's comments. Many candidates had difficultly calculating return on equity and capital employed.

(a) **Accounting ratios before adjustments**

	AXZ	DCB	GFE
Gross profit margin			
$\frac{2,700}{8,300} \times 100$; $\frac{600}{1,900} \times 100$; $\frac{800}{2,200} \times 100$	32.5%	31.6%	36.4%
Profit before tax as a % of sales			
$\frac{1,461}{8,300} \times 100$; $\frac{335}{1,900} \times 100$; $\frac{420}{2,200} \times 100$	17.6%	17.6%	19.1%
Return on equity			
$\frac{1,095}{4,820} \times 100$; $\frac{201}{1,350} \times 100$; $\frac{315}{1,931} \times 100$	22.7%	14.9%	16.3%
Return on total capital employed			
$\frac{1,461+105}{4,820+1,500} \times 100$; $\frac{335+25}{1,350+500} \times 100$;	24.8%	19.5%	
$\frac{420+65}{1,931+650} \times 100$			18.8%
Non-current asset turnover			
$\frac{8,300}{9,950}$; $\frac{1,900}{1,680}$; $\frac{2,200}{2,400}$	0.83 times	1.13 times	0.92 times
Gearing			
$\frac{1,500}{4,820} \times 100$; $\frac{500}{1,350} \times 100$; $\frac{650}{1,931} \times 100$	31.1%	37.0%	33.7%

Accounting ratios after adjustments

	AXZ	DCB	GFE
Gross profit margin			
$\frac{2,700}{8,300} \times 100$; $\frac{667}{1,900} \times 100$; $\frac{800}{2,200} \times 100$	32.5%	35.1%	36.4%

	AXZ	DCB	GFE

Profit before tax as a % of sales

$$\frac{1,461}{8,300} \times 100; \quad \frac{402}{1,900} \times 100; \quad \frac{415}{2,200} \times 100$$

	AXZ	DCB	GFE
	17.6%	21.2%	18.9%

Return on equity

$$\frac{1,095}{4,820} \times 100; \quad \frac{268}{1,552} \times 100; \quad \frac{310}{1,831} \times 100$$

	AXZ	DCB	GFE
	22.7%	17.3%	16.9%

Return on total capital employed

$$\frac{1,461+105}{4,820+1,500} \times 100; \quad \frac{402+25}{1,552+500} \times 100;$$

	AXZ	DCB
	24.8%	20.81%

$$\frac{415+70}{1,831+750} \times 100$$

	GFE
	18.8%

Non-current asset turnover

$$\frac{8,300}{9,950}; \quad \frac{1,900}{1,882}; \quad \frac{2,200}{2,400}$$

	AXZ	DCB	GFE
	0.83 times	1.00 times	0.92 times

Gearing

$$\frac{1,500}{4,820} \times 100; \quad \frac{500}{1,552} \times 100; \quad \frac{750}{1,831} \times 100$$

	AXZ	DCB	GFE
	31.1%	32.2%	40.1%

Workings

1   *Reworked figures after accounting adjustments*

	DCB	GFE
	$'000	$'000
Revenue	1,900	2,200
Cost of sales (W2)	(1,233)	(1,400)
Gross profit	667	800
Distribution costs	(60)	(65)
Administrative expenses	(180)	(250)
Finance costs (W3)	(25)	(70)
Profit before tax	402	415
Income tax expense	(134)	(105)
Profit for the period	268	310
Total equity (1,350 + 202)	1,552	
(1,931 − 100)		1,831
Non-current liabilities	500	
(650 + 100)		750
Non-current assets (W2)	1,882	2,400

2   *Depreciation adjustment – DCB*

Non-current assets

$1,680 = \text{Cost} - ((12.5\% \times \text{cost}) \times 3)$

Let cost = x

$$1,680 = x - 37.5\%x$$

$$1,680 = 62.5\%x$$

$$x = 2,688$$

Net book value of non-current assets adjusted:

2,688 − ((2,688 × 10%) × 3 = 1,882

∴ Adjustment to equity = 1882 − 1,680
= 202

Depreciation charge for year was 2,688 × 12.5% = 336

Adjusted depreciation charge 2,688 × 10% = 269

Cost of sales = 1,300 − 336 + 269 = 1,233

3   *Finance cost adjustment – GFE*

GFE finance costs = 65 + ($100,000 × 5%)
= 70

No effect on equity as this was charged in the statement of changes in equity. However, equity will be reduced by $100,000 as the shares are moved to borrowings.

Non-current liabilities increase to $750,000

(b)   REPORT

To: Directors of AXZ
From: Management Accountant
Date: November 20X6
Subject: Potential acquisition targets

I have assessed the financial statement information provided for DCB and GFE as requested and have calculated our key accounting ratios (see Part (a)) for these companies both based upon their original figures provided and based upon figures that are adjusted to bring their financial statements into line with IFRS.

Before adjusting for IFRS and local GAAP

On balance the **preferred investment would probably have been GFE** as its gross and operating profit margins were higher than ours whereas DCB's were either lower or the same as ours. However the drawback with GFE is that its **return on equity** and **return on capital employed** are both considerably **lower** than our own and would reduce our figures significantly.

After adjusting for IFRS and local GAAP

After adjusting the figures to bring them in line with IFRS the picture is somewhat **different**. These show a dramatic **improvement in the profitability** figures for **DCB** which now has a higher gross profit margin than ourselves (although still lower than that of GFE) and a higher operating profit margin than both ourselves and GFE. Perhaps more importantly the return on equity and return on capital employed for DCB are now only slightly lower than our own therefore would have only a marginal effect on our own ratios when combined.

Based upon the adjusted figures **GFE does not seem to be an appropriate target** as the return ratios for GFE are all considerably lower than our own despite its higher profit ratios. The reason for GFE's poor level or return can be seen if the total asset turnover is considered rather than the non-current asset turnover:

	AXZ	*DCB*	*GFE*
Total asset turnover	1.31 times	0.99 times	0.85 times

As we can see both companies are **less efficient** than ourselves in the use of their total funding but GFE is considerably so.

On top of that the **gearing level of GFE is considerably higher than our own** and a combination with GFE would increase our own gearing level to 33.5%. Whereas a combination with DCB would only increase our combined gearing level to 31.4%.

Conclusion

On the basis of the figures provided and the adjustments made to bring the accounting treatments in line with IFRS on balance an **investment in DCB would be preferred**. This would increase our gross and operating profit margins and only marginally reduce our return on equity and return on total capital employed. There would also only be a very slight increase in our overall gearing level.

59 DPC

Text references. The topics in this answer are covered in Chapters 2-6 and 17.

Top tips. You are required to prepare draft projected financial statements for DPC assuming first that PPS becomes an associate of DPC or alternatively under the second option or subsidiary.

Given the summary financial statements part (a) should be straightforward provided you note and properly account for the fact that the acquisition is to be settled from existing cash resources and an increase in borrowings.

The ratios in part (b) are also straightforward although their calculation relies on the correct preparation of part (a). For part (c) make sure you identify the *reasons* for the differences between the ratios under the different scenarios.

Easy marks. It should be fairly easy to gain full marks for part (a). Make sure you show your workings clearly for both parts (a) and (b). You will gain most of the marks for part (b) if your approach is correct even if some of the numbers from part (a) are not quite right.

A reasonably detailed discussion and identification of the reasons for the differences in ratios should help you gain most of the marks for part (c).

(a) (i) **DPC acquires 40% of the ordinary shares of PPS on 1 January 20X8**

BALANCE SHEET

	$	$
Non-current assets		50,400
Investment in associate		
Cost	3,500	
Share of post-acquisition profits (40% × 700,000)	280	
		3,780
Current assets ($82m-$1m payment out of cash resources)		81,000
		135,180
Equity (31,400,000 + 280,000)		31,680
Long-term liabilities (10,000,000 + 2,500,000)		12,500
Current liabilities		91,000
		135,180

INCOME STATEMENT

	$
Revenue	60,300
Share of profits of PPS	280
	60,580
All expenses including income tax	(55,300)
	5,280

(ii) **DPC acquires 60% of the ordinary shares of PPS on 1 January 2008**

BALANCE SHEET

	$
Goodwill (W1)	4,020
Non-current assets (50,400 + 9,800)	60,200
Current assets (82,000 + 16,000 – 3,000)	95,000
	159,220

		$
Issued equity capital		10,000
Retained earnings (W3)		21,820
		31,820
Minority interest (W2)		1,600
		33,420
Long-term liabilities (10,000 + 93,000 + 3,000)		22,300
Current liabilities		103,500
		159,220

Workings

1   *Goodwill calculation*

	$	$
Cost of investment		6,000,000
Net assets at the date of acquisition		
Issued share capital	100,000	
Retained earnings	3,200,000	
	3,300,000	
Group share (60%)		1,980,000
Goodwill		4,020,000

2   *Minority interest*

This is 40% of the net assets of PPS: 40% × $4,000,000 = $1,600,000.

3   *Consolidated retained earnings*

	$
Retained earnings of DPC	21,400,000
60% of post-acquisition retained earnings of PPS	420,000
	21,820,000

INCOME STATEMENT

	$
Revenue (60,300,000 + 10,200,000)	70,500
All expenses including income tax (55,300,000 + 9,500,000)	(64,800)
Profit for the period	5,700

	$ 000
Attributable to:	
Equity holders of the parent	5,420
Minority interst (40% × 700,000)	280
	5,700

(b)   The EPS is calculated as follows

$$EPS = \frac{Earnings}{Number\ of\ shares}$$

The EPS for the three cases is shown in the table below. The number of shares remains the same in all three cases. Consolidated earnings when DPC acquires 60% of PPS are defined as net of minority interest.

	DPC and its existing subsidiaries	DPC including the acquisition of an associate interest in PPS	DPC including the acquisition of a subsidiary interest in PPS
Earnings	$5,000	$5,280	$5,420
Number of shares	10,0000,000	10,0000,000	10,0000,000
EPS	$0.5	$0.53	$0.54

The gearing ratio is defined as

$$\frac{\text{Total long-term debt}}{\text{Equity}}$$

	DPC and its existing subsidiaries	DPC including the acquisition of an associate interest in PPS	DPC including the acquisition of a subsidiary interest in PPS
Total long-term debt	$10,000	$12,500	$22,300
Equity	$31,400	$31,680	$31,820
Ratio	31.85%	39.46%	70.08%

The non-current asset turnover ratio is defined as:

$$\frac{\text{Revenues}}{\text{Non-current assets}}$$

	DPC and its existing subsidiaries	DPC including the acquisition of an associate interest in PPS	DPC including the acquisition of a subsidiary interest in PPS
Revenues	$60,300	$60,300	$70,500
Non-current assets	$50,400	$54,180	$64,220
Ratio	1.20	1.11	1.10

(c) **Earnings per share** will increase when DPC acquires part of PPS since the acquisition is not funded by issuing new shares and there is no increase in the number of shares.

The **non-current asset turnover ratio** measures the **efficiency** of **non-current assets**. Before any acquisition for every $1 invested in assets, DPC produces $1.20 in revenues. This falls to 1.11 when it acquires 40% of PPS because the asset base increases without a corresponding increase in revenue. The ratio falls to 1.10 when DPC acquires 60% of PPS. This fall is due to the fact that the **non-current asset turnover ratio** for PPS is much lower at $\frac{10,200}{9,800} = 1.04$, and on consolidation it affects the ratio of the combined entity.

The **gearing ratio** will increase in both cases because the acquisition in both cases is partly funded by long-term borrowing. The increase in borrowing is larger when the company acquires 60% of PPS and the impact on the **gearing ratio** is more severe.

60 DAS

To: A. Smith
From: J. Brown
Date: XX.XX.XX
Subject: Report on DAS plc

The available financial statements cover a period of only two years and it is therefore difficult to discern long-term trends in the underlying performance of DAS. It is possible, however, to express a view on the short-term prospects of the company.

Business prospects

In 20X6, the company sold 1,080 new houses, whereas in 20X7, it sold only 675. The reason for the fall in the number of houses sold was the concentration of the company resources in the development of a new site from which it expects to sell 225 houses in 20X8. The average price per house in 20X6 was $225,000 whereas the average price per house sold in 20X7 was $233,900. The average price of a house from the new development is expected to be $513,000. Thus in 20X8 the company should expect revenues of about $115 million from the new development alone.

The economic environment

The demand for housing for the last two financial years was strong, resulting in significant increases in house prices. Revenues in the next financial year and beyond will be determined by the demand for new houses. If interest rates remain at the same level and general economic conditions such as growth and employment remain favourable, then the demand for new houses will remain buoyant. If interest rates on the other hand are expected to increase, then it is possible that the demand for new houses will slow down, resulting in lower revenue growth.

Financial analysis

Given the economic conditions, the ability of the company to take advantage of these conditions, as well as to withstand adverse developments, will depend on its financial characteristics. We look at the following financial ratios which measure different aspects of the financial performance of the company.

Gross profit margin

The gross profit margin ratio is defined as $\dfrac{\text{sales less cost of sales}}{\text{Sales}}$. The value of the ratio for the last two years is:

20X7	20X6
$\dfrac{31.4}{157.9} \times 100 = 19.9\%$	$\dfrac{50.3}{243} \times 100 = 20.70\%$

The gross margin has remained fairly constant in both periods with small decrease in 20X7 over the previous year.

Asset turnover ratio

The asset turnover ratio is defined as $\dfrac{\text{Revenues}}{\text{Total assets}}$. This ratio measures the efficiency with which assets are used.

20X7

$\dfrac{157.9}{283} = 0.558$

20X6

$\dfrac{243}{291.3} = 0.834$

Asset efficiency has fallen between 20X6 and 20X7. This is primarily due to the reduction in revenue which has fallen by 35% over the previous year, whereas total assets fell by only marginally by 2.9%. It would appear that the fall in asset efficiency should not be of concern. The fall in revenue is expected to be reversed in 20X8 if economic conditions remain buoyant and demand for housing reflects the 20X6 and 20X7 prevailing conditions.

This is because, although sales have been agreed fro nearly half of the new developments and deposits have been received, DAS does not recognise revenue until legal completion.

Return on equity

The return on shareholders' funds is defined as $\dfrac{\text{Profits attributable to equity holders}}{\text{Equity}} \times 100$. This ratio measures the performance of the business and its ability to generate a return to equity contributors that covers the cost of equity capital. The higher the return on shareholders' funds the healthier the prospects for the company.

20X7

$\dfrac{7.2}{86.4} = 8.33$

20X6

$\dfrac{19.4}{79.2} = 24.49$

There has been a significant fall in the return on equity due to a fall in profits which it may be temporary.

Current ratio

The current ratio is defined as $\dfrac{\text{Currrent assets}}{\text{Current liabilities}}$. This ratio measures the short-term liquidity of a company.

20X7

$\dfrac{273.7}{81.9} = 3.34$

20X6

$\dfrac{281.5}{100.1} = 2.81$

The liquidity of the company has slightly increased.

Gearing ratio

The gearing ratio is defined as $\dfrac{\text{Total long-term debt}}{\text{Equity}}$

20X7

$\dfrac{114.7}{86.4} = 1.33$

20X6

$\dfrac{112.0}{79.2} = 1.41$

The gearing ratio has improved which means that the risk of insolvency has been reduced.

Interest cover

Interest payments in 20X7 fell relative to 20X6, but the significant drop in revenues has led to a deterioration in the interest cover ratio which is defined as

$$\frac{\text{Profits before interest and tax}}{\text{Interest expense}}$$

20X7   *20X6*

$$\frac{31.4-9.2}{12.2} = 1.82 \qquad \frac{50.3-8.6}{13.4} = 3.11$$

However, with interest payments remaining the same over the next financial year as result of the level of debt remaining the same, and increased revenues, the interest coverage ratio will rise.

Taking together the two ratios it seems that the solvency risk of DAS is relatively small, and it is not expected that the company will face financial difficulties.

Conclusion

The analysis of the business conditions and prospects of the company as well as the financial ratios show that the company may have experienced a short-term fall in profits in the last financial year, but the prospects of the company remain healthy and there is very little risk of financial difficulties which may result in laying-off employees.

61 FJK

Report

To: Kay
From: Accountant
Date: XX.XX.X8

(a)   **Analysis and interpretation of the draft financial statements and discussion of performance and position of the FJK**

The purpose of the analysis is to ascertain whether it would be in Kay's interest to contribute the requested amount of $250,000. The main consideration is an examination of the performance of the last two years in order to predict both future performance and any risks that may arise from the new strategy that the company has adopted.

In order to analyse the performance of FJK from the information provided in the financial statements we shall use a number of ratios that summarise information and allow comparisons across time. The ratios we shall employ measure the **profitability** of the operation and the **efficiency**, **liquidity** and **solvency** of the company.

Profitability Analysis

Both **revenues** and **costs** have increased between 20X7 and 20X8. Revenue has increased by around 54% and profit before tax by over 44%. On the face of this, the strategy of expansion may appear successful in terms of increased profitability. However, it is helpful to look at **profitability** in terms of **returns** rather than in absolute terms and to this end the following ratios have been calculated:

Gross profit margin: $\dfrac{\text{Gross profit}}{\text{Revenue}} \times 100$

Distribution costs as % of revenues: $\dfrac{\text{Distribution costs}}{\text{Revenue}} \times 100$

Administrative costs as % of revenue: $\dfrac{\text{Administrative expenses}}{\text{Revenue}} \times 100$

Net profit as % of revenue: $\dfrac{\text{Profit before finance costs}}{\text{Revenue}} \times 100$

Return on assets $\dfrac{\text{Profit before finance costs}}{\text{Total assets}} \times 100$

The net profit margin has been reduced from 18.3% in 20X7 to 17.8% in 20X8. On the other hand the gross profit margin defined as gross profit over revenue has increased slightly from 26.2 % in 20X7 to 27.7% in 20X8.

Contrasting the marginal expenses increase in the **gross profit margin** with the decrease in the **net profit margin** implies that administrative and distribution costs as percentages of revenue must have increased at the same time. The table below summarises the movement of the profit and cost ratios from 20X7 to 20X8.

	20X8	*20X7*
Gross profit margin	$\dfrac{1,655}{5,973} \times 100 = 27.7\%$	$\dfrac{1,018}{3,886} \times 100 = 26.2\%$
Distribution costs as % of revenue	$\dfrac{270}{5,973} \times 100 = 4.5\%$	$\dfrac{106}{3,886} \times 100 = 2.7\%$
Administrative expense as % of revenue	$\dfrac{320}{5,973} \times 100 = 5.4\%$	$\dfrac{201}{3,886} \times 100 = 5.2\%$
Net profit as % of revenue	$\dfrac{968 + 97}{5,973} \times 100 = 17.8\%$	$\dfrac{671 + 40}{3,886} \times 100 = 18.3\%$
Return on assets	$\dfrac{968 + 97}{4,815 - 167} \times 100 = 22.9$	$\dfrac{671 + 40}{2,661} \times 100 = 26.7\%$
Total asset turnover	$\dfrac{5,973}{4,815 - 167} = 1.29$	$\dfrac{3,886}{2,661} = 1.46$

The increase in both distribution and administrative costs relative to revenues may be due to the new markets in which the company has expanded and the presence of teething problems in establishing new distribution channels. On the other hand it may show inability to control administrative expenses arising in new operations due to the managerial model employed. Both types of expenses therefore need further analysis in order to understand the reasons for the increase.

Another indicator of profitability, the **return on assets** (ROA) also shows a decrease, falling from 26.7% in 20X7 to 22.9% in 20X8. The ROA is the product of **net profit margin** and **total asset turnover** as given below.

$$\text{ROA} = \frac{\text{Profit before finance costs}}{\text{Total assets}} = \frac{\text{Profit before finance costs}}{\text{Revenue}} \times \frac{\text{Revenue}}{\text{Total assets}}$$

Therefore, the **return on assets** is affected by both profitability and the efficiency with which the assets are used which is measured by the **total asset turnover**. However, like net profits **total asset turnover** has also fallen from 1.46 to 1.29 so the **return on assets** was reduced both as a result of less efficient use of the assets as well as due to falling profit margins.

Property, plant and equipment has increased significantly over the two years. At the end of 20X8 property plant and equipment at $3,413,000 is more than double the figure of $1,586,000 at the end of 20X7. Even after removing the effect of revaluation it appears that a significant investment in non-current assets has been made. It may be reasonable to assume that the benefits of this investment will be apparent in 20X8/X9 and future years.

Efficiency

A number of efficiency ratios can be used to analyse performance, in addition to the **total asset turnover** used before and the ones employed are summarised below:

Non-current asset turnover : $\dfrac{\text{Revenue}}{\text{Non-current assets}}$

Inventory: $\dfrac{\text{Inventory}}{\text{Cost of sales}} \times 365$

Trade receivables: $\dfrac{\text{Trade receivables}}{\text{Revenues}} \times 365$

The values of the ratios are given below:

	20X8	20X7
Non-current asset turnover	$\dfrac{5,973}{3,413 - 167} = 1.8$	$\dfrac{3,886}{1,586} = 2.5$
Inventory:	$\dfrac{677}{4,318} \times 365 = 57.2 \text{ days}$	$\dfrac{510}{2,868} \times 365 = 64.9 \text{ days}$
Trade receivables:	$\dfrac{725}{5,973} \times 365 = 44.3 \text{ days}$	$\dfrac{553}{3,886} \times 365 = 51.9 \text{ days}$

The **non-current asset turnover** ratio like the **total asset turnover** ratio shows a deterioration in the efficient use of the asset of the firm. The other efficiency ratios however show some improvement. More specifically the **trade receivables** ratio shows that revenues are received within a shorter period of time whereas the **inventory ratio** shows that inventories are reduced freeing cash to meet short term liabilities. This reduction in inventory should of course been seen in terms of the requisite level of inventories for the level of business in which the company is as there is always the risk of not being able to meet customer demand if the level of inventories is too low.

Liquidity

Liquidity is measured by the **current ratio** defined as $\dfrac{\text{current assets}}{\text{current liabilities}}$ which for 20X7 was $\dfrac{1,075}{845} = 1.27$

In order to calculate the **current ratio** for 20X8 we need to take into account the tax liability for 20X8. The effective tax rate for 20X7 is $\dfrac{164}{671} = 0.244$

Applying the same effective tax rate for 20X8 results in a tax liability of $0.244 \times 968 = 236$.

The additional tax liability for 20X8 should therefore be $236 - 164 = 72$.

The current ratio for 20X8 will be $\dfrac{1,402}{1,718 + 72} = 0.78$

The **current ratio** has fallen from 1.27 in 20X7 to 0.78 in 20X8 which represents a significant worsening of the liquidity position of the company.

Solvency

Solvency is measured using the **gearing ratio** and the **interest cover** ratio. The gearing ratio is defined as $\dfrac{\text{Debt}}{\text{Equity}}$ and the interest cover as $\dfrac{\text{Profits}}{\text{Finance costs}}$. The values of the two ratios for 20X7 and 20X8 are given in the table below.

	20X8	20X7
Gearing ratio	$\dfrac{763 + 327}{2,334 - 167} = 0.503$	$\dfrac{453 + 103}{1,363} = 0.408$
Interest cover	$\dfrac{968 + 97}{97} = 11$	$\dfrac{971 + 40}{40} = 17.8$

The **gearing ratio** has increased significantly over the period as a result of increased borrowing. Total borrowings at the end of March 20X8 reached $1,090,000 (763 + 327) from $556,000 (453 + 103) at the end of March 20X7 an increase of nearly 100%. This will increase the riskiness of the company and may make the servicing of debt more difficult. The interest cover, the value of which has fallen from nearly 18 to 11 as a result of a doubling in the finance costs, is still not a cause for concern and it indicates that ability to service the debt may not have been impaired. However, since one third of the liabilities is short term (it falls due within one year) it may put pressure on profits in the short-term.

(b) **Risks and problem areas revealed by the financial statements**

The company has achieved in the **short-term** an impressive **increase in revenues**, but the speed with which this growth has been achieved gives cause for concern. Costs have not been able to be controlled and profitability as a result has declined. There has been a significant increase in the assets of the company but because these were funded by borrowings, both the gearing of the company and its finance costs have increased. The short-term nature of the debt will put additional pressure on the company and exacerbate the already difficult **liquidity** position of the company. The injection of **new capital** will help alleviate the liquidity problems of the company and depending on the ability of the company to increase profit margins FJK may be a reasonably good investment.

62 BHG

(a) (i) **Earnings per share**

Earnings per share (EPS) is defined as follows:

$$EPS = \frac{\text{Earnings attributable to ordinary shareholders}}{\text{Weighted average of the number of ordinary shares in issue}}$$

It is the only **financial ratio** that listed companies must disclose under IFRS and it is used as a measure of the **financial performance** of a company.

As an **investment appraisal tool** it is of limited use because it only looks at the current performance of a company. Comparison with earlier years may also be difficult for an investor because the ratio can be affected by both accounting policies that may affect the numerator and by the number of outstanding shares.

Finally, the ratio may be misleading because of the dilutive effect that convertible bonds or options may have on the earnings attributable to shareholders.

When EPS is used in conjunction with the price of a share to calculate the price/earnings ratio, it can be used to compare whether shares in a listed company are cheap or expensive relative to other listed companies.

(ii) **Dividend yield**

Dividend yield is the ratio of the dividend to the market value of a share. The dividend yield is the cash component of the total return of an investment. Historically only a small proportion of the total return from equity investments is attributable to dividends, the bulk being attributed to the capital gain from the investment. For this reason, the dividend yield is not normally a good indication of the potential return from an equity investment.

A high dividend yield may be an indication that a company lacks investment opportunities and it prefers to return cash to its shareholders in the form of dividends rather than investing in new projects and returning value to its shareholders in the form of higher share prices. In some countries where the tax system is more favourable to capital gains rather than dividends, a low dividend yield may simply indicate, not the financial strength of a company but an optimal response to the tax treatment. Finally, dividend payments are sometimes perceived as signalling the financial robustness of a company (the so called **signalling effect**) and must be paid even if paying them leads to the abandonment of profitable investment opportunities.

As an investment criterion it would be of limited use to BHG in selecting a suitable target for acquisition.

(iii)   Gearing

Gearing measures the long-term debt liabilities of a company either in relation to the company's share capital or in comparison to the total assets of the company. Since debt holders have first claim to the earnings and the assets of a company, the higher the level of debt, the higher the uncertainty of the equity holders regarding their claim on the residual earnings or assets of the company.

Highly geared companies will be **cheaper** to acquire than **low geared** companies. However, what matters in an acquisition is not the gearing of the target entity, but the gearing of the resulting combined entity. If the resulting gearing is relatively low, the high gearing of the target company may be irrelevant. When looking at the gearing of the target company, equal attention should therefore be paid to the potential benefits that will result for the combined entity in the form of revenue or cost synergies.

(iv)   Gross profit margin

This ratio is defined as

$$GPM = \frac{Gross\ profit}{Sales\ revenue}$$

Gross profit margin is an indicator of a company's pricing policies and its ability to control costs. The higher a company's profit margin compared to its competitors, the better. A low profit margin indicates a low margin of safety and a higher risk that a decline in sales will erase profits and result in a net loss. Other things being equal, a company with a higher GPM is more attractive as an acquisition target compared to a low GPM company. A proper evaluation of a company on the basis of this ratio will require the calculation of the GPM for a number of years in order to see the performance of the company over time. However, like most ratios that involve profits, this may be difficult because profits are affected by both financial and accounting policies that may render comparisons across time meaningless. Similarly, the sources of revenues need to be identified and the contribution of each source of revenue properly understood in order to be able to assess the sustainability of revenue beyond the acquisition.

(v)   Asset turnover ratios

There is a variety of asset turnover ratios all of which are calculated by dividing revenue by the value of specific assets owned by the company. These ratios measure the efficiency of asset use since they compare the amount of revenues generated per unit of assets owned by the company. The ratio can be defined in terms of the total assets of a company or in terms of sub-categories, for example, non-current and current assets.

The ratio can be used as an investment criterion and a company will prefer a target with a higher asset turnover ratio to one with a low one. However, care should be taken in calculating such ratios, because the assets need to be measured at market values, which for non-current assets may be very difficult. The revenues can also be affected by revenue recognition policies that individual entities may have in place.

(b)   Accounting ratios summarise financial information and make the assessment of the historical financial performance of a company easier. However, they have several limitations that should be taken into account when accounting ratios are calculated, and some aspects that need to be taken into account are stated below.

Accounting standards

Although there is a movement towards a common set of accounting standards globally, there are still significant variations in the accounting regulations of most European countries that follow IFRS and the US where companies follow US GAAP. For example the LIFO method of valuing inventories is allowed under US GAAP whereas it is not allowed under IFRS. Even within each set of standards different treatments may be applied to different types of companies, for example listed versus unlisted companies. It is therefore important that ratios are based on comparable sets of financial statements in order to be used in investment appraisal or performance analysis.

Accounting policies

Under both IFRS and US GAPP, companies are afforded great flexibility in the selection of accounting policies in certain areas such as revenue recognition, research and development, asset valuation, depreciation and other areas that affect both the balance sheet and the income statement. Although companies need to be consistent over time in terms of the accounting option they select, problems may still arise when comparing financial ratios which have been constructed under different accounting policies.

Type of business entities

Finally accounting ratios may differ because companies are in different lines of business. For example companies in the services sector have higher asset turnover ratios compared to industrial companies, since the latter require a significantly higher level of assets. Another aspect that may be important, is the different way that industries behave over the economic and business cycles. For example the construction industry may have a different cycle and therefore revenues may be affected earlier than say the pharmaceutical industry. This comment is also relevant to international comparisons when countries are subject to different economic cycles.

Even when companies operate in broadly similar lines of business, there are likely to be differences that make comparisons difficult.

63 Preparation question: EPS

(a)

Date	Narrative	Shares	Time	Bonus fraction	Weighted average
1.1.X1	b/d	5,000,000	$\times \frac{1}{12}$	$\times \frac{2.00}{1.95} \times \frac{11}{10}$	470,085
31.1.X1	Rights issue	+ 1,250,000			
		6,250,000	$\times \frac{5}{12}$	$\times \frac{11}{10}$	2,864,583
30.6.X1	FMP	+ 125,000			
		6,375,000	$\times \frac{5}{12}$	$\times \frac{11}{10}$	2,921,875
30.11.X1	Bonus issue	+ 637,500			
		7,012,500	$\times \frac{1}{12}$		584,375
					6,840,918

TERP	4 @ 2	=	8.00
	1 @ 1.75	=	1.75
	$\underline{5}$		$\underline{9.75}$

$$\therefore 1.95$$

$$\text{EPS for y/e } 31.12.X1 = \frac{\$2,900,000}{6,840,918} = 42.4c$$

$$\text{Restated EPS for y/e } 31.12.X0 = 46.4c \times \frac{1.95}{2.00} \times \frac{10}{11} = 41.1c$$

(b) (i) **Sinbad Co**

$$\text{Basic EPS} = \frac{\$644,000}{10,000,000} = 6.44c$$

Earnings	
P.A.T.	644,000
Interest saving 1,200,000 @ 5% × 70%	42,000
	686,000

Number of shares

Basic	10,000,000
On conversion	4,800,000
	14,800,000

Diluted EPS = $\dfrac{\$686,000}{14,800,000}$ = 4.64c

(ii) **Talbot Co**

Basic EPS = $\dfrac{540,000}{5,000,000}$ = 10.8c

Diluted EPS:

Consideration on exercise
$$400,000 \times \$1.10 = \$440,000$$

Shares acquired at FV
$$\$440,000/\$1.60 = 275,000$$

∴ Shares issued for no consideration
$$(400,000 - 275,000) = 125,000$$

EPS = $\dfrac{540,000}{5,000,000 + 125,000}$ = 10.5c

(c) (i) **Determine incremental EPS**

	Increase in earnings $	Increase in shares No.	Earnings per incremental share $
Options (W1)	Nil	2,400,000	Nil
Convertible preference shares	2,000,000	4,000,000	50c
Bonds	1,400,000	10,000,000	14c

Workings

1 *Options*

 – issued at FV
$$\frac{12m \times \$6.00}{\$7.50} = 9.6m$$

 – issued for no consideration
 $(12m - 9.6m) = 2.4m$

2 *Convertible bond*

 Interest saved

 $\$100m \times 2\% \times 70\% = \$1.4m$

 Shares issued on conversion

 $^{100m}/_{1000} \times 100 = 10m$

(ii) **Determine which potential shares to include**

	Profit from continuing operations attributable to ordinary equity holders of P	Ordinary shares	EPS
	$	No.	$
As reported	25,000,000	50,000,000	0.5
Options	Nil	2,400,000	
	25,000,000	52,400,000	0.48
Bonds	1,400,000	10,000,000	
	26,400,000	62,400,000	0.42
Preference shares	2,000,000	4,000,000	
	28,400,000	66,400,000	0.43

Since diluted EPS is increased when taking the convertible preference shares into account (from $0.42 to $0.43), the convertible preference shares are anti-dilutive and are ignored in the calculation of EPS. Therefore, based on the profit for continuing operations, diluted EPS is $0.42.

(iii) Based on the total profits of $30 million:

Basic EPS $= \dfrac{30}{50} = 60c$

Diluted EPS

Earnings (30 + 1.4)	= $31.4 million
Shares	= 62.4 million
EPS	= 50.3c

64 JKL

Text reference. EPS is covered in Chapter 15.

Top tips. No huge complications in this basic and diluted EPS question: Start off by calculating the theoretical ex rights price to get the bonus fraction. In calculating diluted EPS, don't forget to add back the post tax interest saved. In part (b), don't just talk about EPS generally – you need to focus on diluted EPS.

Easy marks. Obviously the calculation of basic EPS is a source of easy marks. Part (b) has 3 marks – you are bound to get at least one of these if you put pen to paper and say something sensible.

(a) Basic earnings per share $= \dfrac{\$2,763,000}{6,945,922}$ (W2)

$= 39.8$ c

Diluted earnings per share $= \dfrac{\$2,858,200}{9,045,922}$ (W3) (W4)

$= 31.6$ c

Workings

1   *Theoretical ex rights price*

Theoretical ex rights price = 141c

		c
4 shares @ 145c		580
1 share @ 125c		125
5 shares @ 141c		705

2   *Weighted average number of shares in issue for year ending 31 August 20X4*

Date	Narrative	Shares	Time	Fraction	Weighted average
1.9.X3	B/F	6,000,000	$\times\,^{5}/_{12}$	$\times\,^{145}/_{141}$	2,570,922
1.2.X4	Rights issue				
	(6m $\times\,^{1}/_{4}$)	1,500,000			
		7,500,000	$\times\,^{7}/_{12}$		4,375,000
					6,945,922

3   *Diluted earnings*

	$
Basic earnings	2,763,000
Add post tax interest saved (2,000,000 $\times$ 7%) $\times$ (1 − 0.32)	95,200
Diluted earnings	2,858,200

4   *Diluted number of shares*

	Number
Basic weighted average number of shares	6,945,922
Convertible loan 2,000,000/100 $\times$ 105	2,100,000
	9,045,922

(b)   **Historical information**, such as most of the contents of a set of financial statements, is **not always useful** for making economic decisions. **Forecasts** and projections for the future can be much more appropriate for **decision making**.

The **diluted** earnings per share figure is an attempt to provide **information about the future to current holders of shares**. Where financial instruments have been issued which will potentially dilute future earnings, the diluted EPS figure shows how the current earnings would be diluted, or shared out amongst the new as well as the current shareholders. This gives the current shareholders an idea of the effect that these dilutive financial instruments may have on their shareholding in future.

There are, however, **limitations** to the use of these figures. The most basic limitation is that the diluted EPS is based upon the **current earnings** figure which **may not be relevant in future years**. The calculation for **convertible loan stock** also **assumes that all holders will convert** to ordinary shares rather than having their loan stock redeemed. As the share price currently stands at significantly higher than the redemption value then this is currently a fairly safe assumption to make but it may not always be the case.

65 CB

(a)   Earnings for year ended 31 Jan 20X5 = $725,000

Weighted average number of shares:

Date	Narrative	Shares	Time	Bonus Fraction	Weighted average
1 Feb 20X4	B/F	3,000,000	$\times \frac{1}{12}$	$\times \frac{7.50}{7.30}$	256,849
1 Mar 20X4	Right issue $(\frac{1}{4})$	750,000			
		3,750,000	$\times \frac{11}{12}$		3,437,500
					3,694,349

Earnings per share = $\dfrac{\$725,000}{3,694,349}$

= 19.6 cents

P/E ratio = $\dfrac{625c}{19.6c}$

= 31.9

Working: theoretical ex rights price

	$
4 shares @ $7.50	30.00
$\frac{1}{5}$ share @ $6.50	6.50
	36.50

Theoretical ex rights price = $36.50/5 = $7.30

Bonus fraction = $7.50/$7.30

(b)   The price earnings ratio is an **indicator of the stock market's view of a share**. In general terms a high P/E ratio indicates that the stock market views this share favourably and that it is a sound and safe investment. Conversely a low P/E ratio indicates that the market views the investment as more risky and volatile.

CB's P/E ratio is **higher than the industry average**, indicating that the market views the shares in CB fairly favourably and that it is probably a less risky investment than some shares in this sector. CB's principal competitor however has a significantly higher P/E ratio than CB, indicating that the market views the competitor as a better investment than CB.

66 EPS ratio

(a) Earnings per share (EPS) is important because it is used as a **summary measure of an entity's performance** and because it is the **denominator in the P/E ratio** which is accepted as one of the most significant indicators of an entity's prospects.

(b) EPS is calculated by dividing earnings attributable to ordinary shareholders by the number of outstanding ordinary shares.

The **numerator** in the definition of EPS is earnings attributable to shareholders which **can be manipulated** by management.

For example a company may manipulate the timing of payments and receipts and it can therefore affect the earnings figure in a particular year.

Earnings per share may also differ from company to company due to **different accounting policies** in relation to revaluation of assets and depreciation.

Earnings could also be affected by **'one-off' items** that may affect earnings for only one period.

Finally earnings are affected by the capital structure of the company and a change in the capital structure will affect funds attributable to shareholders. It is very difficult to predict future earnings unless one is able to predict the future funding policies of the firm.

The **number of shares** may also change if the company has issued convertible instruments or employee share options that may lead to future dilution of earnings and to a lower EPS.

67 Preparation question: Operating segments

(a)   Ignoring comparative figures, Multitrade group's segment report would look like this.

CLASSES OF BUSINESS

	Group $'000	Division A $'000	Division B $'000	Division C $'000
Revenue				
Total sales	1,200,023	846,071	226,949	127,003
Inter-segment sales	335,962	304,928	31,034	–
Sales to third parties*	864,061	541,143	195,915	127,003
Result				
Segment profit/(loss)	172,818	162,367	18,754	(8,303)
Unallocated corporate expenses**	96,724			
	76,094			
Net interest	10,028			
Profit	66,066			
Assets				
Segment assets	608,823	322,753	80,656	205,414
Unallocated corporate assets	96,871			
Consolidated assets	705,694			

GEOGRAPHICAL SEGMENTS

	Group $'000	Home $'000	Middle East $'000	Pacific fringe $'000	Europe $'000	North America $'000
Revenue						
Sales to third parties*	864,061	57,223	406,082	77,838	195,915	127,003

*   Revenue, profit, net interest and assets should be the same as those shown in the consolidated accounts.

**   Unallocated corporate expenses are those items in the consolidated accounts which cannot reasonably be allocated to any one segment nor does the group wish to apportion them between segments. An example of a common cost is the cost of maintaining the holding company share register, and an example of an unallocated asset might be the head office building.

(b)   **What do we learn** from Multitrade's segment report?

(i)   The relative sizes of each division. Here, A is obviously the most important.

(ii)   The profitability of each division. A has the highest net profit margin and return on capital employed. C is a loss maker.

(iii)   A depends most heavily on inter-segment sales.

(iv)   A high proportion of the group's sales are to areas with a high political risk and nearly 95% are export, exposing it to considerable exchange risks.

What *don't* we learn from the report?

(i)   Which division trades in the riskiest areas?

(ii)   How old are each division's assets?

(iii)   How many staff does each division employ?

(iv)   How much of a mark-up do A and B earn on their sales to other divisions?

(v)   Which divisions are benefiting from inter-segment purchases at potentially advantageous prices?

As usual with ratio analysis, the information provided in segment reports can only suggest further avenues of enquiry. However, such reports are useful in indicating **which parts of a business are out of step** with the rest in terms of:

(i) Profitability
(ii) Potential for future growth
(iii) Rate of past growth
(iv) Degree of business or economic risk

68 Price

(a) (i) The case for segmental reporting is that **disaggregated information is more useful than aggregated information**. By providing an analysis of the asset base, revenue and profits relating to operating segments, the relative performance of each can be assessed. The more profitable segments which may represent countries, regions or markets or business components can be separately identified from the less profitable. Furthermore, those areas of the business that are expanding or declining can more easily be identified.

Managers should always have such detailed information but there is debate about how much of this detail should be disclosed in published accounts. Shareholders and financial analysts are particularly concerned with the 'quality' of earnings, by which they usually mean their volatility and the capacity of the business to continue to produce a reliable and increasing earnings per share. Segment information can reveal the relative volatility of earnings from different elements of the business.

(ii) It is often asserted that the benefits of **segment reporting are largely illusory** and that the **costs are excessive**. The benefits cannot easily be measured and, since the definition of geographical and business segments is largely that of the management, it is unlikely that information will be disclosed which would present directors in a bad light. Yet one of the objectives of segment reporting is to facilitate assessment of the efficiency of management as well as of the inherent relative merits of the business segments.

Furthermore, there is **no standardisation of geographical or business segments**, even between entities in the same industry, so that inter-firm comparison is not assisted by segmental reporting. However, IAS 14 does closely define what is meant by a 'reportable segment' and the standard contains detailed guidance to be used in order to determine the materiality of a reportable segment and the aggregation of immaterial segments.

The **costs of segment reporting are both direct and indirect**. The **direct costs** comprise the costs of collecting, analysing and publishing the data. Since much of the data for major internationals will be analysed by computers, the programming and processing costs can be substantial. These will be further increased should any changes in the analysis be required, since prior year comparative data will have to be derived. The costs of providing the information are borne by the preparers while the benefits are obtained by the users. Consequently, the users have no incentive to limit their demands for additional information and for changes in its composition and analysis.

The **indirect costs** relate to the commercial damage that an enterprise may suffer if confidential information becomes public. For example, the disclosure that margins in a particular geographical or business segment are above average could prompt a company's competitors to enter the market or the host government to increase taxation.

It is also argued that management may adopt a **more conservative stance** if segmental analyses are published because they do not wish to risk making losses which cannot be hidden by other segments' profits. This could inhibit innovation and encourage a short-term outlook amongst analysts and investors as well as managers.

(b)

MEMORANDUM

To: Mr A
From: An investment analyst
Subject: Financial statements of PriceDate: 21 November 20X1

As requested, I have examined the extracts from the financial statements of Price for the year ended 31 July 20X1. I set out my comments below.

Point 1

> **Top tips.** This point was poorly answered in the exam. You need to identify the key factors causing a drain on cash flow.

You note that although the company made a profit and raised additional finance during the year, there was a decrease in cash in the same period. The published financial statements of Price should have included a **cash flow statement**, as required by IAS 7 *Cash flow statements.* I note that this was not included in the information that you provided. However, there is sufficient information to reconstruct the cash flow statement and this is shown below.

CASH FLOW STATEMENT
FOR THE YEAR ENDED 31 JULY 20X1

	$'000	$'000
Cash flows from operating activities		
Profit before finance cost and tax	5,700	
Depreciation	4,000	
Increase in inventories (8,700 – 7,500)	(1,200)	
Increase in trade and other receivables (13,000 – 12,000)	(1,000)	
Increase in trade payables (8,000 – 7,800)	200	
Cash generated from operations	7,700	
Interest paid	(1,600)	
Income taxes paid	(1,200)	
Equity dividends paid	(1,600)	
Net cash from operating activities		3,300
Cash flows from investing activities		
Purchase of property, plant and equipment (W1)	(11,200)	
Net cash used in investing activities		(11,200)
Cash flows from financing activities		
Issue of zero coupon bonds	5,400	
Net cash from financing activities		5,400
Net decrease in cash and cash equivalents		(2,500)
Cash and cash equivalents at the beginning of the year		1,500
Cash at cash equivalents at the end of the year (1,200 – 200)		(1,000)

The cash flow statement explains **how and why** the company suffered a **net cash outflow** of $2.5 million, despite making a profit. It shows that **net cash from operations** was actually $2 million higher than profit from operations and that this more than covered interest, tax and equity dividend payments. However, the company invested $11.2 million in **new non-current assets** during the year. This was partly financed by the zero coupon bonds (and was almost certainly the reason why they were issued). The remainder of the investment was financed from operations and by means of the bank overdraft.

Given that both revenue and profit are increasing, the **capital investment** should probably be taken as a **healthy sign**. It should result in increased profits in future periods. Although gearing (debt as a proportion of the company's total capital employed) has increased from 22.7% to 29.2% (W2) this is **not dangerously high**.

It is not normally desirable to finance long term investments from a **bank overdraft** as this is a **short term method of finance**. I note also that **working capital** (inventories, receivables and payables) has increased during the period and that $2 million cash has been absorbed as a result. These two factors may be a sign that the company is **not managing its cash and working capital as effectively as it might**. However, given the overall profitability of the company it is likely that the bank overdraft is a short term measure and that there is **little real cause for concern**.

Point 2

You note that the $5 million gain on **revaluation of properties** is not shown in the income statement, but that it has been reported in the statement of changes in equity. This treatment is correct and is required by IAS 16 *Property, plant and equipment.*

IAS 16 allows properties and other non-current assets to be included in the balance sheet **either at historic cost or at fair value**. Price has evidently revalued its properties during the year to 31 July 20X1. When an asset's carrying amount is increased as a result of a revaluation, the increase should be credited **directly to equity** under the heading of **revaluation surplus**. The reasoning behind this is that the properties have not been sold and therefore the revaluation gain is unrealised. In many countries, unrealised gains cannot be distributed to shareholders. They are not included in the income statement but are taken directly to an undistributable reserve.

Although the gain is unrealised it is still recognised as part of the company's performance for the year. Therefore it is disclosed separately in the statement of changes in equity.

Point 3

You note that interest has been charged on the zero coupon bonds. Although the bonds do not carry interest as such, the company will **repay them at a premium** over the amount originally received. This premium amounts to $1,802,450 and is in substance **a finance charge**.

It is correct that IAS 39 *Financial instruments: recognition and measurement* does require some types of financial instrument to be stated at fair value. However, **the bonds are neither derivatives** nor are they **held for trading** and therefore they are treated differently. IAS 39 states that immediately after issue, a financial liability should be stated at cost ($5 million). Thereafter, this type of financial liability should be **measured at amortised cost**. Amortised cost is cost plus the difference between cost and the amount repayable on maturity (the finance cost). The finance cost is allocated to periods over the term of the bonds using the effective interest rate.

Therefore the **accounting treatment** adopted by the company **is correct**. The rate of interest implicit in the zero coupon bonds is 8% (W3). Interest of $400,000 ($5 million × 8%) has been charged in the income statement. The liability is shown in the balance sheet at $5.4 million (cost of $5 million plus amortisation).

Workings

1   *Purchase of property, plant and equipment*

PROPERTY, PLANT AND EQUIPMENT

	$'000		$'000
Balance b/f	32,000	Depreciation	4,000
Revaluation	5,000		
Purchases (balancing figure)	11,200	Balance c/f	44,200
	48,200		48,200

2   *Gearing*

	20X1		20X0	
$\dfrac{\text{Long term liabilities} + \text{overdraft}}{\text{Capital employed (inc overdraft)}}$	$\dfrac{16,600}{56,900}$	= 29.2%	$\dfrac{10,000}{44,000}$	= 22.7%

3   *Zero coupon bonds*

Effective rate of interest: $\dfrac{5,000,000}{6,802,450} = 0.735 = 8\%$ (from tables)

69 STV

(a)   Many entities carry on several classes or different types of business or operate in several geographical areas. Although the purpose of consolidated financial statement is to aggregate all of the information about a group into an understandable form from the perspective of the entire entity, if the financial statements are for a diverse group it is also useful to have disaggregated information in the notes about these different businesses or geographical areas.

To assess risks and returns

In an entity with different products or different geographical areas of operation it is likely that **each business or area will have different rates of profitability, different opportunities for growth, different future prospects and different degrees of risk**. The overall risks and returns of the entity can only be fully assessed by looking at the individual risks and returns attached to each of these businesses or geographical areas.

To assess past performance and future prospects

Segment reporting should help investors to appreciate the results and financial position of the entity by permitting better understanding of past performance and thus a better assessment of its future prospects. It should also help investors to be aware of the impact that changes in significant components of a business may have on the business as a whole and to assess the risks and returns of the business.

(b)   **REPORT**

To: Investor
From: Accountant
Date: November 20X5
Subject: Segment analysis of STV

I have looked at the segment analysis note from STV's financial statements and have made the following analysis of the figures shown which may be of use to you. The detailed calculations upon which this analysis has been based are included in the appendix to this report.

From the segment analysis we can add more information to our overview of the results of the organisation.

Profit margin

The **overall profit margin of the group has increased slightly** from 24% in 20X4 to 25% in 20X5. We can also see that this is **nothing to do with road haulage** as its profit margin has stayed the same but is in fact due to a 2% increase from 31% to 33% for airfreight and the change from an operating loss in 20X4 of 25% for the new secure transport business to an operating profit in 20X5 of 6%.

ROCE

Similarly with return on **capital employed** the overall figure is an increase from 27% in 20X4 in 29% in 20X5. However, this is **solely** due to the performance of the **secure transport activities**. Road haulage shows a slight decrease in ROCE but air freight shows a decrease from 57% to 52%.

Summary

Although the figures for the secure transport business are still small with low profit margins it is clearly improving as the investment in the infrastructure starts to feed through to the profits. However for the other two divisions the position is either only slightly better than last year or worse.

I hope that this additional information has been of use to you.

APPENDIX

Key Ratios

		20X5	20X4
Profit margin			
Road haulage	169/653	26%	
	168/642		26%
Air freight	68/208	33%	
	62/199		31%
Secure transport	6/98	6%	
	(16)/63		-25%
Group	243/959	25%	
	214/904		24%
Return on capital employed			
Road haulage	169/(805 – 345)	37%	
	168/(796 – 349)		38%
Air freight	68/(306 – 176)	52%	
	62/(287 – 178)		57%
Secure transport	6/(437 – 197)	2.5%	
	(16)/(422 – 184)		-6.7%
Group	243/(1,548 – 718)	29%	
	214/(1,505 – 711)		27%

Note to appendix. When the group ratios were calculated the figures did not include unallocated expenses or assets/liabilities in order to be able to compare directly with the segmental figures.

(c) Even though segment reporting can be very useful to investors it does also have some limitations.

Defining segments

IFRS 8 *Operating segments,* which replaces IAS 14 *Segmental reporting* with effect from 1 January 2009, does not define segment revenue and expense, segment results or segment assets and liabilities. It does, however, require an explanation of how segment profit or loss, segment assets and segment liabilities are measured for each operating segment.

IFRS 8 requires operating segments to be identified on the basis of internal reports about components of the entity that are regularly reviewed by the chief operating decision maker in order to allocate resources to the segment or assess performance.

Consequently, entities have discretion in determining what is included under segment results, which is limited only by their reporting practices.

Although this should mean that the analysis is comparable over time, it is unlikely to be comparable with that of another business.

Common costs

In many cases it will not be possible to allocate an expense to a segment and therefore they will be shown as unallocated expenses as in STV's segmental analysis. If these unallocated costs are material it can distort the segment results and make comparison with the overall group results misleading. Also if costs are allocated to segments on an arbitrary basis then this can distort the segment results.

Unallocated assets/liabilities

In a similar way to common costs it may be that some of the entity's assets and/or liabilities cannot be allocated to a particular segment and must be shown as unallocated assets/liabilities as in STV. Again this can make the results and comparisons misleading.

Finance costs

Finance is normally raised centrally and allocated to divisions etc as required therefore the normal treatment for finance costs is to show them as an unallocated expense. However if some areas of the business rely more heavily on debt finance than others then this exclusion of finance costs could be misleading.

Tax costs

As with finance costs the effects of tax are normally shown as a total rather than split between the segments. If however a segment had a significantly different tax profile to other segments again this information would be lost.

70 Glowball

Text references. Environmental reporting is covered in Chapter 18 and provisions in Chapter 14.

Top tips. This question looks daunting at first because there is a lot of information in it. However, this is actually a good thing, because you can use the information in your answer. As you know, apart from rules on provisions, there is not much that is mandatory about environmental reporting, so you can draw on whatever knowledge you have.

Easy marks. Obviously, setting out a report format is an easy way to earn marks. The main advice would be to keep going – you can always say something.

REPORT

To: The Directors, Glowball plc
From: Ann Accountant
Date: 28 May 20X3

Environmental Reporting

Introduction

The purpose of this report is to provide information about current reporting requirements and guidelines on the subject of environmental reporting, and to give an indication of the required disclosure in relation to the specific events which you have brought to my attention. We hope that it will assist you in preparing your environmental report.

Current reporting requirements and guidelines

Most businesses have generally ignored environmental issues in the past. However, the use and **misuse** of **natural resources** all lead to environmental costs generated by businesses, both large and small.

There are very few rules, legal or otherwise, to ensure that companies disclose and report environmental matters. Any **disclosures tend to be voluntary**, unless environmental matters happen to fall under standard accounting principles. Environmental matters may be reported in the accounts of companies in the following areas.

- Contingent liabilities
- Exceptional charges
- Operating and financial review comments/management discussion and analysis
- Profit and capital expenditure focus

In Europe, the EU Accounts Modernisation Directive brought in a requirement for an expanded directors' report, the 'business review' to present shareholders with a fair review of the business, including relevant analysis of environmental and social aspects.

This has been brought into UK law in Companies Act 2006 where the required contents of the business review include information about environmental matters (including the impact of the company's business on the environment).

While there is little compulsory detail on how this should be done there are a number of **published guidelines** and **codes of practice**, including:

- The sustainability Reporting Guidelines of the Global Reporting Initiative (GRI)
- The UK Department for Environmental, Food and Rural Affairs (DEFRA) General Guidelines on Environmental Reporting
- The Sigma (Sustainability – Integrated Guidelines for Management) Guidelines (a project launched by a partnership including the British Standards Institution, Forum for the Future and Account Ability)

The question arises as to verification of the environmental information presented. Companies who adopt the Eco Management and Audit Scheme must have the report validated by an external verifier. In June 1999, BP Amoco commissioned KPMG to conduct an independent audit of its greenhouse gas emissions in the first ever **environmental audit**.

Comments on 'environmental events'

(a) Of relevance to the farmland restoration is IAS 37 *Provisions, contingent liabilities and contingent assets*. Provisions for environmental liabilities should be recognised where there is a **legal or constructive obligation** to rectify environmental damage or perform restorative work. The mere existence of the restorative work does not give rise to an obligation and there is no legal obligation. However, it could be argued that there is a constructive obligation arising from the company's approach in previous years, which may have given rise to an **expectation** that the work would be carried out. If this is the case, a provision of $150m would be required in the financial statements. In addition, this provision and specific examples of restoration of land could be included in the environmental report.

(b) The treatment of the **fine** is straightforward: it is an obligation to transfer economic benefits. An estimate of the fine should be made and a **provision** set up in the financial statements for $5m. This should be mentioned in the environmental report. The report might also **put the fines in context** by stating how many tests have been carried out and how many times the company has passed the tests. The directors may feel that it would do the company's reputation no harm to point out the fact that the number of prosecutions has been falling from year to year.

(c) These statistics are good news and need to be covered in the environmental report. However, the emphasis should be on **accurate factual reporting** rather than boasting. It might be useful to provide target levels for comparison, or an industry average if available. The emissions statistics should be split into three categories:

- Acidity to air and water
- Hazardous substances
- Harmful emissions to water

As regards the aquatic emissions, the $70m planned expenditure on **research** should **be mentioned in the environmental report**. It shows a commitment to benefiting the environment. However, **IAS 37 would not permit a provision** to be made for this amount, since an obligation does not exist and the **expenditure is avoidable**. Nor does it qualify as development expenditure under IAS 38.

(d)   The environmental report should mention the steps the company is taking to minimise the harmful impact on the environment in the way it sites and constructs its gas installations. The report should also explain the policy of dismantling the installations rather than sinking them at the end of their useful life.

Currently the company builds up a provision for decommissioning costs over the life of the installation. However, IAS 37 does not allow this. Instead, the **full amount must be provided** as soon as there is an **obligation** arising as a result of **past events**, the **settlement** of which is **expected** to result in an **outflow of resources**. The obligation exists right at the beginning of the installation's life, and so the full $407m must be provided for. A corresponding asset is created.

71 FW

Text references. Provisions are covered in Chapter 14 and financial analysis in Chapter 17.

Top tips. This is not an easy question to answer and in the exam was avoided by most candidates. Make sure that your starting point in Part (a) is to calculate the ratios before and after the provision as many candidates did not even attempt this leading to ill-informed and often incorrect comments. You should work out the adjustments required as a result of the provision and recalculate any ratios. Then you need to discuss the effects of the provision. In the discussion of the advantages and disadvantages of an environmental report, there is scope for you to have ideas of your own, since there are no hard and fast rules.

Easy marks. The easy marks, if you have learnt your stuff are in the description of the GRI framework. However, the marks are fairly evenly distributed in all parts of the question. Again do not get bogged down in the ratio calculations.

Examiner's comments. Part (a) was badly done in almost all cases. Part (b) was better. Part (c) varied, depending on whether candidates had done their homework.

(a)   **Briefing paper**

From: Assistant to CFO

This briefing paper considers the effect on our key financial ratios of including a provision for $500 million for potential legal costs, fines and compensation. The key ratios for 20X5 both before any provision and after the provision together with the ratios for 20X4 are included as an appendix to this paper.

The effect of making the provision is seen in all of the key financial ratios and **each one shows a poorer position once the provision has been made**. However, in comparison to the 20X4 ratios the return on equity, and return on net assets are only marginally lower than the 20X4 ratios once the provision is made and the level of gearing is only marginally higher than 20X4.

The **main area of damage** to the key financial ratios is in the **operating profit margin** and earnings per share. If the provision is made the operating profit margin falls to 7.7% from 10.1% in 20X4 and earnings per share is just 8.4 cents compared to 12.2 cents in 20X4.

If all the ratios are considered together, **even after making the provision**, it would be clear that **the business is sound and profitable**, particularly if the analysts take into account the reasons for the provision. In fact they may well feel that it is better to be aware of the worst case scenario. However the concern with the public and market perception of the company is that earnings per share in particular is often looked at by investors in isolation and this shows a marked drop of over 31%. When this is taken together with a 24% drop in operating profitability then there is concern that this could have an adverse effect on the market perception of the company.

APPENDIX

Key financial ratios

	20X5 before provision (W)	20X5 after provision (W)	20X4
Return on equity	18.8%	9.9%	24.7%
Return on net assets	21.8%	17.0%	17.7%
Gearing	78.0%	85.5%	82.0%
Operating profit margin	10.2%	7.7%	10.1%
Earnings per share	16.7 cents	8.4 cents	12.2 cents

Workings

	20X5 before provision	20X5 after provision

Return on equity

$$\frac{\text{Profit after tax}}{\text{Average share capital} + \text{reserves}} \times 100$$

$$\frac{1{,}002}{(4{,}954 + 5{,}656)/2} \times 100 \qquad\qquad 18.9\%$$

$$\frac{1{,}002 - 500}{(4{,}954 + (5{,}656 - 500))/2} \times 100 \qquad\qquad\qquad\qquad 9.9\%$$

Return on net assets

$$\frac{\text{Operating profit}}{\text{Average net assets}} \times 100$$

$$\frac{2{,}080}{(9{,}016 + 10{,}066)/2} \times 100 \qquad\qquad 21.8\%$$

$$\frac{2{,}080 - 500}{(9{,}016 + (10{,}066 - 500))/2} \times 100 \qquad\qquad\qquad\qquad 17.0\%$$

Gearing

$$\frac{\text{Long term loans}}{\text{Share capital} + \text{reserves}} \times 100$$

$$\frac{4{,}410}{5{,}656} \times 100 \qquad\qquad 78.0\%$$

$$\frac{4{,}410}{5{,}656 - 500} \times 100 \qquad\qquad\qquad\qquad 85.5\%$$

Operating profit margin

$$\frac{\text{Operating profit}}{\text{Revenue}} \times 100$$

$$\frac{2{,}080}{20{,}392} \times 100 \qquad\qquad 10.2\%$$

$$\frac{2{,}080 - 500}{20{,}392} \times 100 \qquad\qquad\qquad\qquad 7.7\%$$

	20X5 before provision	20X5 after provision

Earnings per share

$$\frac{\text{Profit for the year}}{\text{Number of shares}}$$

$$\frac{1,002}{6,000} \quad 16.7 \text{ cents}$$

$$\frac{1,002 - 500}{6,000} \quad 8.4 \text{ cents}$$

(b)   **Advantages of publishing an environmental and social report**

Many businesses are reacting to stakeholder information requirements and now providing **additional reporting** within the annual financial statements, in particular in the area of **environmental and social reporting**. The production of such a report would most probably **enhance the reputation** of FW as a good corporate citizen and we would appear to be responding to the needs of our stakeholders. If there is genuine information about our corporate achievements, environmentally and socially, then an environmental and social report would appear to an appropriate document for FW to prepare.

Disadvantages of publishing an environmental and social report

However, there are also **disadvantages** in providing this information and preparing an environmental and social report. Such a report will be a **costly** exercise. It is not something that we are likely to be able to 'pull together' and may not be able to produce it in time to go out with the annual report. The form of the report must be considered and the key performance indicators that would be reported. We may then need to consider our accounting system which may not currently be able to easily produce the figures we need for these performance indicators.

For an environmental and social report to be taken seriously and to reflect well upon the company then it must not be perceived as simply a public relations exercise but a **genuine attempt to provide additional information to users of the reports**. Such a report must also be at least as good as those of our competitors as if it is not then this will disadvantage FW rather than enhancing the company.

In deciding which performance indicators to report regarding environmental and social issues, it must be considered that once reported there will be **expectations** that they will continue to be reported even if the performance indicator in that area declines.

(c)   The three principal sustainability dimensions covered by the GRI's framework of performance indicators are:

(i)   **Economic.** This should include performance indicators to reflect the direct economic impacts of the entity on those with which it deals such as customers and suppliers

(ii)   **Environmental.** This should include performance indicators relating to the environmental impact of the company's operations such as those concerned with emissions, effluents and waste

(iii)   **Social.** This should include performance indicators relating to labour practises, human rights and product responsibility

72 Widespread

> **Text reference.** This topic is covered in Chapter 19.
>
> **Top tips.** In line with the aims of the current syllabus, expect lots of report writing. Make sure that you have put your answer into the correct report format, otherwise you will lose marks in the exam.

REPORT

To: The managing director
From: The management accountant
Subject: Reconciliation statement

1 Introduction

1.1 The following report deals with the questions you have raised.

   (a) Why a reconciliation statement is necessary.
   (b) The accounting issues underlying each item in the reconciliation.

2 Reconciliation statement

2.1 Financial statements have to be prepared in accordance with generally accepted accounting principles (GAAP). However GAAP in the USA are different to IFRS.

2.2 The subsidiary Dixie Inc has to prepare its local accounts under US GAAP. Therefore it sends us its figures in the US GAAP format.

2.3 The group accounts are prepared under IFRS. Therefore Dixie Inc's accounts need to be restated in the UK GAAP format.

2.4 The reconciliation statement is, therefore, necessary to take account of the difference between Dixie Inc's accounts as published and the figures included in the group accounts.

3 Accounting issues

3.1 There are three main issues arising from the reconciliation statement.

   (a) Development expenditure
   (b) Capitalised interest
   (c) Inventory valuation

3.2 Development expenditure in the USA has to be written off to the income statement. However, in the UK, certain expenditure can be capitalised and then written off (amortised) over the periods when the revenue should arise from the project.

3.3 In the USA, certain interest must be capitalised. However in under IFRS capitalisation is decided by the company. The group policy is not to capitalise interest and so adjustments have to be made.

3.4 Inventory valuation in the USA includes LIFO (last in, first out). However this basis is forbidden in the UK, as it produces lower taxable profits. The preferred method under IFRS is FIFO (first in, first out).

Signed: Management Accountant

73 Nearby

> **Text reference.** This topic is covered in Chapter 19.
>
> **Top tips.** This question is still topical as it deals with harmonisation. Remember to adjust the cost of sales for the valuation of inventory. Note also that the goodwill will need to be added back as the write off to revenue reserves is not allowed.

INCOME STATEMENT
FOR THE YEAR ENDED 30 SEPTEMBER (RESTATED)

	20X1	20X0
	LC'000	LC'000
Revenue	56,000	53,000
Cost of sales (W1)	(33,800)	(32,100)
Gross profit	22,200	20,900
Other operating expenses	(10,000)	(9,800)
Finance costs	(4,000)	(3,800)
Profit before tax	8,200	7,300
Income tax expense (W3)	(3,072)	(2,764)
Profit for the period	5,128	4,536

STATEMENT OF CHANGES IN EQUITY
FOR THE YEAR ENDED 30 SEPTEMBER 20X1

	20X1	20X0
	LC'000	LC'000
Balance brought forward (W4)	50,192	48,056
Profit for the period	5,128	4,536
Dividends	(2,500)	(2,400)
Balance carried forward	52,820	50,192

Workings

1   *Cost of sales*

	20X1	20X0
	LC'000	LC'000
Per question	34,000	32,000
Adjustment (1,800 – 2,000)	(200)	
Adjustment (1,000 – 900)		100
	33,800	32,100

2   *Goodwill on acquisition*

	LC'000
Cost	50,000
Net assets acquired	(30,000)
	20,000

3   *Tax*

	20X1	20X0
	LC'000	LC'000
Per question	3,000	2,800
Tax on inventory adjustment (200 × 36%)	72	
Tax on inventory adjustment (100 × 36%)		(36)
	3,072	2,764

4   *Retained earnings brought forward*

YEAR ENDED 30 SEPTEMBER

	20X1	20X0
	LC'000	LC'000
Per question	30,000	27,800
Increase in inventory due to FIFO	300	400
Tax on above at 36%	(108)	(144)
Goodwill (W2)	20,000	20,000
Retained earnings	50,192	48,056

74 Current issues

Text references. Environmental issues are covered in Chapter 18 and international issues in Chapter 19.

Top tips. A straightforward question. Remember to set out your answer as a report. Note that, although you will not get a 20-mark question in this exam, we have included this question because of the importance of the topics it covers.

MEMORANDUM

To: The Chief Executive Officer of Clean
From: The Management Accountant
Date: 30 November 20X2
Subject: Current reporting practice

1 Introduction

1.1 Following your memorandum, I attach a report on current reporting practice.

2 US filing

2.1 At the moment, there has been **no firm decision** about allowing entities to file accounts in the US under IFRS.

2.2 Discussions have been going on since the 1990s and there is still only a **recommendation** that IFRSs be accepted for US filing purposes.

2.3 US standards are **more detailed** than IFRSs. Therefore if Clean had to file US accounts, the accounts would have to be **restated** using US GAAP. This would be **time consuming** and **expensive**.

2.4 However, if Clean wishes to raise funds on the US markets, we may well be required to prepare accounts using US GAAP for prospective lenders.

3 Environmental reporting

3.1 **Environmental reporting** refers to a business's activities to **maintain and enhance the environment**.

3.2 There is **no IFRS requiring** environmental reports. However, many entities are **giving this information in their financial statements voluntarily**.

3.3 The reasons for doing this include the following.

- Public interest in pollution and other environmental issues
- Investor pressure
- Good public relations

3.4 However if Clean's activities result in **environmental liabilities**, eg clean up costs, then IAS 37 requires that provision is made in the financial statements or that a **contingent liability** is disclosed in the notes.

4 Human resource accounting

4.1 Competitive advantage is largely gained by **effective use of people**.

4.2 The **case for** regarding people as assets is as follows.

(i) People are a **resource** which needs to be **effectively managed**.
(ii) The organisation needs to **protect its investment** by retaining and developing its human assets.
(iii) Deterioration in motivation and attitude represents a cost to the business.

4.3 Nevertheless, there is a strong case against putting employees on the balance sheet, based on the IASB's *Framework*. The *Framework* defines assets as 'a resource controlled by the entity as a result of past transactions and events and from which future economic benefits are expected to flow'. It could be argued that, since a contract of employment cannot, and does not force an employee to work to provide benefits to the entity, it is questionable whether this definition is met.

4.4   Furthermore, for an asset to be recognised, it has to be capable of reliable measurement. It is virtually impossible to measure an employee's worth objectively in this way. There would be too many uncertainties about which specific economic benefits could be regarded as attributable to that employee. In addition, how would one depreciate a human asset.

4.5   In conclusion, there are at present too many practical problems associated with human resource accounting for it to be used in financial statements.

5   **Conclusion**

5.1   If you wish to discuss these matters further, please do not hesitate to contact me.

       Management Accountant

75 Intellectual capital

Text reference. Human resource accounting is covered in Chapter 18.

Top tips. You can say any number of things about intellectual capital. The important thing to note is that it does not meet the definition of an asset.

Easy marks. You will pick up marks for any sensible comments about intellectual capital.

Examiner's comments. Generally candidates were more successful in identifying arguments **against** rather than **for** the proposition.

Intellectual capital includes all of the **intangible resources** that contribute to the creation of value for an organisation. These include **knowledge, competence and skills of people** as well as working methods, processes and systems. It can also be argued that it includes the culture that supports the people, the image in the market place and the relationships with customers, alliance partners and suppliers.

Arguments for capitalisation

The principal **argument for capitalisation** of intellectual capital is that it is an important asset of an organisation, even though a complex asset, and as such should be shown on the balance sheet. If this asset is not shown on the balance sheet then the **balance sheet bears no real approximation to the value of the company** as is evidenced by the gap between the market capitalisation of many companies and their balance sheet value. If a company owns a factory in which products are made which are then sold to earn revenue for the company then that factory appears on the balance sheet as an income earning asset. Why, therefore, should other income earning assets such as the employees of the business not appear on the balance sheet as well?

A balance sheet that does not include all of the assets of the business, whether tangible or intangible, is not only meaningless but also **misleading**. Return on capital employed is calculated by comparing the profits earned from the income statement to the capital employed (net assets) recorded in the balance sheet. The **profit figure** therefore **includes the benefits from the human resources** employed but the **capital employed** figure **excludes** them rendering the resulting ROCE meaningless.

The exclusion of intellectual capital from the balance sheet also hinders any form of **comparison** between companies. Comparisons can only be made based upon information that is known. If there is no information about the intellectual capital of individual businesses then they cannot be validly compared as there is a large amount of information missing.

Arguments against capitalisation

The arguments against capitalisation of intellectual capital centre largely around the fact that it **does not actually meet the definition of an asset** and that it would be incredibly difficult to value.

The IASB's *Framework for the Preparation and Presentation of Financial Statements* defines an asset as 'a resource controlled by the entity as a result of past events and from which future economic benefits are expected to flow to the entity'. Intellectual capital or human resources meet most of these requirements to be an asset. They are a 'resource', they 'result from past events' (employing the people) and it is expected they will bring 'future economic benefits' to the company. The problem however is that these resources are **not 'controlled'** by the entity. Employees are free to leave and to work elsewhere (even if restrictions on this are sometimes put in place) therefore they cannot be described as being controlled by the company.

A further problem with the capitalisation of intellectual capital is the IASB's **recognition criteria** for assets. For an asset to the recognised it must meet three criteria:

(a) It meets the **definition** of an asset.
(b) It is probable that the future economic benefits will flow to the entity.
(c) It has a cost or value that can be measured reliably.

It is the **last of these that is so unhelpful** for capitalisation of intellectual capital. How in practice do you place a reliable monetary value on your employees? It can be argued that an employee's value should reflect the age and experience and their future earning power for the company but there is no getting away from the fact that any valuation made in practice would be **arbitrary**.

76 Convergence project

(a) In 2002 the FASB and IASB issued the Norwalk agreement on convergence formalising their commitment to the convergence of US and international financial reporting standards.

The main objectives of this project include:

- improving comparability of financial statements for international markets
- removing barriers for international companies who seek to obtain a listing in the US

Short term projects have been undertaken to address and remove where possible some of the differences. In 2006 a memorandum of understanding (MOU) reaffirmed the boards' shared objective .

Although the new MOU does not represent a change in the convergence project, it reflects the 'roadmap' of the Securities and Exchange Commission (SEC) in the US for the removal of the reconciliation requirement for non-US companies that use IFRS and wish to register in the United States. Events moved faster than expected, and in November 2007 the SEC announced that non-US filers could report under IFRS for years ended after 15 November 2007.

Some of the results to date of the convergence project are the following:

IFRS 5 *Non-current assets held for sale and discontinued operations*
IFRS 8 *Operating segments*
IAS 1 *Presentation of financial statements* (revised 2007)
IFRS 3 *Business combinations (revised 2008)*

(b) Many differences between US GAAP and IFRS still exist. Examples include:

General Approach

- IFRS: The general approach of IFRS is 'principles based' and application guidance tends to be limited.
- US GAAP: The US follows a 'rules based', more prescriptive approach with detailed application guidance.

IAS 2 Method of determining inventory cost

- IFRS: LIFO is not permitted.
- US GAAP: LIFO is permitted.

IAS 28 Different accounting policies of investor and associate

- IFRS: Policies must be aligned.
- US GAAP: No requirement for policies to be aligned.

IAS 37 Disclosures that may prejudice seriously the position of the entity in a dispute

- IFRS: In extreme rare cases amount and details need not be disclosed, but disclosure is required of the general nature of dispute and why details not disclosed.
- US GAAP: Disclosure is required.

IAS 38 Development costs

- IFRS: Capitalise, if certain criteria are met.
- US GAAP: Expense (except some website development costs and certain internal software).

77 Environmental disclosure

Text reference. These topics are covered in Chapter 18.

Top tips. Note that the question is asking you to explain the principal arguments *against* voluntary disclosures of their environmental policies, impacts and practices.

Easy marks. Identifying and clearly explaining at least four principal arguments should gain you virtually full marks.

The **voluntary** as opposed to the **statutory nature** of **environmental disclosures** presents a number of problems such as:

(a) Not all entities report **environmental information** which makes the evaluation of their **environmental policies** and impacts difficult

(b) There is **no consistency** in **reporting practice** and companies may report in a way that shows their environmental policies in a more flattering way.

(c) The information provided may be unreliable, as environment statements **do not need** to be **audited**.

(d) There is no provision for companies in more **environmentally damaging industries** to provide more information on their impact on the environment.

(e) Those companies who in fact **care most** about environmental reporting are likely to **give more details** than those for whom it is not a priority.

(f) **Competitors** may **exploit honesty** and full disclosure by companies that do report openly on environmental matters.

(g) Conversely, it may be **assumed** that the companies that give the **most information** on environmental matters are the **most responsible**. This **does not follow**.

78 Mixed bank (1)

1   C   A would result in X's asset turnover being higher than that of its competitor. B and D are both likely to result in increased turnover relative to capital employed and therefore in increased asset turnover.

2   B   Rights issue:

	$
2 shares @ $1.75	3.50
1 share @ $1.25	1.25
	4.75
Theoretical ex-rights price	$1.58

$$\text{Bonus fraction} = \frac{1.75}{1.58}$$

Weighted average no of shares:

Date	Narrative	Shares	Time	Bonus Fraction	Weighted average
1.1.X3	B/F	10,000,000	$\times \, {}^3/_{12}$	$\times \, {}^{1.75}/_{1.58}$	2,768,987
31.3.X3	Rights issue ($^1/_2$)	5,000,000			
		15,000,000	$\times \, {}^6/_{12}$		7,500,000
30.9.X3	Issue at FMP	5,000,000			
		20,000,000	$\times \, {}^3/_{12}$		5,000,000
					15,268,987

Earnings per share:

20X3: $\dfrac{2,100,000}{15,268,987} = 13.75$ cents

20X2: $\dfrac{1,800,000}{10,000,000} \times \dfrac{1.58}{1.75} = 16.25$ cents.

3   A   Group gross profit excludes the group's share of the profit of the associate, which is reported on a separate line in the consolidated income statement.

	$'000
Savoy	700
Spring	550
	1,250

4

	$'000
Sale proceeds	3,600
Less net assets sold (80% × 3,310)	(2,648)
Less goodwill (2,360 – 80% × 2,240)	(568)
	384

5   C

	$'000
Sale proceeds	6,500
Less net assets sold (45% × 12,500)	(5,625)
Less goodwill (5,000 – (60% × 8,000)) $\times {}^3/_4$	(150)
	725

6    $25,000

MINORITY INTERESTS

	$'000		$'000
Dividend (balancing figure)	25	Balance b/f	260
Exchange loss (20 × 20/80)	5	Income statement	35
Balance c/f	275	Revaluation gain (25% × 40)	10
	305		305

7   Although the coupon rate of interest is 3%, the entity will have to pay a premium on redemption, which represents a finance cost. The effective rate of interest must be applied, so that the debt is measured at amortised cost (IAS 39).

At the time of issue, the loan notes are recognised at their net proceeds of $449,800 (450,000 – 200). The carrying amount of the loan notes at 31 December 20X3 is calculated as follows:

	$
Initial cost	449,800
Interest @ 12%	53,976
Less: interest paid (450,000 × 3%)	(13,500)
	490,276

8 C Receivables collection period $\dfrac{\text{Trade receivables}}{\text{Sales}} = \dfrac{690}{5,600} \times 365 = 45$ days

Payables payment period $\dfrac{\text{Trade payables}}{\text{Cost of sales}} = \dfrac{250}{4,500} \times 365 = 20$ days

If the working capital cycle is 105 days, inventories turnover must be 80 days (105 + 20 – 45).

Inventories turnover is $\dfrac{\text{Inventories}}{\text{Cost of sales}}$ so inventories are $\dfrac{80}{365} \times 4,500 = \$986,000$

9 B Rights issue:

	$
3 shares @ $2.50	7.50
1 share @ $2.00	2.00
	9.50
Theoretical ex-rights price	$2.37

Bonus fraction = $\dfrac{2.50}{2.37}$

Weighted average no of shares:

Date	Narrative	Shares	Time	Bonus Fraction	Weighted average
1.1.X5	B/F	15,000,000	$\times\,^9/_{12}$	$\times\,^{2.5}/_{2.37}$	11,867,087
30.9.X5	Rights issue ($^1/_3$)	5,000,000			
		20,000,000	$\times\,^3/_{12}$		5,000,000
					16,867,087

Earnings per share $\dfrac{1,500,000}{16,867,087} = 8.89$ cents

10 $2,100,000

	$'000
B (10% × 6,100)	610
C (28% × 5,000)	1,400
	2,010

79 Mixed bank (2)

1 $149,800

	$'000	$'000
Cost of combination		400
Fair value of net assets acquired		
Sassoon: Share capital	100	
Pre acquisition retained earnings	200	
Less: cost of investment in Thomas	(100)	
90% ×	200	(180)
Thomas: Share capital	50	
Pre acquisition retained earnings	80	
54% ×	130	(70.2)
		149.8

Note: Thomas comes into group *control* on 1 January 20X5 when Owen takes control of Sassoon, so pre-acquisition earnings for both subsidiaries are taken as at that date.

2 $1,875,000

After the disposal, Geranium retains a 15% holding in Rose. This is treated as a simple non-current asset investment and valued at the date of disposal using the equity method.

	$'000
Share capital ($1 ordinary shares)	5,000
Retained earnings at 1 January 20X9	6,500
Retained profit to date of disposal (2,000 × 6/12)	1,000
	12,500
Group share (15%)	1,875

3   **B**   Subsidiary B is clearly an extension of Parent's own activities and therefore it almost certainly has the same functional currency as the parent.

4 $1,902,000

	$'000	$'000
Rat		1,900
Mole: closing net assets (960 @ 2.5)	384	
opening net assets (720 @ 2.0)	(360)	
	24	
Group share (75%)		18
Retranslation of goodwill (160 @ 2 – 160 @ 2.5)		(16)
		1,902
Goodwill		
Cost of investment (350 × 2)		700
Net assets acquired (75% × 720)		(540)
		160

5   **C**   The premium on redemption of the preferred shares represents a finance cost. The effective rate of interest must be applied so that the debt is measured at amortised cost (IAS 39).

At the time of issue, the loan notes are recognised at their net proceeds of $599,800 (600,000 – 200).

The finance cost for the year ended 31 December 20X4 is calculated as follows:

	$
1.1.X3 Cash	599,800
Effective interest at 12 %	71,976
31.12.X3 Cash	671,776
Effective interest at 12 %	80,613
	752,389

6   This is clearly a hyper-inflationary economy and following IAS 29 the calculation is:

30 million × 1,100/100 ÷ 12 = $27.5 million

7   **C**   At 31 December 20X0, the entity recognised a provision of $24,240,000 (60 million × 0.404). Because the expenditure gives the entity access to future economic benefits the entity also recognises a non-current asset of $24,240,000.

The charge to the income statement is made up of two elements:

	$'000
Unwinding of the discount (24,240 × 12%)	2,880
Depreciation (24,240 ÷ 8)	3,030
	5,910

8   **B**   MNO has no inventories, moderate levels of land and property, low levels of other non-current assets and very high trade receivables and trade payables. This suggests that MNO operates in a service industry. An insurance broker is the only one of the four that fits this profile.

9   **D**   Statement (i) is not true, but the other three statements are correct.

10   A

		$
Proceeds		4,000,000
Net assets at date of disposal (35% × (8,500 + (800 × 6/12))		(3,115,000)
Less goodwill not written off (1,000 × 35/75)		(466,667)
		418,333

80 Mixed bank (3)

1   Dividend paid to minority interest = $2.7m

MINORITY INTEREST ACCOUNT

	$m		$m
Cash paid (balance figure)	2.7	Opening balance	3.6
		Income statement	2.0
		Acquisition (25% × 6.4)	1.6
Closing balance	6.0	Revaluation	1.5
	8.7		8.7

2   Consolidated retained earnings of F = $7.68m

Effective interest in F   = 80% × 60%
                                 = 48%

Post acquisition profits in F   = 48% × (30 − 14)
                                 = $7.68m

3   C   Statement (i)   Untrue – There is a presumption that L would be an associate of K but this is rebuttable for example if another party held say 70% of the shares whilst K only held 30%

         Statement (ii)   True – If K controls L then L will be a subsidiary not an associate

         Statement (iii) True – There is no elimination of balances for an associate as the associate is not part of the group.

4   C

	$m
Opening liability	35
Expected return on assets	(60)
Unwinding of discount	30
Current service cost	45
Additional benefits	10
Pension contributions	(40)
Actuarial loss (balance figure)	20
Closing liability	40

5   Value to the business is the lower of replacement cost and recoverable amount.

     Recoverable amount is the higher of realisable value and value in use.

6   If an entity operates in a hyper-inflationary economy and reports in that currency then its financial statements should be stated in terms of the measuring unit that is current at the balance sheet date.

7   Consolidated profit on disposal = $24,000

	$
Disposal proceeds	125,000
Net assets disposed of	
(20% × 400,000)	(80,000)
Goodwill not written off to income statement (impairment)	
(120,000 – 36,000) × 20,000/80,000	(21,000)
Consolidated profit on disposal	24,000

8   Mark up on cost   = 20,000/80,000 × 100%
                          = 25%

     Unrealised profit in inventory   = $16,000 × 25/125 × 25%
                                        = $800

In the consolidated income statement $800 is deducted from 'share in profits of associates'. Only the group share is eliminated.

In the consolidated balance sheet $800 is deducted from the value of the consolidated inventory.

81 Mixed bank (4)

1   A   HI and JK did not become part of the FG group until 31 December 20X1. Therefore we need the post acquisition profits from that date using the effective interest in JK of 60% (80% × 75%).

	$
HI (12,200,000 – 10,000,000) × 80%	1,760,000
JK (10,600,000 – 7,600,000) × 60%	1,800,000
	3,560,000

2   B

	$
Cash 80% × 3,000,000 × $1.20	2,880,000
Shares 80% × 3,000,000 × 2 × $1.50	7,200,000
Acquisition fees	400,000
	10,480,000

3   D

4   C   The only cash inflow from TP is the dividend received by the shareholders. TP paid a dividend of $100,000 after NS had acquired its shares therefore NS received 30% of this dividend – $30,000.

5   D

6   (i)   **Debt.** The preference shares require regular distributions to the holders but more importantly have the debt characteristic of being redeemable. Therefore according to IAS 32 *Financial instruments: presentation* they must be classified as debt.

     (ii) **Equity.** According to IFRS 2 Share based payment the grant of share options must be recorded as equity in the balance sheet. It is an alternative method of payment to cash for the provision of the services of the directors.

7   A

8   The substance of the transaction is not that it is a sale of the land but rather the receipt of a loan that is secured on the value of the land. The effective interest on the loan is the increase each year in the amount of the repurchase price. IAS 39 *Financial instruments: recognition and measurement* requires such a transaction to be recorded as a liability together with the related interest expense.

Journal entry

	$'000	$'000
DEBIT Suspense account	7,200	
DEBIT Interest expense ($7.7 – $7.2)	500	
CREDIT Non-current liabilities		7,700

82 Mixed bank (5)

> **Examiner's comment.** Section A produced the full range of marks, with several candidates scoring the maximum of 20. It was a little surprising that so many candidates were unable to calculate the correct figure for minority interest in question 1.1. Similarly, in question 1.7, quite a substantial minority of candidates were unable even to state correctly the initial journal entry for the acquisition of an investment.

1

	$
Ordinary share capital	60,000
Retained earnings	215,000
Fair value adjustment (15,600 – 10,200)	5,400
Less additional depreciation (5,400 × 6/48)	(675)
	279,725

	$
Minority share 279,725 × 25%	69,931
Minority share of preferred shares 75% × 20,000	15,000
Minority interest	84,931

2   The unrealised profit is $5,000 and the inventory is still held by AB. Therefore the adjustment must be to credit inventory. However, as EF is an associate, the amount is only the group share of the unrealised profit 30% × 5,000 = $1,500.

3   C   Proportionate consolidation is the preferred method.

4   Any two of:

    (a)   The general population prefers to keep its non-monetary assets in a relatively stable foreign currency. Amounts of local currency held are immediately invested to maintain purchasing power.

    (b)   The general population regards monetary amounts not in terms of local currency but in terms of a relatively stable foreign currency. Prices may be quoted in that currency.

    (c)   Sales and purchases on credit take place at prices that compensate for the expected loss of purchasing power during the credit period, even if the period is short.

    (d)   Interest rates, wages and prices are linked to a price index.

    (e)   The cumulative inflation rate over three years approaches, or exceeds, 100%.

5   D

	$
Issue costs	120,000
Interest $6,000,000 × 3.5% × 7	1,470,000
Premium on redemption	1,100,000
Total finance cost	2,690,000

6   A

	$
Closing defined benefit obligation	6,600,000
Current service cost	875,000
Benefits paid	(650,000)
Increase in PV of liabilities	540,000
Actuarial gain (balancing figure)	(165,000)
Closing defined benefit obligation	7,200,000

7	11 Feb 20X5	
	DEBIT Investment 60,000 × 0.85	$51,000
	CREDIT Cash	$51,000
	31 March 20X5	
	DEBIT Investment 60,000 × 0.025	$1,500
	CREDIT Increase in fair value (income statement)	$1,500

83 Mixed bank (6)

1

	$m	$m
Cost of combination		1.45
Net assets acquired		
Book value of net assets	1.35	
Fair value adjustments	0.10	
Contingent liability	(0.20)	
Net assets	1.25	
Group share 80% × 1.25		1.00
Goodwill		0.45

In accordance with IFRS 3, restructuring provisions can only be included in the goodwill calculation if there is an existing liability for the restructuring in accordance with *IAS 37 Provisions, contingent liabilities and contingent assets.* In this case JKL has no such existing liability and therefore the provision is excluded.

2   **C**   You need to account for cash in transit.

3   If a subsidiary has been acquired and is held exclusively with a view to its subsequent sale then according to *IFRS 5 Non-current assets held for sale and discontinued operations* the subsidiary can be treated as 'held for sale'. The 'exclusion' is from full line by line consolidation and the subsidiary would be presented on two lines in the group balance sheet 'non-current assets classified as held for sale' and 'liabilities directly associated with non-current assets classified as held for sale'. However, the investment can only be treated as 'held for sale' if it is intended to dispose of the asset within 12 months of the balance sheet date. Therefore in this case it would only be possible to treat STU in this way if the intention were to sell the investment before 28 February 20X7.

4   **A**   600,000 crowns/7 = $85,714

The closing rate must be used.

5   In accordance with IAS 39 *Financial instruments: recognition and measurement* gains and losses on designated hedging instruments and the items that they hedge may be netted off against each other. However any unhedged elements must be recognised in profit or loss. Therefore only any gain or loss on the unhedged element of the investment in DEP will be shown in the income statement.

6

> **Top tip** The method to use here is to find the present value of the principal value of the bond, $500,000 (10,000 × $50) and the interest payments of $25,000 annually (5% × $500,000) at the market rate for non-convertible bonds of 6%, using the discount factor tables. The difference between this total and the principal amount of $500,000 is the equity element.

	$
Present value of principal $500,000 × 0.747	373,500
Present value of interest $25,000 × 4.212	105,300
Liability value	478,800
Principal amount	500,000
Equity element	21,200

7   An actuary will determine the value of a pension plan's assets and liabilities. In order to do this, the actuary will make a number of assumptions. In subsequent years actual events may not in fact coincide with the actuary's assumptions.

A gain or loss on the pension plan is where either value of the assets of the plan exceed the value of the liabilities or vice versa. The element of this gain or loss which is due to the actuarial assumptions not having been the same as the actual outcomes is known as the experience gain or loss.

8   D   Following IFRS 2 a charge must be made to the income statement.

84 Mixed bank (7)

1   A

ASSOCIATE

	2006		20X6
	$'000		$'000
Opening balance	6,600	Dividend (bal fig)	90
Share of profit (420 – 180)	240	Closing balance	6,750
	6,840		6,840

2    $291,350

DYQ and EZR became members of the CXP group on 1 November 20X5. Therefore post-acquisition profits are taken from that date.

CXP has an effective interest in EZR of 48.75% (75% × 65%).

	$
CXP	266,000
DYQ (178,000 – 152,000) × 75%	19,500
EZR (214,000 – 202,000) × 48.75%	5,850
	291,350

3    $19,700

Goodwill calculation

	$	$
Cost of combination		250,000
Net assets acquired		
Share capital	50,000	
Reserves	186,000	
	236,000	
Group share 236,000 × 80%		188,800
Goodwill on acquisition		61,200

Profit on disposal

	$
Proceeds	95,000
Less net assets disposed of (20% × 275,000)	(55,000)
Less goodwill (61,200 × 10,000/40,000)	(15,300)
Profit on disposal	24,700

4   Earnings per share   = $3.70

Diluted earnings per share   = $3.16

Basic EPS = $100m/27m

      = $3.70

Diluted EPS

		$
Basic earnings		100.0
Add back interest (50m × 12%)		6.0
Less tax relief (6m × 30%)		(1.8)
		104.2

Number of shares	=	27m + ($50m/$100 × 12)
	=	27m + 6m
	=	33m

Diluted EPS	=	$104.2/33m
	=	$3.16

5   Total finance cost = $3.15m

	$'000
Issue costs	150
Coupon interest ($5m × 2.5% ×10)	1,250
Premium	1,750
	3,150

6   D

7   The comparison of the measure of asset backing between entities may be invalid due to any of the following.

(a)   Different accounting policies in the entities

(b)   Whether or not the entities revalue their non-current assets

(c)   The age of their non-current assets

(d)   Companies of identical value could have different numbers of shares in issue

85 Mixed bank (8)

1   D   DEBIT   Revenue $100,000
            CREDIT Cost of sales $100,000

> **Top tips.** Intra-group revenue must be eliminated in full from revenue as income and costs are wholly intra-group. As there is no unsold inventory at the year end and, therefore, no unrealised profit, the adjustment to costs is the same as the adjustment to revenue.

2   A   The subsidiary has been acquired exclusively with a view to subsequent disposal

> **Top tips.** Before the issue of IFRS 5 *Non-current assets held for sale and discontinued operations*, IAS 27 *Consolidated and separate financial statements* allowed the exemption from consolidation of subsidiaries acquired with a view to resale.
>
> Although IFRS 5 has removed the IAS 7 exemption and all subsidiaries have to be consolidated, a short-cut method of consolidating and re-measuring a subsidiary held exclusively for resale is allowed by IFRS 5. This short-cut method is not a traditional line by line consolidation. The acquired entity's assets and liabilities including intangibles do not need to be separately identified. The subsidiary is initially measured at fair value less disposal costs. Subsequent measurement is at the lower of its carrying amount and fair value less costs to sell.
>
> Exclusion for dissimilar activities is not permitted because adequate information should be available from IFRS 8 *Segment reporting*.

3

	$
Book value of BLK's net assets	1,300,000
Fair value adjustment for plant (W)	50,000
Market value for patent	150,000
Provision for rationalisation programme	(250,000)
Fair value at 31 July X7	1,290,000

The provision should be recognised because the directors of BLK were committed to the programme before the acquisition.

The patents have been excluded from the fair value due to the fact that the criteria for recognition do not appear to have been met.

- Patents do not appear to be separable.
- Patents do not appear to be capable of being reliably measured.

Working

	$
Replacement cost of plant	700,000
Less: accumulated depreciation for 3 years out of 6, on a straight line basis	
(700,000 × 3/6)	(350,000)
	350,000
Less: book value of plant included in the net assets	(300,000)
Increase in net assets	50,000

4   C $80,000

$100,000 sales in transit include a mark-up of 25% which needs to be eliminated. Sales at cost, excluding the mark-up are therefore ($100,000 × 100%)/125% = $80,000

5   The general rule is that financial liabilities should be measured at amortised cost using the effective interest rate method.

6   BLT GROUP
STATEMENT OF CHANGES IN EQUITY
FOR THE YEAR ENDED 31 AUGUST 20X7

	Group	MI	Total
	$'000	$'000	$'000
Balance at 1 September X6	449,600	127,000	576,600
Acquisition [(127,000 × 100%/40%) + (30,000 × 6/12)] x 20%	–	(66,500)	(66,500)
Profit (98,970 + (30k × 6/12 × 60%) + (30k × 6/12 × 80%))	119,970	9,000 *	128,970
Dividend	(40,000)		(40,000)
Balance at 31 August 20X7	530,200	69,500	599,700

* (30k × 6/12 × 40%) + (30k × 6/12 × 20%))

7   C $53,000

PROPERTY, PLANT AND EQUIPMENT

	$'000		$'000
NBV b/fwd	207	Disposals (NBV)	Nil
Additions (bal. fig.)	53	Deprecation charge	32
		Balance c/fwd	228
	260		260

8   The two conditions which must exist in order for hedge accounting to be permitted under IAS 9 *Financial Instruments: Recognition and Measurement* are as follows:

(a)   The hedging relationship must be formally designated and documented.

(b)   The hedge must be expected to be highly effective and its effectiveness must be capable of being reliably measured.

86 Mixed bank (9)

1   C   36%

The effective interest of AB in EF is 60% of 60% = 36%

2

	Sh'000	Sh'000	Rate	$'000
Cost of combination		3,000		
Less: FV of identifiable NA:				
Share capital	1,000			
Pre-acq'n reserves	1,500			
Group share	70%	(1,750)		
		1,250	5	250.0
Exchange gain/(loss) – 20X8 *				β 15.9
		1,250	4.7	265.9

*   The exchange gain did not need to be calculated here but is included for future reference.

3   C $34,500

The consolidated revenue for inclusion in MNN's group income statement is calculated as follows:

	$
LMN	21,500
OPQ (1/3 × 5,400)	1,800
RST	12,600
	35,900
Intra-group sales	(1,400)
	34,500

4   The purpose of the cost of sales adjustment (COSA) is to eliminate realised holding gains on inventory. It represents the difference between the replacement cost and the historic cost (HC) of goods sold.

The COSA ensures that profit is reduced by the amount that must be consumed in replacing the inventory item sold so that trading can continue at the same levels.

The exclusion of holding gains from current cost profit is therefore required in order to maintain operating capacity.

5   Non-redeemable shares are categorised according to the rights attached to them. If distributions were entirely at the discretion of the issuer, the shares would be classified as equity.

Where distributions are compulsory, the non-redeemable shares would be classified as debt. In this case, the issuer, CPP, is able to carry distributions forward but cannot avoid them. Therefore, the shares will be classified as debt.

6   Unrealised profit in IYC's books

	$
Unrealised profit on transfer (200,000 – 150,000)	50,000
Less proportion depreciated by year end (50,000 × 2% × 6)	(6,000)
	44,000

Adjusting entry on consolidation

		$	$
DEBIT	Group retained earnings	44,000	
CREDIT	Property, plant and equipment		44,000

7   The liability of $300,000 falls due two years after the acquisition date so the fair value of the liability at 1 March 20X7 was:

$300,000 × 0.857 = $257,100

The adjustment to unwind the discount for the year to 29 February 20X8 is:

		$	$
DEBIT	Interest ($257,100 × 8%)	20,568	
CREDIT	Liability		20,568

Therefore after taking into account the adjustment for the unwinding of the discount the profit for the period for YQS is $47,032 (being $67,600 – $20,568).

The share attributable to the equity shareholders of XPR is $28,219 (being 60% of $47,032).

8   The amount to be recognised as the net plan liability in the balance sheet of NST is the total of the following:

- The present value of the defined benefit obligation,

plus

- Unrecognised actuarial gains

minus

- The fair value of the assets of the plan.

	$m
Present value of pension obligation	18.6
Unrecognised actuarial gains	0.7
Fair value of plan assets	(16.9)
Net plan liability	2.4

9   IAS 39 requires financial assets classified as 'held-for-trading' to be accounted for at fair value. Any gains or losses on such assets are accounted for through profit or loss in the period in which they occur.

Mock Exams

CIMA – Managerial Level

Paper P8

Financial Analysis

Mock Examination 1

Instructions to candidates:

You are allowed three hours to answer this question paper.
In the real exam, you are allowed 20 minutes reading time before the examination begins during which you should read the question paper, and if you wish, highlight and/or make notes on the question paper. However, you will **not** be allowed, **under any circumstances**, to open the answer book and start writing or use your calculator during this reading time.
You are strongly advised to carefully read ALL the question requirements before attempting the question concerned (including all parts and/or sub-questions).
Answer the ONE compulsory question in Section A. This has ten objective test sub-questions.
Answer ALL THREE questions in Section B.
Answer TWO of the THREE questions in Section C.

DO NOT OPEN THIS PAPER UNTIL YOU ARE READY TO START UNDER EXAMINATION CONDITIONS

SECTION A – 20 marks

(The indicative time for answering this question is 36 minutes)

Answer ALL TEN sub-questions

The answers to the ten sub-questions in Section A should ALL be written in your answer book.

Your answers should be clearly numbered with the sub-question number and then ruled off, so that the markers know which sub-question you are answering. **For multiple choice questions, you need only write the sub-question number and the letter of the answer option you have chosen.** You do not need to start a new page for each sub-question.

1 Mixed bank (Mock 1)

1.1 Peach purchased 75% of the equity share capital of Damson many years ago. On 30 September 20X6 Peach sold one third of its holding in Damson. During the year ended 31 December 20X6, Damson made a profit after tax of $240,000.

What is the minority interest in the consolidated income statement for the year ended 31 December 20X6?

A	$45,000
B	$60,000
C	$90,000
D	$180,000

(2 marks)

1.2 Gateway is a manufacturer. It has set up an overseas subsidiary in order to sell Gateway's products in Europe. This subsidiary is 100% owned. The exchange gain arising from the translation of the subsidiary's accounts for the year ended 30 June 20X4 was $20,000.

On 1 June 20X4 Gateway purchased raw materials from a European supplier for E250,000. It paid for the materials on 31 July 20X4. Relevant exchange rates were:

	E=$1
1 June 20X4	1.6
30 June 20X4	1.61
31 July 20X4	1.63

In respect of these items, what is the exchange gain that should be included in the consolidated income statement for the year ended 30 June 20X4? **(3 marks)**

1.3 When a parent has a subsidiary that is a foreign operation, which rates of exchange should be used to translate the items below into local currency?

	Non-current assets	Receivables	Non-current liabilities	
A	Closing rate	Closing rate	Closing rate	
B	Historic rate	Closing rate	Closing rate	
C	Historic rate	Historic rate	Closing rate	
D	Historic rate	Historic rate	Historic rate	**(2 marks)**

1.4 Bishop had several subsidiaries and a 25% associate, Pawn. Bishop's investment in Pawn (as shown in its consolidated balance sheet) was $490,000 at the beginning of the year and $550,000 at the end of the year.

The summarised income statement of Pawn for the year is shown below:

	$'000
Profit from operations	510
Interest payable	(120)
Profit before tax	390
Income tax expense	(90)
Profit after tax	300

What amount should appear under 'dividends from associate' in the consolidated cash flow statement for the year?

A $15,000
B $37,500
C $75,000
D $135,000   **(2 marks)**

1.5   On 1 January 20X2, Gascony acquired 90% of the equity share capital of Toulouse. The consideration was made up of 100,000 $1 equity shares in Gascony, valued at $2.50 each, plus $300,000 in cash.

At 1 January 20X2 Toulouse had the following assets and liabilities:

	$'000
Property, plant and equipment	460
Inventories	230
Receivables	280
Cash at bank and in hand	10
Bank overdraft	(60)
Payables	(190)
Non-current borrowings	(150)
	580

What amount is reported under 'purchase of subsidiary' in the consolidated cash flow statement for the year ended 31 December 20X2?   **(2 marks)**

1.6   JK operates a defined benefit pension plan. The following information relates to the plan for the year ended 31 August 20X7:

Contributions paid to the plan	$9 million
Estimated current service cost	$10 million
Expected return on plan assets	$8 million
Actuarial gains less losses give net loss of	$12 million
Unwinding of discount on pension plan liabilities	$5 million

According to IAS 19 *Employee benefits*, what is the charge to the income statement in respect of retirement benefits for the year ended 31 August 20X7?   **(1 mark)**

1.7   The assets and liabilities of an entity include the following:

(1)   an option to subscribe for shares in another entity
(2)   a forward contract for foreign currency
(3)   a bank loan
(4)   10% loan stock

Which of these items is a financial instrument as defined by IAS 32 and IAS 39?

A   (2)
B   (1) and (2)
C   (1), (2) and (4)
D   All of them   **(2 marks)**

1.8   CDE has an overseas subsidiary, FGH. The financial statements of FGH have been prepared in accordance with UK GAAP.

FGH has adopted the following accounting policies:

•   Deferred tax is calculated using the full provision method.
•   Positive purchased goodwill is amortised over its useful life.

In the financial statements of FGH, which items will need to be adjusted for the purpose of preparing the consolidated financial statements of the CDE Group under IASs?

A	Deferred tax only	
B	Positive purchased goodwill only	
C	Positive purchased goodwill and deferred tax	
D	Neither positive purchased goodwill nor deferred tax	**(2 marks)**

1.9 What would be the immediate effect on an entity's P/E ratio and dividend yield of an announcement which caused a substantial rise in the share price?

	P/E ratio	*Dividend yield*
A	Decrease	Decrease
B	Decrease	Increase
C	Increase	Decrease
D	Increase	Increase

(2 marks)

1.10 An entity wishes to increase its return on capital employed (ROCE). Which of the following courses of action will help to achieve this in the short term?

A	Increase sales	
B	Increase the level of dividends paid to equity shareholders	
C	Issue ordinary shares	
D	Revalue land and buildings upwards	**(2 marks)**

(Total for Section A = 20 marks)

SECTION B – 30 marks

(The indicative time for answering this Section is 54 minutes.)

Answer ALL THREE questions

2 DCB and GFE

DCB is a manufacturing and trading entity with several overseas operations. One of its subsidiaries, GFE, operates in a country which experiences relatively high rates of inflation in its currency, the crown. Most entities operating in that country voluntarily present two versions of their financial statements: one at historical cost, and the other incorporating current cost adjustments. GFE complies with this accepted practice.

Extracts from the income statement adjusted for current costs for the year ended 30 September 20X5 are as follows.

	Crowns 000	Crowns 000
Historical cost operating profit		750
Current cost adjustment		
Cost of sales adjustment	65	
Depreciation adjustment	43	
Loss on net monetary position	16	
		124
Current cost operating profit		626

Required

(a)   Explain the defects of historical cost accounting in times of increasing prices.   **(4 marks)**

(b)   Explain how *each* of the three current cost accounting adjustments in GFE's financial statements contributes to the maintenance of capital.   **(6 marks)**

(Total = 10 marks)

3 ABC and DEF

ABC is currently expanding its portfolio of equity interests in other entities. On 1 January 20X5, it made a successful bid for a controlling interest in DEF, paying a combination of shares and cash in order to acquire 80% of DEF's 100,000 issued equity shares. The terms of the acquisition were as follows.

In exchange for each $1 ordinary share purchased, ABC issued one of its own $1 ordinary shares and paid $1.50 in cash. In addition to the consideration paid, ABC agreed to pay a further $1 per share on 1 January 20X7, on condition that the profits of DEF for the year ended 31 May 20X6 will exceed $6,000,000. ABC's directors consider that it is more likely than not that the additional consideration will be paid. The market value of a $1 share in ABC at January 20X5 was $3.50, rising to $3.60 at ABC's 31 May 20X5 year end.

Total legal, administrative and share issue costs associated with the acquisition were $60,000. This figure included $20,000 paid to external legal and accounting advisors, an estimated $10,000 in respect of ABC's own administrative overhead and $30,000 in share issue costs.

The carrying value of DEF's net assets at 1 January 20X5 was $594,000. Carrying value was regarded as a close approximation to fair value, except in respect of the following.

(a)   The carrying value of DEF's property, plant and equipment at 1 January 20X5 was $460,000. Market value at that date was estimated at $530,000.

(b)   DEF had a contingent liability in respect of a major product warranty claim with a fair value of $100,000.

(c)   The cost of reorganising DEF's activities following acquisition was estimated at $75,000.

(d)   DEF's inventories included goods at an advanced stage of work-in-progress with a carrying value of $30,000. The sales value of these goods was estimated at $42,000 and further costs to completion at $6,000.

Required

Calculate goodwill on the acquisition of DEF, in accordance with the requirements of IFRS 3 *Business combinations*, explaining your treatment of the legal, administrative, share issue and reorganisation costs.   **(10 marks)**

4 US GAAP v IFRS

At a recent staff seminar on accounting standards, a senior member of your firm's accounting staff made the following observation:

'International Standards have now been adopted in many countries across the world. Unfortunately though, they can never be truly international because US GAAP will continue to dominate accounting in the USA and therefore in many multinational businesses.'

Required

Explain the rationale for this observation, illustrating your explanation with examples of significant differences and similarities between US GAAP and International Financial Reporting Standards.   **(10 marks)**

(Total for Section B = 30 marks)

SECTION C – 50 marks

(The indicative time for answering this Section is 90 minutes.)

Answer TWO questions out of THREE

5 Expand

You are the management accountant of Expand, an entity incorporated in Dollarland. Expand is seeking to grow by acquisition and has identified two potential investment opportunities. One of these, Hone, is also incorporated in Dollarland. The other, Over, is incorporated in Francland.

You have been presented with financial information relating to both entities. The financial information is extracted from their published financial statements. In both cases, the financial statements conform to domestic accounting standards. The financial statements of Hone were drawn up in $s while those of Over were drawn up in Francs. The information relating to Over has been expressed in $s by taking the figures in Francs and dividing by 1.55 – the $/Franc exchange rate at 31 December 20X0. The financial information is given below.

INCOME STATEMENTS

	Hone		Over	
Year ended	31 March 20X1	31 March 20X0	31 December 20X0	31 December 20W9
	$ million	$ million	$ million	$ million
Revenue	600	550	620	560
Cost of sales	(300)	(250)	(320)	(260)
Gross profit	300	300	300	300
Other operating expenses	(120)	(105)	(90)	(85)
Profit before interest and tax	180	195	210	215
Finance cost	(20)	(18)	(22)	(20)
Profit before tax	160	177	188	195
Income tax expense	(50)	(55)	(78)	(90)
Profit for the period	110	122	110	105

STATEMENTS OF CHANGES IN EQUITY

	Hone		Over	
Year ended	31 March 20X1	31 March 20X0	31 December 20X0	31 December 20W9
	$ million	$ million	$ million	$ million
Balance brought forward	470	418	265	240
Profit for the period	110	122	110	105
Dividends	(70)	(70)	(80)	(80)
Balance carried forward	510	470	295	265

BALANCE SHEETS

	Hone		Over	
Year ended	31 March 20X1	31 March 20X0	31 December 20X0	31 December 20W9
	$ million	$ million	$ million	$ million
Property, plant and equipment	600	570	455	440
Inventories	60	50	55	50
Trade receivables	80	75	90	80
Cash	10	20	15	15
	750	715	615	585

Year ended	Hone 31 March 20X1 $ million	Hone 31 March 20X0 $ million	Over 31 December 20X0 $ million	Over 31 December 20W9 $ million
Share capital	150	150	110	110
Retained earnings	360	320	185	155
	510	470	295	265
Long-term borrowings	150	150	240	240
Current liabilities	90	95	80	80
	750	715	615	585

Expand is more concerned with the profitability of potential investment opportunities than with liquidity. You have been asked to review the financial statements of Hone and Over with this concern in mind.

Required

(a) Prepare a short report to the directors of Expand that, based on the financial information provided, assesses the relative profitability of Hone and Over. **(14 marks)**

(b) Discuss the validity of using this financial information as a basis to compare the profitability of the two entities. **(11 marks)**

(Total = 25 marks)

6 Walsh

Walsh, a public limited company, acquired 80% of the ordinary share capital of Marsh, a public limited company, on 1 April 20X3 when the retained earnings of Marsh were $350 million (credit). The cost of the shares of Marsh was $544 million and the share capital acquired by Walsh was 120 million of the $1 ordinary shares. On 1 July 20X6 Walsh sold 20 million shares of $1 of Marsh for $350m. There has been no change in the ordinary share capital of Marsh since 1 April 20X3.

On 1 April 20X6 Walsh acquired 85% of the 200 million shares of $1 of Short, a public limited company at a cost of $900 million. The capital of Short comprises ordinary shares and retained earnings. There is no share premium account.

The draft income statements for the year ended 31 December 20X6 are:

	Walsh $m	Marsh $m	Short $m
Revenue	10,000	8,000	2,000
Cost of sales	(7,000)	(5,500)	(800)
Gross profit	3,000	2,500	1,200
Sundry expenses	(880)	(570)	(180)
Distribution costs	(1,310)	(830)	(240)
Interest expense	(7)		(4)
Bank interest receivable	5	–	–
Profit before tax	808	1,100	776
Income tax expense	(250)	(350)	(200)
Profit for the period	558	750	576
Retained earnings at 1.1.X6	1,500	1,650	675

The following information is relevant to the preparation of the group accounts.

(a) The sale of the shares in Marsh has not been accounted for in the accounting records of Walsh (ignore the taxation aspects of the sale).

(b) Short sold goods to Walsh to the selling value of $80 million on 1 August 20X6 at cost plus 20%. Walsh had sold $62 million of these goods at the year end.

(c) Assume that the fair values of the net assets of the subsidiary companies were the same as the book values at the date of acquisition.

(d)   Assume that profits accrue evenly and there are no other reserves than the retained earnings reserve.

No dividends have been paid during the year.

Required

Prepare a consolidated income statement for the Walsh Group for the year ended 31 December 20X6 in accordance with International Financial Reporting Standards. **(25 marks)**

7 Global

You are the management accountant of Global. Global has operations in a number of different areas of the world and presents segment information on a geographical basis in accordance with IAS 14 *Segment reporting*. The segment information for the year ended 30 June 20X2 is given below.

	Europe		America		Africa		Group	
	20X2 $m	20X1 $m	20X2 $m	20X1 $m	20X2 $m	20X1 $m	20X2 $m	20X1 $m
Revenue								
External sales	700	680	600	550	400	200	1,700	1,430
Inter-segment sales	20	5	10	10	40	5	70	20
Total revenue	720	685	610	560	440	205	1,770	1,450
Result								
Segment result	70	69	90	90	(20)	(40)	140	119
Unallocated corporate expenses							(25)	(20)
Profit from operations							115	99
Interest expense							(22)	(18)
Interest income							4	3
Share of profits of associates	10	9	12	5	–	–	22	14
Income taxes							(35)	(30)
Net profit							84	68
Other information								
Segment assets	610	560	610	560	300	270	1,520	1,390
Investment in equity method associates	55	52	36	30			91	82
Unallocated corporate assets							200	175
Consolidated total assets							1,811	1,647
Segment liabilities	260	240	250	230	100	90	610	560
Unallocated corporate liabilities							80	75
Consolidated total liabilities							690	635

Your chief executive officer has reviewed the segment information above and has expressed concerns about the performance of Global. He is particularly concerned about the fact that the Africa segment has been making losses ever since the initial investment in 20X0. He wonders whether operations in Africa should be discontinued, given the consistently poor results.

Required

(a)   Prepare a report for the chief executive officer of Global that analyses the performance of the three geographical segments of the business, based on the data that has been provided. The report can take any form you wish, but you should specifically refer to any reservations you may have regarding the use of the segment data for analysis purposes. **(20 marks)**

(b)   Discuss two other bases of segment reporting that Global could have adopted. **(5 marks)**

(Total = 25 marks)

(Total for Section C = 50 marks)

Answers

**DO NOT TURN THIS PAGE UNTIL YOU HAVE
COMPLETED THE MOCK EXAM**

A plan of attack

The exam may look daunting at first. You need to adopt a calm approach. The following plan of attack is just a suggestion.

First things first

Part A contains ten objective testing (OT) and short answer questions of varying degrees of difficulty designed to cover the whole syllabus. Part A tests your knowledge and understanding and provides the opportunity for the well-prepared candidate to score high marks.

Both Parts A and B are compulsory, so you may as well start with Part A and the OT and short answer questions. Remember the instructions for dealing with these OTs and MCQs at the beginning of the Kit. Do not exceed the time limit of **36 minutes** for this section. Answer the easy questions first.

Part B

Part B is also compulsory so you may as well deal with these three ten-mark questions next. This section, in keeping with the style of the real exam, is a combination of discursive and numerical questions. Do not get bogged down in the detail and remember to allow yourself only **54 minutes**, allocating equal time to each question. The first question is testing the limitations of historic cost accounting and requires you to explain how current cost accounting adjustments contribute to the maintenance of capital. Make sure you say something about *each* of the adjustments. The second question requires the calculation of goodwill on acquisition. Note that in addition to the calculation you are required to explain your reasoning for your treatment of costs. In Question four, on IFRS versus US GAAP, make sure your arguments are well balanced.

Part C

Part C has **two questions** to answer out of three. Choose the question that you know most about to answer first. Remember to answer only **two** questions. If you try parts of all three, only the marks for your best two questions will count, so you will have wasted your time **and possibly failed** the exam.

In choosing your questions, have regard to your strengths and weaknesses.

Question 5. A financial analysis report involving both calculations and commentary requires you to assess the relative profitability of two potential acquisition targets. You can always say something, so we would advise you to have a go. Make sure your report looks critically at the ratios calculated.

Question 6. A rather complicated consolidation, but there are easy marks for standard consolidation aspects even if you can't do the disposal.

Question 7. If you were really put off by the partial disposal in Question 6, this is a good question to do even if your knowledge of segment reporting is not very good. (We recommend Question 5 in any event.)

Remember

Always – well nearly always – **allocate your time** according to the marks for the question in total and then according to the parts of the question. The only exception is if the question is compulsory, say in Section B, and you really know nothing about it. You may as well try to pick up marks elsewhere. And **always**, **always follow the requirements** exactly.

You've got spare time at the end of the exam ... ?

If you have allocated your time properly then you **shouldn't have time on your hands** at the end of the exam. But if you find yourself with five or ten minutes to spare, **go back to the questions** that you couldn't do or to **any parts of questions that you didn't finish** because you ran out of time.

Forget about it!

And don't worry if you found the paper difficult. More than likely other candidates will too. If this were the real thing you would need to **forget** the exam the minute you leave the exam hall and **think about the next one**. Or, if it's the last one, **celebrate**!

SECTION A

1 Mixed bank (Mock 1)

1.1   A
     $

Profit after tax
     25% × 9/12 × 240,000   45,000

Damson became an associate on 30 September 20X6 and therefore there is no minority interest for the last three months of the year.

1.2   Exchange gain:

     $

Purchase from European supplier:
     1 June 20X4 (250,000 @ 1.6)   156,250
     30 June 20X4 (250,000 @ 1.61)   (155,280)
     970
Gain on translation of subsidiary   20,000
     20,970

The overseas subsidiary has the same functional currency as the parent (ie it is not a semi-autonomous operation) and therefore the translation gain of $20,000 is reported in the consolidated income statement.

1.3   A   Non-current assets are always closing rate, not historic rate, for foreign operations.

1.4   A
INVESTMENT IN ASSOCIATE

	$'000		$'000
Balance b/f	490	Dividend (balancing figure)	15
Share of net profit (25% × 300)	75	Balance c/f	550
	565		565

1.5 $350,000

	$'000
Cash paid to acquire subsidiary	300
Cash acquired with subsidiary	(10)
Bank overdraft acquired with subsidiary	60
	350

1.6 $7m

	$m
Current service cost	10
Unwinding of discount	5
Less expected return on assets	(8)
	7

1.7   D   A financial instrument is any contract that gives rise to both a financial asset of one entity and a financial liability or equity instrument of another entity.

1.8   C   Z must disclose transactions with group entities in its financial statements as these are related parties (see IAS 24).

1.9   B   Under IFRS 3, positive purchased goodwill is not amortised, but carried forward at cost and reviewed for impairment annually.

1.10   A   An increase in sales will probably lead to an increase in operating profit. There will be no increase in capital employed.

     Increasing the level of dividends (option B) has no effect on ROCE. Revaluing land and buildings upwards (option D) decreases ROCE, because it increases capital employed and reduces profits. Issuing ordinary shares (option C) increases capital employed and decreases ROCE in the short term, although the issue proceeds can be used to generate additional profit and this may help to increase ROCE in the longer term.

SECTION B

2 DCB and GFE

(a)   In a time of increasing prices there are a number of **defects in historical cost accounting**:

    (i)   As historical cost accounting **ignores the current value of assets** therefore the balance sheet gives an unrealistic figure for capital employed.

    (ii)   **Profits in the income statement tend to be overstated** as depreciation charges are based on out of date costs for non-current assets.

    (iii)   Profits are also overstated as cost of sales is valued at historic cost rather than current cost.

    (iv)   A combination of understated asset values and overstated profits means that **key ratios** such as return on capital employed can be **overstated and meaningless**.

    (v)   The fact that profits are overstated with no distinction being made between operating gains and holding gains means that **dividends may be too high** and the operating capacity of the business may not be maintained.

    (vi)   There is no attempt to recognise that in a time of rising prices there is a **loss from holding fixed monetary assets** and a **gain in holding fixed monetary liabilities**.

    (vii)   **Trend information is misleading** if no account is taken of changes in the real value of money – revenue and profits may appear to be increasing in monetary terms but not in real terms.

(b)   **The cost of sales adjustment**

This is due to the fact that under historical cost accounting only the historical cost of inventory items is charged to cost of sales. This adjustment increases cost of sales from historical cost to current cost or replacement cost of the items that have been sold. This adjustment helps to ensure that the operating capacity of the business is maintained in that a similar number of goods could be purchased out of retained profits as were sold in the previous year.

The depreciation adjustment

This is to charge the additional depreciation that should have been charged if the non-current assets of the business were included in the balance sheet at current value rather than historical cost. Again this helps to maintain the operating capital by ensuring that with lower profits lower dividends are paid and more is retained within the business for the replacement of non-current assets when required.

The charge for loss on net monetary position

This is a recognition that in times of rising prices the holding of net monetary assets causes a loss to the business as when the cash is received for those assets it is worth less than when the assets were created. Again as this is a charge to the income statement then less profits are available for the payment of dividends and more are retained within the business.

3 ABC and DEF

Text reference. Goodwill and fair values are covered in Chapter 4.

Top tips. This is a tricky question. It requires a computation of goodwill, but there are complications both in the consideration (share issue and contingent consideration) and in the fair value of the net assets acquired.

Easy marks. This is unusual for a ten mark Section B question, in that there are none of the easy marks found in most consolidation questions. However, if you are able to show a working for goodwill and deal with some of the easier fair value items such as the cash and the shares issued on the consideration side and the adjustment regarding the property, plant and equipment on the net assets acquired side, some easy marks would be earned.

Examiner's comment. Many candidates, although by no means all, gained useful marks on this question. A substantial group of candidates did not know how to deal with the issue, administration and legal costs A smaller, but still significant, group included the provision for reorganisation costs when calculating goodwill.

	$
Fair value of consideration	
Ordinary shares issued 80,000 × $3.50	280,000
Cash 80,000 × $1.50	120,000
Deferred consideration 80,000 × $1.00	80,000
	480,000
Add legal and accounting fees	20,000
	500,000

Note that normally the deferred consideration would be discounted to its present value but as no appropriate discount rate has been given in the question this has been ignored.

	$
Fair value of net assets	
Carrying value	594,000
Add revaluation (530,000 − 460,000)	70,000
Less contingent liability	(100,000)
Add work in progress (36,000 − 30,000)	6,000
	570,000

	$
Goodwill	
Fair value of consideration	500,000
Fair value of net assets acquired (570,000 × 80%)	456,000
Goodwill	44,000

The **legal fees** have been added to the **fair value** of the consideration as they are directly attributable costs of the business combination.

The **administrative fees** have not been included as part of the consideration as they cannot be directly attributed to the combination.

The **share issue costs** are not directly attributable to the combination and therefore are not part of the consideration. Instead they should be deducted from the proceeds of the equity issue.

There is **no present obligation** to incur the **reorganisation costs** as at the date of acquisition. Therefore they do not meet the definition of a liability and therefore they should not be recognised as part of the fair value adjustment.

4 US GAAP v IFRS

Text reference. International issues are covered in Chapter 19.

Top tips. This question required a discussion of similarities and differences between US GAAP and International Accounting Standards, and of whether US GAAP has too much influence on IAS. This is topical, and you should be familiar with this area.

Easy marks. There were easy marks to be gained for any valid points made.

Examiner's comment. Where marks were gained on this question, it was generally for identifying some of the differences between US GAAP and international standards. Only a handful of candidates were able to identify and explain examples of convergence and very few knew about the Norwalk agreement.

It is fair to say that at the current time there are **two main accounting systems** throughout the world – International Financial Reporting Standards (**IFRSs**) and US Generally Accepted Accounting Principles (**US GAAP**). Previously overseas companies seeking a listing in the US had to prepare accounting in line with US GAAP or reconcile their accounts to US GAAP. As US GAAP is generally extremely prescriptive this has often been costly and problematic for companies. Therefore it could be argued that for such companies US GAAP will prevail.

Convergence

However, in recent years there have been significant **changes to the relationship between IFRSs and US** GAAP. In May 2000 endorsement of the old IASC's core standards was given by IOSCO. As the most powerful member of IOSCO the US Securities and Exchange Commission (SEC) has therefore evidenced its support of the new IASB. It is now generally felt that with this commitment from the US, **US GAAP and IFRSs will probably rapidly converge over the next few years**. Neither the US nor the IASB are likely to issue new accounting standards which are not acceptable to the other.

Further evidence of the attempted convergence between US GAAP and IFRSs is the current SEC sanctioned **IASB-FASB convergence project**. The current head of the IASB Sir David Tweedie readily admits that currently there are two sets of global standards – his own and US GAAP. The reconciliation between IFRS financial statements and US GAAP is also recognised as a problem for big companies but the SEC has now said that there is a way forward to achieve getting rid of this reconciliation by eliminating the accounting differences on several specific issues.

So clearly there are currently two sets of accounting standards in the world but there is progress being made to converge these two. The other factor to consider is how far apart IFRSs and US GAAP actually are. Over recent years the divergence between IFRS and US GAAP have become significantly less in key areas.

Similarities

Under both accounting systems goodwill in a business combination must be capitalised and carried in the balance sheet without amortisation but subject to annual impairment review. Similarly in both systems all business combinations must be treated as acquisitions with the 'pooling of interests' or 'uniting of interests' method being prohibited. With regards to deferred tax both IAS 12 and US GAAP require the liability method with full provision being based on temporary differences.

In September 2002, the FASB and IASB entered into the **Norwalk agreement**, which includes an agreement to undertake a convergence project to amend certain of their standards that do not require comprehensive reconsideration, to eliminate differences by adopting the best solution available. In some case that solution will be the IASB standard, while in other cases it will be the FASB standard. In yet other instances, the best solution may be contained in another standard-setters' standard and both FASB and IASB standards will change.

Differences

However, there are **still significant differences** between the requirements of IFRS and US GAAP. IAS 16 allows non-current assets to be carried at either cost or valuation but US GAAP requires cost with no alternative of revaluation. Development costs in the US must be written off as incurred but under IAS 38, if certain criteria are met, then the development costs must be capitalised and amortised. Under US GAAP capitalisation of borrowing costs is required for certain assets whereas under IAS 23 the preferred treatment is to recognise borrowing costs as an expense with the allowed alternative being capitalisation. Finally US GAAP allows the LIFO method of inventory valuation whereas IAS 2 no longer permits LIFO as an allowed alternative.

Note. The number of differences continues to decrease. For example IAS 23 has been revised to *require* capitalisation of borrowing costs (although this revision only takes effect from 2009).

SECTION C

5 Expand

> **Text reference**. Financial analysis is covered in Chapter 17.
>
> **Top tips**. The main point of this question is the different accounting standards being used by the target entities. However, do not forget to mention the limitations of the data given for comparison purposes. Also part (a) should focus on the question asked, ie profitability aspects.
>
> **Easy marks**. These are available for part (b), which is a standard add on to any ratio analysis question.

(a) **REPORT**

To: The Board of Directors of Expand
From: Management Accountant
Date: 23 May 20X1
Subject: Profitability of Hone and Over

1   Introduction

1.1   As requested, I have attempted to assess the relative profitability of Hone and Over. My assessment has been based on the financial information provided. Ratio calculations are set out in the attached Appendix.

2   Profitability

2.1   Over appears to be the more profitable of the two entities overall, as its return on capital employed is significantly higher than that of Hone for both years. Return on shareholders' funds for Over is also much higher than that of Hone. However, both entities are facing a reduction in profitability, despite increasing revenue in both cases. This appears to be due to falling margins, rather than inefficient use of assets.

2.2   Hone has slightly higher gross profit margins than Over, but this advantage is offset by significantly higher operating costs. One possible reason for this is Hone's higher asset values, which are likely to have resulted in higher depreciation charges.

3   Other points

3.1   Over appears to suffer a significantly higher effective rate of tax than Hone, although it should be noted that this has decreased during the period under consideration. It is also much more highly geared than Hone, although the effective rate of interest on its borrowings appears to be lower. This explains why the return on shareholders' funds of Over compares very favourably with that of Hone. The level of interest cover is adequate for both entities.

4 Conclusion

4.1 On the basis of this comparison, Over appears to be the more profitable of the two companies and therefore the better investment.

4.2 However, much more information, including forecast earnings and details of factors that could affect the companies' future profitability, should be obtained before any investment decision is taken.

(b) **Limitations of using this financial information as a basis to compare the profitability of the two companies**

These are as follows.

(i) The information provided relates to previous periods. It does not take account of events that have occurred since the balance sheet date or of factors that could affect the future earnings and prospects of the two entities.

(ii) There is no information about the nature of the operations of either entity. The two entities almost certainly operate in different geographical markets and may well carry out completely different businesses. This means that comparisons are unlikely to be meaningful.

(iii) The two sets of accounts cover different periods. If one or both businesses are seasonal it will be difficult to make valid comparisons between the two.

(iv) The financial statements have been drawn up under different accounting standards. There are likely to be significant differences between the accounting standards of Dollarland and those of Francland. The financial statements will not be comparable unless they are restated in accordance with the same accounting standards and using the same accounting policies.

(v) The financial statements of Over have been translated into dollars using the exchange rate in force at 31 December 20X0. This approach is over simplistic as the financial statements cover the two years ending on that date. The information would have been more meaningful if the balance sheet at 31 December 20W9 had been translated at the closing rate on that date and if both income statements had been translated using the average rate for the year.

Appendix – Ratios

	Hone		Over	
	20X1	*20X0*	*20X0*	*20W9*
Return on capital employed				
$\dfrac{\text{Profit before interest and tax}}{\text{Capital employed}}$	$\dfrac{180}{660} = 27.3\%$	$\dfrac{195}{620} = 31.5\%$	$\dfrac{210}{535} = 39.3\%$	$\dfrac{215}{505} = 42.6\%$
Return on shareholders' funds				
$\dfrac{\text{Profit after tax}}{\text{Shareholders' funds}}$	$\dfrac{110}{510} = 21.6\%$	$\dfrac{122}{470} = 26.0\%$	$\dfrac{110}{295} = 37.3\%$	$\dfrac{105}{265} = 39.6\%$
Gross profit margin				
$\dfrac{\text{Gross profit}}{\text{Revenue}}$	$\dfrac{300}{600} = 50.0\%$	$\dfrac{300}{550} = 54.5\%$	$\dfrac{300}{620} = 48.4\%$	$\dfrac{300}{560} = 53.6\%$
Operating profit margin				
$\dfrac{\text{Profit before interest and tax}}{\text{Revenue}}$	$\dfrac{180}{600} = 30.0\%$	$\dfrac{195}{550} = 35.4\%$	$\dfrac{210}{620} = 33.9\%$	$\dfrac{215}{560} = 38.4\%$
Asset turnover				
$\dfrac{\text{Revenue}}{\text{Capital employed}}$	$\dfrac{600}{660} = 0.91$	$\dfrac{550}{620} = 0.89$	$\dfrac{620}{535} = 1.16$	$\dfrac{560}{505} = 1.11$
Gearing				
$\dfrac{\text{Borrowings}}{\text{Capital employed}}$	$\dfrac{150}{660} = 22.7\%$	$\dfrac{150}{620} = 24.2\%$	$\dfrac{240}{535} = 44.9\%$	$\dfrac{240}{505} = 47.5\%$

	Hone		Over	
	20X1	20X0	20X0	20W9
Interest cover				
$\dfrac{\text{Profit before interest and tax}}{\text{Interest payable}}$	$\dfrac{180}{20} = 9$	$\dfrac{195}{18} = 11$	$\dfrac{210}{22} = 10$	$\dfrac{215}{20} = 11$
Effective interest rate				
$\dfrac{\text{Interest payable}}{\text{Borrowings}}$	$\dfrac{20}{150} = 13.3\%$	$\dfrac{18}{150} = 12.0\%$	$\dfrac{22}{240} = 9.2\%$	$\dfrac{20}{240} = 8.3\%$
Effective tax rate				
$\dfrac{\text{Tax}}{\text{Profit before tax}}$	$\dfrac{50}{160} = 31.3\%$	$\dfrac{55}{177} = 31.1\%$	$\dfrac{78}{188} = 41.5\%$	$\dfrac{90}{195} = 46.2\%$

6 Walsh

Text reference. Disposals are covered in Chapter 8.

Top tips. This question is more complicated than you would get in the exam, but is useful practice. You have both an acquisition and a partial disposal. Note that Marsh is still a subsidiary and still needs to be consolidated.

Easy marks. Once you've taken on board the fact that Marsh is still a subsidiary, you will be able to gain easy marks for setting out the proforma and adding the figures correctly. There is also some very easy intragroup trading.

WALSH GROUP
CONSOLIDATED INCOME STATEMENT
FOR THE YEAR ENDED 31 DECEMBER 20X6

	$m
Revenue (W2)	19,420
Operating costs (W3)	(16,928)
Profit on disposal of shares in subsidiary (W5)	36
Finance costs (W6)	5
Profit before tax	2,523
Income tax expense (W7)	750
Profit for the period	1,773
Attributable to	
Equity shareholders of the parent	1,509
Minority interests (W8)	264
	1,773

Workings

1   *Timeline*

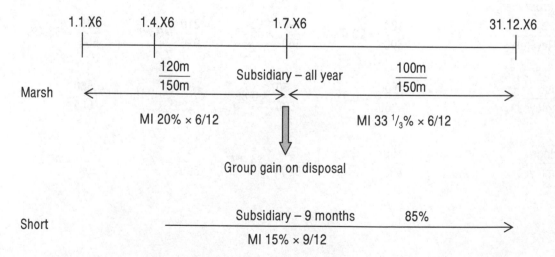

2 Revenue

	$m
Walsh	10,000
Marsh	8,000
Short ($^9/_{12} \times 2,000$)	1,500
Inter-company revenue	(80)
	19,420

3 *Operating costs*

	$m	$m
Cost of sales		
Walsh		7,000
Marsh		5,500
		12,500
Short: $^9/_{12} \times 800$	600	
Inter-company sales	(80)	
Inter-company profit: $(80 - 62) \times {}^{20}/_{120}$ ←	3	
		523
		13,023
Sundry expenses		
Walsh	880	
Marsh	570	
Short: $^9/_{12} \times 180$	135	
		1,585
Distribution costs		
Walsh	1,310	
Marsh	830	
Short: $^9/_{12} \times 240$	180	
		2,320
		16,928

4 *Goodwill: Marsh*

	$m	$m
Cost of combination		544
Fair value of identifiable net assets acquired		
Share capital	150	
Retained earnings	350	
	500	
Group share	80%	400
Goodwill		144

5 *Profit on disposal of shares*

	$m	$m
Proceeds		350
Share of net assets sold (at 31.12.X6)		
Share capital	150	
Retained reserves		
At 1.1.X6	1,650	
6 months to 31.7.X6 ($6/12 \times 750$)	375	
	2,175	
Holding sold	$13^1/_3$%	290
		60
Less related goodwill ($144 \times 20/120$)		(24)
Profit on disposal		36

Nock exa

6　*Finance costs*

	$m
Walsh (7–5)	2
Short: $^9/_{12} \times 4$	3
	5

7　*Taxation*

	$m
Walsh	250
Marsh	350
Short: $^9/_{12} \times 200$	150
	750

8　*Minority interests*

	$m
Marsh	
$20\% \times {}^6/_{12} \times 750$	75
$33^1/_3 \times {}^6/_{12} \times 750$	125
	200
Short	
$15\% \times ({}^9/_{12} \times 576) - 3)$	64
	264

7 Global

> **Text reference**. Segment reporting is covered in Chapter 14.
>
> **Top tips.** Remember that the question asks for a report in part (a) and so you should use the correct format. There is a lot of information given to you, but resist the temptation to just calculate a lot of ratios. The ratios must be relevant to your report.
>
> **Easy marks.** In part (a) the obvious easy marks are for setting out a report as requested. Also a strong hint is given in the question that you should mention some of the limitations of segment data, which you can list from memory – assuming you've learnt them. As always with analysis questions, make sure you keep making points. As long as they are sensible, they don't need to be exactly the same ones as our model answer, but you won't get marks at all if you don't write anything.

(a)　　　　　　　　　　　　　　　　　**REPORT**

To: The Chief Executive Officer of Global
From: The Management Accountant
Date: 31 August 20X2
Subject: Segmental analysis

1　Introduction

1.1　As requested, I attach an analysis of the performance of the European, American and African segments of the Group.

2　European segment

2.1　The profitability of the European segment has **slightly declined** over the period.

2.2　The European and American segments have the **same asset bases**, but the American segment **performs significantly better** than the European segment. It is not clear from the data why this should be so.

2.3　**Revenue generated** in Europe is **slightly higher than** from America, but the **net profit is lower**. It could be that European costs are higher for a number of reasons, eg higher wages, higher exchange rate costs, higher interest costs. However, this is not clear from the data.

3 American segment

3.1 The profitability of the American segment has also **slightly declined** over the period.

3.2 The **profit margin** in America is **significantly higher** than in Europe. However, the reason for this is not clear from the data provided.

3.3 The profitability of the **associates has doubled** over the period, although no explanation of the reason can be ascertained from the figures.

3.4 It may be worthwhile looking into the **reason why** the associates have produced such good results, with a view to **increasing the group's share**.

4 African segment

4.1 Although the African segment has been **making losses**, **profitability** has in fact **increased** over the period.

4.2 Income **has doubled** and the **loss has halved**.

4.3 The **net assets used** in the segment have only increased from $180m to $200m, an **increase of only 11%**.

4.4 Therefore the segment is producing a **much better return**.

4.5 **Inter-segment sales have grown** from $5m in 20X1 to $40m in 20X2. So the segment appears to be having a big effect on other segments.

4.6 Based on this information, it seems **unwise to discontinue** the African operations without further research.

5 Reservations

5.1 Given the **limited data available**, it is not possible to make a complete analysis of the operations in the various segments.

5.2 **Further information** is needed before any decisions should be taken. In particular:

- Capital structure
- Financing
- Cash flows
- Analysis of expenditure
- Analysis of assets and liabilities

5.3 Therefore this report has only concentrated on the **profitability** of the various segments.

APPENDIX – RATIOS

	Europe		America		Africa	
	20X2	20X1	20X2	20X1	20X2	20X1
Return on net assets	$\frac{70}{(610-260)}$	$\frac{69}{(560-240)}$	$\frac{90}{(610-250)}$	$\frac{90}{(560-230)}$	$\frac{(20)}{(300-100)}$	$\frac{(40)}{(270-90)}$
	= 20.0%	= 21.6%	= 25.0%	= 27.3%	= (10.0)%	= (22.2)%
Profit margin	$\frac{70}{720}$	$\frac{69}{685}$	$\frac{90}{610}$	$\frac{90}{560}$	$\frac{(20)}{440}$	$\frac{(40)}{205}$
	= 9.7%	= 10.1%	= 14.8%	= 16.1%	= (4.5)%	= (19.5)%
Asset turnover	$\frac{720}{350}$	$\frac{685}{320}$	$\frac{610}{360}$	$\frac{560}{330}$	$\frac{440}{200}$	$\frac{205}{180}$
	= 2.10	= 2.10	= 1.70	= 1.70	= 2.20	= 1.14
Acid test ratio	$\frac{610}{260}$	$\frac{560}{240}$	$\frac{610}{250}$	$\frac{560}{230}$	$\frac{300}{100}$	$\frac{270}{90}$
	= 2.35	= 2.33	= 2.44	= 2.43	= 3.0	= 3.0
Profitability of associates	$\frac{10}{55}$	$\frac{9}{52}$	$\frac{12}{36}$	$\frac{5}{30}$		
	= 18.2%	= 17.3%	= 33.3%	= 16.7%		

> **Top tips.** It is also permissible to use the external sales figure instead of total revenue. Students will not lose marks for using the alternative basis.

(b) Segmental reporting does not have to be based solely on geographical segments. The segments could be based on different **business types** or **product groups**.

(i) **Business types**

The group may comprise a number of different businesses, that can be grouped together. For example, a group could comprise an engineering business, a carrier business and a service business.

(ii) **Product groups**

The group may be operating over a number of different products, that can be grouped separately. For example, an engineering business could manufacture aircraft, cars and military tanks. The segments could then be divided among those three different types of product.

CIMA – Managerial Level

Paper P8

Financial Analysis

Mock Examination 2: May 2007

Instructions to candidates:

You are allowed three hours to answer this question paper.
In the real exam, you are allowed 20 minutes reading time before the examination begins during which you should read the question paper, and if you wish, highlight and/or make notes on the question paper. However, you will **not** be allowed, **under any circumstances**, to open the answer book and start writing or use your calculator during this reading time.
You are strongly advised to carefully read ALL the question requirements before attempting the question concerned (including all parts and/or sub questions).
Answer the ONE compulsory question in Section A. This has nine objective test sub-questions.
Answer ALL THREE questions in Section B.
Answer TWO of the THREE questions in Section C.

DO NOT OPEN THIS PAPER UNTIL YOU ARE READY TO START UNDER EXAMINATION CONDITIONS

SECTION A

[Indicative time for answering this section is 36 minutes]

Answer ALL NINE sub-questions

The answers to the nine sub-questions in Section A should ALL be written in your answer book.

Your answers should be clearly numbered with the sub-question number and then ruled off, so that the markers know which sub-question you are answering. **For multiple choice questions, you need only write the sub-question number and the letter of answer option you have chosen.** You do not need to start a new page for each sub-question.

1 Mixed bank (5/07)

1.1 On 1 January 20X5, CD purchased 30% of the ordinary share capital of EF for $280,000, which gave it significant influence over EF's activities. In the financial year ended 31 December 20X5, EF reported pre-tax profits of $62,000. The tax charge was $20,000. During the financial year ended 31 December 20X5, EF paid a total dividend of $5,000 to its shareholders.

In the year ended 31 December 20X6, EF made a pre-tax loss of $18,000, with a tax credit of $4,000. A review of CD's investment in EF at 31 December 20X6 concluded that an impairment had taken place. An impairment loss of $45,000 was charged in CD's consolidated financial statements for the year.

The carrying amount of the investment in EF to be included in CD's consolidated balance sheet at 31 December 20X6 was:

A $241,900
B $243,400
C $246,700
D $258,000   **(2 marks)**

1.2 STV owns 75% of the ordinary share capital of its subsidiary TUW. At the group's year end, 28 February 20X7, STV's payables include $3,600 in respect of inventories sold to it by TUW.

TUW's receivables include $6,700 in respect of inventories sold to STV. Two days before the year end STV sent a payment of $3,100 to TUW that was not recorded by the latter until two days after the year end.

The in-transit item should be dealt with as follows in the consolidated balance sheet at 28 February 20X7:

A $2,325 to be included as cash in transit
B $3,100 to be added to consolidated payables
C $3,100 to be included as inventories in transit
D $3,100 to be included as cash in transit   **(2 marks)**

1.3 The directors of BN, an unlisted entity, have approached the directors of DL, a smaller listed entity, to propose an agreed takeover of BN by DL. The net assets of BN are approximately three times as great as those of DL.

The type of arrangement proposed is known as a:

A   fresh start acquisition
B   merger
C   reverse acquisition
D   listed acquisition   **(2 marks)**

1.4 IAS 21 *The effects of changes in foreign exchange rates* permits an entity to choose a presentation currency that is different from its functional currency.

Identify ONE reason why an entity might choose to exercise this choice. **(2 marks)**

1.5 At 31 March 20X7, the present value of AZB's pension obligation is $1,634,000. The fair value of the pension plan assets is $1,337,000. Unrecognised actuarial losses are $224,000.

What is the amount of the liability in respect of the pension scheme that should be recognised in the balance sheet?

A $73,000
B $297,000
C $521,000
D $1,634,000 **(2 marks)**

1.6 In respect of deprival value, which ONE of the following statements is correct?

A   Value to the business is the higher of replacement cost and recoverable amount
B   Value to the business is the lower of value in use and realisable value
C   Recoverable amount is the higher of value in use and realisable value
D   Recoverable amount is the lower of realisable value and replacement cost **(2 marks)**

1.7 An analyst is comparing the non-current asset turnover ratios of two listed businesses engaged in similar activities. The non-current asset turnover ratio of one entity is almost 50% higher than that of the other entity, and she concludes that the entity with the higher non-current asset turnover ratio is utilising its assets far more effectively.

Identify TWO possible reasons why this conclusion might not be valid. **(2 marks)**

1.8 Several years ago DVS acquired 75% of the ordinary share capital of EWT at a cost of $1.7 million. The fair value of the total net assets of EWT at the date of acquisition was $1.8 million. Net assets of EWT at 31 January 20X7 totalled $4.7 million. On that date DVS disposed of 10% of the ordinary share capital of EWT, leaving it holding 65% of EWT's ordinary shares. The disposal proceeds were $900,000. A capital investment gains tax of 30% is charged to DVS on its profit on disposal. There has been no impairment of goodwill since the acquisition of the shares in EWT.

Calculate the amount of gain or loss on disposal that, net of tax, should be included in the consolidated financial statements of the DVS group for the year ended 31 January 20X7.

Work to the nearest $. **(4 marks)**

1.9 HGG, whose functional currency is the $, has invested 4.75 million euro in purchasing a majority shareholding in JXF. The investment in JXF is financed by a loan in euro. The directors of HGG decide to designate the loan as a hedging instrument and the investment as the related hedged transaction.

Describe the accounting treatment of any gains or losses arising on the investment and the loan, assuming that the hedging relationship meets all the conditions required by IAS 39 *Financial instruments: recognition and measurement* to qualify for hedge accounting. **(2 marks)**

(Total for Section A = 20 marks)

SECTION B – 30 marks

[Indicative time for answering this Section is 54 minutes]

Answer ALL THREE questions

2 AB and CD

On 1 November 20X5, AB purchased 75% of the issued share capital of CD at a cost of $204,000. CD's issued share capital at the date of acquisition was $50,000 in $1 shares, and its retained earnings were $142,000 (there were no other reserves).

At that date, the carrying value of CD's property, plant and equipment was $150,000, split as follows:

	$
Land and buildings (including land at cost of $35,000)	105,000
Plant and equipment	45,000
	150,000

The fair value exercise carried out at acquisition showed that the fair value of CD's land and buildings was $125,000, of which $45,000 was attributable to land. The carrying value of plant and equipment approximated to fair value, and no adjustment was considered necessary. An intangible asset representing intellectual property rights, which had previously been unrecognised by CD, was recognised at a value of $10,000 at the date of acquisition. The directors decided that this asset should be amortised at the rate of 2.5% each month on the straight line basis. The intangible asset and the revaluation of land and buildings are recognised as consolidation adjustments only; they are not recognised in CD's own financial statements.

At 1 November 20X5, the remaining useful life of CD's buildings was estimated at 21.5 years. Depreciation on buildings is calculated each month on the straight line basis.

A further revaluation exercise was conducted at 1 November 20X6. The fair value of CD's land and buildings had increased by a further $20,000, half attributable to land and half to buildings. The estimate of the remaining useful life of the buildings was consistent with the estimate on 1 November 20X5. AB's group policy is to adopt the revaluation model in respect of land and buildings.

At the group's year end on 30 April 20X7, the retained earnings of AB were $365,000 and the retained earnings of CD were $183,000. During the financial year, CD had started supplying goods to AB at a mark-up of 17% on cost. AB's inventories at 30 April 20X7 included $6,000 in respect of goods supplied by CD.

Since 1 November 20X5, CD has been AB's only subsidiary.

Required

Calculate the amounts to be included in the consolidated balance sheet of the AB group at 30 April 20X7 for:

(a)   Goodwill (assuming that there has been no impairment of goodwill since acquisition)
(b)   Consolidated retained earnings
(c)   Minority interest

Work to the nearest $. **(10 marks)**

3 BAQ

BAQ is a listed entity with a financial year end of 31 March. At 31 March 20X7, it had 8,000,000 ordinary shares in issue.

The directors of BAQ wish to expand the business's operations by acquiring competitor entities. They intend to make no more than one acquisition in any financial year.

The directors are about to meet to discuss two possible acquisitions. Their principal criterion for the decision is the likely effect of the acquisition on group earnings per share.

Details of the possible acquisitions are as follows:

1 **Acquisition of CBR**

- 100% of the share capital of CBR could be acquired on 1 October 20X7 for a new issue of shares in BAQ.
- CBR has 400,000 ordinary shares in issue.
- Four CBR shares would be exchanged for three new shares in BAQ.
- CBR's profit after tax for the year ended 31 March 20X7 was $625,000 and the entity's directors are projecting a 10% increase in this figure for the year ending 31 March 20X8.

2 **Acquisition of DCS**

- 80% of the share capital of DCS could be acquired on 1 October 20X7 for a cash payment of $10.00 per share.
- DCS has 1,000,000 ordinary shares in issue.
- The cash would be raised by a rights issue to BAQ's existing shareholders. For the purposes of evaluation it can be assumed that the rights issue would take place on 1 October 20X7, that it would be fully taken up, that the market value of one share in BAQ on that date would be $5.36, and that the terms of the rights issue would be one new share for every five BAQ shares held at a rights price of $5.00.
- DCS's projected profit after tax for the year ending 31 March 20X8 is $860,000.

BAQ's profit after tax for the year ended 31 March 20X8 is projected to be $4.2 million. No changes in BAQ's share capital are likely to take place, except in respect of the possible acquisitions described above.

Required

Calculate the group earnings per share that could be expected for the year ending 31 March 20X8 in respect of each of the acquisition scenarios outlined above.

(10 marks)

4 Knowledgeable about IFRS

You have been asked by a colleague to present a brief paper to accounting students at the local university about recent attempts at convergence between International Financial Reporting Standards (IFRS) and US Generally Accepted Accounting Practice (GAAP). The students are knowledgeable about IFRS, but have not studied US GAAP in any detail.

Required

Prepare the paper, describing the progress to date of the convergence project, including some examples of areas of accounting where convergence has taken place.

(10 marks)

(Total for Section B = 30 marks)

SECTION C – 50 marks

[Indicative time for answering this Section is 90 minutes]

Answer TWO questions out of THREE

5 BSP

BSP, a listed entity, supplies, installs and maintains burglar alarm systems for business clients. As a response to increased competition and falling margins in the burglar alarm market, the entity's directors decided, towards the end of 20X5, to extend its operations into the provision of fire alarm and sprinkler systems. A training programme for staff was undertaken in the early months of 20X6 at a cost of around $200,000. An aggressive marketing campaign, costing $250,000, was launched at the same time. Both costs were incurred and settled before the 31 March 20X6 year end. BSP commenced its new operations with effect from the beginning of its financial year on 1 April 20X6.

BSP's cash resources were at a low level in early 20X6, so, in order to finance the costs of the new operation and the necessary increase in working capital to fund the new operations, BSP made a new issue of shares. The issue took place in May 20X6. During March 20X7, BSP disposed of its two overseas subsidiaries in order to concentrate on operations in its home market. Both were profitable businesses and therefore sold for an amount substantially in excess of carrying value. These subsidiaries accounted for almost 10% of group sales during the 20X6/20X7 financial year.

As the finance director's assistant you have been responsible for the preparation of the draft financial statements, which have been circulated to the directors in advance of a board meeting to be held later this week.

The marketing director, who was appointed in June 20X6, has sent you the following e-mail:

'When I did my university course in marketing I studied a module in finance and accounting, which covered the analysis of financial statements. Unfortunately, it was a long time ago, and I've forgotten quite a lot about it.

I'm puzzled by the cash flow statement, in particular. The income statement shows a loss, which is obviously bad news, especially as the budget showed a profit for the year. However, the cash resources of the business have actually increased by quite a large amount between March 20X6 and March 20X7. It is said that 'cash is king', so I'm assuming that the poor profitability is a short-term problem while the new operation settles down.

As you know, we almost managed to achieve our sales targets in both the fire and burglar alarm sectors for the year, (although of course we did have to offer some customers special discounts and extended credit as inducements). I'm assuming, therefore, that the lack of profitability is a problem of cost control.

It would be really helpful if you could provide me with a brief report, in advance of this week's meeting, which tells me what this cash flow statement means. You could include ratios, provided that you show how they are calculated.'

The consolidated cash flow statement for the year ended 31 March 20X7 (with comparative figures for 20X6) is as follows:

BSP: CONSOLIDATED CASH FLOW STATEMENT FOR THE YEAR ENDED 31 MARCH 20X7

	20X7		20X6	
	$'000	$'000	$'000	$'000
Cash flows from operating activities				
(Loss)/profit before tax	(453)		306	
Adjustments for				
Depreciation	98		75	
Foreign exchange loss	22		37	
Profit on sale of investments	(667)		–	
Interest expense	161		45	
		(839)		463
Increase in inventories		(227)		(65)
Increase in receivables		(242)		(36)
Increase in payables		62		12
Cash (outflow)/inflow from operations		(1,246)		374
Interest paid		(157)		(42)
Tax paid		(38)		(55)
Net cash (outflow)/inflow from operating activities		(1,441)		277
Cash flows from investing activities				
Proceeds from sale of investments	2,320		–	
Purchase of property, plant and equipment	(661)		(425)	
Income from associates	23		26	
Net cash inflow/(outflow) from investing activities		1,682		(399)
Cash flows from financing activities				
Proceeds from issue of share capital	850		–	
Dividends paid	–		(200)	
Net cash inflow/(outflow) from financing activities		850		(200)
Net increase/(decrease) in cash		1,091		(322)
Cash at start of period		27		349
Cash at end of period		1,118		27

Additional information

Revenue in the 20X5/X6 financial year was $12.11 million. In the 20X6/X7 financial year, total revenue was $12.32 million, $10.93 million of which arose in respect of the sale of burglar alarms.

Inventories at the start of the 20X5/X6 financial year were $591,000, and receivables were $1,578,000. There was no increase in long-term borrowings throughout the two year period covered by the cash flow statement above.

Required

Analyse and interpret the information given, and produce a report to the marketing director. The report should explain the difference between cash and profit, and should discuss the business's profitability and working capital position. It should also discuss, to the extent possible from the information given, the prospects for BSP's future.

(25 marks)

6 TYD

You are the accounting adviser to a committee of bank lending officers. Each loan application is subject to an initial vetting procedure, which involves the examination of the application, recent financial statements, and a set of key financial ratios.

The key ratios are as follows:

- Gearing (calculated as debt/debt + equity, where debt includes both long- and short-term borrowings)
- Current ratio
- Quick ratio
- Profit margin (using profit before tax)

Existing levels of gearing are especially significant to the decision, and the committee usually rejects any application from an entity with gearing of over 45%.

The committee will shortly meet to conduct the initial vetting of a commercial loan application made by TYD, an unlisted entity. As permitted by national accounting law in its country of registration, TYD does not comply in all respects with International Financial Reporting Standards. The committee has asked you to interview TYD's finance director to determine areas of non-compliance. As a result of the interview, you have identified two significant areas for examination in respect of TYD's financial statements for the year ended 30 September 20X6.

1   Revenue for the period includes a sale of inventories at cost to HPS, a banking institution, for $85,000, which took place on 30 September 20X6. HPS has an option under the contract of sale to require TYD to repurchase the inventories on 30 September 20X8, for $95,000. TYD has derecognised the inventories at their cost of $85,000, with a charge to cost of sales of this amount. The inventories concerned in this transaction, are, however, stored on TYD's premises, and TYD bears the cost of insuring them.

2   Some categories of TYD's inventories are sold on a sale or return basis. The entity's accounting policy in this respect is to recognise the sale at the point of despatch of goods. The standard margin on sales of this type is 20%. During the year ended 30 September 20X6, $100,000 (in sales value) has been despatched in this way. The finance director estimates that approximately 60% of this value represents sales that have been accepted by customers; the remainder is potentially subject to return.

The financial statements of TYD for the year ended 30 September 20X6 are as presented below. (Note: at this stage of the analysis only one year's figures are considered.)

TYD: INCOME STATEMENT FOR THE YEAR ENDED 30 SEPTEMBER 20X6

	$'000
Revenue	600
Cost of sales	450
Gross profit	150
Expenses	63
Finance costs	17
Profit before tax	70
Income tax expense	25
Profit for the period	45

TYD: STATEMENT OF CHANGES IN EQUITY FOR THE YEAR ENDED 30 SEPTEMBER 20X6

	Share capital $'000	Retained earnings $'000	Total $'000
Balances at 1 October 20X5	100	200	300
Profit for the period		45	45
Balances at 30 September 20X6	100	245	345

TYD: BALANCE SHEET AT 30 SEPTEMBER 20X6

	$'000	$'000
ASSETS		
Non-current assets		
Property, plant and equipment		527
Current assets		
Inventories	95	
Trade receivables	72	
Cash	6	
		173
		700
EQUITY AND LIABILITIES		
Equity		
Called up share capital	100	
Retained earnings	245	
		345
Non-current liabilities		
Long-term borrowings		180
Current liabilities		
Trade and other payables	95	
Bank overdraft	80	
		175
		700

Required

Prepare a report to the committee of lending officers that:

(a) Discusses the accounting treatment of the two significant areas identified in the interview with the FD, with reference to the requirements of International Financial Reporting Standards (IFRS) and to fundamental accounting principles **(8 marks)**

(b) Calculates any adjustments to the financial statements that are required in order to bring them into compliance with IFRS (ignore tax) **(5 marks)**

(c) Analyses and interprets the financial statements, calculating the key ratios before and after adjustments, and making a recommendation to the lending committee on whether or not to grant TYD's application for a commercial loan **(12 marks)**

(Total = 25 marks)

7 AT

AT holds investments in three other entities. The draft income statements for the four entities for the year ended 31 March 20X7 are as follows:

	AT	BU	CV	DW
	$'000	$'000	$'000	$'000
Revenue	2,450	1,200	675	840
Cost of sales	(1,862)	(870)	(432)	(580)
Gross profit	588	330	243	260
Distribution costs	(94)	(22)	(77)	(18)
Administrative expenses	(280)	(165)	(120)	(126)
Interest received	–	2	–	–
Finance costs	(26)	–	–	–
Profit before tax	188	145	46	116
Income tax	(40)	(50)	(12)	(37)
Profit for the period	148	95	34	79

Notes

1   *Investments in BU, CV and DW*

Several years ago AT purchased 75% of the ordinary shares of BU. On 30 September 20X6 it purchased a further 5% of BU's ordinary shares. In 20X3 AT, together with two other investor entities, set up CV. Each of the three investors owns one-third of the ordinary shares in CV. All managerial decisions relating to CV are made jointly by the three investor entities. On 1 January 20X7, AT purchased 35% of the ordinary shares in DW. AT exerts significant influence over the management of DW, but does not control the entity.

2   *Intra-group trading*

BU supplies inventories to AT, earning a gross profit margin of 20% on such sales. During the financial year ended 31 March 20X7, BU supplied a total of $80,000 at selling price to AT. Of these items, 25% remained in AT's inventories at the year end. AT supplies a range of administrative services to BU, at cost. $12,000 is included in BU's administrative expenses, and in AT's revenue, in respect of such services supplied during the year ended 31 March 20X7.

3   The group has a policy of adopting proportional consolidation wherever permitted by International Financial Reporting Standards.

4   Revenue and profits accrue evenly throughout the year, unless otherwise stated.

5   *Finance costs*

The finance costs in AT's income statement are in respect of short-term bank borrowings only. Finance costs in respect of its long-term borrowings have not yet been included, and an appropriate adjustment must be made. On 1 April 20X4, AT issued bonds at par in the amount of $1,000,000. Issue costs were $50,000. The bonds carry a coupon rate of interest of 5% each year, payable on the last day of the financial year. The interest actually paid on 31 March 20X7 has been debited to a suspense account, which is included under current assets in AT's draft balance sheet. The bonds will be repaid on 31 March 20X9 at a premium of $162,000. The effective interest rate associated with the bonds is 9%, and the liability is measured, in accordance with IAS 39 *Financial instruments: recognition and measurement*, at amortised cost.

6   *Financial asset*

From time to time BU uses available cash surpluses to make short term investments in financial assets. Such assets are 'held-for-trading' and are invariably sold within a few months. At 31 March 20X7, BU held 4,000 shares in a listed entity, EX. The shares had been purchased on 20 January 20X7 at a price of 1332¢ per share. At 31 March 20X7, the market price per share was 1227¢. No adjustment has been made to the draft income statement above in respect of this financial asset.

Required

Prepare the consolidated income statement for the AT group for the financial year ended 31 March 20X7. Show full workings.   **(25 marks)**

Note. 8 marks are available for the adjustments in respect of notes 5 and 6.

Work to the nearest $100. For the purposes of this question it is not necessary to make adjustments to income tax.

(Total for Section C = 50 marks)

Answers

DO NOT TURN THIS PAGE UNTIL YOU HAVE
COMPLETED THE MOCK EXAM

A plan of attack

The exam may look daunting at first. You need to adopt a calm approach. The following plan of attack is just a suggestion.

First things first

Parts A and B are compulsory, so you may as well start with Part A comprising 9 OT and short answer questions. Remember the instructions for dealing with these OTs and MCQs at the beginning of the Kit. Do not exceed the time limit of **36 minutes** for this section. Answer the easy questions first.

Part B

Part B is also compulsory so you may as well deal with these three next. Do not get bogged down in the detail and remember to allow yourself only **54 minutes**, allocating equal time to each question.

Part C

Part C has **two questions** to answer out of three. Choose the question that you know most about to answer first. Remember to answer only **two** questions. If you try parts of all three, only the marks for your best two questions will count, so you will have wasted your time **and failed** the exam.

In choosing your questions, have regard to your strengths and weaknesses.

Question 5. A financial analysis question which requires both calculations and commentary. You need to discuss the difference between cash and profit and analyse the profitability and capital position of the entity. We would advise you to have a go at this question, as you can score marks for relevant discussion and a critical evaluation of the ratios.

Question 6. Another financial analysis question which starts by requiring adjustment for incorrectly accounted transactions and an appreciation of the issues of substance over form. This question combines both accounting adjustments and financial analysis and is in three parts. A methodical approach to parts (a) and (b) and a critical analysis in part (c), together with the calculation of key ratios, should help you score good marks.

Question 7. The question required the preparation of a consolidated income statement including the accounting for the finance costs of a bond.

Remember

Always – well nearly always – **allocate your time** according to the marks for the question in total and then according to the parts of the question. The only exception is if the question is compulsory, say in Section B, and you really know nothing about it. You may as well try to pick up marks elsewhere. And **always**, **always follow the requirements** exactly.

You've got spare time at the end of the exam ... ?

If you have allocated your time properly then you **shouldn't have time on your hands** at the end of the exam. But if you find yourself with five or ten minutes to spare, **go back to the questions** that you couldn't do or to **any parts of questions that you didn't finish** because you ran out of time.

Forget about it!

And don't worry if you found the paper difficult. More than likely other candidates will too. If this were the real thing you would need to **forget** the exam the minute you leave the exam hall and **think about the next one**. Or, if it's the last one, **celebrate**!

SECTION A

1 Mixed bank (5/07)

1.1   A $241,900

		$'000	$'000	$'000
Cost of investment				280.00
Add: post acquisition retained profits/(losses)				
2005	profit		62	
	Tax	(20)		
	dividends	(5)		
			(25)	
2006	loss	(18)		
	tax credit	4		
			(14)	
			23	
CD group share 30% × $23,000				6.90
				286.90
Less impairment				(45.00)
				241.90

1.2   D $3,100 to be included as cash in transit.

The payment sent by STV the holding company to its subsidiary TUW should be included as cash in transit on consolidation.

1.3   C   Reverse acquisition

Identifying the acquirer in a business combination is based on the concept of control. Normally in an acquisition the legal parent company's shareholders control the combined group through majority shareholding.

However, the position may sometimes be reversed with the legal subsidiary company's shareholders having effective control of the combined group even though the other party is legally the parent.

The circumstances given in this question are an example of a reverse acquisition in that a larger unlisted company arranges to have itself acquired by a significantly smaller listed company.

Although the listed company DL is legally considered as the parent and the unlisted company BN is regarded as the subsidiary, the legal subsidiary BN is identified as the acquirer due to the fact that its net assets are significantly greater than those of the other entity's.

1.4   IAS 21 *The effects of changes in foreign exchange rates* permits an entity to choose a presentation currency that is different from its functional currency.

Any **one** of the following reasons would be appropriate. (Please note that you are asked for **one** reason).

(a) In a globalised economic environment a large group may not have a single functional currency but rather comprise a number of different functional currencies where it may not be clear why one currency may be preferable to another.

(b) The entity's main investors may use a currency other than the functional currency of the entity.

(c) In some jurisdictions, entities are required to present their financial statements in the local currency even if this is not the functional currency. To avoid presenting two sets of financial statements (ie ones that comply with local regulations and ones presented in the functional currency) entities may use the local currency as presentation currency.

(d) The entity may be seeking investment resources from investors whose functional currency is not the same as the entity's.

(e) The functional currency may not be well known or widely used and the entity may wish to use a more widely used one.

1.5 A $73,000

The amount of the liability to be recognised in the balance sheet in respect of the pension scheme is calculated as follows:

	$'000
Present value of the obligation	1,634
Less: fair value of plan assets	(1,337)
unrecognised actuarial losses	(224)
Liability recognised in the balance sheet at 31 March 20X7	73

1.6 C Recoverable amount is the higher of value in use and realisable value.

The deprival value of an asset is the loss which a business entity would suffer if it were deprived of the use of the asset. An entity would not sell an asset if it would earn more from using it than from selling it.

A statement describing deprival value is given diagrammatically below:

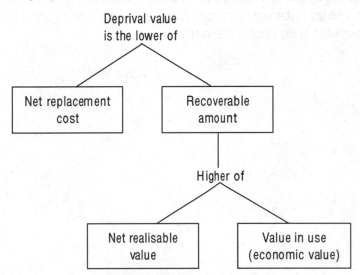

1.7 There are two possible reasons why this calculation may not be valid.

(a) **Average age of non-current assets**. The asset turnover ratio is affected by the average age of the assets. It is possible that the entity with the higher non-current asset turnover ratio has older non-current assets. These would have lower net book values and would give rise to a higher non-current asset turnover ratio.

(b) **Valuation model used for non-current assets**. The revaluation of non-current assets where the revalued amounts are higher than net book values would give rise to a lower non-current asset turnover ratio. Comparing this ratio with that of an entity that uses the cost model could give rise to misleading conclusions.

1.8

	$
Investment at cost	1,700,000
Less 75% of fair value of net assets (75% × $1.8m)	(1,350,000)
Goodwill on acquisition	350,000

Tax on disposal

	$
Proceeds on disposal	900,000
Less investment at cost ($1.7m ×$^{10}/_{75}$) (*Note*)	(226,667)
Gain on disposal	673,333

Tax on gain 30% × $673,333 = $202,000

	$	$
Proceeds of sale		900,000
Less: share of net assets at date of disposal $4.7m × 10%	(470,000)	
goodwill related to the disposal $^{10}/_{75}$ × $350,000	(46,667)	
tax on gain	(202,000)	
		(718,667)
Consolidated gain on disposal		181,333

Note. DVS disposed 10% of the ordinary share capital of EWT, not 10% of its own shareholding, thus leaving it holding 65% of the total shares in EWT.

Therefore, the cost of the investment disposed of is $^{10}/_{75}$ of the original cost of $1.7 million.

$1.7 million represents 75% of the cost of the investment.

1.7 million × $^{10}/_{75}$ represents 10% of the cost of the investment.

1.9 The transaction entered into by HGG is a hedging transaction of a net investment in a foreign entity. The loan is the hedging instrument and the investment in JXF is the hedged item.

As the loan has been designated as the hedging instrument at the outset and the transaction meets the hedging criteria of IAS 39, the exchange movements in both items should be recognised in equity through the statement of changes in equity. Any ineffective portion of the hedge should be recognised in the income statement.

SECTION B

2 AB and CD

> **Text reference**. Group financial statements for the purposes of this question are covered in Chapters 2-4.
>
> **Top tips.** To determine the goodwill for inclusion in the consolidated balance sheet, you will need to calculate the fair value (FV) of the net assets at the date of acquisition. Make sure you incorporate correctly the FV adjustments. To determine the minority interest you will need to use the net assets at the balance sheet date.
>
> **Easy marks.** Calculating the goodwill and correctly incorporating the FV adjustments would have earned you two easy marks. The calculation of net retained earnings would have earned five out of the total of ten marks.
>
> **Examiner's comments.** The question was generally answered well although some students failed to incorporate the revaluation adjustments in the calculation of goodwill.

(a) **Goodwill**

	$	$
Cost of investment		204,000
Less fair value of assets acquired		
Share capital	50,000	
Retained earnings	142,000	
Fair value adjustments		
land and buildings	20,000	
Intangible assets	10,000	
	(222,000)	
Group share: $222,000 × 75%$		(166,500)
Goodwill		37,500

(b) **Consolidated retained earnings at 30 April 20X7**

	AB	CD
	$	$
Per question	365,000	183,000
Amortisation of intangible (W1)		(4,500)
Deprecation adjustment (W2)		(942)
Provision for unrealised profit		(872)
		176,686
Retained earnings at acquisition		(142,000)
		34,686
AB's share of CD's retained earnings 75 × 34,686	(26,015)	
	391,015	

(c) **Minority interest**

		$	$
CD's net assets at balance sheet date per question			
	Equity	50,000	
	Retained earnings	183,000	
			233,000
Fair value adjustments			
	Intellectual property rights	10,000	
	Land and buildings	20,000	
	Land and buildings – further revaluation	20,000	
			50,000
Other adjustments (post-acquisition)			
Amortisation of intangibles (W1)		(4,500)	
Depreciation		(942)	
Provision for unrealised profit		(872)	
			(6,314)
			276,686
× Minority share 25%			69,171

Workings

1   *Amortisation of intangible*

1 November 20X5 to 30 April 20X7 $10,000 × 2.5% per month × 18 months = $4,500

2   *Depreciation adjustments on revalued buildings*

	$
Additional depreciation on fair value adjustment at acquisition	
Fair value adjustment attributable to buildings	
$(125,000 – 45,000) – (105,000 – 35,000) = 80,000 – 70,000 = $10,000	
Additional depreciation $\dfrac{1.5 \text{ years}}{21.5 \text{ years}} \times \$10,000$	698
Additional depreciation on post-acquisition revaluation on 1 November 20X6	
Fair value adjustment attributable to buildings $20,000 × \frac{1}{2} = $10,000	
$\dfrac{0.5 \text{ years}}{20.5 \text{ years}} \times \$10,000$	244
	942

3   *Provision for unrealised profit on inventory*

$6,000 × 17/117 = $872

3 BAQ

Text reference. Earnings per share are covered in Chapter 17.

Top tips. You need to calculate projected group earnings for each of the acquisition scenarios and the weighted average number of shares before calculating the projected earnings per share.

Easy marks. The DCS acquisition would have carried more marks than the CBR acquisition.

Examiner's comments. Common errors included taking the full twelve months of CBR's earnings rather than six months.

1   **Acquisition of CBR**

	$
Projected group earnings for the year ended 31 March 20X8	
BAQ's for year ended 31 March 20X8	4,200,000
CRB's for six months to 31 March 20X8 (£625,000 × 110% × 6/12)	343,750
	4,543,750
Weighted average number of shares in issue	
1 April 2007 to 30 September 2007 $^6/_{12}$ × 8,000,000	4,000,000
1 October 2007 to 31 March 2008 (($^3/_4$ × 400,000) + 8,000,000) × $^6/_{12}$	4,150,000
	8,150,000

Projected group earnings per share if CGB acquisition takes place $\dfrac{\$4{,}543{,}750}{8{,}150{,}000}$ = 55.8 cents

2   **Acquisition of DCS**

	$
Projected group earnings for the year ended 31 March 20X8	
BAQ's projected earnings for year ended 31 March 20X8	4,200,000
DCS's projected earnings for six months to 31 March 20X8	
$860,000 × 80% × $^6/_{12}$	344,000
	4,544,000
Weighted average number of shares in issue	
1 April 20X7 to 30 September 20X7	4,045,283
$^6/_{12}$ × 8,000,000 × $\dfrac{5.36}{5.30}$ (W1)	
1 October 20X7 to 31 March 20X8	
$^6/_{12}$ × 9,600,000 (W2)	4,800,000
	8,845,283

Projected group earnings per share if DCS acquisition takes place $\dfrac{\$4{,}544{,}000}{8{,}845{,}283}$ = 51.4 cents

Workings

1   Theoretical ex-rights price (TERP)

	$
5 × $5.36	26.80
1 × $5.00	5.00
	31.80

$$\text{TERP} = \frac{\$31.80}{6} = \$5.30$$

$$\text{Bonus fraction} = \frac{\$5.36}{5.30}$$

2   Number of BAQ shares in issue after 1 October 20X7

($^1/_5$ × 8,000,000) + 8,000,000 = 9,600,000

4 Knowledgeable about IFRS

Text reference. Convergence between IFRS and US GAAP is covered in Chapters 1 and 19.

Top tips. Make sure you do not exceed the time allocation for this ten-mark question by making points not directly relevant. The issue of US GAAP/IFRS convergence is the most important contemporary issue in financial reporting. Note that the question does not ask for a list of differences between US GAAP and IFRS.

Easy marks. Appreciation of the difference between a principles-based and rules-based approach would have earned you the first couple of easy marks. The background to convergence and examples of outputs and long-term projects in the pipeline would have earned you additional marks.

Examiner's comments. The question was badly answered with most students not being aware of instances where convergence had taken place.

The convergence project

In September 2002 the US accounting standards setter, the Financial Accounting Standards Board (FASB) and the International Accounting Standards Board (IASB) reached an agreement, committing themselves to a project with the objective of reducing the number of differences between US GAAP and IFRS.

The two standard setters are co-ordinating their work programs so that in the long-run the two sets of standards are fully compatible. The first commitment was to reduce differences in existing standards in the short term and the second commitment is long-term compatibility.

Traditionally the two accounting bodies had a different approach to standard setting, with the FASB adopting a rules band approach as opposed to a principles based one adopted by the IASB. Convergence has, however, been possible with the FASB adopting a more principles based approach.

Although significant progress has been made to date, many differences remain between US GAAP and IFRS. Several of the current on going projects are first phases of larger and longer term projects. An example of a long-term project is the convergence of the conceptual framework and the principles of revenue recognition.

Another long-term project is the presentation of financial statements. The recent revision to IAS 1 *Presentation of Financial Statements* represents the first phase of a longer-term project.

To date, the joint work of the FASB and the IASB has produced the following:

- IFRS 5 *Non-current assets held for sale and discontinued operations*
- Business combinations – Exposure drafts issued in June 2005
- IFRS 8 operating segments issued in November 2006
- Revision of IAS 1 *Presentation of Financial Statements* issued in September 2007.

SECTION C

5 BSP

> **Text reference**. Financial analysis is covered in Chapter 17.
>
> **Top tips.** There are a number of different possible ways to approach the answer. Including calculations in an appendix would be one of them.
>
> **Easy marks.** Commenting on the distinction between cash and profit would have earned you the first easy three marks. Comments on sources of cash and unusual items such as inventories and receivables would have earned you further marks. Correct and relevant calculations, neatly presented, would have earned at least five marks.
>
> **Examiner's comments.** Some students did not show an adequate understanding of the difference between cash flow and profit. The approach to financial analysis tended to be mechanistic, lacking in interpretation.

To: Marketing Director of BSP

From: Assistant to Finance Director

Report on draft cash flow statement for the financial year ended 31 March 20X7

1   *The difference between cash and profit*

The main difference between **cash** and **profit** is that the latter is an **accounting concept** based on the **accruals principle**, whereas the former reflects the **cash receipts** or **payments** within an accounting period. Profit is affected by **non-cash elements** such as **depreciation**. Cash cannot be manipulated by management through **earning smoothing practices**. Cash and profits will therefore differ and the two statements should be studied together in order to get a **complete picture** of the **financial health** of an entity.

The **cash flow statement** of BSP shows a healthy amount of cash accumulated at the end of the accounting period. However, a closer examination of the cash flow statement, a summary of which is shown below, reveals that the **cash accumulation** came primarily from the **net sale of assets**, and from **raising new funds**. Both sources of funds are **not sustainable** in the **long-term**. The **cash flow from operations**, on the other hand, shows a **significant deterioration**, in relation to the previous year, which is an unwelcome development.

	20X7
	$'000
Cash at the beginning of the year	27
Cash from operations	(1,441)
Cash from investments	1,682
Cash from financing activities	850
Cash at end of period	1,118

2   *Profit and loss*

The loss before tax for 20X7 stood at $453,000.

Whereas the profit for the year ended 31 March 20X6 was $306,000. It is worth noting that the loss before tax in the year ended 31 March 20X7 is reduced by the **profit on disposal** of the **foreign subsidiaries**. If this profit is excluded, the loss from operations amounts to $1,120,000. The **deterioration in profit** that occurred in the year 20X7 is even more significant if the **one-off costs of training** ($200,000) and **marketing** ($250,000) that were included in the results of the previous year are excluded.

3   *Working capital*

Working capital increased in the year ending 31 March 20X7, with **increases** in both **inventories** and **receivables**. Inventories increased by 35 percent in the year ended 31 March 20X7, which seems excessive compared to the increase in revenue over the same period.

Receivables also **increased substantially** in the year ended 31 March 20X7. Assessing the increase in receivables to the increase in revenues can be done by constructing the days receivable ratio for the two accounting periods as follows:

20X6

$$\text{Days receivable ratio} = \frac{(365 \times \text{Accounts receivable})}{\text{Sales}}$$

$$= \frac{(365 \times 1,614)}{(12,110)}$$

$$= 48.6 \text{ days}$$

Where 1,614 = beginning of period receivables + increase in the year

20X7

$$\text{Days receivable ratio} = \frac{(365 \times \text{Accounts receivable})}{(0.9 \times \text{Sales})}$$

$$= \frac{(365 \times 1,856)}{(0.9 \times 12,320)}$$

$$= 61.1 \text{ days}$$

Where 1,856 = beginning of period receivables + increase in the year

The sales figure for the year ended in 31 March 20X7 has been adjusted to reflect the fact that the accounts receivable do not reflect any amounts from the subsidiaries that have been disposed of.

The figures for the two years show that there has been an **extension** of the **credit period**. This may have boosted revenues in the short term, but it may have increased the exposure to credit risk of the company in the long term.

4   *Prospects for the future*

With revenue increasing slightly, the decline in the profitability that BSP suffered for the year ending 31 March 20X7 must be attributed to increased costs. The real question in deciding on the future prospects is whether this is a short-term problem, due to the new line of business settling down, or a manifestation of a longer term trend which will affect long-term performance.

Looking into the **longer term**, the **growth of sales** needs to be estimated, in the light of the **disposal** of the **subsidiaries**. In the **short term**, the **impact on revenue** may not be reflected in the profit figure. However, unless the remaining businesses increase their revenues to make up for the disposal, the impact will manifest itself in the long-run.

The source of revenues is also important for the long term prospects of the company. Two years after moving into fire alarms and sprinklers, the revenue from this product accounts for only 11 percent of total revenues. Given the pressures on profit margins for the burglar alarm business, the prospects for revenue growth are not very good.

Other factors may also play a role in deterring **future profitability**. The lower interest charges, resulting from reduced borrowing needs will also increase profits and may mitigate the impact of reduced revenues.

As it was mentioned above, the cash accumulation was due to the new shares issue but also to the fact that no dividend was paid out. This is not a **sustainable position** regarding the investors, and a dividend payment may be due in the accounting period 20X7/20X8.

5   *Conclusion*

Looking at the profit figures and the information contained in the **cash flow statement**, some worrying trends can be discerned. First, if there is no improvement in the **operating performance** the cash balances will disappear. Secondly, **revenue growth** should be maintained or even increased to make up for the loss of revenue from the **disposal of subsidiaries**. **Costs should be controlled** and **working capital management** should be **improved**.

6 TYD

To: Lending Committee
From: Accounting adviser
Subject: TYD's loan application

(a) **Treatment of two significant items in TYD's financial statements**

Revenue recognition on sale with purchaser's option to resell.

The sale of $85,000 to HPS, a banking institution, which took place on 30 September 20X6 does not meet the criteria set out in IAS 18 *Revenue* for inclusion as a sale.

The existence of an option which is exercisable by the bank reflects the economic reality of the transaction. TYD effectively agrees to repurchase the inventory at a higher price and is obliged to do so if the bank exercises its option to resell.

The economic substance of the transaction is effectively a loan from the bank to TYD secured on the inventory.

The difference between the amount advanced by the bank for the 'sale' on 30 September 20X6 of $85,000 and the amount for which the inventories will be repurchased in two years time of $95,000 represents what is effectively interest on the loan.

Additional evidence that the risks and rewards of ownership remain with TYD is that the inventory remains on TYD's premises and TYD is responsible for insuring it.

The principle of **substance over form**, relevant to the above transaction, is recognised in the IASB's *Framework* as significant to the reliability of financial statements.

Although there is no IFRS currently, addressing specifically the concept of **substance over form** the *Framework* requires that transactions should be accounted for with due regard to their substance and economic reality not simply their legal form.

The second transaction is a *sale or return transaction*. Past experience indicates that about 40% of the value of the sale is likely to be returned. The accounting treatment of the sale should reflect this and only 60% of the value should be reflected in revenue.

(b) **Adjustment to TYD's financial statements**

The required adjustments have been made to the financial statements in order to be able to assess the loan application fairly.

Income statement for the year ended 30 September 20X6

	Original $	Adjusted $
Revenue	600 (*Note 1*)	475
Cost of sales	450 (*Note 2*)	333
Gross profit	150	142
Expenses	63	63
Finance costs	17	17
Profit before tax	70	62
Income tax expense	25	25
Profit for the period	45	37

| Jnl 1 | DEBIT | Sales | $85,000 | |
| | CREDIT | Cost of sales | | $85,000 |

Being reversal of *sale with option to resell* transaction with HPS banking institution (inventory being at cost).

| Jnl 2 | DEBIT | Inventories | $85,000 | |
| | CREDIT | Long-term loan | | $85,000 |

Being recording of substance of above transaction as long-term loan.

| Jnl 3 | DEBIT | Sales | $40,000 | |
| | CREDIT | Receivables | | $40,000 |

Being adjustment for *sale or return* transaction where 40% of sales of $100,000 need to be reversed as likely to be returned.

| Jnl 4 | DEBIT | Inventories | $32,000 | |
| | CREDIT | Cost of sales | | $32,000 |

Being reversal of the related cost of sales figure on journal 3 representing 80% × $40,000 = $32,000

Note 1: The adjustment represents reversal of sales of $85,000 + $40,000 = $125,000
Note 2: The adjustment represents reversal of cost of sales of $85,000 + $32,000 = $117,000

Balance sheet for the year ended 30 September 20X6

	Original $'000	$'000	Adjusted $'000
ASSETS			
Non-current assets			
Property, plant and equipment		527	527
Current assets			
Inventories	95		212
Trade receivables	72		32
Cash	6		6
		173	
		700	
			777

	Original		Adjusted
	$'000	$'000	$'000
EQUITY AND LIABILITIES			
Equity			
Called up share capital	100		100
Retained earnings	245		237
		345	337
Non-current liabilities			
Long-term borrowings		180	265
Current liabilities			
Trade and other payables	95		95
Bank overdraft	80		80
		175	
		700	
			777

(c) **Key ratio calculations and analysis**

Gearing

Before adjustment	After adjustment
$\dfrac{180+80}{180+80+345} \times 100 = 43\%$	$\dfrac{265+80}{265+80+337} + 100 = 50.6\%$

Current ratio

$\dfrac{173}{175} = 0.99{:}1$	$\dfrac{212+32+6}{175} = 1.43{:}1$

Quick ratio

$\dfrac{72+6}{175} = 0.45{:}1$	$\dfrac{32+6}{175} = 0.22{:}1$

Profit margin

$\dfrac{70}{600} \times 100 = 11.7\%$	$\dfrac{62}{475} \times 100 = 13.1\%$

TYD is highly geared. After the required adjustment to reflect the loan from HPS the gearing is over 50%.

The current ratio improves due to the increase in inventories after the reversal of the 'sales' transactions. However, more significantly, the more useful quick ratio worsens as a very high proportion of current assets is made up of inventory.

The quick ratio is a more useful guide of short-term liquidity as it does not take into account inventory which may not be as easily realised into cash.

The profit margin improves after adjustment but is likely to deteriorate when what is effectively a finance or interest charge is accounted for on the sale and repurchase agreement.

Recommendation

It is recommended that the loan application be rejected.

7 AT

Consolidated income statement for the year ended 31 March 20X7

	Working	$'000
Revenue	1	3,783.00
Cost of sales	2	(2,800.00)
Gross profit		983.00
Distribution costs	3	(141.70)
Administrative expenses	4	(473.00)
Interest received		2.00
Loss on investment in financial asset		(4.20)
Finance costs		(118.20)
Share of profit of associate		6.90
Profit before tax		254.80
Income tax expense		(94.00)
Profit for the period		160.80
Attributable to		
Equity holders of the parent		141.10
Minority interest		19.70
		160.80

Workings

1   *Revenue*

	$'000	$'000
AT	2,450	
BU	1,200	
CV	225	
		3,875
Less: elimination of intra-group sales		
inventories	(80)	
administration services	(12)	
		(92)
		3,783

2 *Cost of sales*

	$'000
AT	1,862
BU	870
CV ($^1/_3 \times 432,000$)	144
	2,876

Add: provision for unrealised profit
      closing intra-group inventories $80,000 × 25% = $20,000

unrealised profit at 20% × $20,000	4
Less: intra-group sales of inventories	(80)
	2,800

3 *Distribution costs*

	$'000
AT	94.00
BU	22.00
CV ($^1/_3 \times$ $77,000)	25.70
	141.70

4 *Administrative expenses*

	$'000
AT	280
BU	165
CV ($^1/_3 \times$ $120,000)	40
	485
Less: intra-group purchase of administrative services	(12)
	473

5 Loss on investment in financial asset 4,000 shares × ($13,320 – $12,270) = $4,200

6 *Finance costs*

Y/E 31 March	Principal b/fwd	Effective interest	Interest charge	c/fwd
20X5	950.0	85.5	(50)	985.5
20X6	985.5	88.7	(50)	1,024.5
20X7	1,024.5	92.2	(50)	1,066.4
20X8	1,066.4	96.0	(50)	1,112.4
20X9	1,112.4	100.1	(50)	1,162.5

7 *Share of profit of associate*

$79,000 × $^3/_{12}$ × 35% = $6,900

8 *Taxation charge*

	$'000
AT	40
BU	50
CV ($^1/_3 \times$ 12,000)	4
	94

9   *Minority interest*

		$'000
Profit of BU for the period		95
Less provision for unrealised profit		(4)
		91

		$
Split into 6 months to 30 September 20X6		45.50

		$
Split into 6 months to 31 March 20X6		45.50
Less loss on financial asset (W5)		(4.20)
		41.30

Minority share of profit

		$
6 months to 30 September 20X6	45.5 × 25%	11.40
6 months to 31 March 20X7	41.3 × 20%	8.30
		19.70

CIMA – Managerial Level

Paper P8

Financial Analysis

Mock Examination 3: November 2008

Instructions to candidates:

You are allowed three hours to answer this question paper.
In the real exam, you are allowed 20 minutes reading time before the examination begins during which you should read the question paper, and if you wish, highlight and/or make notes on the question paper. However, you will **not** be allowed, **under any circumstances**, to open the answer book and start writing or use your calculator during this reading time.
You are strongly advised to carefully read ALL the question requirements before attempting the question concerned (including all parts and/or sub-questions).
Answer the ONE compulsory question in Section A. This has seven objective test sub-questions.
Answer ALL THREE questions in Section B.
Answer TWO of the THREE questions in Section C.

DO NOT OPEN THIS PAPER UNTIL YOU ARE READY TO START UNDER EXAMINATION CONDITIONS

SECTION A

[Indicative time for answering this section is 36 minutes]

Answer ALL SEVEN sub-questions

The answers to the seven sub-questions in Section A should ALL be written in your answer book.

Your answers should be clearly numbered with the sub-question number and then ruled off, so that the markers know which sub-question you are answering. **For multiple choice questions, you need only write the sub-question number and the letter of answer option you have chosen.** You do not need to start a new page for each sub-question.

For sub-questions 1.3 and 1.7, you should show your workings as marks are available for method for these sub-questions.

1 Mixed bank (11/07)

1.1   On 31 August 20X7, the consolidated balance sheet of MIP included minority interests of $77,600. One year later, on 31 August 20X8, the minority interests balance was $64,700. During the year ended 31 August 20X8, MIP had disposed of its holding of 75% of the ordinary share capital of its subsidiary NJZ. At the date of disposal the net assets of NJZ totalled $64,000. The minority interests in the MIP group's profits for the year ended 31 August 20X8 was $6,500.

What amount was included in the consolidated cash flow statement as a dividend paid to the minority interests during the year ended 31 August 20X8?

A $3,100
B $3,400
C $19,400
D $22,400   **(2 marks)**

1.2   BJJ is planning to acquire a subsidiary, XZZ, for $1.3 million. The fair value of the net assets recognised by XZZ in its own financial statements amounts to only $400,000. BJJ's directors are confident that the difference between the amounts is accounted for principally by unrecognised intangible assets. BJJ's directors wish, if possible, to recognise these assets on acquisition.

Describe the conditions that must be met, in accordance with IFRS 3 *Business Combinations*, in order to be able to recognise intangible assets upon acquisition of a subsidiary.   **(2 marks)**

1.3   JSX, a listed entity, has a defined benefits pension scheme. The following information relates to the pension scheme for the year ended 31 October 20X8:

	$
Current service cost	362,600
Contributions to scheme	550,700
Benefits paid	662,400
Fair value of scheme assets at 1 November 20X7	10,660,000
Fair value of scheme assets at 31 October 20X8	11,204,000
Interest cost in respect of defined benefit obligation	730,600

The expected return on scheme assets for the year ended 31 October 20X8 was 6.2%.

Calculate the actuarial gain or loss on JSX's pension scheme assets for the year ended 31 October 20X8.
                                                                              (4 marks)

1.4 Describe the principal characteristics common to joint venture arrangements, as identified by IAS 31 *Interests in Joint Ventures*. **(2 marks)**

1.5 During its 20X8 financial year GZP makes the following investments:

1 A loan of $1,000,000 to one of its suppliers. The loan agreement stipulates that GZP will not transfer or assign the loan to a third party. The supplier is obliged to repay the loan in five years' time and to pay interest at 2% over bank base rate annually during the term of the loan.

2 Purchase of a small holding of shares in a listed company, ANG. GZP's intention is to realise this investment towards the end of its financial year when seasonal fluctuations in its business make a cash shortfall probable.

Neither asset is classified by GZP as being at fair value through profit or loss.

Explain how each of these financial assets should be:

(i) Initially classified

(ii) Measured, subsequent to initial classification, in accordance with IAS 39 *Financial Instruments: Recognition and Measurement* **(4 marks)**

1.6 Which ONE of the following statements is correct?

A derivative financial instrument

A can be recognised only if it is highly effective.
B requires little or no initial net investment.
C invariably forms part of a hedging relationship.
D should be valued at cost. **(2 marks)**

1.7 On 1 April 20X5, APL bought 30% of the 1 million $1 ordinary shares of CST for $1.2 million, thus achieving significant influence over CST's operations and policies. The retained earnings of CST at the date of acquisition were $1.6 million.

Between the date of acquisition and 30 September 20X8, APL group's financial year end, CST had earned profits of $320,000.

APL sells goods to CST at a mark up of 25%. At 30 September 20X8, CST's inventories included $100,000 of goods at cost that had been purchased from APL.

In the financial year ended 30 September 20X7, CST paid a dividend of 10¢ per share to its investors. Before that, no dividend had been paid by CST since 1 April 20X5, and there have been no changes in its issued share capital.

Identify the method of accounting that APL should use for CST in its consolidated financial statements and, using this method, calculate the amount of the investment in CST for inclusion in the consolidated balance sheet at 30 September 20X8. **(4 marks)**

(Total for Section A = 20 marks)

SECTION B – 30 marks

[Indicative time for answering this Section is 54 minutes]

Answer ALL THREE questions

2 Intellectual capital

CIMA's Official Terminology defines intellectual capital as 'knowledge which can be used to create value'.

Currently, IFRS permit the recognition of only a limited range of internally generated intellectual assets including, for example, copyrights.

Required

(a)   Explain the advantages that could be gained by entities and their stakeholders if the scope of IFRS were expanded to permit the recognition in the balance sheet of a wider range of intellectual assets, such as know-how, the value of the workforce, and employee skills.   **(5 marks)**

(b)   Explain the principal reasons why IFRS do not currently permit the recognition in the balance sheet of intellectual assets such as know-how, the value of the workforce, and employee skills.   **(5 marks)**

(Total = 10 marks)

3 AGZ

AGZ is a listed entity. You are a member of the team drafting its financial statements for the year ended 31 August 20X8. Extracts from the draft income statement, including comparative figures, are shown below:

	20X8	20X7
	$million	$million
Profit before tax	276.4	262.7
Income tax expense	85.0	80.0
Profit for the period	191.4	182.7

At the beginning of the financial year, on 1 September 20X7, AGZ had 750 million ordinary shares of 50¢ in issue. At that date the market price of one ordinary share was 87.6¢.

On 1 December 20X7, AGZ made a bonus issue of one new ordinary 50¢ share for every three held.

In 20X6, AGZ issued $75 million convertible bonds. Each unit of $100 of bonds in issue will be convertible at the holder's option into 200 ordinary 50¢ shares on 31 August 20Y2. The interest expense relating to the liability element of the bonds for the year ended 31 August 20X8 was $6.3 million (20X7 – $6.2 million). The tax effect related to the interest expense was $2.0 million (20X7 – $1.8 million).

There were no other changes affecting or potentially affecting the number of ordinary shares in issue in either the 20X8 or 20X7 financial years.

Required

(a)   Calculate earnings per share and diluted earnings per share for the year ended 31 August 20X8, including the comparative figures.   **(8 marks)**

(b)   Explain the reason for the treatment of the bonus shares as required by IAS 33 *Earnings per Share*.   **(2 marks)**

(Total = 10 marks)

4 DNT

At its year end on 31 August 20X8, DNT held investments in two subsidiaries, CM and BL.

Details of the investments were as follows:

1   Several years ago DNT purchased 850,000 of CM's 1 million ordinary $1 shares when CM's retained earnings were $1,775,000 (there were no other reserves). At 31 August 20X8, CM's retained earnings were $2,475,000.

2   On 31 May 20X8, DNT purchased 175,000 of BL's 250,000 $1 ordinary shares. At 1 September 20X7, BL's retained earnings were $650,000 (there were no other reserves). During the year ended 31 August 20X8, BL made a loss after tax of $40,000. It can be assumed that BL's revenue and expenses accrue evenly throughout the year.

No adjustments to fair value of the subsidiaries' net assets were required at either of the acquisitions.

On 1 March 20X7 CM sold an item of machinery to DNT for $75,000. The carrying amount of the item at the date of sale was $60,000, and CM recorded a profit on disposal of $15,000. The remaining useful life of the item at the date of sale was 2.5 years. The group depreciation policy in respect of machinery is the straight line basis with a proportionate charge in the years of acquisition and of disposal.

DNT's retained earnings balance at 31 August 20X8 was $2,669,400.

Required

Calculate the amounts of consolidated retained earnings and minority interest for inclusion in the DNT group's balance sheet at 31 August 20X8. **(10 marks)**

SECTION C – 50 marks

[Indicative time for answering this Section is 90 minutes]

Answer TWO questions out of THREE

5 DX

On 1 November 20X3, DX invested in 100% of the share capital of EY, a new entity incorporated on that date. EY's operations are located in a foreign country where the currency is the Franc. DX has no other subsidiaries.

The summary financial statements of the two entities at their 31 October 20X8 year end were as follows:

Summary income statements for the year ended 31 October 20X8

	DX	EY
	$'000	Franc 000
Revenue	3,600	1,200
Cost of sales, other expenses and income tax	(2,800)	(1,000)
Profit for the period	800	200

Summary statements of changes in equity for the year ended 31 October 20X8

	DX	EY
	$'000	Franc 000
Brought forward at 1 November 20X7	5,225	1,500
Profit for the period	800	200
Dividends	(200)	–
Carried forward at 31 October 20X8	5,825	1,700

Summary balance sheets at 31 October 20X8

	DX	EY
	$'000	Franc 000
Property, plant and equipment	5,000	1,500
Investment in EY	25	–
Current assets	4,400	2,000
	9,425	3,500
Share capital	1,000	50
Retained earnings	4,825	1,650
Current liabilities	3,600	1,800
	9,425	3,500

Relevant exchange rates were as follows:

1 November 20X3	1$ = 2.0 francs
31 October 20X7	1$ = 2.3 francs
31 October 20X8	1$ = 2.7 francs
Average rate for year ended 31 October 20X8	1$ = 2.6 francs

Required

(a) Explain the meaning of the term 'functional currency' as used by IAS 21 *The Effects of Changes in Foreign Exchange Rates*, and identify THREE factors that an entity should consider in determining its functional currency. **(4 marks)**

(b) Prepare the following:

    (i) The summary consolidated income statement for the year ended 31 October 20X8 **(2 marks)**

    (ii) The summary consolidated balance sheet at 31 October 20X8 **(6 marks)**

(c) Prepare the summary consolidated statement of changes in equity for the year to 31 October 20X8 and a calculation that shows how the exchange gain or loss for the year has arisen. **(13 marks)**

(Total = 25 marks)

Work to the nearest $

6 SWW

You are assistant to the Chief Financial Officer (CFO) of SWW, a large fashion retailer. SWW's merchandise is sourced from many different suppliers around the world. SWW's senior management has a business policy of building lasting relationships with suppliers either by investing in their shares, or by making loans to them at favourable rates of interest.

A request has recently been received from a supplier, TEX, for a loan of $25 million to allow it to invest in up to date machinery. The directors of TEX claim that the investment will result in efficiency improvements which, in the short to medium term, will allow it to reduce prices to its customers. SWW is a major customer of TEX, buying approximately 10% of TEX's annual output of cotton clothing.

In support of the application, TEX's CFO has supplied a one page report on the state of the business, and a balance sheet and income statement for the year ended 30 September 20X8. The 20X8 figures are unaudited. TEX has not paid a dividend in the last five years. TEX's shares are listed on a local stock exchange, although the entity's founding family has retained a minor holding. TEX's functional and presentation currency is the $, and its financial statements are prepared in accordance with IFRS.

The financial statements supplied by TEX are as follows:

TEX: Consolidated income statement for the year ended 30 September 20X8

	20X8 $million	20X7 $million
Revenue	256.3	281.7
Cost of sales	(226.6)	(243.1)
Gross profit	29.7	38.6
Selling and distribution costs	(9.2)	(8.9)
Administrative expenses	(18.7)	(15.6)
Finance costs	(5.4)	(6.2)
Share of losses of associate	(1.3)	(6.8)
(Loss)/profit before tax	(4.9)	1.1
Income tax expense	1.5	(0.4)
(Loss)/profit for the period	(3.4)	0.7
Attributable to:		
Equity holders of parent	(3.2)	0.6
Minority interest	(0.2)	0.1
	(3.4)	0.7

TEX: Consolidated balance sheet at 30 September 20X8

	20X8		20X7	
	$million	$million	$million	$million
ASSETS				
Non-current assets				
Property, plant and equipment		221.4		227.3
Investment in associate		13.8		15.1
Available for sale investments		2.6		4.8
		237.8		247.2
Current assets				
Inventories	132.4		125.6	
Trade and other receivables	51.7		58.2	
Cash	–		4.8	
		184.1		188.6
		421.9		435.8
EQUITY AND LIABILITIES				
Equity				
Share capital ($1 shares)	25.0		25.0	
Retained earnings and other reserves	103.2		106.2	
Minority interest	13.7		13.9	
		141.9		145.1
Non-current liabilities				
Long-term borrowings	57.2		67.1	
Deferred tax	18.0		25.8	
Defined benefit obligation	26.0		24.2	
		101.2		117.1
Current liabilities				
Trade and other payables	150.1		161.2	
Borrowings	28.7		12.4	
		178.8		173.6
		421.9		435.8

Required

Produce a report to the CFO of SWW that does the following:

(a)   Analyses and interprets the information given above from the point of view of SWW as a potential lender

(20 marks)

(b)   Describes the areas of uncertainty in the analysis and the nature of any additional information that will be required before a lending decision can be made   **(5 marks)**

Note: Up to 8 marks are available in part (a) for the calculation of relevant accounting ratios.

(Total = 25 marks)

7 ABC Corp

Ned is a recently appointed non-executive director of ABC Corp, a listed entity. ABC's corporate governance arrangements permit non-executives to seek independent advice on accounting and legal matters affecting the entity, where they have any grounds for concern. Ned has asked you, an independent accountant, for advice because he is worried about certain aspects of the draft financial statements for ABC's year ended 30 September 20X8.

The ownership of most of ABC's ordinary share capital is widely dispersed, but the three largest institutional shareholders each own around 10% of the entity's ordinary shares. In meetings with management, these shareholders have made it clear that they expect improvements in the entity's performance and position. ABC appointed a new Chief Financial Officer (CFO) at the start of the 20X7/X8 financial year, and the board has set ambitious financial targets for the next five years.

The 20X7/X8 targets were expressed in the form of three key accounting ratios, as follows:

- Return on capital employed (profit before interest as a percentage of debt + equity): 7%
- Net profit margin (profit before tax as a percentage of revenue): 5%
- Gearing (long-term and short-term debt as a percentage of the total of debt + equity): below 48%

The draft financial statements include the following figures:

	$
Revenue	31,850,000
Profit before interest	2,972,000
Interest	1,241,000
Equity	22,450,800
Debt	18,253,500

The key ratios, based on the draft financial statements, are as follows:

Return on capital employed	7.3%
Net profit margin	5.4%
Gearing	44.8%

Ned's copies of the minutes of board meetings provide the following relevant information:

1   On 1 October 20X7 ABC sold an item of plant for $1,000,000 to XB, an entity that provides financial services to businesses. The carrying value of the plant at the date of sale was $1,000,000. XB has the option to require ABC to repurchase the plant on 1 October 20X8 for $1,100,000. If the option is not exercised at that date, ABC will be required under the terms of the agreement between the entities to repurchase the plant on 1 October 20X9 for $1,210,000. ABC has continued to insure the plant and to store it on its business premises. The sale to XB was recognised as revenue in the draft financial statements and the asset was derecognised.

2   A few days before the 30 September 20X8 year end, ABC entered into a debt factoring agreement with LM, a factoring business. The terms of the agreement are that ABC is permitted to draw down cash up to a maximum of 75% of the receivables that are covered under the factoring arrangement. However, LM is able to require repayment of any part of the receivables that are uncollectible. In addition, ABC is obliged to pay interest at an annual rate of 10% on any amounts it draws down in advance of cash being received from customers by LM. As soon as the agreement was finalised, ABC drew down the maximum cash available in respect of the $2,000,000 receivables it had transferred to LM as part of the agreement. This amount was accounted for by debiting cash and crediting receivables.

3   In October 20X7, ABC issued 2,000,000 $1 preference shares at par. The full year's dividend of 8% was paid before the 30 September 20X8 year end, and was recognised in the statement of changes in equity. The preference shares are redeemable in 20Y5, and the entity is obliged to pay the dividend on a fixed date each year. The full $2,000,000 proceeds of the issue were credited to equity capital.

Required

(a) Discuss the accounting treatment of the three transactions, identifying any errors that you think have been made in applying accounting principles with references, where appropriate, to IFRS. Prepare the adjustments that are required to correct those errors and identify any areas where you would require further information. **(15 marks)**

(b) Calculate the effect of your adjustments on ABC's key accounting ratios for the year ended 30 September 20X8. **(7 marks)**

(c) Explain, briefly, the results and the implications of your analysis to the non-executive director. **(3 marks)**

(Total = 25 marks)

Answers

DO NOT TURN THIS PAGE UNTIL YOU HAVE
COMPLETED THE MOCK EXAM

A plan of attack

The exam may look daunting at first. You need to adopt a calm approach. The following plan of attack is just a suggestion.

First things first

Parts A and B are compulsory, so you may as well start with the easier option of Part A with 9 short answer questions. Remember the instructions for dealing with these OTs and MCQs at the beginning of the Kit. Do not exceed the time limit of **36 minutes** for this section. Answer the easy questions first.

Part B

Part B is also compulsory so you may as well deal with these three next. Do not get bogged down in the detail and remember to allow yourself only **54 minutes**, allocating equal time to each question.

Part C

Part C has **two questions** to answer out of three. Choose the question that you know most about to answer first. Remember to answer only **two** questions. If you try parts of all three, only the marks for your best two questions will count, so you will have wasted your time **and failed** the exam.

In choosing your questions, have regard to your strengths and weaknesses.

Question 5.

This question is on groups, so only tackle it if you feel very comfortable with groups. The first three parts are relatively straightforward.

Question 6.

This is a financial analysis question: a good bet as you can always write something. Remember to bear in mind who the report is for.

Question 7.

This is a 'mixed bag' question on sale and re-purchase, debt factories and issue of redeemable preference shares. A good one to do if you know two out of three topics.

Remember

Always – well nearly always – **allocate your time** according to the marks for the question in total and then according to the parts of the question. The only exception is if the question is compulsory, say in Section B, and you really know nothing about it. You may as well try to pick up marks elsewhere. And **always**, **always follow the requirements** exactly.

You've got spare time at the end of the exam … ?

If you have allocated your time properly then you **shouldn't have time on your hands** at the end of the exam. But if you find yourself with five or ten minutes to spare, **go back to the questions** that you couldn't do or to **any parts of questions that you didn't finish** because you ran out of time.

Forget about it!

And don't worry if you found the paper difficult. More than likely other candidates will too. If this were the real thing you would need to **forget** the exam the minute you leave the exam hall and **think about the next one**. Or, if it's the last one, **celebrate!**

SECTION A

Question 1

1.1   B $3,400

	MINORITY INTERESTS		
	$		$
Dividends paid (Bal fig)	3,400	Balance b/d	77,600
Disposal: 25% × 64,000	16,000	Share of profits in year	6,500
Bal c/d	64,700		
	84,100		84,100

1.2   IFRS 3 *Business combinations* requires the acquirer (BJJ) to recognise separately the intangible assets of the acquiree (XZZ) at the acquisition date, if the following conditions are met.

(i)   The intangible asset meets the definition of an intangible asset in IAS 38, and
(ii) The intangible asset's fair value can be measured reliably

This is irrespective of whether the intangible asset or assets had been recognised by the acquiree (XZZ) before the business combination.

1.3

	£
Fair value of plan assts at 1 November 20X7	10,660,000
Expected return on plan assets (6.2% × 10,660,000)	660,920
Contributions	550,700
Benefits paid	(662,400)
Actuarial loss on plan assets (balancing figure)	(5,220)
Fair value of plan assets at 31 October 20X8	11,204,000

1.4   The **principal characteristics** common to joint venture arrangements, as identified as IAS 31 *Interests in joint ventures* are:

(i)   Two or more venturers are bound by a **contractual arrangement**
(ii) The contractual arrangement establishes **joint control**.

IAS 31 emphasises the need for a contractual agreement in order to ensure that there is genuine joint control, and no venturer is in a position to control the entity unilaterally.

If one party exercises unilateral control then the venture is a subsidiary of the controlling party and not a joint venture.

The contractual agreement may be evidenced in a number of ways but it is usually in writing.

1.5   (a)   **Loan of $1,000,000**

    (i)   *Initial classification*

        The loan is a financial asset with fixed repayment in five years and an interest rate linked to base rate. It cannot be assigned or transferred to a third party and it is not traded in an active market. It falls into the category '**loans** and **receivables**' for classification and measurement purposes. It should be recognised at its initial cost of $1,000,000.

    (ii) *Subsequent measurement*

        The loan should be measured at **amortised cost**.

        The effective interest rate method is used to calculate the annual amortisation which is recognised in profit or loss as the asset is amortised.

2   **Holding in ANG**

These are designated as **available for sale financial assets**.

(i)   *Initial recognition*

Initial recognition should be at **fair value** (the transaction price)

(ii)   *Subsequent measurement*

Subsequent measurement is at **fair value** with gains or losses recognised directly in equity and reported in the statement of changes in equity.

Note: IAS 39 para 9(a)

A financial asset is classified as held for trading if it is acquired principally for the purpose of selling in the near term.

Para 9(b) introduces the possibility of financial instruments other than the three classes specified in para 9(a) being 'designated' as fair value through profit or loss.

If the sentence is interpreted as referring to this 'designation' then it would be valid to say that it would be classifed as held for trading and subsequently measured at fair value through profit or loss.

1.6   B   A derivative instrument requires little or no initial net investment.

1.7   Although APL does not have a controlling interest in CST, it can exercise significant influence over the latter's operating and financial policies. CST is consequently an **associate** of APL and should be accounted for under the **equity method** in the consolidated financial statements.

Under the equity method of accounting the initial cost of APL's investment in CST will be increased each year by APL's share of CST's post tax profits. This means that the value of the investment in CST at each balance sheet date is cost plus the APL group share of the associate's post tax profits.

	$'000
Cost	1,200,000
Shares of post acquisition retained earnings: $220,000 (W1) × 30%	66,000
Less unrealised profit (W2)	(6,000)
Investment in associate	1,260,000

Workings

1   *PARE*

	$'000
Per question	320,000
Less dividend paid in 20X7	(100,000)
	220,000

2   *PUP*

Unrealised profit is $\frac{25}{125} \times \$100,000 = \$20,000$

Group share $20,000 × 30% = $6,000

This must be eliminated against the parent's profit

DEBIT	Group retained earnings	$6,000	
CREDIT	Investment in associate		$6,000

SECTION B

Question 2

> **Text references**. This topic is covered in Chapter 18 of the Study Text, but also draws on your P7 knowledge of intangible assets.
>
> **Top tips**. This question is fairly open-ended, so you can make a lot of points, provided you back up your arguments. The key point to note is that intellectual assets – in the form of employees – are difficult to control.
>
> **Easy marks**. This question allows you to earn marks for common sense, as well as technical knowledge.

(a)   A frequent criticism that is levelled against conventional accounting is that the balance **sheet does not reflect the true value of a business** as it fails to recognise the value of intellectual capital, a wide term which includes a range of intellectual assets such as copyrights, patents, the brain power of a company's workforce, customer relationships, information technology networks and management skills.

The criticism that traditional accounting measures fail to account for the intellectual capital and hence the true value of companies, is evidenced by the growing gap between a company's market value and the value of all its tangible assets which has widened significantly over the last two decades.

Most rapidly growing companies tend to be **knowledge intensive** in the fields of microelectronics, biotechnology, new materials industries and telecommunications.

There are several **potential advantages** to be gained by the recognition of intellectual assets.

(i)   **Improved information to investors and potential investors**. Investors as a stakeholder group comprise both shareholders and other capital contributors such as bondholders. Under the existing reporting system, a typical investor does not receive an accurate picture of a company's true value or the sources of value since a company's investment in intellectual capital such as employee training does not appear in the balance sheet. Indeed a company that invests in its future may appear undercapitalised.

(ii)   **Improve profitability through better identification of the company's hidden resources** and better management of investment in the company's intellectual capital. Evaluating intellectual capital can help make a company more efficient, profitable and competitive. By identifying and evaluating intellectual capital a company is better able to:

(1)   Asses its ability to achieve its goals
(2)   Plan and fund research and development
(3)   Plan and fund education and training

(iii)   Provide useful information to **employees and future employees**. Better information about skills and human capital would help recruit and retain motivated staff.

(iv)   Provide useful information to **the local community**. The positive contribution made to the economy by a company that invests in intellectual capital would be apparent.

(b)   The principal reasons why IFRS do not currently permit the recognition of intellectual assets on the balance sheet relate to **proper definition and measurement** of such assets. Defining as well as measuring intellectual capital is fraught with difficulties . A range of intellectual assets such as know-how, the value of the workforce and employee skills are not recognised by IFRS.

The IASB's Framework and IAS 38 *Intangible assets* define an asset as a 'resource controlled by an entity as a result of past events from which future economic benefits will flow to the entity'. IAS 38 *Intangible assets* further defines intangible assets a subset of this group as 'identifiable non-monetary assets without physical substance'.

Not all types of intellectual assets meet the definition of an intangible asset under IAS 38. The three key aspects of the definition are:

(i) **Identifiability**

(ii) **Control**

(iii) The existence of future **economic benefits**

Even if the above three criteria are met, a further criterion for recognition requires that the cost of the asset can be measured reliably.

The main difficulty with treating know-how and intellectual capital such as employee skills as intangibles is the **uncertainty as to whether the entity can control the benefits**. The problem with recognising human resource related assets in the balance sheet is that the **employer cannot normally prevent the employee from changing employment** and from other entities obtaining the future benefits. Moreover, even if the employee was bound to stay with the company, the benefit of know-how and skills would be difficult to quantify.

IAS 38 specifically prohibits the recognition of either a highly skilled workforce or specific management know-how to be recognised as an intangible unless it is protected by legal rights and the entity has control over the expected future economic benefits.

In practice, an example of an intangible skill that is recognised, is in football clubs. In a form of human resource accounting, fees paid for the transfer of players are capitalised and amortised over the players' estimated period of service to the club. This is an example where the criteria of **identifiability**, **control**, **future economic benefits** and **reliable measurement** are met

Question 3

Text reference. This topic is covered in Chapter 15 of the Study Text.

Top tips. Remember that the bonus shares do not affect earnings, only the number of shares. Remember to take account of the tax, when adjusting for the interest on the convertible bonds. Show full workings to make sure you get full credit for correct methods even if you have made a numerical error at some point.

Easy marks. These are available for Basic Earnings per share, and for the explanation in Part (b).

(a) *Basic earnings per share*

	20X8	20X7
Profits attributable to the ordinary shareholders for the year ending 31 August	$191,400,000	$182,700,000
Number of ordinary shares in issue at 31 August	1,000,000,000	750,000,000

Calculation of Earnings per share

$$20X7 = \frac{182.7}{1,000} = 18.27$$

$$20X8 = \frac{194.0}{1,000} = 19.14$$

In the accounts the EPS for the year ending 31 August 20X7 would have appeared as 24.36c (182.7 ÷ 750)

Diluted earnings per share

To calculate dilute earnings per share we need to adjust both earnings and the number of shares. The adjusted earnings are calculated as:

	20X8	20X7
	$	$
Profits attributable to the ordinary shareholders for the year ending 31 August	191,400,000	182,700,000
Add interest on the convertible bonds	6,300,000	6,200,000
Less tax	(2,000,000)	(1,800,000)
Adjusted earnings	195,700,000	187,100,000

The maximum number of shares that the convertible bond holders will receive is 150,000,000. The fully diluted number of shares will be 1,150,000,000 and the fully diluted EPS will be 17.02c. (20X7: 16.27c).

Basic number of shares		1,000,000,000
Additional shares on conversion		
$75m \times \dfrac{200}{100}$	=	150,000,000
		1,150,000,000

Fully diluted EPS

20X8	$\dfrac{195,700,000}{1,150,000,000}$	=	17.02¢
20X7	$\dfrac{187,100,000}{1,150,000,000}$	=	16.27¢

(b) Where a company issues new shares by way of a bonus issue during the period, the effect is to increase only the number of shares outstanding. There is no effect on earnings as there is **no flow of funds** as a result of the issue. Consequently the shares are treated as outstanding as if the issue had occurred at the beginning of the earliest period reported. This means that the number of shares outstanding before the issue must be adjusted so that the effect of the bonus issue does not distort any comparison from one period to the next.

Question 4

Text references. This topic is covered in Chapter 4 of your Study Text.

Top tips. Points to watch are:

BL makes a loss in the year. Make sure you take this into account when calculating retained earnings and working out how much of this is pre-acquisition.

The best way to approach the intragroup sale of the machinery is to eliminate the unrealised profit, then add back the element of that profit that is realised through depreciation.

Easy marks. Easy marks. Even if you don't get the intragroup sale right, there are easy marks just for setting out the workings properly. It is essential that you learn our standard workings.

CONSOLIDATED BALANCE SHEET EXTRACTS

Retained earnings

	DNT	CM	BL
	$	$	$
Retained earnings: per question (W3)	2,669,400	2,475,000	610,000
Unrealised profit (W2)		(6,000)	
Pre acquisition: per question (W3)		(1,775,000)	(620,000)
		694,000	(10,000)
Group share: CM 85%	589,900		
BL 70%	(7,000)		
	3,253,300		

Minority interest

	CM $	BL $
Share capital	1,000,000	250,000
Retained earnings: per question (W3)	2,475,000	610,000
Unrealised profit (W2)	(6,000)	
	3,469,000	860,000
	15%	30%
	520,350	258,000

Minority interest $778,350

Minority interest

Workings

1   *Group structure*

2   *Unrealised profit on intragroup sale of machinery*

	$
Profit on disposal per question	15,000
Realised through depreciation by 31 August 20X8	
$15,000 \times \dfrac{1.5 \text{ years}}{2.5 \text{ years}}$	(9,000)
∴ Unrealised profit	6,000

Adjust in books of seller: CM

3   *Retained earnings of BL*

	$'000
Retained earnings at 1 September 20X7	650
Loss for year	(40)
Retained earnings at 31 August 20X8	610

At acquisition: $(650,000 – (9/12 \times 40,000) = \$620,000$

SECTION C

Question 5

Text reference. Foreign exchange is covered in Chapter 9 of the BPP Study Text.

Top tips. Students often worry about foreign exchange but some parts of it are really straightforward. In this question, there is no minority interest as the subsidiary is 100% owned, and there is no goodwill because the company has been owned since incorporation, when the fair value of the net assets was equal to the book value. Don't forget, in the statement of changes in equity, that you will need to calculate the brought forward balance.

Easy marks. Some very easy marks are available for bookwork in Part (a) and for straightforward translation in Parts (b) and (c).

(a) **Functional currency**

IAS 21 *The effects of changes in foreign exchange rates* defines functional currency as 'the currency of the primary economic environment in which the entity operates'. Each entity, whether an individual company, a parent of a group, or an operation within a group, should determine its functional currency and **measure its results and financial position in that currency.**

Factors to consider in determining functional currency

An entity should consider the following factors:

(i) The currency:

    (1) Is it the currency that mainly **influences sales prices** for goods and services (this will often be the currency in which sales prices for its goods and services are denominated and settled)?

    (2) Is it the currency of the country whose **competitive forces and regulations** mainly determine the sales prices of its goods and services?

(ii) Is it the currency that **mainly influences labour, material and other costs** of providing goods or services? (This will often be the currency in which such costs are denominated and settled.)

The following factors may also provide evidence of an entity's functional currency:

(i) Is it the currency in which **funds from financing activities** are generated?

(ii) Is it the currency in which **receipts from operating activities** are usually retained?

(b) (i) DX GROUP

    CONSOLIDATED INCOME STATEMENT
    FOR THE YEAR ENDED 31 OCTOBER 20X8

	$
Revenue (3,600,000 + 461,538)	4,061,538
Cost of sales, other expense and tax (2,800,000 + 384,615)	3,184,615
Profit for the period	876,923

    Translation of EY's income statement

	Franc	Rate	$
Revenue	1,200,000	2.6	461,538
Cost of sales, other expenses and tax	(1,000,000)	2.6	(384,615)
Profit for the period	200,000		76,923

(ii)　DX GROUP

CONSOLIDATED BALANCE SHEET
AS AT 31 DECEMBER 20X8

	$
Property, plant and equipment: 5,000,000 + 555,555 (W1)	5,555,555
Current assets: 4,400,000 + 740,741 (W1)	5,140,741
	10,696,296
Share capital	1,000,000
Retained earnings (W2)	5,429,630
	6,429,630
Current liabilities 3,600,000 + 666,666 (W1)	4,266,666
	10,696,296

(iii)　DX GROUP

STATEMENT OF CHANGES IN EQUITY
FOR THE YEAR ENDED 31 OCTOBER 20X8

	$
Brought forward at 1 November 20X7 (W3)	5,852,174
Exchange difference arising on foreign operations (note)	(99,467)
Net income recognised directly in equity	(99,467)
Profit for the period (Part (b))	876,923
Total recognised income and expenses	777,456
Dividends paid	(200,000)
Carried forward at 31 December 20X8	6,429,630

Note. Exchange difference on foreign operations

	$
Closing net assets at closing rate (W1)	629,630
Less opening net assets at opening rate 1,500,000 ÷ 2.3	(652,174)
	(22,544)
Less retained profit as translated	(76,923)
Exchange loss on translation	(99,467)

Workings

1　*Translation of balance sheet of EY*

	Franc	Rate	$
Property, plant and equipment	1,500,000	2.7	555,555
Current assets	2,000,000	2.7	740,741
			1,296,296
Share capital	50,000	2	25,000
Retained earnings (all post acquisition)	1,650,000	β	604,630
			629,630
Current liabilities	1,800,000	2.7	666,666
			1,296,296

2　*Retained earnings*

	$
DX (per question)	4,825,000
EY (W1)	604,630
	5,429,630

3   *Equity brought forward*

		$
Share capital		1,000,000
Retained earnings		
DX: 5,225 – 1,000		4,225,000
EY: 604,630 – 76,923 + 99,467		627,174
		5,852,174

Alternative workings

	$
Equity b/f	1,000,000
Retained earning b/f (W4)	4,852,174
	5,852,174

4   *Retained reserves brought forward*

	$	$
DX: 4,825 – (800 – 200)		4,225,000
EY: net assets (b/d)	652,174	
(see note to SOCIE)		
net assets at acquisition*	(25,000)	
		627,174
		4,852,174

*As EY was newly incorporated at the acquisition date, the investment of $25,000 by DX made up the total net assets of the subsidiary at that date.

Question 6

> **Text references**. Ratio analysis is covered in Chapter 17 of your Study Text.
>
> **Top tips**. Make sure you consider what is important from the point of view of a **lender**, Part (b) is open ended, but you need to relate any comments to the situation in the question.
>
> **Easy marks**. These are available for the report format, and for backing up arguments with common sense.

REPORT

To: Chief Finance Officer
            SWW

Subject: **TEX Loan application**

Date: 10 October 20X8

(a)   **Performance**

There has been **a marked deterioration** in the financial performance of TEX between 20X7 and 20X8. Sales in 20X8 were 10% lower compared to 20X7, but the cost of sales fell only by 7% causing the **gross profit margin to go down** from 13.7% to 11.6%.

Sales and administrative **expenses** have also **increased** between 20X7 and 20X8 by 14% from 24.5 to 27.9, resulting in the **collapse of the operating profit** from $14.1m in 20X7 to $1.8m in 20X8. Accordingly, the operating profit margin fell from 5% to 0.7%.

Looking at the performance of the assets of the company, there is a similar pattern. The **return on assets has declined** from 3.24% in 20X7 to 0.43% in 20X8.

Looking at the efficiency of asset usage in producing revenues, the asset turnover ratio indicates that the **same level of efficiency prevailed in both years**. More specifically, the asset turnover ratio was 0.65 in 20X7 and 0.61 in 20X8, indicating a small reduction in efficiency.

Liquidity

Whereas the overall **liquidity position** of the TEX may appear stable, with the current ratio around 1 in both 20X7 and 20X8, the **quick ratio has gone down** from 0.36 to 0.29 indicating that the company has too much working capital tied up in inventory and may have problems meeting its short term liabilities. Furthermore the fact that in 20X8 the company **has no cash balances** and that short-term borrowing has more than doubled make the **liquidity position** of the company **precarious** since it will need to liquidate inventories to meet short term obligations.

Gearing

One of the main considerations of SWW is the **likelihood of default** by TEX as well as the ability of TEX to service its loan. The likelihood of default is a function of the gearing ratio, but this has shown a slight increase (47% to 48%). If short-term borrowings are excluded, the gearing ratio has fallen from 44.7% to 41.6%. If the **defined benefit** obligation is **excluded** from the gearing calculation, however, there is a **slight increase**, from 35.4% (20X7) to 37.7% (20X8).

The **debt/equity** ratio also gives **cause for concern**, as it has **risen** from 55%(20X7) to 60% (20X8).

The **ability to service the debt** will depend on whether the operating profits of the company will be sufficient to cover the interest payments. Looking at the interest cover ratio (operating profits/finance costs) there is a marked **deterioration in the ability of TEX to service its debt**. More specifically, whereas operating profits were 2.3 tIme the interest payments in 20X7, in 20X8 operating profits only covered about 1/3 of interest payments.

The overall picture that emerges from the analysis of the financial statements is that the **sharp fall in revenue** has **affected the profitability of the company and its ability to service debt**. The existence of large fixed costs in the operational model of TEX means that in downturns its ability to survive may be impaired.

The **purpose of the loan** is to **increase efficiency**. This may lead to price reductions, increased sales and higher profitability that TEX may secure the repayment of the debt. On the other hand, the gearing ratio is fairly stable, indicating that default of TEX is not highly probable.

The lending decision

Gearing is the key factor in the lending decision. TEX is already highly geared, and gearing is either stable or increasing depending on how it is calculated. It would be **unwise to lend to a company that already has too much debt**.

(b) The first issue that needs to be investigated is whether the deterioration in the financial performance of TEX is **short-term and cyclical**, or whether it **reflects a long-term trend** and it is permanent. The fall in revenue could be a result of high prices, or change of tastes, or competitor action.

Before SWW lends any money to TEX, if needs to be established whether the decline in financial performance and ability to service its debt is a temporary or permanent one.

Further information is required is required on TEX's **associate company** and the share of TEX' losses in this. Further information is also required on **TEX's subsidiaries** and its their effect on the results for the respective periods. We need to ascertain the extent to which the determination of the results is due to any of the subsidiaries.

Other factors to consider are:

(i)   The nature of the **pension scheme** and any planned changes

(ii) **Terms** of existing borrowing

(iii) **Accounting policies**

(iv) **Budgets and forecasts**, and potential cost-cutting

(v) 'The nature of the '**other reserves**' for example, is there a revaluation reserve, which could be subjective?

(vi) The nature of any **security** for the loan

Financial Ratios used in the analysis

		20X8	20X7

Gross profit margin $= \dfrac{\text{Gross profit}}{\text{Revenue}} \times 100\%$ $\qquad \dfrac{29.7}{256.3} = 11.6\%$ $\qquad \dfrac{38.6}{281.7} = 13.7\%$

Operating profit margin $= \dfrac{\text{PBIT}}{\text{Revenue}}$ $\qquad \dfrac{1.8}{256.3} = 0.7\%$ $\qquad \dfrac{14.1}{281.7} = 5\%$

Return on assets $= \dfrac{\text{PBIT}}{\text{Total assets}} \times 100\%$ $\qquad \dfrac{1.8}{421.9} = 0.43\%$ $\qquad \dfrac{14.1}{435.8} = 3.24\%$

Asset turnover $= \dfrac{\text{Revenue}}{\text{Total assets}} \times 100\%$ $\qquad \dfrac{256.3}{421.9} = 0.61$ $\qquad \dfrac{281.7}{435.4} = 0.65$

Interest cover $= \dfrac{\text{PBIT}}{\text{Interest expense}}$ $\qquad \dfrac{1.8}{5.4} = 0.33$ $\qquad \dfrac{14.1}{6.2} = 2.3$

Current ratio $= \dfrac{\text{Current assets}}{\text{Current liabilities}}$ $\qquad \dfrac{184.1}{178.8} = 1.03 : 1$ $\qquad \dfrac{188.6}{173.6} = 1.09 : 1$

Quick ratio = (Current assets less inventories)/Current liabilities $\qquad \dfrac{184.1 - 132.4}{178.8} = 0.29 : 1$ $\qquad \dfrac{188.6 - 125.6}{173.8} = 0.36 : 1$

Gearing ratio = (Total long-term debt*)/ (Total borrowing + equity) $\qquad \dfrac{101.2 + 28.7}{101.2 + 28.7 + 141.9} = 48\%$ $\qquad \dfrac{117.1 + 12.4}{117.1 + 12.4 + 145.1} = 47\%$

Gearing excluding short term borrowing $\qquad \dfrac{101.2}{101.2 + 141.9} = 41.6\%$ $\qquad \dfrac{117.1}{117.1 + 145.1} = 44.7\%$

		20X8	20X9

Gearing ratio $\dfrac{\text{Long - term debt}}{\text{Long - term debt + equity}}$ $\qquad \dfrac{57.2 + 28.7}{57.2 + 28.7 + 141.9} = 37.7\%$ $\qquad \dfrac{67.1 + 12.4}{67.1 + 12.4 + 145.1} = 35.4\%$
(excluding pensions obligation)

Debt/Equity $\dfrac{\text{Long - term debt}}{\text{Equity}}$ $\qquad \dfrac{85.9}{141.9} = 60\%$ $\qquad \dfrac{79.5}{145.1} = 55\%$

*Borrowings classified as current liabilities (such as a bank overdraft) may be included in long-term debt in this ratio if it is a source of long-term finance, eg, a persistent bank overdraft.

Question 7

(a)   **Transaction 1: Sale and repurchase agreement**

This is a case of **inappropriate revenue recognition**.

(i)   ABC Corp **remains the owner as it retains the risks and rewards of ownership**. ABC Corp continue to insure the plant and store it on its premises.

(ii)   The transaction is **not a true sale** but a financing transaction with the asset as collateral. The transaction involves contracting to sell the financial asset with an express contract to buy it back.

As a result of (i) and (ii) above the **derecognition** criteria for an asset are **not met**.

(iii)   The **price** which ABC will be required to pay to buy the item of plant back is **equivalent to a financing cost** and appears to have no relationship to any appreciation in the value of the item.

(iv)   **XB** is an entity that provides financial services to business and **has no use for the plant**.

As a result of the above, the fundamental principle of substance over form, as identified in the IASB *Framework*, points clearly to a **financing agreement**.

(v)   Moreover, as an item of **plant** is involved, even if this was a true sale, it would **not** have been **shown in revenue**. IAS 18 *Revenue* restricts the **revenue** classification to sales of goods purchased for resale. (The question does not indicate the nature of ABC Corp's business; this answer assumes that the company has used this machine in manufacturing, and that it is not involved in selling plant as a trade.)

The **adjusting entries** should be as follows, assuming the $1,000,000 was received in cash and we need details of the accounting entries made to derecognise the asset in order to reverse these.

DEBIT	Revenue	$1,000,000	
CREDIT	Short-term loan		$1,000,000
DEBIT	Interest expense	$100,000	
CREDIT	Interest payable		$100,000

Transaction 2

This transaction does not meet the derecognition criteria for receivables as per IAS 39 *Financial instruments: recognition and measurement*, as ABC bears the risk of any uncollectible amounts. The **substance** of the transaction is a **financing agreement** with interest of 10% as the finance charge secured by ABC's receivables. The receivables must be re-instated.

The adjusting entries are:

DEBIT	Receivables (75% × $2,000,000)	$1,500,000	
CREDIT	Loan		$1,500,000

To re-instate receivables and account for the loan.

DEBIT	Interest expense	$150,000	
CREDIT	Current liabilities		$150,000

To account for 10% interest expense on loan.

Transaction 3

Under IAS 32 *Financial instruments: presentation*, **redeemable preference shares should be classified as debt**. The preference **dividends** payable should be **classified as interest**.

The fact that the shares are **redeemable** and the obligation to pay **dividends** indicate that the financial instrument is, **in substance**, **a liability** and should be classified as such.

The adjusting entries are:

DEBIT	Interest expense	$160,000	
CREDIT	Statement of changes in equity		$160,000

To account for preference dividends

DEBIT	Equity	$2,000,000	
CREDIT	Non-current liabilities (debt)		$2,000,000

To adjust the incorrect treatment of preference share capital as equity.

Adjustments

	As given	Transaction 1	Transaction 2	Transaction 3	Adjusted figures
	$	$	$	$	$
Revenue	31,850,000	(1,000,000)			30,850,000
Profit before interest	2,972,000				2,972,000
Interest	1,241,000	100,000	150,000	160,000	1,651,000
Equity	22,450,800			(2,000,000)	20,450,800
Debt	18,253,500	1,000,000	1,500,000	2,000,000	22,753,500

(b) **Effect of adjustments on ABC's key accounting ratios for the year ended 30 September 20X8.**

Return on capital employed $= \dfrac{\$2,972,000}{\$22,753,500 + \$20,450,800} \times 100$

$= 6.88\%$

Net profit margin $= \dfrac{\$2,972,000 - \$1,651,000}{\$30,850,000} \times 100$

$= 4.28\%$

Gearing $= \dfrac{\$22,753,500}{\$22,753,500 + \$20,450,800} \times 100$

$= 52.66\%$

(c) The three incorrectly treated transactions resulted in **overestimating revenue, underestimating interest expense, overestimating equity and underestimating debt**.

The result is that **net profit margin and ROCE have been overstated and gearing has been understated** thus appearing to meet the targets and giving a more favourable picture of the company's **profitability** and **solvency** than would have been the case if the transactions had been correctly accounted for.

The transactions appear to have been incorrectly treated in a **deliberate attempt to meet the company's targets**, none of which are met when the transactions are treated correctly.

Mathematical tables

Present value table

Present value of £1 = $(1+r)^{-n}$ where r = interest rate, n = number of periods until payment or receipt.

Periods (n)	Discount rates (r)									
	1%	**2%**	**3%**	**4%**	**5%**	**6%**	**7%**	**8%**	**9%**	**10%**
1	0.990	0.980	0.971	0.962	0.952	0.943	0.935	0.926	0.917	0.909
2	0.980	0.961	0.943	0.925	0.907	0.890	0.873	0.857	0.842	0.826
3	0.971	0.942	0.915	0.889	0.864	0.840	0.816	0.794	0.772	0.751
4	0.961	0.924	0.888	0.855	0.823	0.792	0.763	0.735	0.708	0.683
5	0.951	0.906	0.863	0.822	0.784	0.747	0.713	0.681	0.650	0.621
6	0.942	0.888	0.837	0.790	0.746	0.705	0.666	0.630	0.596	0.564
7	0.933	0.871	0.813	0.760	0.711	0.665	0.623	0.583	0.547	0.513
8	0.923	0.853	0.789	0.731	0.677	0.627	0.582	0.540	0.502	0.467
9	0.914	0.837	0.766	0.703	0.645	0.592	0.544	0.500	0.460	0.424
10	0.905	0.820	0.744	0.676	0.614	0.558	0.508	0.463	0.422	0.386
11	0.896	0.804	0.722	0.650	0.585	0.527	0.475	0.429	0.388	0.350
12	0.887	0.788	0.701	0.625	0.557	0.497	0.444	0.397	0.356	0.319
13	0.879	0.773	0.681	0.601	0.530	0.469	0.415	0.368	0.326	0.290
14	0.870	0.758	0.661	0.577	0.505	0.442	0.388	0.340	0.299	0.263
15	0.861	0.743	0.642	0.555	0.481	0.417	0.362	0.315	0.275	0.239
16	0.853	0.728	0.623	0.534	0.458	0.394	0.339	0.292	0.252	0.218
17	0.844	0.714	0.605	0.513	0.436	0.371	0.317	0.270	0.231	0.198
18	0.836	0.700	0.587	0.494	0.416	0.350	0.296	0.250	0.212	0.180
19	0.828	0.686	0.570	0.475	0.396	0.331	0.277	0.232	0.194	0.164
20	0.820	0.673	0.554	0.456	0.377	0.312	0.258	0.215	0.178	0.149

Periods (n)	Discount rates (r)									
	11%	**12%**	**13%**	**14%**	**15%**	**16%**	**17%**	**18%**	**19%**	**20%**
1	0.901	0.893	0.885	0.877	0.870	0.862	0.855	0.847	0.840	0.833
2	0.812	0.797	0.783	0.769	0.756	0.743	0.731	0.718	0.706	0.694
3	0.731	0.712	0.693	0.675	0.658	0.641	0.624	0.609	0.593	0.579
4	0.659	0.636	0.613	0.592	0.572	0.552	0.534	0.516	0.499	0.482
5	0.593	0.567	0.543	0.519	0.497	0.476	0.456	0.437	0.419	0.402
6	0.535	0.507	0.480	0.456	0.432	0.410	0.390	0.370	0.352	0.335
7	0.482	0.452	0.425	0.400	0.376	0.354	0.333	0.314	0.296	0.279
8	0.434	0.404	0.376	0.351	0.327	0.305	0.285	0.266	0.249	0.233
9	0.391	0.361	0.333	0.308	0.284	0.263	0.243	0.225	0.209	0.194
10	0.352	0.322	0.295	0.270	0.247	0.227	0.208	0.191	0.176	0.162
11	0.317	0.287	0.261	0.237	0.215	0.195	0.178	0.162	0.148	0.135
12	0.286	0.257	0.231	0.208	0.187	0.168	0.152	0.137	0.124	0.112
13	0.258	0.229	0.204	0.182	0.163	0.145	0.130	0.116	0.104	0.093
14	0.232	0.205	0.181	0.160	0.141	0.125	0.111	0.099	0.088	0.078
15	0.209	0.183	0.160	0.140	0.123	0.108	0.095	0.084	0.074	0.065
16	0.188	0.163	0.141	0.123	0.107	0.093	0.081	0.071	0.062	0.054
17	0.170	0.146	0.125	0.108	0.093	0.080	0.069	0.060	0.052	0.045
18	0.153	0.130	0.111	0.095	0.081	0.069	0.059	0.051	0.044	0.038
19	0.138	0.116	0.098	0.083	0.070	0.060	0.051	0.043	0.037	0.031
20	0.124	0.104	0.087	0.073	0.061	0.051	0.043	0.037	0.031	0.026

Cumulative present value table

This table shows the present value of £1 per annum, receivable or payable at the end of each year for *n* years.

Periods (n)	Discount rates (r)									
	1%	**2%**	**3%**	**4%**	**5%**	**6%**	**7%**	**8%**	**9%**	**10%**
1	0.990	0.980	0.971	0.962	0.952	0.943	0.935	0.926	0.917	0.909
2	1.970	1.942	1.913	1.886	1.859	1.833	1.808	1.783	1.759	1.736
3	2.941	2.884	2.829	2.775	2.723	2.673	2.624	2.577	2.531	2.487
4	3.902	3.808	3.717	3.630	3.546	3.465	3.387	3.312	3.240	3.170
5	4.853	4.713	4.580	4.452	4.329	4.212	4.100	3.993	3.890	3.791
6	5.795	5.601	5.417	5.242	5.076	4.917	4.767	4.623	4.486	4.355
7	6.728	6.472	6.230	6.002	5.786	5.582	5.389	5.206	5.033	4.868
8	7.652	7.325	7.020	6.733	6.463	6.210	5.971	5.747	5.535	5.335
9	8.566	8.162	7.786	7.435	7.108	6.802	6.515	6.247	5.995	5.759
10	9.471	8.983	8.530	8.111	7.722	7.360	7.024	6.710	6.418	6.145
11	10.37	9.787	9.253	8.760	8.306	7.887	7.499	7.139	6.805	6.495
12	11.26	10.58	9.954	9.385	8.863	8.384	7.943	7.536	7.161	6.814
13	12.13	11.35	10.63	9.986	9.394	8.853	8.358	7.904	7.487	7.103
14	13.00	12.11	11.30	10.56	9.899	9.295	8.745	8.244	7.786	7.367
15	13.87	12.85	11.94	11.12	10.38	9.712	9.108	8.559	8.061	7.606
16	14.718	13.578	12.561	11.652	10.838	10.106	9.447	8.851	8.313	7.824
17	15.562	14.292	13.166	12.166	11.274	10.477	9.763	9.122	8.544	8.022
18	16.398	14.992	13.754	12.659	11.690	10.828	10.059	9.372	8.756	8.201
19	17.226	15.678	14.324	13.134	12.085	11.158	10.336	9.604	8.950	8.365
20	18.046	16.351	14.877	13.590	12.462	11.470	10.594	9.818	9.129	8.514

Periods (n)	Discount rates (r)									
	11%	**12%**	**13%**	**14%**	**15%**	**16%**	**17%**	**18%**	**19%**	**20%**
1	0.901	0.893	0.885	0.877	0.870	0.862	0.855	0.847	0.840	0.833
2	1.713	1.690	1.668	1.647	1.626	1.605	1.585	1.566	1.547	1.528
3	2.444	2.402	2.361	2.322	2.283	2.246	2.210	2.174	2.140	2.106
4	3.102	3.037	2.974	2.914	2.855	2.798	2.743	2.690	2.639	2.589
5	3.696	3.605	3.517	3.433	3.352	3.274	3.199	3.127	3.058	2.991
6	4.231	4.111	3.998	3.889	3.784	3.685	3.589	3.498	3.410	3.326
7	4.712	4.564	4.423	4.288	4.160	4.039	3.922	3.812	3.706	3.605
8	5.146	4.968	4.799	4.639	4.487	4.344	4.207	4.078	3.954	3.837
9	5.537	5.328	5.132	4.946	4.772	4.607	4.451	4.303	4.163	4.031
10	5.889	5.650	5.426	5.216	5.019	4.833	4.659	4.494	4.339	4.192
11	6.207	5.938	5.687	5.453	5.234	5.029	4.836	4.656	4.486	4.327
12	6.492	6.194	5.918	5.660	5.421	5.197	4.988	4.793	4.611	4.439
13	6.750	6.424	6.122	5.842	5.583	5.342	5.118	4.910	4.715	4.533
14	6.982	6.628	6.302	6.002	5.724	5.468	5.229	5.008	4.802	4.611
15	7.191	6.811	6.462	6.142	5.847	5.575	5.324	5.092	4.876	4.675
16	7.379	6.974	6.604	6.265	5.954	5.668	5.405	5.162	4.938	4.730
17	7.549	7.120	6.729	6.373	6.047	5.749	5.475	5.222	4.990	4.775
18	7.702	7.250	6.840	6.467	6.128	5.818	5.534	5.273	5.033	4.812
19	7.839	7.366	6.938	6.550	6.198	5.877	5.584	5.316	5.070	4.843
20	7.963	7.469	7.025	6.623	6.259	5.929	5.628	5.353	5.101	4.870